Pan Breakthrough Books

The Business of Communicating

Improving Communication Skills

Nicki Stanton

A Pan Original
Pan Books, London and Sydney

First published 1982 by Pan Books Ltd,
Cavaye Place, London SW10 9PG

9 8 7 6 5 4 3

© Nicki Stanton 1982

ISBN 0 330 26750 7

Printed and bound in Great Britain by
Richard Clay (The Chaucer Press) Ltd, Bungay, Suffolk

If you wish to study the subject-matter of this book in more
depth, write to the National Extension College, 18 Brooklands
Avenue, Cambridge CB2 2HN, for a free copy of the
Breakthrough Business Courses leaflet. This gives details of
the extra exercises and professional postal tuition which are
available.

Pan Breakthrough Books

Pan Breakthrough Books open the door to successful self-education. The series provides essential knowledge using the most modern self-study techniques.

Expert authors have produced clear explanatory texts on business subjects to meet the particular needs of people at work and of those studying for relevant examinations.

A highly effective learning pattern, enabling readers to measure progress step-by-step, has been devised for Breakthrough Books by the National Extension College, Britain's leading specialists in home study.

Nicki Stanton is Head of Department of Business Studies at Swindon College and was previously Senior Lecturer in Business Communication at Bristol Polytechnic. Before starting her teaching career, she worked for Josiah Wedgwood & Sons and Berni Inns. Her activities have included teaching at diploma and degree level, management training in the South West Regional Management Centre, and consultancy work. Her interest in business education curriculum development has led to her appointment as Business Education Council moderator and member of the BEC Bl Board and Validation Committee. She is also a UK member of the American Business Communication Association, and has contributed to the book International Business Communication: Theory, Practice, Teaching Throughout the World, *published by the University of Michigan.*

Pan Breakthrough Books

Other books in the series

Acknowledgements

No idea can really be said to be original – for every 'new idea' is a development of the countless ideas which have gone before. Any book is therefore merely an expression of the knowledge, experience and skill acquired during the author's lifetime of contact with other people. To all those people who have in any way been influential in my own development and learning and who have therefore contributed, often without my knowing, to the ideas expressed in this book, I owe my gratitude.

However, my special thanks are due to my head of department, Gordon Bolt, and my colleagues at Bristol Polytechnic, and to all my students, young and old with whom over the years I have learned about the process of communication.

For their patient and tireless, practical and moral support I thank my husband, Mike, and my two children, Matthew and Abigail; and for her awe-inspiring speed and efficiency I thank Jackie May who helped me type the manuscript.

Contents

Appendices

Introduction

Why? The purpose of this book is to help anyone who is interested in improving his communication skills and his knowledge of the way in which communication functions in business, by providing a self-contained book which will both stand on its own without the aid of a teacher, and complement a taught course.

It is intended to take the general principles of communication covered in the companion volume, *What Do You Mean, 'Communication'?*, one stage further and provide the reader with particular guidance on those communication tasks most commonly used in business today.

Who? Like its companion volume, it is intended to help:

- students on BEC National and Higher level courses and students on other professional courses to improve their skills in writing and speaking by learning and practising techniques on their own;
- teachers in colleges, whether communication specialists or not, who are concerned to improve their students' communication skills, but who find there is never enough time in the timetable to give students sufficient chance to get the practice which is so essential if their knowledge and skills are really to develop satisfactorily; and
- anyone interested in communication and keen to become a more effective communicator but who is unable to take advantage of a course of study at a college.

What? The book covers the main communication tasks with which you are likely to be confronted – telephoning, interviewing, meetings and giving talks and oral presentations in the first part; writing letters, reports (long and short), questionnaires, memos and so on, in the second part. In addition you will find a chapter on visual communication – graphs, charts, etc. – in Part 1 and a chapter on the use of visual aids – boards, projectors, films and so on – in Part 2.

The final part (Part 3) deals with the basic elements of English grammar and usage and is intended either to help you brush up your knowledge of English or to act merely as a quick reference section together with some useful reference lists in the appendices at the back of the book

How? In order to help you check your progress as you work through the book, you will frequently come across questions and exercises.

Self-checks are usually short questions or exercises to test your understanding of what you have just read, or to find out what you know already, before reading on. Try not to read on to the discussion of these questions until you have at least attempted an answer for yourself. Try not to cheat – it will only hinder your progress – but if you are really stuck, then read on or check back over the last few pages.

Reviews are similar to self-checks but come at the end of a chapter or section to test your understanding of the whole chapter. Again, if you have difficulty answering these, go back over the previous section or chapter.

Activities are longer exercises usually at the end of chapters to help you apply your knowledge and practise the skills and techniques you have learned. However, sometimes these activities occur in the middle of a chapter and ask you to carry out some observations or do some research over a longer period of time. Make a note of them when you get to them to remind you what to do or what to look out for during the next few days or weeks.

When? Although it is preferable to have first read this book's companion volume, *What Do You Mean, 'Communication'?*, since it deals with the process of communication, organizational communication and the general rules which apply to all communication in much more detail, nevertheless this volume can be used separately in its own right.

Just as this volume builds on the material covered in its companion volume, so the chapters in this book inevitably develop from one another. However, just as the book is intended to help you without necessarily having to refer to its companion volume, so each chapter is designed to be complete and self-contained, enabling you to pick up the book and make use of those odd hours between other demands on your time.

Where? Armed only with this book and a pen and paper, you should be able to work through the various chapters at home, at college, in a library, on buses, trains or even planes. However, in some of the chapters that deal with speaking skills you may find a small tape-recorder useful, in which case you may prefer to work in privacy.

So – good luck, and above all, enjoy yourself! Learning should be fun and the way in which human beings communicate is always fascinating even when we fall short of perfection, which we all too often do.

Before we get down to details

Human communication is fraught with problems and difficulties. How often do we say or hear statements like 'I didn't really mean that' or 'You still don't see what I mean', or 'You don't seem to have grasped the point'? Whatever we try to communicate, something often seems to get in the way and we are not understood in the way we intended. But even when we are understood we often fail to get people to think or behave in the way we would wish.

Self-check

Can you suggest four general objectives which are true of all efforts to communicate?

The objectives of communication

Whether we are writing or speaking, trying to persuade, inform, entertain, explain, convince or educate or any other objective behind the particular communication task we are engaged in, we always have four general objectives:

- to be received (heard or read)
- to be understood
- to be accepted
- to get action (change of behaviour or attitude)

– and when we fail to achieve any one of these, we have failed to communicate. This can often lead to frustration and resentment expressed in phrases like 'Don't you understand plain English?'

But, what is plain English? English after all is only a code which we use to express the thoughts in our head, and a code can only be understood if both parties give the same meaning to the symbols that are used. Words are only symbols that represent things and ideas, and we attach slightly different meanings to the words that we hear and use. The meanings that we give to words result from the way we each interpret the world around us, and for each of us that world is seen and understood differently.

The meaning of words

It is therefore our individuality that is the main barrier to effective communication. While it is true that as we all went through the process of learning our mother tongue, we learned to give *roughly* the same meaning to words as those around us, we must nevertheless recognize that the only connection between a word and the thing it represents is whatever association a particular group of people has chosen to make.

Self-check

What does the word 'dap' mean to you?

Well, depending on what part of the country you come from, it may mean nothing, or it may mean what others may call a 'plimsoll', 'tennis shoe', or 'pump' or 'sandshoe'. The thing itself may be roughly the same but what you call it will depend on what the community you lived in, when you learned the word, agreed rather arbitrarily to call it.

With concrete words – words which describe things we can touch, feel, hear, see or smell – we may have fewer difficulties in explaining what we mean because if all else fails we can point to the thing and providing that the other person has experienced that thing before, he will recognize it and therefore understand us. But what about abstract words – words that describe sensations, feelings, emotions, ideas? How can you be sure that someone else gives the same meaning as you to words like 'danger', 'love', 'hate' 'beautiful' and so on? The meanings attached to these words will be the result of each person's past experience. For example, if you spend much of your life climbing mountains or driving racing cars the word 'dangerous' will have a very different meaning from that given to the word by, say, the mother of a toddler, or a high-powered business tycoon.

The importance of non-verbal communication

Of course we don't only use words to communicate. Every time we communicate we are sending out messages by means of all sorts of other things. In fact, even when we are not actually writing or speaking we are still communicating something, even if unintentionally.

 Self-check

 Make a list of the other ways we communicate when we speak or write – the non-verbal means of communication.

Well, obviously we may use pictures to communicate our message, either to replace words or more importantly to reinforce our verbal message. But, consciously or unconsciously, when we speak we will also communicate by means of:

- facial expression – a smile, a frown
- gestures – movement of hands and body to help explain or emphasize our verbal message
- body posture – how we stand or sit
- orientation – whether we face the other person or turn away
- eye contact – whether we look at the other person or not, and the length of time that we look at the other person
- body contact – a pat on the back, an arm round the shoulder
- proximity – the distance we stand or sit from the person
- head-nods – to indicate agreement or disagreement or to encourage the other to go on
- appearance – physical grooming and choice of clothes
- non-verbal aspects of speech – variations of pitch, stress and timing; voice quality and tone of voice (these are sometimes called 'paralanguage')
- non-verbal aspects of writing – handwriting, layout, organization, neatness and visual appearance generally

All these non-verbal elements of communication are sometimes called 'metacommunication', from the Greek word *'meta'* meaning 'beyond' or 'in addition to'. 'Metacommunication' is therefore something 'in addition to the communication' and we must always be aware of its existence.

It is essential to remember that the metacommunication which accompanies any message is very powerful. The receiver will use these clues to help him interpret what you mean, but more importantly he will often take the meaning from the metacommunication rather than from the words themselves, particularly when what you are saying conflicts with what you are 'doing'. If, for example, you are angry but trying to hide your anger you must be aware of your body posture, the way you use your eyes, gestures and facial expressions, and the tone of your voice, which may well give you away.

The context or situation

Just as the words (the verbal message) and the non-verbal message may be interpreted differently by different people, so the same person may attribute different meanings to the same words at different times and in different contexts. After all, we don't communicate in a vacuum; the act of communication always takes place within a situation or context. The situation will have a history and particular characteristics which will make it different from any other situation. Certainly in order to communicate at all, we learn to recognize similarities in situations so that we can learn from our experiences. This is obviously essential or we would never know what to do or what to expect.

But, just as this looking for similarities in situations can be helpful, it can also be harmful for there is always a danger that we will *assume* a situation is familar and therefore *assume* we know what to say and do. For example, supposing you have only met a person once, and on that occasion he behaved in an arrogant and dictatorial manner. Is it not likely that when you meet him again you will expect him to behave in the same way? However, while you are assuming that the situation is the same and that therefore his behaviour will be the same, you may have neglected to recognize that the two situations are different and that therefore he may well behave very differently in each. The danger lies in your expectations: for, if you expect him to be arrogant and dictatorial, you may react to him in an aggressive way and it may be precisely that aggression which causes him to feel insecure and under attack, resulting in his adopting an arrogant and dictatorial stance in order to stand up to you. You leave him, content that your first impressions were right – he *is* arrogant and dictatorial and therefore unpleasant. But, in a different situation he may behave and therefore speak very differently.

Barriers to communication

Now let's look at some factors which can cause problems for communication and which we must be aware of if we are to overcome them or communicate in such a way as to minimize their effect.

Differences in perception The way we view the world is largely determined by our past experiences so people of different ages, nationalities, cultures, education, occupation, sex, status, personality and so on will each have different perceptions, will each perceive situations differently. Differences in perception are often at the root of many of the other barriers to communication.

Jumping to conclusions We often see what we expect to see, and therefore hear what we expect to hear, rather than what is actually there. This may lead us, as the saying goes 'to put two and two together and make five'.

Stereotyping Because we have to learn from our experiences, we run the risk of treating different people as if they were the same: 'You've met one copper/student/foreman/shop steward/car salesman, you've met them all!' we often hear, or words to that effect.

Lack of knowledge It is difficult to communicate effectively with someone who has a very different background from yours, or whose knowlege of the particular subject of discussion is considerably less than yours. Of course, it is possible, but it requires skill on the part of the communicator to be aware of the discrepancy between the levels of knowledge and communicate accordingly.

Lack of interest One of the greatest barriers to overcome is the receiver's lack of interest in your message. You should always be alert to this as a possibility, since it is so easy to assume that everyone is as concerned about our interests as we are. Where the lack of interest is obvious and understandable you must work particularly hard to angle your message to appeal to the interests and needs of the receiver.

Difficulties with self-expression If, as the communicator, you have difficulty finding the words to convey your ideas this will clearly be a barrier and you must work at improving your vocabulary. But lack of confidence, which can be boosted by careful preparation and planning, can also cause difficulties in expression.

Emotions The emotions of either receiver or communicator can also prove to be a barrier – any strongly felt emotion is liable to prevent almost anything but the emotion being communicated. The moral of course is to try to avoid communicating when a strong emotion is liable to make you incoherent or when it will totally distort what you mean to say. However, any audience knows that a speaker with no emotion and enthusiasm in his voice is likely to be a dull speaker – so emotion can be a good thing.

Personality In the example above about someone who appeared to be arrogant and dictatorial we saw that it is not just the differences in people's personalities that can cause problems. So often our judgement of someone's personality is affected by our own and our resulting behaviour can then affect the behaviour of the other person. This kind of 'clash of personalities' is one of the most common causes of communication failure. We may not be able to change the personality of others but at least we should be prepared to consider our own personality to see if a change in our behaviour may result in more satisfactory relationships – however unpalatable this sort of self-analysis may be.

Well, these are only a few of the many factors which can cause communication to be less than effective or even fail completely. But it is quite a good place at which to end this discussion of potential barriers because it leaves us with the recognition that it is up to *us* either as the receiver or the communicator to make conditions as satisfactory as possible so that communication – a far from perfect process – stands a chance of being effective.

So far we have looked very briefly at some of the more important factors which affect our success in communicating. You will find a more detailed explanation of the process of communication in Part 1 of *What Do You Mean, 'Communication'?*. Now let's move on to examine ways in which we might make sure that we communicate as effectively as possible. The first golden rule is to *think ahead*. If we can predict some of the likely problems *before* we communicate, we may be able to avoid them.

Self-check

What are the six essential questions we should always consider when we are about to communicate a message?

If you have already worked through *What Do You Mean, 'Communication'?*, the six simple questions and some of their supplementary questions will probably already be ingrained on your memory. But, if you need a gentle reminder here is a checklist:

Why? (purpose)
- Why am I communicating?
- What is my real reason for writing or speaking?
- What am I hoping to achieve? Action? Change of attitude? Change of opinion?
- What is my purpose? To inform? To persuade? To influence? To educate? To sympathize? To entertain? Etc.

Who? (receiver)
- Who exactly is my audience?
- What sort of person is he? Personality? Education? Age? Status?
- How is he likely to react to the content of my message?
- What does he know already about the subject of my message? A lot? Not much? Nothing? Less/more than I do?

Where and when? (place and context)

- Where will he be when he receives my message? In his office close to other relevant material? Or, isolated from the problem so that I may need to remind him of the facts?
- At what point in the total matter does my message come? Am I replying to something he has raised? Or, will my message represent the first he has heard about this topic/problem/issue?
- What is my relationship with the receiver? Is the subject of my message the cause of controversy between us? Is the atmosphere strained or cordial?

Answers to these questions will help you to find answers to the next set of questions more easily than if you jump straight in with 'What do I want to say?'

What? (subject)

- What exactly do I want to say?
- What do I need to say?
- What does he need to know?
- What information can I omit?
- What information must I include in order to be –
    clear
    concise
    courteous
    constructive
    correct
    complete
  – the six C's of effective communication.

How? (tone and style)

- How am I going to communicate my message? With words? Or pictures? Or both? Which words? Which pictures?
- Which medium of communication will be most appropriate? Written or spoken? A letter or a personal chat or interview? A report or an oral presentation? A memo or a telephone call?
- How will I organize the points I want to make? Shall I use deductive sequence (start with my main point and then go on

to the explanation/examples/illustrations)? Or inductive sequence (start with the explanation/examples/illustrations and build up to the main point at the end)?

● How am I going to achieve the right effect? What tone must I use to achieve my objective? Which words must I use/avoid in order to create the right tone?

In some cases the answers to these questions will come quickly. In fact, they may seem obvious. But, beware – it is very easy to jump to conclusions, to see the problem from your point of view and forget that your listener or reader may see things differently. It is always worthwhile going through these questions before you communicate anything difficult or of some length and it is useful to bear them in mind even when you are communicating spontaneously. They act as a gentle discipline to stop you 'opening your mouth without thinking'.

But with more difficult problems or sensitive issues, it is often worthwhile pondering over these questions even for several days and sometimes weeks before you write or speak.

Planning the message

Only when you have given some thought to these six essential questions are you ready to plan your message.

Stage 1 – Write down your objective It is always a good idea to write down (preferably in one or two sentences) exactly what you are trying to achieve by your message. You will then have it always before you to help you to organize your material and avoid straying from the point.

Stage 2 – Assemble the information Using notes on paper or index cards if it is to be a fairly long message like a report or oral presentation of some kind, jot down all the ideas or points which you think you need to make.

At this stage you need to *select* only the essential, relevant information and *reject* the irrelevant however much you may feel tempted to include it. Ask yourself questions like 'Is this really relevant to my message?' 'Does my audience (listener or reader) really need to have this information if he is to understand my message?' 'Will this help me to achieve my objective?'

Stage 3 – Group the information Now consider your list and look for links between the bits of information. Rewrite your notes in clear groups. It helps to give each group a heading. The groups will probably become the paragraphs or sections in your finished message and the headings will either remain as headings (if headings are appropriate) or contain the gist of each group and will therefore help you to compose the main sentence of the paragraph, often called the 'topic sentence'. Remember that all paragraphs should have only one main idea. All the other ideas in the paragraph will be supporting material – examples, elaboration, illustrations and so on, of the main idea.

Stage 4 – Put the information into logical sequence Your next task is to put the groups of information (still only in note-form) into some sort of sensible order which your reader can follow.

Self-check

What are the most commonly used methods of ordering material?

Perhaps *the* most common method is *chronological order* (or historical order) which merely presents the material in the order in which it occurred or occurs in time. On occasions presenting the material chronologically is the most appropriate order to adopt, but don't use this method without some critical thought. Since most of the things we need to write about in business have a time sequence, there is always a temptation to use this method even when it is not the most appropriate. Always try to look for some other logical link between the sections of your material. Consider the following:

- *Spatial (or place) order* – effective for describing machinery, buildings, furniture, geographical location. Facts are presented on a geographical basis – from place to place: from north to south, top to bottom, left to right, high to low, in and out, up and down or near to far.
- *Order of importance* – descending order of importance (or deductive order): starting with the most important point to gain the reader's attention; ascending order of importance (or inductive order): starting with the least important point. This

order is not usually advisable in business writing except in persuasive writing where it can be very effective.

- *Ascending order of complexity* – simpler ideas first followed by increasingly difficult or complex material.
- *Descending order of familiarity* – moving 'from the known to the unknown'.
- *Cause and effect* – put simply cause and effect means '*because of this, then that*'. In other words, 'because this happened, that happened'.
- *Topical* – sometimes of course there appears to be no real link between the chunks of material and no obvious pattern of development. In this case, all you can do is deal with each chunk on a topic by topic basis.

Stage 5 – Produce a skeleton outline By working through the previous four stages you will have produced in effect a plan or skeleton outline of your finished message but if this outline is not clearly on a piece of paper and your message is fairly long, it is essential to produce this plan which you can then use to work from. It will make the job of writing or presenting your final message much easier and the receiver's job of understanding you also much easier.

Stage 6 – Write the first draft Now you are ready to start writing. Write the first draft to yourself. Don't worry at this stage about the style and the words – that can come later. Many people find that actually starting to write, particularly anything of any length and complexity, is the most difficult barrier to get through. However, if you take this advice and you have done the necessary preparation and planning including some thoughts on what you are going to put in the introduction, the main body of the message and the conclusion, you will probably find that the words themselves come much more easily.

Stage 7 – Edit the rough draft and write the final draft Once you have written the first rough draft you are now required to put yourself in the shoes of your receiver. Read your draft through his eyes, checking for ambiguities, errors, awkward expressions, lack of signpost words ('first', 'second,' 'finally', 'on the other hand', 'consequently', etc.) which are essential to guide your reader along the route of your argument, and, above all, aiming for a concise, easily understood style

The following tips may help you:

- Vary the length of the sentences but keep them on the shorter side.
- Paragraphs should have only one main idea.
- Use words that the reader will understand.
- Avoid unbusinesslike colloquialisms (e.g. 'to cut a long story short').
- Omit unnecessary words.
- Use the shorter rather than the longer word or phrase, if appropriate.
- Avoid hackneyed expressions (clichés – 'please find enclosed', 'thanking you in anticipation', for example).
- Avoid needless repetition of words and phrases – find alternatives, wherever possible.
- Use sincere words – don't overstate or exaggerate.
- Use positive words rather than negative words if possible.
- Use the active rather than the passive voice (for an explanation of this and other aspects of grammar and style refer to Part 3: 'The bricks and mortar of English').

Part 1
The business of speaking

In the opening pages of this book we have looked
at some of the general principles which lie behind
communicating any message. You should always
bear these principles in mind as we turn now to
look at more specific applications of them to
typical business communication tasks.

Perhaps because speaking is such an essential
part of our everyday life we tend to take some of
the less formal speaking occasions for granted.
For this reason, Part I opens with some general
information about the way we speak and some
advice on how to make the most of your voice. It
then goes on to look at one of the most common
business communication activites of all – talking
on the telephone, before dealing with the
problems of interviewing, being interviewed for a
job, communicating in small groups and meetings
and the most formal and perhaps therefore the
most alarming occasion of them all – giving a talk.
The final chapter in this part introduces the
variety of visual aids available to the speaker and
outlines the major advantages and disadvantages
of each together with some tips on how to use
them effectively and confidently.

1 | Effective speaking

'Mike, come here a moment, will you?'

'What's the matter, Jim?'

'Well, while you were away, the men decided to go ahead with their request for a common room. I'm supposed to see the boss about it tomorrow.'

'Oh?'

'Well, I've thought about it and I think we'd stand a better chance if you come too. You're a better talker than I am.'

'Well, thanks but I'm really not sure . . .'

'Oh! Don't worry, I'll give you all the details. We decided that . . .'

Supposing someone did ask you to do this. How would you react? Would you go along and just trust to luck that the right words would occur to you when you needed them? Or would you plan your approach? If the boss didn't give in easily to your request, would you become aggressive? Or would you keep calm? If Jim wasn't presenting a very good case, would you butt in impatiently and take over?

How do you estimate your ability at effective speaking? Not just the formal occasion but in face-to-face discussions and interviews, at meetings and on the telephone?

Perhaps because we learn to speak before we write, or perhaps because speaking is so much a part of our everyday life, we are liable to take speaking for granted and as the joke card implies, 'open our mouth before engaging our brain'. But it is not just the 'big occasion' which requires care and attention.

In *What Do You Mean, 'Communication'?* and *The Business of Communicating* we have looked so far at the problems inherent in the communicating process when listening, reading and writing. But the same principles apply in the countless speaking situations which present themselves at work. They may involve you in simply answering a telephone call; on the other hand, they may involve participation in group discussion, giving information, instructing someone new in the procedures of your department, presenting an idea at a union meeting, or making oral reports to your manager or head of department. They may also involve you in giving short talks at work or as part of your club activities. Later on, they may involve interviewing and chairmanship. In the next few chapters we shall look in more detail at each of these situations. In each of them you will be drawing on the range and flexibility of your communication skills as you try to express what you have to say in clear, precise and forceful English.

Let's look first in this chapter at the basic skills of speaking which apply in any situation: (a) personal qualities and (b) vocal qualities – enunciation and pronunciation.

Basic speaking skills

Activity

First of all, think of someone whose speaking ability you admire. What are the qualities and characteristics which contribute to his success when speaking? Make a list.

Has he any qualities which distract or irritate you? List these.

Now think of someone you regard as a poor speaker. Add to your list ways in which you think he could improve his skill at speaking.

Keep this list – it represents what you think constitutes good and poor oral communication and it should form the basis for all your efforts to increase your own skills as a speaker.

Personal qualities

Speak clearly To be a good speaker you need first and foremost to be able to express your ideas clearly. Your language should be simple and your material organized so that it can be easily followed. You should avoid trying to impress by using long complicated words. Of course, you may have to use specialized vocabulary or jargon in some situations but you should take care to explain any terms that may be unfamiliar to your audience.

As well as clear thinking, speaking clearly also means uttering the words distinctly so that they are easily recognizable.

Speak accurately You should also make sure that the words you use say exactly what you mean. You therefore need a reasonably wide vocabulary so that you can choose words with precise meanings to suit your purpose.

The facts you use should be correct, so you should take care to research your subject thoroughly and ensure that any authorities you quote are reliable. You should also avoid making statements which go beyond the facts and which might therefore be challenged. Statements which begin 'Everybody thinks . . .' or 'Nobody in their right mind would accept . . .' are always dangerous and open to challenge, especially since they are likely to create a hostile reaction.

Show empathy Always try to be courteous and friendly. However angry you feel, try to control your emotions and at least remain calm. Perhaps the best way to be courteous and polite is to put yourself in the other person's place. Try to make yourself feel what the other person is feeling. Putting yourself in the other person's place in this sense helps you to establish *empathy* for that person. This doesn't mean that you have to agree with them or their ideas but it does help you to be understanding and patient. Facial expression and tone of voice are obviously important here especially in group discussions and interviews.

Be sincere This really means being natural. There is always a danger when talking to strangers or people of higher status of becoming stiff and awkward, and trying to put on an act. This usually stems from lack of confidence. Of course, when you talk to your boss you will not talk in exactly the same manner that you would when you talk to a friend or colleague, but you should strive to be yourself as much as you can in all situations.

Activity

Consider how you normally speak when talking to friends
or members of your family. Then think about how you
speak when talking to your boss or someone very senior to
you.

Does your voice sound much the same in both instances?

If so, then you probably speak in a natural way most of
the time. (Of course, your choice of words and phrases
may, and probably should, be rather different.)

Do you freeze up when talking to certain people?

Does your voice become higher or lower?

Does your rate of speech speed up or slow down?

Do your movements and posture become stiff and
awkward?

Relax The best way of getting rid of these unnatural speech
characteristics is to relax. When our muscles are tense, we have
difficulty expressing ourselves naturally. Awkward movements
are also the result of tension.

Try taking a deep breath. This may help you to relax. If you
freeze up with tension, you probably begin holding your breath
without realizing it. If you can remind yourself to breathe in a
natural manner, or even more deeply than usual, your muscles
will be more relaxed, and you will be too.

Eye contact In Chapter 15 of *What Do You Mean, 'Communication'?* which looks at the importance of body language, we have
already seen that *direction of gaze* and *length of gaze* are important factors in synchronizing speech and signifying desire to be
friendly, but it is worth reminding ourselves here how crucial eye
contact is whenever people are speaking to one another.

Activity

Have you ever been in conversation with someone who
seems unwilling to look you in the eye and intent on
looking almost anywhere but at you? How does this make
you feel?

A speaker who never looks at his listeners may be conveying messages like 'I am not very interested in you', 'I don't like you', 'I am not very sure of myself', 'I am not sure about what I am saying', or even 'Don't believe what I am saying.'

So when you are speaking give your listeners their fair share of eye contact. Don't keep your eyes on the desk, or in your lap or out of the window, and when you are talking to a large group move your eyes around the room treating them as individuals. Your audience will prefer a slightly hesitant speaker who shows his interest in them by looking at them to a highly fluent speaker who reads with his head down over his notes.

Appearance How you look can affect how well others understand you. Your appearance reflects how you see yourself – 'self-image'. Since your listeners cannot help but notice your appearance, they will receive metacommunications from the way you dress and your general grooming. In most speaking situations (apart from telephone conversations and the radio) people see the speaker and form judgements about him even before he speaks.

Attractive dress and good grooming are obviously important in formal situations: the public meeting, the job interview and so on. But being 'dressed up' or 'dressed formally' is not always practicable or even appropriate and in some jobs it would be absurd. Supposing you are in the middle of a dirty job and you are called to the manager's office or asked to explain something to a visitor, what then? Well, your personal appearance should commend you. Even oil-stained overalls can convey the impression that they are well cared for and that you consider personal cleanliness and tidiness is important even when you have a dirty job.

The two important things to consider are therefore:

● personal cleanliness and tidiness
● dress and appearance appropriate to the situation

Even as a new employee, you should realize that the way you look affects the impression you make. Take your cues from the others around you and dress accordingly. This doesn't mean losing your individuality completely but it does mean being flexible and ready to adapt your appearance to suit particular circumstances. So, if you like going in for extremes in fashion when you are not at work, tone things down for work.

Posture Good posture is also important. Someone who props up the wall or slouches in his chair as he speaks conveys a message to his listeners which may surprise him. His attitude is showing. He is either tired or bored or careless, or all three! And his listeners are not likely to be impressed.

Another important reason for examining your posture – how you sit and stand when you are talking – is that posture is related to voice quality.

If you slouch over, hang your head or let your shoulders droop, the quality of your voice will not be good, because your breathing is affected. You cannot draw as much breath into your lungs, nor do you have complete control over how you let out the air.

Furthermore, if you slouch or bend your head down, your throat muscles, jaw and vocal chords do not operate as freely as they should, with the muffled poorly pronounced results we have already seen.

Poor posture also affects your voice psychologically as well as physically. The sense of not caring about yourself or about anything – communicated by poor posture – creeps into your voice as well. If you have a hangdog look, your voice will probably have a hangdog sound. It will be listless and spiritless. A whining quality which most people find unpleasant may very well colour the tone of your voice.

By improving your posture when talking, you can do much toward instilling in your voice and your whole manner four characteristics of good voice quality: alertness, pleasantness, distinctness and expressiveness.

Techniques of effective speaking

Don't think that you can't change the way you speak. You can and do control your voice all the time. Listen to the way you use your voice in different situations, raising and lowering the volume, adjusting the tone to suit particular circumstances and so on. You can improve your voice if you want to, but you have to work at it. The first step is to be aware of the factors which affect the sound of your voice.

The mechanics of speech Speech involves many mechanical skills. It requires a complicated manipulation of the diaphragm, the lungs and muscles of the chest as well as vocal chords, mouth, tongue and lips.

The vocal chords are rather like rubber bands stretched across the interior of a kind of box called the larynx behind what we call the adam's-apple. As the air in your lungs is forced up through the larynx and past the vocal chords, sound is produced. The sounds are affected first by the vocal chords, and then successively by the position of the jaw, the interior of the mouth, the tongue, teeth and lips. Of course, you are not aware of all this when you speak, unless excessive speaking, tiredness or emotion draws your attention to your voice.

To ensure that the sounds you produce are clear, your throat muscles must be relaxed, your jaw must not be taut or rigid and your lips must be flexible and capable of assuming a variety of positions. If you have ever had an anaesthetic injection at the dentist you will know what it does to your ability to move your lips properly to pronounce the words.

Pitch A person whose voice has a high pitch may sound thin or squeaky or shrill. A person with low pitch will sound deep or throaty. When your vocal chords are stretched tight, the higher the sound will be as the air is forced past them causing them to vibrate (like plucking a tight elastic band).

When people are frightened or tense, their vocal chords stretch tight and their voices tend to squeak. One way to relax your throat muscles is to practise this simple exercise:

Activity

Take a deep breath then, as your breathe out, say several short syllables, for example:

She gave us all a . . .

Try it. Notice how the tightness disappears as you exhale.

It is, in fact, physically impossible to breathe out and keep the muscles tight at the same time. This is why deep breathing can help you to relax.

People with high pitch must work to control it. Generally, listeners don't react favourably to voices that are pitched very high and are very thin and shrill. If your voice is high, practise lowering and varying the pitch if you can. But don't worry about this too much because the normal voice under normal circumstances is rarely pitched so high as to be unpleasant. The thing to avoid is allowing emotional stress to raise the pitch of your voice even higher.

People with very low pitch have a different problem. They need to be careful to speak up clearly. People with this kind of voice sometimes muffle their words and make it very difficult for their audience to follow what they are saying.

Volume Volume is more easily controlled than pitch, but practice is still required to get the right volume. Proper breathing is essential to volume control and good speaking. Practise taking deep breaths and letting out the air with just enough force to generate the right volume. Learn how to *project* your voice so that you can be heard at great distances without yelling or sounding strained.

If you can control your voice and speak clearly without appearing to strain or shout or run out of breath, you will impress your listeners by the quality of your voice alone. They are very likely to assume that you also know what you are talking about and will find it worth their while to listen to you.

The right volume depends on the situation. You should therefore note:

- where you are speaking (in a small room or a large lecture room; in a room where sound carries well; in a room where sound echoes; indoors or out in the open), as the location will affect how well your words can be heard
- the size of the group to whom you are speaking
- background noise, e.g. the low hum of machinery

Diction Diction – the way in which you say or pronounce words – is acquired. To some extent it is affected by your accent. Someone from the North will have different diction from someone who comes from London or the South. Diction depends on 'articulation' and 'enunciation', which are terms used to describe how you pronounce words:

- articulation refers to the way people pronounce *consonants*
- enunciation refers to the way people pronounce *vowels*

If a person articulates and enunciates well, i.e. clearly, they will have good diction. Good diction is generally considered to be the result of being well educated and well informed.

However, it is important not to confuse diction with accent. Whatever your accent, you should pronounce your words clearly. Listen to television and radio announcers to hear the difference between accent and diction. There was a time when BBC English was held up as 'the way to speak'. Nowadays, every possible regional accent is represented and is quite acceptable because the speakers pronounce their words clearly; so like your accent, your diction will tell your listeners something about you.

If you mispronounce words, for example 'labratry' instead of 'laboratory', or drop your 'h's' or final 't's', or slur your words, you won't impress your listeners. In some situations this may not matter. In others such as a job interview, it could mean the difference between getting something you want or need, or not getting it.

Activity

Record your voice and think about the way you speak – the physical process you use to produce the sounds.

Blurred, indistinct speech can be caused by a tight, rigid jaw or tight lips.

If your throat is tight, it is almost certain that your jaw will be tight. The jaw should be relaxed and ready to open and close freely as required. If it doesn't do this, the sounds come through a half-closed mouth and consequently are unclear. It is also almost impossible to get expression into a voice produced under these conditions and the result is a voice which lacks vitality and sounds monotonous.

Activity to test your jaw movement

Test this for yourself. Tighten (i.e. half-close) your jaw and say, 'A cleverly devised scheme'. Notice that your teeth and lips hardly moved.

Now relax your jaw and let your teeth and lips move freely while you say the phrase again. You should be able to detect the difference quite easily. If not, try it again with a tape-recorder. Repeat the exercise and see if you can detect the difference.

Activity to relax your jaw

Grit your teeth and tighten your jaw. Hold this position for a few seconds.

Then let your lower jaw sag. (It may help to let your mouth drop open as you do this – best done in private perhaps!) Note that while your lower jaw is sagging you can put your tongue between your teeth. This tells you that your jaw is relaxed.

Thought! Often when we are lying down and think we are relaxed, our jaw is tight as a result of inner tension. Practising this exercise when trying to get off to sleep can be very effective.

Tight lips, or lips which do not move very much during speech also affect the sounds which are made.

Billy Connolly, a Glaswegian, when asked if he made an effort to change his accent when he came south of the border said: 'No! I just open my mouth more. Glaswegians have mouths like letter-boxes. They don't open their mouths much when they speak.'

This emphasizes the difference between accent and diction. If you have a strong regional accent, don't try to change it, but do make sure you open your mouth and use your lips flexibly to pronounce your words.

Activity

Try this experiment. Set your lips in a straight line (like a letter-box!) and try to say the words 'bit', 'team', 'fill', 'kite', 'see' and 'chap' without changing the position of your lips. Now try 'hip', 'load', 'murmur', 'no', 'rain', 'yet' and 'weigh'.

Notice how the pronunciation was affected. This is because the lips should take a different position in order to produce the first letters in each of these words.

Now try saying the words again naturally.

The good speaker would have ranged through all the lip positions.

A small range of movements automatically means that some consonants and vowels become difficult to distinguish and this results in poor communication.

Even listeners with good hearing rely more than they think on 'lip-reading'. If the speaker's lips don't move very much, the words can be more difficult, if not impossible to understand.

Activity

If you are aware that you don't move your lips very much when you speak, practise this exercise.

Say 'soon', 'seen', 'sand', 'sawn', 'sow', 'side', 'such' – concentrating on putting your lips in clearly different positions.

At first you will find it helpful to exaggerate each movement, but don't exaggerate your lip movement when you are talking to other people; although when you are speaking in a very large room to a very large audience, it may be helpful to make your lip movements slightly more pronounced than normal, to cope with the distance your sounds must carry.

Speed The speed at which you talk will also affect the message you are sending. Speaking very quickly conveys a sense of urgency or an emergency to the listener. This may be useful at times, but speaking rapidly all the time, pouring out your words in a great rush, may cause your listeners to switch off. They will react negatively to the implied emergency that they have learned does not really exist. Speaking too quickly may also make it difficult for you to be understood, and you probably won't pronounce each word clearly and carefully.

Most people who speak in public actually speak at a slower rate than they do in normal conversation, but, of course, this depends on their normal speed. And they cannot afford to speak so slowly that the minds of their listeners wander or their listeners become bored or lose track of what they are saying.

The good speaker varies his pace according to the relative importance of what he is saying; thus unimportant words and phrases are spoken quickly while important words or phrases will be spoken more slowly.

The use of the pause If you spoke with long pauses between each word or series of words, you would very quickly lose your audience. However, the pause, carefully used, can be a very effective device for getting your message across.

A good speaker will pause briefly at the appropriate places to give his listeners the opportunity to take in what he has said. He will also occasionally pause before or after a word to give it emphasis, or before making a particularly important point.

Tone The inflection, or up-and-down movement of your voice – tone – also affects the way in which your message is received. Variations in tone are often associated with pitch and speed in giving interest and emphasis to your speech.

However, quite apart from the words you are saying, tone can betray your attitudes and emotions. Your attitude to your listener or listeners and to your message or subject is often indicated by the tone of voice you use.

Your tone can convey whether you are happy or angry or sad. You can sound humble and frightened, or commanding and patronizing. You can even make the same word mean several different things by the tone you give it:

'I've finished all those letters.'

'Good.'

'They're being typed now and should go out this afternoon.'

The word 'good' could mean 'I understand' or 'Well done –
you've worked amazingly fast' or 'It's about time too!' depending
on the tone of voice used.

It is easy to give the wrong impression by carelessly using the
wrong tone and, of course, it is easy to convey what you *really*
think even when you don't want to.

Just as tone is important in informal speaking, so it is an
essential part of a talk given in a formal situation. If you are
speaking on a subject which is of no interest to you, it is easy for
the listeners to detect this in the tone of your voice. Of course, if
you are enthusiastic about it and pleased to be speaking on a
particular subject, it is good to let the audience recognize this.
But negative, adverse feelings should be disguised. If the subject
really *is* a bore, then concentrate on doing a good job in spite of
it, and you'll find the tone of your voice will work with you and
not against you.

In other words, it is important to guard against letting your
tone betray your attitude and feelings unless you want it to do
so.

Qualities to aim for when speaking

Alertness gives your listener the impression that you are aware
of and interested in what is happening around you and what you
are saying. They are more likely to feel it is worthwhile to listen
to you.

Pleasantness is partly being polite, but also striving to give a
friendly tone to your voice by smiling and looking pleasant.

Distinctness is speaking clearly so that your listener can hear and
understand your words without straining. This includes pronunciation, of course. It requires you to breathe properly, to move
your lips, tongue and jaw freely and easily. It also requires you
to talk directly to the listener.

Expressiveness is putting feeling into your voice. To be expressive, you must avoid the low droning monotone which will turn
off your listener. It is easier to be expressive when you maintain

good posture, and are interested in your subject and concerned about your listener.

Activity

Choose a passage from a book or magazine article and read it aloud (tape-recording if possible) four times: first concentrating on sounding alert, then concentrating on sounding pleasant (smiling helps!), then concentrating on sounding distinct, and finally, aiming for expression.

Now play back the four versions of the passage. Can you hear any difference between them? Did you succeed in emphasizing each of the four qualities?

Finally, read and record the passage again aiming for *all four* qualities this time.

2 | Talking on the telephone

'Hello.'

'Hello.'

'I'm ringing up to report a pothole in the road outside my house. It's been getting bigger and bigger and it's time something was done about it before someone has an accident. Can you get someone to see to it?'

'Yes, we'll see to it. Where exactly is the pothole?'

'Right outside my house.'

'Yes, but . . . where is that?'

'Oh, I see . . . yes, you want my address – it's 29 Maud Rise . . . Have you got that?'

'Yes. Thanks for letting us know.'

The girl wrote '25 Moor Drive' on a piece of paper and immediately went along to the Highways Section to report the pothole.

Activity

What do you think might have been the likely outcome of this telephone conversation? Imagine the possible sequence of events. Make a list and then alongside, list what should have been done to avoid these consequences.

Nowadays the telephone is probably the most common means of communication in business, and used efficiently it has two advantages:

- it is fast
- it allows people who can't meet to converse

We can communicate in seconds with people not only within our own organization, but across the country, and nowadays across the world by means of satellites, under-sea cables and radio. Indeed, the telephone has now been joined by telex which transfers a written message, and video conference links which allow several people in far distant places to confer with one another and see one another by means of video equipment; before long, video telephone and electronic equipment to convey exact replicas of written documents will no doubt be as commonplace as the telephone that we have learned to love – and hate.

For the telephone, for all its convenience and speed, also has the power to convey rapidly a poor impression of the efficiency of individuals and organizations and create considerable confusion and irritation.

Self-check

List the ways in which inefficient use of the telephone has irritated you.

Cost

Certainly telephone calls seem cheaper than sending a letter. Many organizations calculate that the average cost of sending a letter, taking into account the staff time involved and overheads as well as postage, is about £5, which would buy quite a lot of telephone time even at current rates. But telephone calls do not necessarily save time – and in business time is money. We have all suffered from the irritating waste of time caused by:

- trying to get a line
- person required not available
- being left hanging on by an operator who appears to have gone to lunch
- being passed from department to department in an effort to find someone who can answer the query
- wrong numbers or numbers engaged
- a caller who seems to have all the time in the world to chat when we are busy

Any one of these time-wasters can take longer than it takes to dictate a letter.

First impressions count

But the telephone can exact other costs. Frequently, the first contact a caller has with an organization is with the person who answers his first call. That person, either through lack of courtesy, lack of knowledge about the organization, or how to use the telephone itself, can, however innocently, create an initial bad impression of the organization which it is difficult to correct.

The faceless voice

Perhaps the principal cause of much of this apparent inefficiency is that although the telephone allows oral communication, it does not transmit visual communication. We have already seen how important non-verbal messages can be in complementing the verbal message. Facial expressions, gestures and posture not only help to convey the real meaning of words, but are often the principal means of feedback in face-to-face conversation, allowing misunderstandings to be instantly corrected. Without this visual communication and consequent feedback these problems are typical of those which occur during telephone calls:

- words are missed
- words are misheard
- the message is misunderstood because the visual cues and feedback are missing

Not only does this lack of visual communication cause messages to be *received* incorrectly, but it can also cause messages to be *transmitted* incorrectly by putting callers at what they feel to be a psychological disadvantage. Many people have developed a positive dislike of the telephone because they cannot see whom they are talking to, to the extent that they lack the confidence to make and answer calls clearly and efficiently.

Given the importance of the telephone in modern business operations and the prevalence of bad telephone habits (of which we are all guilty at times), it is surprising that very few books on business communication offer more than a paragraph or two on the subject of telephone technique. For this reason, this chapter is aimed at correcting the balance somewhat by providing guidance on making and answering calls efficiently and therefore cutting the costs of telephoning.

First requirements

Be brief – but not at the expense of making yourself clearly understood and not to the extent of being abrupt and discourteous. Lack of telephone confidence often causes people to talk for longer than they would in face-to-face conversations.

Be courteous This is especially important when telephoning to avoid creating a bad impression which is so difficult to correct. Your tone of voice is as crucial in conveying a courteous, cheerful impression as the words you use. Remember too, that even if you are not yet using a video phone, your facial expression affects the tone of your voice. Smile! A smile can be heard – in your tone of voice, which will sound pleasant and interested. If you scowl or frown, your tone will be unfriendly and uninterested.

Be resourceful Don't be clueless. Always think of ways in which you can be most helpful. If you are taking a message for someone else, use your local knowledge to suggest helpful ways of getting the caller and the recipient of the message in touch with one another so that the caller can judge in an informed way what he wants to do. If the caller has been put through to your department but no one in your department knows anything about the matter, think quickly. Who else in the organization might know something and be able to help? If you really can't help, sound sincerely concerned, not uninterested.

Speak clearly Enunciate and articulate your words particularly clearly to counteract both the poorer acoustic quality of a telephone line and the absence of lip movements to help the listener. When giving names and numbers, if there is any possible ambiguity use the Post Office alphabetical code which is reproduced below:

A for Andrew	F for Frederick	K for King
B for Benjamin	G for George	L for Lucy
C for Charlie	H for Harry	M for Mary
D for David	I for Isaac	N for Nellie
E for Edward	J for Jack	O for Oliver

P for Peter	T for Tommy	X for Xmas
Q for Queenie	U for Uncle	Y for Yellow
R for Robert	V for Victory	Z for Zebra
S for Sugar	W for William	

And remember that 5 and 9 sound very similar. Take a tip from the police who say 'fife' and 'nina' to distinguish between them.

Speak more slowly When you are talking on the telephone it is a good idea to slow your speech down. When your voice is being mechanically transmitted, the words seem to move together faster. That is one reason television announcers often speak at a slower rate than is normal in everyday conversation. Remember too that someone may be trying to take notes as you talk.

Telephone operators

Although telephone operator training is standard practice, it would seem that some organizations put their least able employee on the switchboard.

> ### Self-check
>
> We have all suffered at the hands of switchboard operators who behave as if taking a call is an inconvenient interruption. If you were selecting a switchboard operator, which six personal qualities would you look for?

The operator is typically regarded by callers as the representative of the whole organization and in a booklet published by the British Association for Commerical and Industrial Education (BACIE) called *A Guide to the Use of the Telephone in Business* the author justifiably suggests that telephone operators should be very carefully selected and trained and should possess these essential qualities:

- verbal intelligibility
- speed
- courtesy
- accuracy
- discretion
- resourcefulness

They are just as essential to *anyone* who is allowed near a business telephone.

Help the operator

The good switchboard operator is indeed an organization's hostess: she welcomes your callers, introduces you, apologizes for your absence or tries to get you on another line, often takes messages – and is frequently blamed for your shortcomings.

Help her by:

- understanding how the telephone system used in your organization works
- giving the number you want (including the STD code)
- not disappearing immediately you have asked her to ring a number for you
- answering the phone after the first ring (when she calls you back)
- acting upon her messages without delay
- telling her in advance when you are likely to be absent

Making a call

Before

1 Answer the six questions of effective communication (see pp. 19–21).
2 Make notes of what you want to achieve, the main points/queries you must include and any dates, facts, etc., you may need to refer to.
3 Have ready any files, correspondence, etc., you *may* need in the course of the conversation. Don't keep your receiver waiting while you ferret around for the relevant papers.
4 Have ready a plain piece of paper for your own notes.
5 Know whom you need to speak to. Sometimes this may be impossible but, at least, keep a personal telephone directory of names and numbers you ring regularly.
6 Remember there are certain times when calls are cheaper – can your call wait?

7 Dial the number carefully (or tell the operator clearly). Wrong numbers are the most common cause of frustration and time-wasting, but are usually the fault of the caller.

During

1 Give a greeting ('Good morning', etc.). State your name (and organization) and the name of the person you want to speak to.

2 Wait patiently to be put through. You may be put through to a secretary or the department telephone, in which case you will have to go through Step 1 again.

3 If you are cut off, replace the telephone receiver, wait a few seconds and ring again.

4 Keep it short. Most calls can achieve their purpose in twenty seconds. Twenty seconds . . . time to run 200 yards! Time for a jet to fly four miles!

5 State your subject/query clearly – enough to put the receiver in the picture.

6 Refer periodically to your notes.

7 Pause occasionally to get feedback that your message is understood.

8 Spell names and addresses. Repeat any numbers.

9 Take notes, especially name and number of person to whom you are speaking.

10 Summarize main points of a long conversation at the end and always conclude by confirming any action required or date to be met.

11 If you have to leave a message for someone else, help the person who answered the phone to take the right message. Don't just ramble on making him get the gist of it. Tell him which are the main points to write down.

12 Be polite. Thank the receiver for his help, even if you haven't got the information you wanted. Fostering goodwill is not just part of being courteous, but will help future relations.

13 Telephone etiquette officially requires that if you are the caller *you* decide when the call ends but since not everyone knows this, use your judgement.

After

Immediately, before you forget:

1 Fill in your notes so that they will be comprehensible at a later date.
2 Date the note and file it.
3 Put any relevant dates for future action or follow-up in your diary.
4 Pass on the results of your call to anyone concerned with the matter.

Getting 'research' information through telephone calls

In gathering information for the preparation of a report, or merely as part of your day-to-day job, we have seen that you may need to contact original or primary sources of information, or someone else who has access to secondary information you need. Telephone calls are widely used by business and industrial firms who may need certain information very quickly, and made correctly these calls can be very effective.

Before

- Work out exactly what information you need.
- Frame a series of increasingly specific questions which will give you what you want to know, e.g.

    'Do you have the unemployment figures for the Bristol area over the last six months?'

    'Does this include a breakdown by age groups and sex?'

    'Can you tell me the unemployment figures for girls aged sixteen to twenty-five for each month since June?'

    . . . And so on, to the level of detail that you need to go.
- Decide which firm, individual, office, government agency, organization or business might possibly have at hand the information you need.

During

- When you get through, be polite but specific. Don't say: 'I wonder if you happen to have anyone there who knows something about unemployment . . .' etc. Instead say: 'I need some information concerning the unemployment figures for the Bristol area over the last six months. Can you help me?' (Remember politeness and courtesy can be conveyed in your tone of voice.) Then, depending on the response, go on to ask a more specific question.

If they can't help say: 'Could you please give me the name of someone who can?'

- Don't get discouraged if the first place you try can't help you. Try another place. You will eventually get what you want if you keep trying. (Providing that it is not your telephone technique which is putting them off!)
- Make sure you are talking to the right person. Ask to speak to the 'personnel manager' or 'the person in charge of buying' or whatever is appropriate.
- Write down the information immediately. Don't rely on your memory. Read it back to the person you are questioning.
- Remember to say 'thank you'.

Answering the telephone

In some organizations the job of answering the telephone is given to the most junior employee. This is unwise as far as the organization or department is concerned, and unfair on the junior, who through lack of confidence and lack of experience in the organization usually creates a poor impression.

However, more senior employees may be just as guilty: through laziness, apathy or thoughtlessness they can create an equally poor impression.

Anyone who answers a telephone must be courteous, helpful and efficient.

Before

1 Know how the telephone system in your organization works, especially how to transfer a call. (Being cut off is probably one of the most frustrating experiences – it wastes time and creates a bad impression.)
2 Never answer a telephone without a pencil and paper.
3 Keep near your own telephone:

- a pencil and message pad
- an internal telephone directory
- an appointment diary (if appropriate)

4 Stop talking to anyone else and reduce any other noise *before* picking up the telephone receiver.

During

1 Think about the needs of the receiver and give him as far as possible everything he needs to know, e.g.

- announce your name and department or section (in a cheerful voice!)
- if the call has come through the operator, the receiver will already have been given the name of your organization
- if the call is directly from outside, announce the name of your organization first, and then your name and department (if relevant)

NB A common fault is to start speaking a second or two before picking up the receiver or more commonly on the switchboard, before pressing the button on the console. I have heard half the name of more organizations than I care to remember, e.g. '. . . oyce Ltd. Good morning.' '. . . dons Ltd. Good morning.'

Many organizations have a standard practice for greeting a caller – know your house rules, e.g. 'Simmonds, Personnel Director, speaking', 'Mr Boff's secretary speaking', 'Good morning. The Dispatch Department, Mrs Jones speaking.'

Don't rush this greeting. Because you have to say it so often it is tempting to rattle it off, with the result that it is usually incomprehensible to an outsider and therefore pointless.

2 Be willingly prepared to answer the query, or take a message for someone who can, or transfer the call.

3 If you are acting as secretary you may be expected to filter calls for your boss. Know whether:

- he may wish to be 'unavailable'
- he wants some people put straight through to him (if so, know who they are)

- he wants you to deal with certain routine calls yourself (if so, know which types of call you should deal with)

You will therefore have to ask for the name of the caller and politely ask the purpose of the call. But use tact. Don't be over protective or you might cause resentment from the caller and your boss.

4 Listen carefully to what the caller has to say and take notes. They will form the basis either of your action or of a message if you have to pass one on. Check that you have the right facts in the message. Don't assume the recipient of the message will know what it's all about.

5 Don't hesitate to ask the speaker to slow down or to spell names and addresses if they are unclear, and always read them back.

6 Compensate for the lack of visual communication. The nods of normal conversation must be conscientiously replaced by verbal equivalents, e.g. 'Yes, I see . . .', 'Fine, I'll let him know . . .', 'I'm not sure I agree with that . . .', 'Really?'

But avoid using overfamiliar or slang expressions like 'You don't say!', 'Yeah', 'Good God!' – and, if the message is for someone else, avoid speaking *for* them, committing them or imagining negative attitudes on their behalf, unless you are authorized to do so. For instance: 'Oh he'll be over the moon about *that*!' (said either sincerely or in a sarcastic tone of voice).

7 Don't be distracted by anything going on around you, or someone else trying to attract your attention and *never* try to hold two conversations at once.

8 Be just as keen as your caller should be to save time and money.

9 Avoid asking the caller to 'hold the line' whilst you go on a paper chase. Offer to call back.

10 If you are cut off, put the telephone down and wait for the caller to call you back.

11 Before the call ends, repeat back the main points of the conversation and always read back any names, addresses, numbers, dates and times, to give the caller a chance to correct any errors or omissions.

12 Agree what happens next, especially if you are taking a

message for someone else, e.g. 'I will tell him that you will ring again on Thursday morning', or 'I will ask him to ring you back as soon as possible.'

13 Telephone etiquette requires that since the caller is paying, he should be the one to decide when the call ends. However since not everyone seems aware of this, be prepared to use your judgement.

After

1 Fill in your notes so that they will be comprehensible to you later and particularly to the recipient if you have taken a message.

2 Act on the notes immediately, telling anyone else who is concerned. Write any letters or memos now, if possible, while the matter is clear in your mind.

3 If you have a message for someone else, put the date and time of the call on the message and deliver it immediately or place it in a prominent position on the person's desk if he is out. Remind him when he returns.

4 Update any documents necessary; write dates in your diary.

Remember! When you speak on the telephone the efficient reputation of both you and your organization is in your hands.

Review

1 *Telephone messages*
What problems might arise for the recipient of the messages at the top of page 53?

2 Most organizations have their own telephone message pads or obtain them from stationery suppliers. Design a telephone message pad for your organization (or your home).

3 Reduce the length of this telephone conversation making it more efficient on both sides (invent any extra details which seem necessary):
The number is ringing . . .
'Miss Jefferies. Can I help you?'
'Er . . . Are you Mr Sloan's secretary? Is he about?'
'Well, he's in the building, but I'm afraid he's not

Jim
J. Mr Strange rang. Can you meet him in
the bar today to discuss some problems.

b. Your something workshop on Monday is
cancelled. They will let you know the new
time.

c. The chap from Dawsons rang says its all fixed.

available at the moment. Can I get him to ring you back?
Could you give me your name and number?'

'Yes – tell him it's Trent of Partridge's. My number is
Manchester 6750716 but I won't be in after 4 o'clock this
afternoon.'

'Can I tell him what it is about?'

'Well – I've arranged to meet him in London tonight
and I said I'd let him know when I'd be arriving at the
airport. He thought he might be able to meet me at the
airport.'

'Well, I'll get him to ring you back before 4.00.'

'When do you expect him back?'

'Well, he said he'd be back by 3.00 p.m. but you know
what these meetings are like. They usually natter on
even when the business is done.'

'Oh – but supposing he hasn't rung me before I leave
for the airport? I shan't know whether he's meeting me
or not.'

(Silence)

'Are you still there?'

'Yes. I was just thinking . . . Well, I can't see what
else I can do. He never likes to be disturbed in these
meetings.'

'So you'll try to get him to ring me then?'

'Yes, I'll do what I can. Thank you. Goodbye, Mr
Trent.'

'I've just thought of . . .' (sound of receiver being put
down).

ANSWERS

1 a What does 'today' mean? Since the message has no date,
Jim will not necessarily know which day 'today' refers to. If
Jim is out all day on the day the message is received, when
he comes in the next day he would be justified in assuming
'today' refers to that day. It is therefore possible that he will
miss the appointment and turn up on the wrong day to find
no one there.

Furthermore, what does 'lunch time' mean? This will
depend on whether the lunch hour is taken at the same time
every day for both Mr Strange and Jim.

Finally Jim has no means of finding out the answers to
any of these queries because the message is not signed, so
he has no idea who took it.

*Telephone messages should always include the date and
time the message was taken and the name of the person who
took the message.*

b Same deficiencies as **1a**. It also does not include the name of
the person to whom it is addressed. The message is very
vague suggesting that the message-taker has not heard the
words very clearly and has not read it back to the caller. If
the message-recipient has no idea what the message is about
he may even wonder if it really is for him. He cannot check
with the message-taker (no name), he cannot check with
the caller (caller's name not given) and he is probably left,
either to ignore it and hope he will eventually find out what
it is all about, or to start a detective hunt perhaps starting
with appointments in his diary on Mondays (he doesn't
know *which* Monday).

Make sure the message contains all the necessary details.

c *Who* rang? *What's* all fixed? Now, the message-recipient has
just been talking to a chap at Dawson's asking him to
arrange a special delivery, so perhaps the message refers to
that and he can rest assured that his requirements will be
met. On the other hand, he spoke to someone else at
Dawson's the day before about another matter in which a

special price was being negotiated. That chap also said he'd ring back and let him know if the price had been accepted.

Perhaps the message refers to that matter. Perplexed, the recipient has no alternative but to make another, otherwise unnecessary, call to clear up the confusion.

Perhaps a worse consequence of this kind of incomplete message is that the message-recipient could have assumed wrongly that the message referred to the most recent matter.

Never assume that the message-recipient will know what the message is all about.

2   This illustration shows a message pad with all the headings necessary to remind the message-taker what he should make a note of. But no message pad can ensure that the details of the actual message are taken down clearly and completely – *that is up to you*:

```
Date: .....................    Time: ....................
Message for: ............................................
Message from: (Name) ...................................
             (Address) ................................
                       ................................
             (Tel. no.) ...............................
Message: ...............................................
.......................................................
.......................................................
Message taken by: ......................................
```

3   The conversation could have been like this:
   'Miss Jefferies. Mr Sloane's secretary. Can I help you?'
   'Good afternoon. This is Trent of Partridge's. Is it possible to speak to Mr Sloane? I'm meeting him in London tonight.'
   'I'm afraid he's at a meeting at the moment, Mr Trent. Can I give him a message?'
   'Yes please.' (Trent thinks quickly.) 'He said he might be able to meet me at the airport. Tell him: Trent (Partridge's,

Manchester) is arriving at Heathrow at 6.27 p.m. on Flight
No. ML-367. That's Terminal One. I will wait until 7 p.m. If
he has not arrived by then I will make my own way to
Tudor's where we've booked dinner for 8 p.m. If he wants
to ring me I shall be at Manchester 6750716 until 4 o'clock
this afternoon.'

'Can I just check that, Mr Trent?' (She reads back the
message.) 'Is that correct?'

'Fine. Thanks very much.'

'I'll see he gets it as soon as possible, but in any case
before he leaves the office this afternoon.'

'Thank you. Goodbye.'

'Goodbye, Mr Trent.'

Where possible, the conversation has been shortened by
giving the essential details early on in the conversation.
However, it cannot be greatly reduced because Mr Trent
must give the necessary information and the secretary must
read the message back to check that she has heard correctly
and written down what Mr Trent wants written down.

The major difference, however, between this and the
original conversation is that Trent knows exactly what is
going to happen and has built in a contingency plan which
will operate if Sloane can't meet him. Providing the secretary passes on the message (and she sounds efficient)
everyone will know what is happening. If by any chance she
fails to contact her boss, Trent's contingency plan will work
and they will meet for dinner at 8 p.m. All this has been
completed in one phone call instead of possibly two in the
original situation.

This was achieved because Trent thought in advance
about the call; worked out at least two possibilities – he
might speak to Sloane himself or he might have to leave a
message; thought of a contingency plan in case Sloane
couldn't meet him so that an additional call was not necessary; and had all the details at his fingertips.

Despite making the call as brief as possible, consistent
with being clearly understood, both parties were polite and
helpful, and the purpose of the call was achieved. Efficient
telephoning!

Activity

1 Find out *now* how your organization's telephone system works, including these points:

- Does a call come straight through to you, or through an operator?
- Does your organization expect you to answer a telephone call in a particular way? If so, how?
- How do you transfer an internal call? An external call?
- How do you get an outside line? Ask the operator? Or dial a particular number?

2 Find out when telephone calls are charged at the cheap rate, and what the different rates are.

3 Decide on a particular piece of information you need, work out which firms or organizations might be able to help you and make the necessary telephone calls to get the information.

   If you are not successful, analyse your telephone method and work out why.

   Try again – for some new information.

3 | Interviewing

For many people, interviewing means job hunting. Indeed, for many of us the job or selection interview is probably the most important interview we ever take part in. However, employment is only one of many reasons for participating in an interview. Every business day millions of interviews occur for purposes of giving and receiving instructions, selling ideas or products, appraising performance, handling complaints and grievances or solving problems. Add to that list the number of interviews that occur between doctors and their patients, lawyers and their clients, teachers and their students, police and the public, journalists and the public and so on, and it is easy to see that interviewing and being interviewed are something we are all involved in everyday – talking and listening to people, at home, at work and at leisure.

Perhaps it is because we are all involved in this activity so often that we tend to take all but the most formal occasions for granted. We become complacent and as with so many other communication activities interviews can often be ineffective and a waste of time.

Activity

Think back over the interviews that you have taken part in during the last week. Perhaps your boss called you into his office to discuss something, or asked to see you at a specific time; perhaps you made an appointment to see him; perhaps you visited the doctor; or had occasion to speak to a tutor at college on a one-to one basis. In some of the interviews you may have been the 'interviewer' – the one who asked for the interview – in others you may have been the 'interviewee' in that the other person may have been in control. In either case, think about these interviews critically and jot down a list of things which you feel were wrong with them, things which prevented the interview being as effective as it might have been.

Your list will probably include some of the following:

- Took longer than necessary.
- Rambled off the point into a discussion of irrelevancies.
- One or other party talked too much, not letting the other get a word in edgeways.
- Left you feeling dissatisfied in that the interview didn't achieve what you had expected or hoped.
- Left you wondering what the purpose of the interview really was.
- Developed into an argument or even a slanging match.
- Did more harm than good.

Activity

Now focus on one of those interviews and ask the following questions (write down the answer to the first question, if you know the answer):

1 Why did the interview take place?
2 Was the purpose of the interview clear? To both of us?
3 Was it with the right person?
4 Was it held at the right time and in the right place?
5 What did I expect or hope to achieve by it?
6 Did I achieve what I had hoped or expected?
7 Did I listen sufficiently? Did I talk more than I should have done?
8 Did I consider the other person's point of view fairly?
9 Did he consider mine fairly?
10 How long did the inverview take? How long should it have taken?

11 Was the time well spent?

Now write down ways in which you could improve the interview if you could go through the same interview again.

In general terms, interviewing consists of talking and listening and forming conclusions. Although talking and listening to other people are the basis of good communications at work and in our personal relationships, it is not just a question of encouraging people to talk to one another more, but a question of improving the *quality* of the talking and listening that takes place.

This chapter will therefore be concerned not just with the more formal kinds of interview, but with general principles which apply to all interviews, even fairly informal interviews which it is all too easy to take for granted.

What is an interview?

For the purpose of this chapter we shall define an interview as being:

any planned and controlled conversation between two (or more) people which has a purpose for at least one of the participants, and during which both speak and listen from time to time.

Chance meetings in corridors, lifts or canteens often result in conversations, but we shall not consider these interviews as such, since the definition we are using contains the crucial idea of *purpose*, as well as the aspect of planning and controlling the conversation. In remembering the reasons why some interviews you have taken part in were unsatisfactory, you may well have deduced that many interviews tended to become merely meandering chats precisely because no one seemed to be too clear exactly what the interview was intended to achieve or, if there had once been a purpose, it somehow got forgotten as the conversation explored various blind alleys.

To be effective, therefore, an interview must have:

- purpose
- planning
- controlled interaction

Whether you are likely to be mainly the interviewer or the interviewee will depend, of course, on your circumstances, but you can learn a great deal about the art of 'being interviewed' by learning how to 'interview'. From understanding the objectives of an interviewer and being aware of the methods used to achieve those objectives, you can gain insight into how best to perform as the interviewee, and to cope with or help the less-than-good interviewer, of whom there are many.

The purposes of the interview

The purpose of an interview may be very specific – selecting someone for a job; hearing about someone's complaint; reprimanding or disciplining someone for a misdemeanour; or determining how someone is progressing – and there are many more. But all interviews will be concerned with:

- obtaining information
- passing on information
- clarifying information

– or in other words, *exchanging information.*

It is the *reason* why this information is exchanged which forms the purpose of a particular interview, and researchers normally conceive of four basic purposes of interviews:

1 Dissemination of information (teacher–student interviews, news/journalism interviews).
2 Seeking belief or behaviour change (sales, discipline, counselling, performance appraisal).
3 Problem-solving and decision-making (employment interviews, performance appraisal, medical interviews, counselling, grievance procedures, parent–teacher discussions).
4 Research and discovery of new information (academic and social casework, market research, polls and opinion surveys, police interrogation, academic and writer research).

Most interviews, whatever their overall purpose, will be concerned with eliciting or exchanging information of various kinds.

Types of interview information

Statements of description The interviewee is required to provide information concerning something he has observed or experienced and may be questioned much as a witness is by a lawyer.

Statements of factual knowledge The interviewee is required to pass on an explanation of information he possesses (e.g. an interview with an expert or specialist).

Statements of behaviour The interview defines the previous, present and future behaviour of the interviewee.

Statements of attitude and belief Information of a more subjective nature revealing attitudes, personality, ambition and motivation. These statements represent the interviewee's evaluations (good/bad) and opinions of the truth and falseness about things, e.g. 'I think that may be true but . . .', 'I get frustrated when I don't have enough to do', etc.

Statements of feelings These messages reveal physical and/or emotional levels which reflect the state of the individual, e.g. 'I am fed up with always being ordered about by someone for whom I've no respect', 'I'm thoroughly enjoying this new responsiblity', etc.

Statements of value These statements convey long-standing belief systems that are highly treasured by the respondent, e.g. 'The essential quality in anyone is commitment – a willingess to see things through and stick at the job despite difficulties. Without that, all the qualifications in the world are useless.'

Many of these types of statement, particularly the last three, are concerned with subjective data rather than objective factual or biographical data. The interview has survived as an information-getting tool, despite the expense in terms of time and money, and despite criticism as to its reliability, primarily because it is the only known means of getting certain subjective types of information, and because much of this information can be conveyed by non-verbal messages. Even the questionnaire designed to elicit attitudes, opinions and beliefs is more and more being administered by an interviewer who talks to the interviewee, using the questionnaire as a framework for the interview.

The list below includes some of the more common business interviews.

Types of business interview
- employment
- performance appraisal
- counselling
- discipline
- termination
- induction
- consulting
- sales
- data gathering
- order-giving

Review

1 How does an interview differ from a spontaneous conversation?

2 What is the basic purpose of each of the following interviews?
   a selection/employment interview
   b market research interview
   c interview with the witness of an accident
   d performance appraisal interview
   e sales interview

3 Which types of interview information would you expect to predominate in each of the interviews above?

ANSWERS

1 An interview has a purpose and is planned and controlled.

2 a problem-solving but mainly decision-making
   b research and discovery of new information
   c research and discovery of new information
   d problem-solving and decision-making; seeking behaviour (and perhaps belief) change
   e seeking belief and/or behaviour change

3 a Probably all of them: a good selection interview should not focus on any one type of information.
   b A market research interview could focus on any one or all

of the possible types of information.

c   An interview with a witness will usually focus on description and factual knowledge. It might include statements of the interviewee's behaviour prior to and during the accident, but it should avoid subjective statements of attitudes, beliefs, feelings and values.

d   The performance appraisal interview will concentrate on statements of behaviour. Although the interviewee may be encouraged to express attitudes, feelings and values, the interviewer should avoid making these statements and should concentrate on an objective discussion of facts, i.e. what the interviewee has done, is doing and could do.

e   The sales interviewer will be particularly concerned with eliciting attitudes, beliefs, feelings and values as a basis for his persuasive skills.

Effective interviewing requires planning

Contrary to popular opinion, successful interviews do not 'just happen'. Successful interviews are the result of careful planning and preparation on the part of one or both of the participants. Good interviewers and interviewees are made, not born. They practise the skill until they appear to be able to do it without thinking, but their apparent easy, relaxed behaviour often belies the conscious analysis which has taken place beforehand and the careful monitoring of what is happening during the interview.

Obviously while certain interviews allow for considerable preparation by the interviewer and by the interviewee, this is not always the case. A worker may suddenly surprise his supervisor by using his regular progress interview or performance appraisal session to air a string of grievances, and workers seldom have much advance warning to prepare carefully for discipline or reprimand interviews.

The conversational nature of interviewing precludes the kind of detailed planning which is possible for a public speech. However, at least one of the participants should carefully consider the usual *why? who? what?*, etc. questions prior to the interview. If you can discipline yourself to practise this routine regularly it will not only make the process of interviewing less stressful, but will also mean that when you are surprised by a sudden chance to interview someone or a sudden summons to see someone, you will be able to do some very quick but effective thinking as you walk along the corridor and during the initial stages of the interview.

Why?
What broad type of interview is it?

What exactly do you hope to accomplish?

Are you seeking informaton, giving information? If so, what type of information?

Is the interview seeking change in beliefs or behaviour?

What is the nature of the problem to be solved? If you fail to persuade, have you a fall-back position with which you would be satisfied?

You should never enter an interview which you have initiated without thinking through what you hope to accomplish.

Who?
Analyse the other person. Find out as much as possible about the other person prior to the interview. What are his likely reactions/objections? Does he have the power to make the decisions you require?

Where and When?
Analyse the context. Where will the interview take place? In your office, his office? In a car during a journey? Is it likely to be interrupted? What time of day will it take place? What is likely to have happened just before the interview? What stage are you at in the matter? Will he need to be introduced to the whole matter, or merely reminded or brought up to date on the main events so far?

What?
Determine the topics you will need to cover and the types of question you will need to ask.

How?
Decide on the structure of the interview. How will you accom-

plish your objective? How should you behave? Would it be best
to begin in a friendly manner or come smartly to the point? Are
you going to have to tread carefully? Listen more than talk?

Would it be best to begin with general questions, followed by
more specific ones? Or should you get the detailed information
first and then progress to the wider, philosophical issues? How
are you going to arrange the furniture? How can you prevent
interruptions?

> ### Activity
>
> Now think of one of those interviews you have taken part
> in recently. Imagine you could have your time over again,
> or that you were the interviewer this time, and think
> carefully about how you would answer all the planning
> questions above.

Interview structure

The opening

Regardless of the purpose of the interview, it is essential that the
opening of the interview is handled carefully for on the relationship established during the first few minutes will depend much of
the success of the rest of the interview.

Without taking up too much time, you will therefore need to
'establish rapport' and introduce the main content of the interview. Obviously the opening will depend on the nature of the
interview and it would be impossible to cover all the possibilities,
but here are some which are fairly popular. However, it is
essential that whichever one is chosen it is handled sincerely or
the interviewee will realize it is merely a gimmick.

Ways to start an interview
Summarize the problem facing the interviewee and/or the interviewer. This method is useful, when the interviewee knows
vaguely that the problem exists but is not aware of the details.

Explain how you (the interviewer) discovered the problem.
Suggest he might want to discuss it with you. This helps to
establish the idea that the problem is mutual, and encourages a

cooperative, objective discussion.

Ask for advice or help regarding the particular problem. This must be a sincere request, or it will be recognized as a mere gimmick and set you at a disadvantage.

Suggest a possible advantage to the interviewee of solving the problem/accepting your proposal. Again, this must be seen as sincere and honest by the interviewee.

Open with a startling or striking fact. Effective in a real emergency and when the interviewee tends to be rather apathetic.

Refer to the interviewee's known view on the particular problem. Effective when the interviewee has taken up a position which is well known, has asked you to put forward proposals, or is likely to be strongly opposed to your ideas.

Refer to the background, cause, origin of the problem without actually stating the problem itself. Effective when you suspect the interviewee may be hostile to your ideas but is familiar with the background.

State the name of the person who sent you to the interviewee. Very useful when you need a 'way in' because you don't know the interviewee. But the 'introduction' must be genuine and the person must be respected by the interviewee.

State your organization or company or the group you represent. This can help your prestige, but again only if the organization is respected by the interviewee. It also may provide an explanation for your visit.

Ask for ten minutes/half an hour of his time. Be specific and don't sound too apologetic. Asking for a brief period of time is effective with the busy, impatient or intolerant interviewee.

Ask a question. The question may be leading, anticipating agreement, or direct (see 'Types of question' below). It obliges the interviewee to answer and he automatically becomes involved.

Activity

1 You have been invited to the wedding of an old school-friend, but you have have used up all your annual leave and so need to persuade your boss to allow you to take the Friday off in order to travel. You have made an

appointment to see him, but have not told him what your purpose is. Which type of opening would you use? Write some notes on what you would actually say in raising the subject.

2 You have a temporary job selling 'executive desk-tidies' (containers for pens, pencils and paperclips). Always supposing you manage to get past the secretary and in to see the executive, how would you start the interview?

3 You are having problems getting on with a colleague. He seems to be avoiding you and no one seems to know why. You have mentioned the problem to your boss, who has suggested you first try to speak to the colleague yourself, during a quiet moment. How would you start the interview?

4 You are attending a course at a local college, but you and the other course members are very concerned about a particular member of staff's teaching. You have been advised to speak to the member of staff personally in the hope that an improvement will remove the need to take the matter further. *You* have been elected spokesman by the rest of the course! How will you broach the subject?

The body of the interview

Whichever type of opening you adopt, you should make sure that it doesn't take up too much time: remember one of the typical problems is the interview that never gets to the point.

The major part of the interview should be reserved for asking and answering questions, seeking solutions to problems, or trying to persuade the interviewee to accept your idea or your product. A rough guide is to allow about 95 per cent of a thirty-minute interview for this phase.

Structured and non-structured approaches to interviewing The extent to which you will want to structure the interview will depend on the purpose of the interview, the type of interview and any time restrictions. In a non-structured interview, the interviewer allows the interviewee to steer the interview (e.g. if the interviewee has a complaint or grievance or a personal problem). In a structured interview, the interviewer dominates and controls the interview (e.g. an information-getting interview with severe time limits). Interview structure is frequently described as 'non-structured', 'moderately structured', 'highly structured' or 'highly structured – standardized.'

Non-structured interviews have no prearranged schedule or framing of questions. You simply think about the purpose and make a mental note of a few possible areas or topics which need to be covered. While this is a very effective strategy for certain interviews, particularly those of a counselling nature, you should beware of justifying poorly prepared, badly conducted interviews on this basis.

Moderately structured interviews involve planning and framing the *major* questions you want answered and perhaps some possible follow-up questions to probe deeper if necessary. These follow-up questions are only used if the interviewee doesn't volunteer the information required.

Highly structured interviews All questions are arranged and scheduled in advance. These questions are put to each interviewee in exactly the same way. Some questions may be open-ended but this type of interview tends to rely mainly on close-ended questions; useful when you want to compare interviewees' responses systematically as in market research or opinion surveys but also useful in some fact-finding/investigatory interviews.

Highly structured – standardized interviews All questions are again arranged and scheduled in advance but in addition the potential answers are preplanned in such a way that the interviewee has a restricted choice of answers from which to choose one, e.g. 'If the price of this product were reduced, would you buy more, less or about the same as you do now?' In other words, all the questions are close-ended.

Self-check

Look at the types of business interview listed on p. 63. Which structure would you choose for each type of interview?

Obviously there are no right answers. It would depend entirely on the particular context of the interview and your specific purpose. However, here are my suggestions:

employment   –   moderately structured
appraisal   –   moderately structured
counselling   –   unstructured
discipline   –   moderately structured
termination   –   moderately/highly structured
induction   –   moderately structured
consulting   –   highly structured
sales   –   moderately/highly structured
data-gathering –   highly structured/standardized
order-giving –   moderately structured

Types of question The main body of the interview normally consists of questions and responses but in most interviews the aim of the interviewer is to conduct a conversation rather than an interrogation session. The way in which he frames his questions and the extent to which he talks and listens will directly influence the atmosphere of the interview, the feelings of the interviewee and thus the outcome of the interview. You, therefore, need to be familiar with the basic types of question and their uses.

1 The direct question or close-ended question This kind of question permits the interviewee very little, or no freedom in selecting his response. There is usually one specific answer.

Examples 'What 'O' level subjects did you do?' 'How long have you worked for us now?' 'Where were you when the accident took place?'

> *Self-check*
>
> What would this sort of question be useful for?
> What are the possible disadvantages of direct questions?

Uses When specific replies are sought on a definite topic, direct questioning is most often used. It is particularly useful in seeking objective factual or biographical data, or where straightforward answers are required for comparison with other interviewees' i.e. qualifications for a job, details about an event or accident, statistical or objective facts.

Disadvantages In limiting the response, it does not encourage the interviewee to talk. An interview based exclusively on this type of question is a very cold, lifeless affair which makes the interviewee feel he is being interrogated (which he is) rather than consulted or invited to expand or discuss.

2 Bipolar questions or yes/no questions If the interviewer wants to limit the potential responses beyond the limitations already imposed by direct questions, he can ask a bipolar question, which limits the answer to one of two possible answers, or simply 'yes' or 'no'.

Examples 'Were you actually there when the accident happened?' (yes/no) 'Did you come by train or car?' 'Are you happy in your job?' (yes/no) 'Would you be able to start work by the first of March?' (yes/no)

Self-check

Can you think of possible uses and disadvantages of this type of question.

Uses In a sense, bipolar questions are a form of direct question and therefore have the same uses. Used with a carefully considered purpose, they can be very effective in eliciting definite information quickly.

Disadvantages Because they are so limiting in the answers permitted by the nature of the question, when they are used incorrectly they force the interviewee to opt for one or the other extreme answer, when the answer he really wants to give may be halfway between, e.g. 'Are you happy in your job?' strictly speaking implies either a 'yes' or 'no' answer. A fairly talkative interviewee may answer truthfully and go beyond the limitations of the question, but a quiet person who lacks confidence will be inhibited by this question and feel unable to expand. The interviewer should be aware of these dangers.

3 The leading question or standard-revealing question This is the kind of question which makes it so obvious what the answer should be, or what answer the interviewer expects, that he is in effect 'leading' the interviewee.

Examples 'Don't you think the weather's been awful lately?' 'Don't you think it would be a good idea if we. . . ?' 'There's no reason why someone earning your salary couldn't afford £10 per month, is there?'

These are examples of leads which are expressed in the negative. Usually they get a 'yes' response or, at any rate, are obviously intended to get a 'yes' response. However, the last example gets a 'no' response which is in effect an affirmative answer for the salesman!

Self-check
Again, can you think of the uses and . . . abuses?

Uses Leading questions which expect an affirmative answer in this way are, of course, the weapon of the salesman. If he can prepare a series of questions in this way, he can lead the respondent, and he is well on the way to getting the respondent to accept his idea or product. This technique has been successfully adopted by countless salesmen. Used subtly it can be very effective when the purpose of the interview is persuasive.

Disadvantages or abuses Used aggressively or thoughtlessly it can either make the interviewee feel under severe pressure and attack by revealing the standards by which the interviewer measures people – 'You didn't do very well at school, did you?' – or it allows the interviewee to give the 'right' answer even if he might have unwittingly answered differently if he hadn't been given a clue: 'The person we accept for this position will have to supervise a staff of twenty and be good at handling people and their problems. Do you think you would be capable of this?'

No one but an idiot would answer anything but 'yes' to this question! The interviewer has given away his views or standards, thus helping the interviewee to give the 'right' answer.

Sometimes this type of question is simply a waste of time:'Presumably you are keen to get this job?' 'I suppose you are ambitious?'

4 *The loaded question* Sometimes the use of emotive words in the question indicates the response the interviewer wants: 'Do you think we should accept this crazy idea?' 'What do you think about this whole sorry business?'

‖ *Self-check*

‖ Can you think of any possible uses for this kind of question?

Uses It is difficult to imagine a situation in which this type of question would be anything but useless in terms of eliciting people's *real* feelings and opinions.

However, such questions are sometimes used when the interviewer is trying to find out how able the interviewee is to resist being led, how strongly he holds his own opinions. Taken to an extreme it is also used to discover how an interviewee reacts under stress, and when the interviewer wants to see how far he has to go to get the interviewee to 'crack'.

'I don't agree with employing women. I mean they're a dead loss really, aren't they? They are always taking time off to look after the kids or leaving to have babies. You can't rely on them, can you?' (A question put to a woman applicant for a job!)

This may not be the true opinion of the interviewer. He may be asking it to see how the woman defends the role of women at work, whether she would be able to cope under genuine attacks like this, and *how* she answers the question – aggressively, or with dignity and calm, reasoned arguments.

5 *The open-ended question* Unlike the previous questions, this type of question allows the interviewee maximum freedom in responding.

Examples 'Tell me about yourself.' 'How do you see the problem?' 'What are your feelings on this?' 'How do you think a course in business education or training can help you to do the job better?' As you can see, these questions frequently begin with 'why', 'what', 'how' and 'where'.

‖ *Self-check*

‖ What sort of information might be elicited by open-ended questions?

Uses When selected carefully, these questions can reveal a great deal about a person's attitudes, beliefs and motivation. They also reveal how well he can collect his thoughts, organize what he wants to say, and express himself without guidance or prompting.

Disadvantages Although open questions may provide the interviewer with some measure of the person's ability to think, and may lead to worthwhile areas of discussion not perhaps anticipated by the interviewer, considerable thought should go into their selection and use, otherwise a lot of time may be wasted in gaining answers to only a few very general questions.

6 *The prompting question* This question helps the interviewee who appears to have a mental 'block', or when he is not clear exactly what the interviewer is getting at.

Examples 'Tell me about yourself.' 'Well, starting from your last couple of years at school, what have been the major milestones in your life, what do you see as the most important decisions you've had to make? That sort of thing.'

> ## Self-check
>
> The purpose of this type of question is obvious. Can you think of any snags?

Uses To help the interviewee who has 'gone blank'.

Disadvantages It is easy to jump in too quickly with this type of 'prompt question'. The interviewer should avoid not allowing the interviewee time to think before answering or, prompting in such a way that much of the value of the original open question is lost.

7 *The mirror question* This question 'plays back' to the interviewee the interviewer's understanding of the last response, or summarizes several different statements made by the interviewee.

Examples 'So you're saying that, in general, you would support the idea?' 'If I've understood you correctly, you like the practical aspects of the work, but not the paperwork?'

Self-check

Can you think of one major advantage and one major disadvantage in using mirror questions?

Uses This type of question is one of the most effective ways of ensuring that real communication is taking place. It provides the interviewee with immediate feedback as to how well he is communicating what he really means, and it allows the interviewer to check his understanding. These two advantages improve the quality of listening in the interview and help to promote an atmosphere of empathy and trust.

Disadvantages There is a real danger of 'putting words into the mouth' of the interviewee. He agrees that that is what he meant even if he didn't!

Example 'So you think you're being victimized?' 'Yes.' (Thinks: 'Well, I didn't really see it like that, but it sounds more dramatic, so now I come to think of it – yes!')

8 *The probing question* Frequently, the initial response given to a question may be lacking in detail or may indicate the need for a follow-up question.

Examples 'Could you give me an example of what you mean by poor workmanship?' 'When you say you haven't been late very often, how many times would you say you've been late during the last month, say?' 'I'm not sure I really understand what you mean by that. Can you give me some examples?' 'Which of those causes is the most serious, do you think?'

Probing questions often begin with 'why'. In fact, the simple question 'Why?' is a useful question in itself, particularly if the interviewer doesn't want to run the risk of stopping the interviewee talking.

Self-check

There are several specific uses for the probing question. How many can you think of?

Uses To elicit more detail – example, illustrations, explanations; to encourage the interviewee to keep talking; to move the interview from the general to the specific; to steer the interviewee back on the predetermined route of the interview when it is getting off-course; to encourage the interviewee to stick to specific facts rather than generalizations.

Disadvantages Used aggressively or too persistently this kind of questioning may make the interviewee feel he is in the witness box.

9 The hypothetical question
Example 'Let's assume that you had discovered one of your subordinates was drinking heavily and that it was interfering with his work. What would you do?' 'Imagine I had to introduce a new piece of equipment or process which was going to affect the work routine of my employees. How would you advise me to go about it?'

Self-check
Why might an interviewer use this type of question?

Uses Effective for determining how an interviewee might handle some potential job-related situation, or for discovering how somone imagines his ideas might work out in practice. Also useful in discovering an interviewee's prejudices, stereotypes and other attitudes, beliefs and values.

Disadvantages If the imaginary instance is too far-fetched it will reveal very little of any value about the interviewee and is more likely to say something about the personality of the interviewer!

Example 'Suppose a third world war broke out today. What would you do?'

Review
Now examine the questions below and spot the errors involved. What types of question are they? Now suggest a better alternative in each case.

1 'Did you have a good journey?'
2 'Do you realize that as the supervisor of this section I am

here to carry the can for your weaknesses?'
3 'You say that you're persistent in the face of problems, but three jobs in four years doesn't indicate that you stick at anything for very long, does it?'
4 'Why did you take CSEs instead of 'O' levels in 1969 or perhaps you didn't.' (Looking down at the form.) 'Did you take CSEs in preparation for 'O' levels the next year or because you were in the CSE stream? And did you improve your grade when you took them again – CSEs I mean, not 'O' levels, or was the 'O' level an improvement in each case?'

ANSWERS

1 A direct question allowing only a 'yes' or 'no' answer, so not very useful. Good for opening the interview and putting interviewee at ease but might be better worded: 'How was your journey?'
2 Pulling rank and begging for pity are both inexcusable and it's a leading, if not even a loaded, question. A good alternative would depend on the purpose of the interview, but something along these lines would be an improvement: 'How can I help you to cope better with your job?'
3 A leading question revealing the interviewer's own views on 'job-hopping' and not giving the interviewee a really fair chance to explain what may be perfectly acceptable reasons for his changing jobs. Better: 'Why did you move from . . . to . . . ?'
4 Such a mixture of questions and far too complicated and long-winded for us to analyse let alone for anyone to answer. Ask one question at a time: 'Why did you take a mixture of 'O' levels and CSEs?'

Sequencing the questions When you have thought about the types of question you will use, it is equally important to give some thought to the sequencing of the questions in the interview. You may want to begin with broad, open-ended questions and then move on to increasingly specific questions. This is called 'funnel' sequencing. The 'inverted' funnel sequence begins with close-ended specific questions and moves to more general, open-ended questions. The 'tunnel' sequence, as its name suggests, is a series of similar questions. This type of sequence is particularly suitable when you want to get initial answers to each separate question without asking follow-up probes. For example, a series of questions aimed at discovering attitudes to a number of job-related experiences would be considered a tunnel sequence.

Closing the interview

When your time limit is up; when you have got the information you wanted; when you have managed to persuade the interviewee to accept your suggestions or buy your product; when the problem has been solved; or when it is obvious that continuing the interview will be unproductive, perhaps because more information is needed, or interviews with other people are necessary, you should close the interview.

There are three main things to be accomplished when closing the interview:

- Briefly summarize the achievements of the interview, or the views expressed.
- Thank the interviewee for participating.
- Agree on the next meeting or the actions which will follow.

If you follow the guidelines suggested in this chapter you should be able to cope with even the most difficult interview (and have learned a little about the reason for the methods which an interviewer may adopt when you are the interviewee). However, perhaps the most common type of interview is the fact-finding interview since fact-finding either forms the basis of most interviews or a part of a series of interviews with a more specific purpose. For this reason, you may find the following checklist useful. Try it out when next you have to conduct any interview which involves determining the facts before anything else. You may also like to use it to assess the skill of the interviewer when next you are interviewed!

Checklist for fact-finding interviews

1 Purpose
- To enable the individuals to air the problem.
- To discover the causes of dissatisfaction.
- To establish the facts of the problem situation.

2 Preparation
- Consider individual to be interviewed, check previous record/ history.
- Endeavour to establish circumstances causing dissatisfaction (particularly attitudes, feelings).
- Be aware of company policy which may affect action which can be taken.
- Ensure privacy and no interruptions.
- Allow adequate time.
- Arrange desk and chairs to create the right atmosphere.

3 Conduct
- Put at ease – establish rapport.
- State purpose of interview.
- Don't try to solve the problem before you know what it is (there may not even be a problem!).
- Allow individual to state the problem from their point of view.
- Get feelings as well as facts – feelings are usually more important though less likely to be expressed without encouragement.
- Listen attentively.
- Do not evade the issue or belittle it.
- Probe in depth to ensure all relevant details are known.
- Use 'open' questions.
- Do not commit yourself too quickly appear to take sides.
- If possible get individual to suggest solutions.
- Discuss implications of different solutions (if appropriate).
- Agree a best solution (if appropriate).

It is not always appropriate to arrive at a solution in a fact-finding interview. Other interviews may be necessary before a solution can be determined.

- Agree course of action to
  be taken (if appropriate).
- Review ground covered.
- Arrange next meeting.

4 Follow up
- Investigate facts/information if necessary – interview others
  as appropriate.
- Decide on action in light of investigation.
- Check that results are as required – relationships, attitudes,
  performance.
- Hold follow-up meeting.

> *Activity*
>
> Try to persuade someone you know who does a lot of
> interviewing in the course of his job to allow you to sit in
> during an interview, as an observer. Look at the following
> observation sheet before you go in to the interview and
> then complete it after the interview is over.

INTERVIEWING

	Yes	No	Not sure
1 Was the interviewer prepared for the interview?			
(a) Had he done his homework?			
(b) Was he mentally ready?			
(c) Had he arranged to give his whole attention?			
(d) Had he arranged the room appropriately?			
2 Did he state the objectives of the interview at the outset?			
3 What opening technique did he use?			
4 Did he make the interviewee feel at ease?			
5 Did he make his points clearly and concisely?			
6 Did he give the interviewee a chance to make his/her points?			
7 Did he listen to the interviewee?			

8 Did he frame questions appropriately?
9 Did he give valid reasons for criticism and
   objective evidence for statements made?
10 Did he make suggestions?
11 Did he encourage the interviewee to make
   suggestions?
12 Did he 'back down' under pressure?
13 Did he structure the interview sensibly?
14 Was the interview:
   (a) non-structured?
   (b) moderately structured?
   (c) highly structured?
   (d) highly structured – standardized?
15 Did he allow sufficient time for the
   interview to run its natural course?
16 Did he summarize what had happened for
   the interviewee?
17 Did he end on a positive note of agreed
   action with the interviewee?

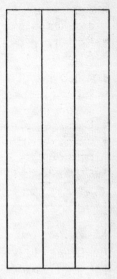

4 | Being interviewed for a job

Stuart Peat was a trainee civil servant in the fast stream for promotion to Principal grade. He was one of the oldest men still in the training grade, and felt he was ready for promotion; he had already been passed over two or three times, and had expressed his view that the promotion system was unsatisfactory. But when the next list for Promotion Board interviews came out, his name was missing. He was not even being considered.

Stuart decided to exercise his right to demand an interview. It took place on the day he always met his brother, Steve, for a lunchtime drink. Stuart walked into the pub looking ashen. 'I don't have to ask how it went,' said Steve. 'No,' answered Stuart, 'it was a disaster. They didn't ask a thing about why I thought I was ready for promotion or about my work. They just asked about why I thought the system was bad; as soon as I walked in. They kept on about it. What would I do if I were given a free hand to put it right? For a whole hour. I was at a loss for words – must have looked a complete idiot.'

Activity

Where did Stuart go wrong?

This chapter is intended to help you in preparing for that all important interview – the job interview. It should provide you with guidance in thinking positively about the interview beforehand, getting to know your strengths and weaknesses, and making the most of yourself at interview.

Preparation

By now, you should be familiar with some of the main types of interview and the ways in which the interviewer can best use the time available to achieve his objective; whether it is to select the best person for the job; deal with a complaint or a problem of discipline; or make that once-a-year appraisal interview more than just a superficial chat. But, unless you have a job which happens to involve a lot of interviewing, you will probably be interviewed many more more times during your life than you will ever be the interviewer. So, let's look at the problems of being on the other side of that table.

Probably the most important interview you ever attend is the job selection interview – important because, whatever else you choose to do with your life, you will probably spend a considerable part of it working, so you might as well try to get a job you will enjoy. It is therefore just as important that you select the right job, as it is that the interviewer selects the right person. For this reason, it seems sensible to use the job interview as a vehicle for exploring some of the techniques of the successful interviewee.

Dealing with nerves

Perhaps the major problem for most interviewees is 'nerves'. Almost everyone's heart sinks at the very idea of being interviewed, because the idea of being 'on trial' causes stress and not being sure what is going to happen causes apprehension. However, you should take comfort from four thoughts:

- Almost everyone is nervous before and probably during an interview as well, so you are in good company.
- 'Nerves' can in fact be beneficial – just as for the actor or the public speaker, a certain degree of nervous tension will make you more alert and better able to perform well. However, it is obviously necessary to learn ways of reducing anxiety to a level where it can be a help rather than a hindrance.

- The interviewer will probably expect you to be nervous, will make reasonable allowances, and will try to help you feel at ease. Remember too, that he may be feeling just as nervous as you!
- 'Nerves' are usually made worse by being unsure of what is going to happen and of how you are going to cope. So the secret is to do some thinking beforehand – positive thinking not negative worrying – about the interview, and about you and your behaviour. In other words – be prepared!

Get some practice

Let us assume that all the hard work necessary to write many application letters has finally paid off, and you have been invited for interview. But suppose that out of the jobs you have applied for, this is the one you like the look of least. You should still go! You have nothing to lose and everything to gain: above all, the best way to become good at being interviewed is to go to lots of interviews.

Secondly, you cannot really judge whether the job is the right one for you until you have found out all you can about the organization; and the best way is to visit the organization, meet someone who actually works there (more than one, possibly) and get a feel for the place.

Any good interviewer recognizes that, though he needs to find out as much as possible about the interviewee, equally important is the need of the candidate to find out as much as possible about the company. It is therefore always a good idea to go for an interview if you are invited.

However, finding out about an organization is not something which can be left entirely to the interview itself. In preparing for the 'big day', you need to do some research, so that you know as much as possible *before* you get there – about the job and the company.

Get some background information

Don't be like the interviewee desperately wanting a job with Rolls-Royce Limited who, when asked by the interviewer about the company's products, replied: 'Well, you make cars, don't you?' Now *you* may be forgiven for not knowing that Rolls-Royce Limited makes aero-engines, but the interviewee wanted a job with the company and should, at least, have taken the trouble to discover that since 1971 the car division had been a completely separate company from the one that makes aero-engines.

Above all, then, you need to know, at the very least, what the organization does. Is it in retailing, or manufacturing, or distribution, or does it provide a service. What does it make, sell or distribute? What service does it provide?

You will probably be applying for a particular job in a particular section or department, so you will also need to know roughly what the department or office does. Obviously, you will not be expected to know everything in great detail. However, there are some basic facts which you should be able to discover in advance.

Self-check

Before we tackle the problem of how and where you might be able to find the information, try listing some of the things it would be useful to know about an organization, in the form of questions:

Questions about the organization
1 **What does it do?**
2
3
4
5

It will obviously depend on the particular organization to which you are applying, but here are some suggestions:

Is it a big organization or a small firm?
Is it part of a group?
Is it in the public or private sector?
How many people does it employ?
Where is it based?
What is its annual turnover?
Is it quoted on the stock exchange? If so, is the share price rising or falling?

Is it in an expanding or contracting industry?
Does it have subsidiaries or branches? If so, where?
Do its employees belong to a union? If so, which one(s)?
Does it have a good industrial relations record?
Have any recent political or economic events been likely to affect it?
Has it been in the news lately? If so, why?
What is the name of the chief executive?
Does it export goods? If so, where to?

Jotting down some questions like this is a good way of starting your research, but of course you could begin by thinking of sources of information which, on investigation, will give you not only the answers to questions like these, but also answers to questions that had not occurred to you.

Where to find out

You should already have discovered something about the organization before you applied for the job. The advertisement itself may have held some clues: Was the address for applications different from the location of the job? To whom were you asked to apply? A personnel officer/manager/director? The manager of a particular department? Did it describe what the organization does? etc. If you are a good detective and you know what to look for, you should already know a little about the organization or at least have some questions which will start you off in your investigation.

When you first applied, the organization may also have sent you some information for candidates, which you should read carefully and questioningly.

Bearing these facts in mind then, where can you get information about an organization? Who can you ask? Who might know something of use?

Self-check

List the possible sources of information about an organization.

Sources of information

The organization itself You may well have been sent some
information when you first applied, but if not, it is always worth
writing to the public relations officer for anything they publish
about their products or activities and, also, for a copy of their
annual report to shareholders, which should contain all sorts of
useful facts as well as the usual financial information, e.g. the
name of the chief executive.

Local public or college library The reference section of most
libraries should provide many sources of information. For example, *Who Owns Whom?* will tell you what kind of company it
is, who owns it, whether there are subsidiary companies and so
on.

It is always worth spending time finding your way around the
reference section of the library, but if you cannot find what you
want, or do not know where to look, explain what you want and
why you need it to the librarian. You should certainly be able to
get all the hard facts about an organization from reference
books.

Television and newspapers When you are in the throes of applying for jobs, it is always advisable to read the newspapers
regularly and listen to news broadcasts. These can be a valuable
source of information on topical events and their effect on
organizations, industries and groups of people like trade unions,
for example.

In addition to the usual news reports, you should also skim
through the business section of newspapers and keep your eye
open for articles in magazines like the *Economist* and TV programmes like *The Risk Business* and *The Money Programme*
which often report on various aspects of business and industry.
Again, the local library should help with copies of current
periodicals and magazines, but a college library will almost
certainly have copies of all the daily papers and journals and
magazines, both current and back copies on file.

Even if you are not a member of the library, there should be
no difficulty in visiting the reference section, and your efforts

will be well repaid if you can make informed comments about the organization and its business during the interview.

Personal contacts Mention the names of the organization when you are talking to friends and relatives. It is surprising how often even a chance acquaintance may know something which will help you to build up a picture. He may have worked there, or know someone who does, and you may learn details which would be impossible to get easily from any other source. But, be careful. Remember to keep a sense of perspective. For every one ex-employee who only remembers the darker side, there are many more currently employed there who might paint a rosier picture.

Prepare some questions

As well as answering many of your questions and providing you with valuable background knowledge, research like this will probably also suggest further questions, which you should make a note of, to ask at the interview when you get the chance.

The famous question 'How much will I be paid?' frequently causes interviewees embarrassment, but it is a very reasonable question and if the interviewer does not bring up the subject, he will not be at all surprised or offended if you ask. You may have some associated questions and can ask about salary together with other conditions and training opportunities, for instance.

Many people find that when they are asked if they have any questions, their mind goes a complete blank. For this reason, it is a good idea to jot the questions down on a card. Then, if you cannot remember them, ask the interviewer if you might refer to it to remind you. Interviewers should regard this as an example of good organization, and it all helps to show that you are sufficiently interested to have thought about the interview beforehand.

Know yourself

The next stage of interview preparation, and probably the most important, is to find out about yourself. This may sound obvious and perhaps you think you already know yourself pretty well. Well, how would you cope if the interviewer suddenly asked: 'What are your strengths and weaknesses?' Or: 'We have many applicants for this job. Tell me why we should take *you*?'

Try it! Without any preparation for these questions, you may well suddenly be struck dumb. At best, and depending on your self-confidence, you may either overstate your strengths or exaggerate your weaknesses. Neither would be viewed very favourably by the interviewer. In a job interview you obviously want to make the most of your strengths and play down your weaknesses, but you can only do this effectively when you have given the matter some considerable thought.

Another reason for reviewing your good and bad points is to be able to consider, in advance, how to admit your weaknesses in as favourable a light as possible and balance them with compensating strengths. Of course, it is always possible that something you regard as a strength may be regarded differently by the interviewer, but of course it might happen the other way round too. In any event, since it is rather unnerving to discover, for the first time in an interview, that a particular characteristic or failure to achieve could be regarded by someone else as a black mark against you, it is far better to consider it beforehand and think about how you might cope.

Finally, then, it is really only possible to plan tactics for the interview itself when you are reasonably sure what your qualities and characteristics are and where your weak spots are. For example, let us take the interviewee who maintains that he is 'no good at interviews'. He can do very little about improving until he has first determined *why* he is bad at interviews. One of his weaknesses may be that he suffers badly from stage fright in strange situations but is not prepared to admit it. Not until he has honestly admitted to himself that he does get nervous can he start to plan ways of reducing his anxiety. He may then be prepared to try some of the techniques suggested in this chapter, like preparing properly for an interview, for example. But even these are no guarantee that stage fright can be completely conquered. Indeed, for many people extreme nervousness during stress is part of their lives. These people must analyse their nervousness and develop strategies for living with it. Our fictitious interviewee may, when he stops to think about it, realize that he suffers from stage fright worse at the beginning of occasions but gradually calms down. He would therefore be better off if he could try to keep the key points he wants to make until later in the interview. On the other hand, he may realize that he can usually begin calmly but becomes progressively more nervous, and would be wiser to inject his better remarks at the beginning and then try to keep the interview as short as possible.

You can see now that by admitting a weakness and analysing it, you may be able to make the best of it.

Activity

It is now time to take a long, hard, honest look at yourself. Don't be shy about your strengths and don't be blind to your weaknesses. Be honest! What do people like about you? What don't they like? What sort of things are you good at? What are you bad at? How would colleagues at work describe you? Are you different at home?

Make a list of as many strengths and weaknesses as you can think of.

Keep the list – you may want to return to it later, perhaps to amend it, as you discover more about yourself.

Activity

Now comes the hardest part of all! Find a friend who seems likely to be cooperative but honest, to write a list of *your* strengths and weaknesses, as he sees them. Then compare the two lists. Try not to be defensive about the weaknesses but get him to give examples and discuss the two lists objectively.

Note: someone who works with you at college or work who knows you fairly well would probably be the most suitable. It might be preferable not to choose someone you are too close to – they may see you through 'rose-tinted glasses' and not want to ruin a beautiful friendship.

If you can bring yourself to do this exercise conscientiously, it will probably be one of the most useful exercises you ever do.

> O wad some Pow'r the giftie gie us
> To see oursels as others see us!
> *Robert Burns*

Awkward questions

The last exercise sprang not only from a sensible need to be prepared for an interview, but also from a particular question posed by many interviewers in one form or another: 'What are your strengths and weaknesses?' In their efforts to discover as much as possible about you in the shortest possible time, they will have thought out carefully and developed preferences for particular questions which are designed not so much to elicit specific facts as to discover how you think, what motivates you, what kind of person you are.

Activity

Here are some very awkward questions sometimes asked by interviewers which have felled many a candidate before you. How would you answer? Make a note of your answers, so that you can refer to them later.

Don't be put off by these questions. Unless you are applying for a fairly high-level job, most interviewers, however inexpert they are, will try to be kind and are unlikely to ask questions quite as blunt as these. However, if you are prepared to answer these, you should be prepared for almost anything and find the more conventional questions easier to answer.

What has been your most valuable experience?
Which do you prefer: money or status?
Are you an aggressive person?
When did you last lose your temper? Why?
Describe yourself in three adjectives.
What is the best idea you've had in the last year?
What is the hardest thing you've done in the last three years?
Are you too young/too old for us?
Tell me about yourself.
What is your worst fault?

What is your proudest achievement?
What would you like to be doing in five years time?
   In ten years time?

You should have answers ready for these questions and be prepared to recognize others with a similar purpose, bearing in mind that the interviewer is not so interested in what you answer as how you answer.

Even if you are not asked these specific questions, just having made yourself think about your answers to them will provide you with things to talk about and that is what the interviewer wants you to do.

Obviously there are no right or wrong answers to the questions – it will depend on you, the job, the organization, the atmosphere of the interview and so on; but one woman, who was asked if she was aggressive, responded that she was assertive rather than aggressive. In other words, she went on, she always sought to be cooperative, but she was very keen to get on in her career. Thus she managed to characterize herself as neither contentious nor passive. Most questions which might seem 'awkward' to you need to be answered in this balanced way.

At the interview

Be yourself

Now we come to the interview itself. In order to give yourself a fair chance make sure that you find out exactly where the interview is to take place, and allow yourself plenty of time to get there early rather than late. The interviewer will probably start the interview with a few general questions about your journey and so on, designed to set you at your ease. Use the time to make yourself comfortable and take a few subtle deep breaths to calm you. He will probably then turn to your application form or letter and ask you questions arising from what you have written. It is always a good idea to keep a copy of your letter and application form to refer to just before the interview. There is nothing worse than finding that you cannot really remember what you wrote and getting flustered into saying something which does not really agree with what the interviewer is looking at.

Projecting a good image

As we have seen, the points you make in an interview have to do with what you say about yourself and what you say about the organization and the job. In one way or another you have to show that you are responsible, hard-working and competent. In sum, that you care about yourself and are firm in your beliefs about your qualities. But you must also show that you are flexible and ambitious enough to learn new skills and gain new qualities. Moreover, you must show that you have performed both competently and creatively – the kind of person who has not only accepted responsibility but also sought it out.

The projection of this image of yourself may sound like a tall order. Perhaps you feel that this description does not fit you at all. But let's take a closer look. Supposing, for example, that you don't think you're hard-working, but basically rather a lazy person. Try to explain to yourself why this may be so. There must have been some occasions during your life when you have been hard-working. What were they? What were the particular characteristics of the situations that prompted you to work hard? Try always to think of examples of occasions when you have displayed the qualities the interviewer may be looking for. He will be looking for *evidence*, not bald statements like 'I think I'm hard working'. Instead of reeling off a list of your characteristics, try using anecdotes which provide evidence of those characteristics: short stories about yourself which involve a demonstration of each quality as part of the story. One young man, for example, described several experiences which he had had as a clerk with a professional football team. In one story his hard work had led him to develop an innovation; in another his flexibility and ambition had got him involved in an interesting problem of personnel work. Your answers to the awkward questions will probably have prompted you to have thought of examples like these which you would be able to use in any interview.

Adopting this approach will ensure that, above all, you are yourself. If you are recounting an incident or experience which you actually took part in, you are likely to talk more naturally and easily. It is when interviewees start to invent things which they think will sound good that they come unstuck in interviews. They try to be someone they're not: they can't produce the evidence and they can't keep the act up. It is the resulting feeling of unease and discomfort that can cause nervousness. So, be yourself but make the most of what you've got!

Be realistic

However, making the most of what they've got can lead people into the other trap: that of being over confident and arrogant. The secret lies in showing your finest feathers in as modest a manner as possible. Demonstrate your ambition but within reason. Most interviewers will expect you to be fairly ambitious, so don't be afraid of admitting that, like many people, you would like to be managing director one day. However, show that you have a sense of perspective and have thought about your own strengths in relation to what you can reasonably expect from your career. Be prepared to say something about your goals, but relate them to time and the experience you hope to gain in five years and in ten years. The use of a time span will demonstrate that you are organized and thoughtful. *You know who you are, what you can do, what you want and where you are going*.

Reveal your qualities in a way that allows them to speak for themselves without having to overstate the case, and be prepared to admit your weaknesses but express them in such a way that you show you are aware of them, but having some success at overcoming them, and compensating for them by making the most of your strengths.

Example: 'I didn't really work as hard as I could have done at school, but my disappointing exam results really taught me a lesson. At the moment I am experimenting with a daily checklist of things to be done, and I am finding that not only do I get a sense of achievement at the end of the day, but that I am more self-disciplined than I thought I was.'

What to avoid

When speaking to an interviewer there are a number of things to avoid. Most important of all are those related to your style of delivery and your posture because as we have seen non-verbal communication can often speak louder than words.

Monotonous delivery A loud, domineering voice will make the interviewer feel threatened; a quiet, low, monotonous voice will bore him. He may lose interest in you; worse still, he may even think *you* are bored and uninterested. Anxiety can often cause people to speak in a lower, more monotonous voice than normal without their realizing it. So concentrate on projecting your voice in a dynamic, enthusiastic tone. Above all, aim at variety – variety of pitch, volume and speed.

Unresponsiveness When people are nervous they are often also less responsive than normal. The interviewer wants to hear about you so if he should ask a question which appears to require only a 'yes' or 'no' answer, try to expand your answer beyond a simple 'yes' or 'no'.

Deliberate unresponsiveness You may of course be asked a question which you really don't want to or can't answer. Women, for example, are often asked questions which they consider embarrassing, like 'Won't you leave to have a baby before long?' Always try to answer honestly if you can – this might be an opportunity to offer your opinion about women working, for example – but always avoid a direct refusal to answer or an argumentative answer. It is far better to adopt the 'political' response. Learn from politicians. They are frequently asked questions which they cannot or do not want to answer, but they reply by steering the question neatly round to a slightly different question which they *are* prepared to answer. However, this technique should only be used when absolutely necessary; it is no alternative to good preparation.

Inappropriate language You should also try to avoid using slang or excessively casual language – 'great', 'smashing', 'OK', 'no way', 'it was all right', 'I mean', 'like . . . I was . . . you know . . . chairman of . . .', 'fantastic', 'like I said . . . Yeh', and 'me and my friend went . . .' – such expressions are not typical of a business professional.

Unnatural posture Slumping and sitting like a stiff tin soldier are both frequent symptoms of nerves. The best impression is created by sitting up straight with legs crossed. This position looks good and allows you to lean forward a little towards the interviewer to make special points or to show special attention. It also provides a natural rest point for your hands but allows you to gesture naturally – without the sweeping movement required if the hands are in your lap or resting awkwardly on the chair seat. Practise sitting on different chairs until you can readily find a comfortable but alert position which looks good and feels easily maintainable without fidgeting.

A negative start Watch the opening of an interview. Avoid making remarks that create a 'negative set' for the rest of the interview, such as 'I'm not really sure that my background is suitable for this job', or 'I'm afraid I haven't had any experience.' Be positive!

Tips to remember

When you are in a strange, formal situation it is easy to forget the obvious things which are second nature on more relaxed occasions, so here are a few tips to remember.

- Arrive in good time – not only because it is polite but because having to rush will leave you feeling hot and flustered, and therefore nervous.
- Be neat and fairly conservative in your appearance.
- Take cues from the interviewer on degree of formality – your sensitivity to non-verbal communication should help you with this. Perhaps be a little more formal than usual – not a stuffed shirt. Be cautious about jokes, sarcastic asides, etc.
- Don't smoke unless invited to do so; and then only if you must, unless the interviewer smokes; but never if there is no ashtray in sight.
- Be prepared to take notes, if it is necessary to record information. But it might be best to ask the interviewer if he would mind if you did. Even then, don't scribble furiously all the way through.

- Be polite, but friendly and don't forget to *smile* (but only when it's appropriate).
- Leave promptly when the interview is over: don't hover. Smile, shake hands and thank the interviewer.

Review

Summarize the things you should and shouldn't do **a** before the interview; **b** during the interview.

SUMMARY CHECKLIST

Before the interview

1 Be informed about the organization: its history, geographical location, general methods of doing business, reputation, etc.
2 Anticipate questions that might be asked: factual questions as well as 'trap' questions.
3 Make a note of questions you want to ask.

During the interview

4 State why you are applying for the job and show you know something about it.
5 Present your qualifications in terms of having something of value to offer the company. Deal as much as possible in specific details and examples – job experiences, interests, travel, activities, offices held, organizations and school.
6 Don't depend merely on a 'smooth front' (appearance and smile) to sell yourself. Provide full information to the prospective employer.
7 Don't hesitate to admit potential weaknesses. Under no circumstances attempt to bluff or fake on these, but wherever possible make a transition from a weakness to a strength; or, at least, when the facts justify it, show some extenuating circumstances for the weakness. (This doesn't mean supplying alibis or excuses!)
8 Generally attempt to expand your responses beyond a simple 'yes' or 'no'.
9 Treat the interviewer as a human being, not an ogre!
10 Remember the normal rules of etiquette.
11 Get as much information as possible about the job requirements and organization, and on 'sensitive' matters such as

salary (usually in terms of range, or the going average).
12 Try never to have an interview concluded without some sort
of understanding about where you stand, what happens next,
who is to contact whom, etc.
13 Try to enjoy it.
14 Be sincere – be yourself.

Activity

Using a tape recorder, your list of strengths and weaknesses and your answers to the awkward questions, imagine that the interviewer has just asked you the question
'Tell me about yourself.'

Try to speak for 3–5 minutes. (NB In a real interview
you may not have so long, as the interviewer may interrupt
you. You would, anyway, have to use your judgement
about when to stop.)

When you have finished, play it back, listening critically
to the tone of your voice, the language you use, the
evidence you provide to back up your statements and so
on. Would *you* be interested, impressed, attracted if you
were the interviewer?

If you're not happy with your performance, try again.

5 | Communicating in groups

A meeting brings together a group of the unfit, appointed by the unwilling to do the unnecessary for the ungrateful.

A camel is a horse designed by a committee.

A meeting is a group of people who keep minutes and waste hours.

A meeting is a meeting of people to decide when the next meeting will take place.

A meeting is a group of people who singly can do nothing and collectively decide that nothing can be done.

Up until now we have tended to treat communication primarily as an individual and/or interpersonal activity, but individual or personal communication is only one aspect of organizational communication. The group meeting as a method of informing and decision-making is as old as man, and has existed ever since people began to work in groups. However, during the last decade or so, it has become increasingly prevalent. This growth is due mainly to the fact that organizations have become larger and more complex, which has led to such a level of specialization that all the information needed to make decisions in this increasingly complex business society can no longer be adequately assimilated, evaluated and decided by one person or specialized area, without reference to other areas in the organization.

Furthermore, research studies into attitudes and motivation of people at work have shown that people need to feel involved and informed and able to participate in the decisions that affect them.

The result has been, as one writer commented, that 'meetings have become big business. Group participation is in vogue and the wheels of modern industry are turned by committees.' And yet according to one expert, of all the thousands of meetings which take place daily up and down the country, only one in ten works efficiently. The other nine out of ten presumably cause the frustration and cynicism which are reflected in the statements quoted at the beginning of this chapter. In fact, many people view the appointment of a committee as a waste of time and energy and as a delay tactic on the part of those who are willing to pay 'lip service' to an idea, but are unwilling to actually *do* anything. Perhaps you have experienced wasted hours in group meetings and agree with those who question the value of meetings, working parties and committees. Maybe you are among those who want quick action, not wasted hours of talking. Or perhaps you are one of those who wonder why other people are apparently prepared to spend hours of their time taking part in an activity about which they complain so volubly. But the problem is not so much the meetings, as the people who attend the meetings, the leader and the participants.

This chapter will look at the differences between individual and group communication, the advantages of group decision-making, why people join groups in the first place and the factors which influence what happens in a group – in short, we will look at the nature of the group communication process in the hope that an understanding of this process will help to explain why you or others have experienced non-productive meetings and to encourage you to become a more effective leader or participant.

Activity

First of all, from your own experience of belonging to groups and attending meetings, however informal, can you think of any advantages which groups have over an individual working on his own?

Advantages of small group decision-making

It is true that an individual analysing a problem alone may perform more effectively and efficiently than would a group. Sometimes after a group discussion it is easy to recognize that one or two people could have reached the same conclusion without help from the others. The problem is, however, that it is usually impossible to determine in advance which particular members are skilled enough to solve the problem alone, or who will be the main participants in any discussion.

More commitment

Research studies have shown that people are more committed to a decision (that is they are more positively disposed towards the decision and more likely to try to carry it out) when they are included in the decision-making process. This can be explained by two factors:

- Involving a group in the process of determining a policy or decision ensures they are familiar with the nature, background and need for the policy. They are, therefore, more likely to understand why the policy is necessary.
- Attitudes tend to be more favourable because of the personal involvement in the decision.

Better decisions

Groups on the whole make decisions which are better than that of an individual working alone. It is true that sometimes for various reasons the interesting, bright ideas of one individual may be stifled by a conservative majority, as we shall see. However groups should be able to make better decisions for four reasons:

1 More available information
In trying to solve a problem, an individual normally has access to his own experience and observation and to the written reports of others. In a group, that individual can be exposed to the experience and observations of other people's personal investigation.

This increased information can make it easier to find the correct solution and allows members to select from a number of alternatives. The number of different ideas tends to increase with group size but levels off at about five or six participants.

It is possible to increase artificially the amount of information produced in a group – especially new, imaginative and creative information – by means of a technique known as 'brainstorming'.

Rules for brainstorming

- The subject or problem must be clearly and simply stated.
- Adverse criticism is not allowed and mental self-criticism should be resisted.

    This is a crucial rule since criticism or negativism inhibits thinking as well as communication. If you think of an idea but know that someone is likely to disagree with it, or criticize it, you are more likely to keep it to yourself. So, in a brainstorming session, evaluation of ideas is suspended until after the session is completed.

- All ideas are recorded.

    Every idea is recorded by a secretary or scribe appointed to the task, or by means of a tape recorder, as the ideas are put forward as rapidly as possible. However, it is a good idea to write the ideas up on a blackboard or series of wall charts so that everyone can see them.

- Free association of ideas is encouraged.

    However 'way out' the ideas may seem, all ideas are encouraged.

- Quantity of ideas is important.

    Members should be encouraged to keep ideas coming thick and fast, since at this stage it is the quantity which is important, not the quality.

- Combining and building on ideas is encouraged.

    One idea may trigger further ideas, or an idea which is a combination of others, or a development of a previous idea.

At the beginning of a brainstorming session, the leader should remind the group of the rules and possibly start with a warm-up session on some quite unrelated subject. The best known subject is probably 'What can you use a brick for?' This warm-up session overcomes the initial inhibitions and guarded poses that might otherwise exist.

Usually after about thirty minutes ideas dry up and the evaluation stage can be started, although it is a good idea to hold the evaluation session a day or two later, if possible.

The results of brainstorming groups in business indicate that through using this method, groups produce more ideas than they would otherwise and, for some problems, produce higher-quality suggestions. It not only increases original thought by participants but also teaches them to have greater empathy and tolerance for the ideas of others. It can therefore increase the morale of the group because interaction is increased and everyone feels they are making a contribution.

For these reasons, it is often worth a try when the situation is appropriate.

2 More and better suggestions

Regardless of the task, groups in a good communication climate will produce more and better suggestions than an individual working alone. It is true that some tasks are not best carried out by groups, but there are others for which groups are uniquely qualified:

- those requiring some kind of division of labour
- those where manual rather than intellectual skills are required
- those for which creativity is desirable
- those where memory or recall of information is important
- those where the object of judgement is ambiguous

Activity

Can you think of the reasons why groups are better at performing these five types of tasks?

Tasks requiring division of labour or manual skills are obviously best suited to a group: six pairs of hands are better than one, and usually faster. Groups are better at tasks requiring judgement, creativity and memory because six heads can usually make more accurate judgements and be more creative as a result of exploring more possibilities, and remember more things for longer than just one.

Groups also in this respect learn faster than individuals since there is less chance of bias disrupting learning. Human perception of experiences and viewpoints can produce a very individualized 'frame of reference' – a blinkered view, if you like. In a group these problems are offset by the different backgrounds and experiences of the individual group members, and this results in one member seeing aspects of the problem under discussion that were not perceived by others. By the time the collective decisions have been brought to bear upon the problem, a high-quality decision should be the result.

3 More courageous decisions

Another interesting difference between group and individual thinking and communication is that people seem to be more willing to accept a more risky decision in a group than they would alone.

> *Self-check*
>
> In your experience, do you think this is true? What reasons could explain this tendency?

There are several theories to explain this phenomenon, but the two most popular are:

- People feel they can share the responsibility for their decision over all the group members, rather than just bearing it themselves.
- Groups somehow invest a risk with 'value'. It can be regarded as brave and courageous, and then no one individual wants to be seen to be cowardly or conservative, or the 'wet blanket' or 'odd one out' by not agreeing with others to accept the 'risky' decision.

Whatever the reason, it is interesting to bear in mind that we can usually expect decisions reached in a group meeting to be more risky than the decisions of those same people if approached individually. For an organization this, of course, could prove an advantage or a disadvantage.

4 Higher productivity

People join groups for very different reasons, as we shall see, but whatever their reason for being there, working together with others on the same task can act as a stimulant to greater productivity since group members often work to gain social approval.

Self-check

In talking about the advantages of group decision-making
I have hinted at some disadvantages. Can you remember
them and think of any others?

Disadvantages of small-group decision-making

All the advantages mentioned above result, of course, from a
'good' group working in a 'good communication climate'. As we
know only too well, the problem with many meetings is that they
do not reach these heights of excellence. Group decision-making
can have disadvantages compared with the individual working
alone, and many of these disadvantages are associated with the
advantages.

Time

In terms of man hours, an individual working alone is far
superior. He does not have the problem of coordinating efforts
with other individuals, does not have to listen to information
already known, does not have to feel out the group climate
before contributing, and runs no real risk of having his efforts
duplicated by others.

Although we considered the different frames of reference as
an advantage earlier, we must now see them as potential disadvantages, if we consider the time required to satisfy each member's desire to comment and react to the comments of other
members.

The length of a meeting rises with the square of the number of people
present.*

This may not be an irrefutable law, but our experience surely
tells us that it has an element of truth in it.

There are times when the necessity of prompt action precludes
the use of committees and meetings.

The length of time required to reach a decision wouldn't be so
bad, if it weren't for the fact that much of that time is *wasted*.

*Eileen Shanahan, quoted from Harold Faber, *New York Times Magazine*,
March 1968.

Self-check

Write down ways in which you have found time is wasted in meetings.

Groups can waste time in a number of ways:

● Too much time is spent pursuing one issue or train of thought, with the result that the agenda cannot be completed.
● Members insist on discussing irrelevant points.
● Members feel obliged to make a 'speech' even when they agree and are only repeating what others have said.
● Members spend so much time maintaining group morale and other human relations matters that time does not permit solving the problem assigned to the committee.

Group pressure

Just as we have hinted that the tendency to make more risky decisions can be an *undesirable* phenomenon in group decision-making, this 'mob psychology' may also result in mediocre decisions. The presence of others can produce a 'group pressure' which influences people to agree with a mediocre decision. Group pressure need not necessarily lead to a mediocre decision, but groups do value compromise, and compromise can lead to mediocrity through the process of accommodation and consensus-seeking.

Talk rather than action

Groups sometimes substitute talk for action. Most people seem not to like making decisions and given half a chance they will avoid having to. Some committees therefore tend to exhibit a willingness to discuss almost any problem but solve none. Certainly a considerable sense of achievement can sometimes be derived simply from discussing an important social or business issue and so some groups are so satisfied with their talk that they never get round to acting to come to a realistic solution.

Review

1 Give two reasons for the trend towards what might be termed 'management by committee'.

2 Give two reasons why decisions made by a group are likely to be better than those made by one individual working alone.

ANSWERS

1 Larger and more complex business organizations have made it impossible for any one person or area to make decisions without consulting other areas in the organization.

People want to be involved, to be given a chance to express themselves and be heard, to be 'given a voice' in matters that concern them. They are then more likely to be committed to the resulting decisions which may affect them.

2 Groups are likely to make better decisions than an individual because (a) more information is available in the form of several people's knowledge and experience, and (b) by dividing responsibilities for research among a number of people, more information can be brought into the discussion.

Taken together these two advantages explain the statement 'two heads are better than one'. A group consisting of five or more people can conduct more interviews, read more reports, or conduct more surveys than one member acting alone.

Effective groups, then, can have considerable advantages over the individual working alone. They can provide the individual member with a sense of satisfaction derived simply from being a member of the group, and they can produce higher productivity. But it must be remembered that not all groups have these results, nor do both results necessarily occur together, and although member satisfaction may result in productivity, productivity does not necessarily result in satisfaction.

Factors affecting small-group communication

The outcome of the group is a result of a very complex set of interconnected factors and it is difficult to discuss intelligently any one factor in small-group communication without first knowing something about all the factors since they are all interdependent and influence one another.

As an example of the way in which these factors are all related, let's look first at an important characteristic of effective groups which will affect the outcome of any group's activity but which in turn can be affected by other factors.

Cohesiveness

Cohesiveness is the attractiveness that a group has for its members. It is sometimes confused with 'morale' but cohesiveness refers to one's desire to belong to a group, while morale refers to one's desire to work towards a goal. Cohesiveness therefore represents an individual's attraction to a group and its members, while morale represents one's satisfaction with these as well as other major aspects of the task and the work situation.

Cohesiveness is circular in nature in that once established in a group it leads to many desirable outcomes, which in turn lead to even stronger cohesion.

There are many causes of cohesiveness. In fact there have been instances where people are attracted to groups which have a history of failure. This probably occurs when an individual is more concerned with the group's membership than with its task.

A cohesive group will have a strong sense of loyalty both from its members and to its members. Obviously, the level of cohesiveness will exert a direct influence on individual members' determination to abide by group decisions. Groups that are high in cohesiveness will generally tend to enjoy one another's company, are interested in the well-being of other group members and tend to help each other with problems. Although highly cohesive groups do tend to develop rigid group standards (or norms) which everyone is expected to abide by, their members are more likely to feel able to disagree *openly* than are members of less cohesive groups.

Activity

You are almost bound to belong, or to have belonged to groups – different groups at work, at college, in your leisure activities. Think about them: which ones did you enjoy belonging to, which ones did you want to join and why?

You may belong to some groups whose cohesiveness is very weak. What do you think the reasons are for this? Make a list of the factors which cause this cohesion or lack of cohesion and compare your list with the many interrelated factors which affect the way in which a group operates.

Variables affecting small-group communication
Uncontrollable variables

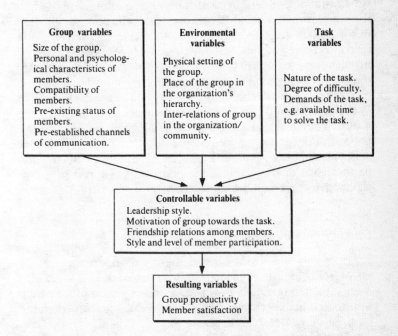

Adapted from *Individual in Society* by Krech, Crutchfield and Ballachey. © 1962 McGraw-Hill Book Company, Inc. Used by permission.

Variables affecting small group decision-making

Look at the diagram on page 109 and you will see that the ultimate outcome of a group – its productivity and member satisfaction – is affected by two main groups of factors or variables:

- uncontrollable (independent) variables
- controllable (intermediate) variables

For example, a group may have been appointed to carry out a certain task. The individual members may have little control over who makes up the group or committee, who they may be working with, in other words; equally they may have little choice over the nature of the task they have to perform; nor will they have much control over the environment within which they act which will impose certain constraints and conditions on the way they operate and which will also determine the physical location in which they meet. All these 'uncontrollable' factors, which in turn affect one another, will have an influence on what happens in the group – the extent to which people interact and participate, the level of motivation of the group, the style of leadership which exists or is adopted, the friendship relationships which develop in the group and so on. These factors are 'controllable' by the group. They are also known as 'intermediate' factors because although they are influenced by the uncontrollable or independent variables, as we have seen, they in turn will influence the performance of the group – the end result in terms of group productivity and member satisfaction.

Uncontrollable variables

It is obvious that in one sense these factors are not totally uncontrollable in that group members could exert influence to change them but usually only over a longer period of time than the group is in existence. As far as the group is concerned, at the moment it comes together as a group, it will have certain conditions imposed upon it. Let's look at the nature of the group itself first of all.

The Group

Self-check

What is the optimum size of a group?
Think about the groups you belong to. Is size important?
Which groups seem to work best and why? Do you think
the size of the group is important?

Size We have already seen that the larger the group the greater
the diversity of information, skills, talent, backgrounds and
experiences available. On the other hand, the larger the group
the less chance there is of an individual participating. However,
the effect of size does not affect everyone in the same way. One
man may find no difficulty in speaking in a group of twenty,
whereas another may find a group of ten too large unless he has
some official role or knows the group well. In larger groups,
more powerful or forceful individuals will tend to dominate the
available communication time; and since studies show that those
who participate most are perceived as having most influence but
do not necessarily have more knowledge or experience, this will
tend to distort what happens in the group. The 'neglected
resource' is a common feature of groups; the silent expert whose
views are never heard because his participation is so low.

There must therefore be a trade-off between the optimum size
for participation and the optimum size for breadth of available
knowledge and experience. Groups of fewer than five will tend
to be less cohesive as splits occur 3:1 or 2:2 and there is insuffi-
cient breadth of experience, variety and intellectual stimulus to
produce good results. Over ten members begins to make face-
to-face contact difficult; over fifteen, low participators will probably stop talking to one another altogether and interaction and
thus creativity are stifled. However, big groups can solve some
types of problem more efficiently than smaller groups, for example where there is a verifiable answer. The more people in the
meeting, the more chance that it contains an expert who knows
the correct answer.

The problem of size is particularly intense where a committee
must include representatives of various interest groups, and this

has given rise to the plethora of subcommittees and working parties which are often formed by a large committee, in an attempt to get the best of both worlds perhaps.

The optimum size is probably between five and seven members but a size of five to ten will allow people to talk almost as much as they want to while still providing a sufficient variety of talent and personality to tackle problems imaginatively.

Size tends to be related to cohesiveness. As the number of members is increased beyond six or seven, cohesiveness begins to decline. This is due mainly to the reduced interaction, the need to divide tasks, the need for stronger more autocratic leadership to keep order and the number of cliques or factions which appear.

Member characteristics and objectives When a group forms or is formed, the members do not arrive with characters like blank sheets. They come complete with different attitudes, values and beliefs and the ways these mix within the group process will again affect the level and style of participation and interaction in the group, and in consequence the productivity and member satisfaction. Effective groups will have a high level of compatibility between the members, but this does not necessarily mean that to be effective a group must have members whose attitudes, beliefs and values are all similar. While this kind of group (homogeneous) tends to promote satisfaction, and heterogeneous groups (groups where members are very dissimilar) tend to exhibit more conflict, heterogeneous groups have been shown to be more productive than homogeneous. The aim is therefore to get a mix of members, or help a group to develop, in such a way that both member satisfaction and productivity is high, and this will be very dependent on the personality and style of the leader. In fact, compatibility can often be achieved when there is agreement and acceptance by the whole group of the leader.

In an effective group, all the members will accept the group's objectives and work to achieve the common goal. However, most people will come to a group with personal objectives of their own – sometimes called 'the hidden agenda'. These can include:

- trying to impress (someone of senior rank perhaps)
- defending the interests of the group you represent
- using the meeting to 'put down' an opponent
- covering up inefficiency or previous errors
- making a particular alliance
- using the meeting as a platform for your own amusement or for an 'ego-trip'

Since it is obviously not possible to satisfy all the individual objectives and group objectives simultaneously some sort of trade-off or give-and-take arrangement has to be arrived at. The extent to which each member is prepared to sacrifice his personal objectives in favour of the objectives of the group as a whole will be dependent on many other factors, but it will be related to the degree of cohesiveness that the group possesses.

Status and roles When a group comes together, they may all be equal members of the group, but they will also each have a pre-existing status in the eyes of the rest of the group. For example, a committee may have been formed to think of ways of reducing accidents and each member may have been picked because of the contribution he can make, but there will inevitably be differences in seniority in the group and some people, whether senior or not, will be regarded as influential by others, before they even open their mouths.

Each member will also see himself as being there to perform a particular role: to stir others up and get some action; to pour oil on troubled waters because there are conflicting interests present in the group; to be the logical thinker, and so on.

Another factor which is important is the existence of pre-established links or friendships. Almost inevitably there will be some people present who know one another from outside the group. The quality and extent of any communication which has taken place before will influence the way they behave inside the group.

In deciding either consciously or unconsciously how he is going to behave, each member has to ask himself three questions:

- *Who am I in this group?* What is my occupational role? What role do others expect me to play? Am I here to be a listener or a leader? Am I here to represent others or am I here in my own right? Who will be judging me on the way I behave?
- *What is the pattern of influence?* Who is likely to have influence? What kind of influence is it? Do I want to change the influence pattern? If so, how am I going to do it?
- *What are my personal needs and objectives?* Are they the same as the group's? Or, at least, compatible with them? If not, should they be? What shall I do if my needs and objectives don't fit with the group's? If I need to be accepted and liked, how important is this to me? Will I be prepared to sacrifice this need, in order to achieve another one?

The Environment

Physical location. The simplest of the so-called 'uncontrollable' factors is the setting of the group, but its importance to the way a group interacts and performs its task is often ignored.

Self-check

In what ways can the physical setting of the group affect the group?

Physical proximity increases interaction. A large room where everyone feels rather distant from his neighbour will hinder cohesiveness. Seating arrangements which separate the leader or chairman from 'the rest' will also discourage interaction, and encourage the leader to adopt a very autocratic style of leadership. Members are more likely to form alliances with those sitting near them and conflicts often occur across a table. Some leaders knowing this will actually arrange the seating so that potential opponents sit along the same side of the table rather than opposite one another.

The location of a meeting gives out signals. If the meeting takes place in the manager's office the pre-existing status relationships are likely to be reinforced, whereas a meeting on neutral ground may lessen the impact of these relationships and encourage everyone to feel they can be themselves.

Shared facilities, even shared discomfort, can encourage cohesiveness by helping group identity. Although the facilities should be suitable for performance of the task, and things like lighting, seating, tables and so on, can be quite significant, even when these are poor, the 'we're all in the same boat' idea can often be helpful to a group in developing a sense of group identity.

Inter-group relations The way a group is regarded by the rest of the organization or community will affect its productivity, cohesiveness and morale. No one wants to belong to a group, or wants to spend hours sitting in meetings of a committee, which is not regarded as being important by the rest of the organization. The extent to which it is perceived to influence events in the organization or outside; the influence it can exert on key figures in the organization; the extent to which it is accepted as important, helpful, cooperative to the overall goals of the organization will all affect the performance of the group and the attitude of individual members to the group.

A member who feels that the group is a waste of time because it is not regarded as being important may react in several ways:

- He may reduce the importance of the group to himself; he may actually stop coming or at least 'withdraw' in the sense that he stops participating.
- He may use his 'negative' or 'nuisance' power by generally being difficult and uncooperative.
- He may encourage the group to become a nuisance, so that at least people notice it.

Expectations of the group The significance of the task for the organization will have implications for the group, as we shall see, but in addition many organizations have a particular 'house style' for meetings. Things are expected to be done in a particular way. In other words, the organization will have norms about ways of conducting meetings, methods of working, reporting and coordinating. A group can often not avoid conforming to these norms and expectations, even if they are not the most appropriate in a particular set of circumstances.

The Task

The nature of the task, the degree of difficulty and any special demands of the task, for instance the time available to complete it, will all affect the attitude of the group members, the way they work and the decisions of the leader about the best way to structure (or not structure) the meeting. Tasks will usually fall into one or more of these four main purposes of meetings:

- information-sharing (exchange of views and information)
- persuasive (recommending action)
- creative/problem-solving (generating ideas)
- decision-making (choosing the best alternative and planning action)

Of these four, 'information-sharing' and 'persuasive' are probably the most common, but meetings which have to solve problems will be concerned with generating ideas and planning action to carry out their decisions.

Information-sharing meetings can usually be larger and more tightly controlled whereas problem-solving meetings will depend on a high degree of interaction and a looser structure which takes more time.

Different tasks will therefore require people to play different roles, and to confuse two different tasks in one meeting will put great strain on the leader and the participants, as one minute they may be expected to contribute ideas in an uninhibited fashion and interact freely, and the next minute conform to a tight timetable and restricted interaction. For this reason, agendas for meetings should try to separate tasks by type rather than lumping everything together in the order it was received by the secretary.

Controllable factors

All the 'uncontrollable' factors will affect what actually happens in a group, and the leader and the participants need to be aware of the potential impact of these factors so that they can arrange their own behaviour accordingly, because the 'controllable' factors are just that: they can be changed and adapted to improve group productivity and member satisfaction. The leader is, of course, central to this adaptation. He may have been appointed by the outside, or he may have emerged from within the group, chosen by them as the most appropriate leader in those circumstances and for that particular task. But whatever the reason for his position as leader, he needs to be aware that there are different styles of leadership and that these styles will have different effects on the group, on their interaction and therefore on the productivity and morale of the group.

Leadership style There are three principal styles of leadership: democratic, autocratic and *laissez-faire*. Each style is likely to cause people to behave in a particular way and to cause certain things to happen.

Self-check

Look at the following statements. Each is a characteristic likely to arise in a group as a result of a particular style of leadership. Look at each one and decide whether it is more likely to occur in meetings with a democratic leader, an autocratic leader or a *laissez-faire* leader.

(Clue: behaviour in meetings can be self oriented (aimed at achieving personal goals), group oriented (aimed at achieving group goals and group member satisfaction) and task oriented (centred mainly on performing the task, with little concern for members' satisfaction and human relations in the group). Generally speaking democratic-style meetings demonstrate *group*-oriented behaviour, autocratic-style meetings demonstrate *task*-oriented behaviour and *laissez-faire*-style meetings demonstrate *self*-oriented behaviour.)

In each section there is one characteristic typical of each leadership style, except in section **d**, Status, where there are two for each.

a *Activity planning*
   1 The activities of the group are planned by the leader. Members are rather uncertain about what the next steps may be.

2 The group plans its activities, technical advice being provided by the leader when necessary.

3 Members of the group are given help by the leader in planning their activities only when it is requested.

b *Discipline*

4 Little stress is placed on discipline, unless imposed by the group. The leader's relation to the members is friendly, helping and tolerant.

5 There is no concern for discipline. Members develop self-assertiveness without regard for others.

6 Considerable stress is placed on discipline and on getting the job done.

c *Responsibilities*

7 Limited responsibility is placed on all members; members are chosen for specific tasks.

8 Leader places no responsibilities on members, who are left to develop activities if they wish.

9 Responsibilities are placed on all members.

d *Status*

10 Leader and members function as equals. Emphasis on status decreases and emphasis on respect increases.

11 Considerable status differences exist between leader and members. Aggressive status-seeking activities develop among members who need status.

12 Few contacts exist between leader and members. Little friendship for the leader develops. Status-mindedness develops, resulting in competitive hostility.

13 Status comes from praise from the leader which is usually personal and subjective.

14 Comments by leader or members are infrequent. Lack of development of feelings of unity, self-confidence or friendliness.

15 Status in the group is earned by the contribution made to the achievement of the group's goals; praise from the leader is objective and factually based.

e *Interaction and participation*

16 Listening improves, resulting in greater acceptance of the

ideas of others.
17 Members listen carefully to leader's instructions; they may
pay little attention to what others say, unless productivity
is at stake.
18 Members focus mainly on their own concerns. Listening to
the comments of others is infrequent.

ANSWERS

Democratic	Autocratic	Laissez-faire
2	1	3
4	6	5
9	7	8
10	11	12
15	13	14
16	17	18

How well did you do? Now copy out the appropriate characteristics for each leadership style and you will have a useful checklist
of the kind of behaviour to expect from each style of leadership.

Self-check

Looking at the three lists how would you rate each leadership style in terms of group productivity and member
satisfaction?

Democratic style Generally speaking since the leader only guides
as needed, working on the fundamental belief that members can
attain their own ends by using their own resources, members
gain satisfaction from his confidence and making their own
decisions. Group productivity is therefore usually fairly high.

Autocratic style The leader's behaviour is governed by a
fundamental belief that constant direction is necessary to achieve
the goals. The task is usually performed and productivity fairly
high but at the expense of member satisfaction.

Laissez-faire Since there is very little concern for goal achievement, the task may not be performed and member satisfaction

will only be derived from achieving personal objectives not from achieving group goals.

However, despite the apparent advantages of a democratic style and the modern trend towards democratic management, there are times when it is inappropriate. The nature of the task, the limited time available, the characteristics of the members and so on may all suggest at a particular moment that another style of leadership is required. The effective leader is the one who is able to be flexible, adapting his style to suit the demands of the occasion.

Interaction patterns The willingness of group members to interact verbally and non-verbally has a significant effect on the type of meeting you will have. Earlier in this chapter, we discovered that group size and the time available could severely limit the member's participation. Many groups seem to assume that the only interaction that takes place is between the leader and the members. If ideas are to be discussed in depth, if the collective wisdom of the group is to be used to advantage, interaction between *all* the members is a must. In groups where the leader adopts a highly structured autocratic style of leadership, the interaction is likely to be highly centralized, whereas in a freer discussion members' comments are directed in any one of many directions rather than exclusively to the leader (see diagrams below).

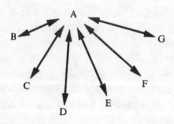

Centralized communication structure

Decentralized communication structure

Neither way is absolutely right or wrong. Both will be appropriate in different circumstances, but you should realize that a tightly controlled discussion 'through the chairman' which is often necessary in large meetings will considerably restrict a group's ability to deal with a task like solving an open-ended problem.

Group roles and behaviour analysis In all human interactions there are two major ingredients – content and process. The first deals with the subject matter or the task upon which the group is working. The second ingredient, process, is concerned with what is happening between and to group members while the group is working. Group process or group dynamics deals with such items as morale, atmosphere, influence, participation, conflict, leadership struggles, competition, cooperation and so on.

In most interactions most people tend to focus their attention on the content or the task and neglect the process even when, as is sometimes the case, it is the major cause of ineffective group action. Sensitivity to the process will enable you to diagnose a group's problems early and deal with them effectively. Since these processes are present in all groups, awareness of them will make you a more valuable and effective member of a group.

Activity

Next time you take part in a meeting observe the way in which the group behaves in terms of things like influence, morale, conflict, leadership struggles, competition and co-operation, as well as the way it performs the task.

It is possible to analyse people's verbal behaviour and then group these different kinds of behaviour into two main groups – those concerned with performing the task and those concerned with maintaining the group as an effective group.

Many people interested in group dynamics have put forward their ideas on the way in which behaviour can be analysed. Most of these behavioural analysts have tended to try to classify behaviour into only ten or perhaps twelve categories, which can then be used by observers to analyse the behaviour of groups. These categories are inevitably all slightly different and so the list below represents an accumulation of the ideas of various analysts.

Activity

Consider the descriptions of the different kinds of behaviour given below and try to think of group meetings you have taken part in. Do you recognize these behaviours? In you? In others?

a *Task roles (functions required in selecting and carrying out a group task)*
1   *Initiating activity* Proposing solutions; suggesting new ideas, new definitions of the problem, new attack on the problem, or new organization of material.
2   *Seeking information* Asking for clarification of suggestions; requesting additional information or facts.
3   *Seeking opinion* Looking for an expression of feeling about something from the members; seeking clarification of values, suggestions or ideas.
4   *Giving information* Offering facts or generalizations; relating one's own experience to the group problem to illustrate points.
5   *Giving opinion* Stating an opinion or belief concerning a suggestion or one of several suggestions, particularly concerning its value rather than its factual basis.

6 *Elaborating* Clarifying, giving examples or developing meanings; trying to envisage how a proposal might work if adopted.

7 *Coordinating* Showing relationships among various ideas or suggestions; trying to pull ideas and suggestions together; trying to draw together activities of various sub-groups or members.

8 *Summarizing* Restating suggestions after the group has discussed them.

b *Group building and maintenance roles (functions required in strengthening and maintaining group life and activities)*

1 *Encouraging* Being friendly, warm, responsive to others; praising others and their ideas; agreeing with and accepting contributions of others.

2 *Gatekeeping* Trying to make it possible for another member to make a contribution to the group by saying, 'We haven't heard anything from Jim yet'; or suggesting limited talking time for everyone so that all will have a chance to be heard.

3 *Standard setting* Expressing standards for the group to use in choosing its content or procedures or in evaluating its decisions; reminding the group to avoid decisions which conflict with group standards.

4 *Following* Going along with decisions of the group; thoughtfully accepting ideas of others; serving as audience during group discussion.

5 *Expressing group feeling* Summarizing what group feeling is sensed to be; describing reactions of the group to ideas or solutions.

Some behaviours serve both functions at the same time: they help the group to perform its task while contributing to the maintenance of the group as well.

c *Both group task and maintenance roles*

1 *Evaluating* Submitting group decisions or accomplishments to comparison with group standards; measuring accomplishments against goals.

2 *Diagnosing* Determining sources of difficulties, appropriate

steps to take next; analysing the main blocks to progress.

3 *Testing for consensus* Tentatively asking for group opinions in order to find out whether the group is nearing agreement on a decision; sending up trial balloons to test group opinions.

4 *Mediating* Harmonizing; conciliating differences in points of view; making compromise solutions.

5 *Relieving tension* Draining off negative feeling by jesting or pouring oil on troubled waters; putting a tense situation in a wider context.

For any group to be effective, these task and maintenance functions will have to be performed by some member or members of the group, at some time or another. Of course, it is the ultimate responsibility of the leader to ensure that they are performed, but although he will perform some himself, the extent to which he and the others share the responsibility for their performance will be determined by his choice of leadership style. In some groups, all members may, at some point, perform each of these functions.

Of course, from time to time, people behave in non-functional ways that do not help the group and the work it is trying to do, and sometimes actually harm the group and its proceedings.

d *Types of non-functional behaviour*
1 *Being aggressive* Working for status by criticizing or blaming others; showing hostility against the group or some individual; deflating the ego or status of others.

2 *Blocking* Interfering with the progress of the group by going off on a tangent; citing personal experiences unrelated to the problem; arguing too much on a point, rejecting ideas without consideration; difficulty stating.

3 *Self-confessing* Using the group as a sounding board; expressing personal, non-group-oriented feelings or points of view.

4 *Competing* Vying with others to produce the best idea, talk the most, play the most roles, gain favour with the leader.

5 *Seeking sympathy* Trying to induce other group members to be sympathetic to one's problems or misfortunes; deploring one's own situation, or disparaging one's own ideas to gain support.

6 *Special pleading* Introducing or supporting suggestions related to one's own pet concerns or philosophies; lobbying.
7 *Horsing around* Clowning; joking; mimicking; disrupting the work of the group.
8 *Seeking recognition* Attempting to call attention to oneself by loud or excessive talking, extreme ideas, unusual behaviour.
9 *Withdrawal* Acting indifferent or passive; resorting to excessive formality; daydreaming; doodling; whispering to others; wandering from the subject.

You should be careful in using the classification above not to blame either yourself or someone else who demonstrates non-functional behaviour. It is more helpful to see such behaviour as a symptom that all is not well with the group's ability to satisfy individual needs through group-centred activity. You should also be alert to the fact that each person may interpret such behaviours differently. For example, there are times when what appears to be non-functional behaviour may not necessarily be so, for the content and the group conditions may also have to be taken into account. Sometimes aggressive behaviour may serve a useful purpose in clearing the air and stirring the group into action, for example.

Any group is strengthened and enabled to work more efficiently if its members

- become more conscious of the role function needed at any given time
- become more sensitive to and aware of the degree to which they can help to meet the needs through what they do
- undertake self-training to improve their range of role functions and skills in performing them.

Review

1 Name two uncontrollable variables and two controllable variables which may interact and affect the resulting variables – group productivity and member satisfaction.
2 What is the optimum size of a group? Why?

3   For a group to be effective, is it essential for all the members to have similar personalities?
4   What does the 'hidden agenda' mean?
5   Which three main questions does a member of a group ask himself either consciously or subconsciously on joining a group?
6   How can the physical setting affect the group?

ANSWERS

1   Look back at the diagram on p. 109.
2   The optimum size of group is five (certainly no more than seven), as this size allows complete interaction among the members and yet provides sufficient variety of talent and personality to tackle problems imaginatively.
3   No. A group needs to be compatible, and this means that personalities should be complementary. A group consisting of members who all have dominant personalities and want to lead would probably not be effective.
4   The 'hidden agenda' refers to the personal objectives of individuals in a group. These personal objectives may conflict with the group's objectives and to be effective a group must, by some means or another, encourage individuals to see the group's objectives as more important than their own.
5   Who am I in this group? What is the pattern of influence? What are my personal needs and objectives?
6   Physical proximity increases interaction. The location of the meeting communicates a message. Shared facilities, even poor facilities, can encourage cohesiveness in a group.

Self-check

Using the role functions described on pp. 122–5 say what kind of function each of the following statements might perform in a meeting. Remember one behaviour may serve more than one function.

1   'What do you think about that for an idea, John?'
2   'OK, so let's just see where we've got to. Some of you think the best plan would be to . . . but the others

think that might be counter-productive.'

3 'I get the impression that deep down none of us is really happy about this.'

4 'Oh, that's a daft idea!'

5 'Remember, though, that whatever we do, we have agreed to have the report ready by November at the latest.'

6 'Well, I think, and I suspect the chairman will agree with me, that . . .'

7 'In the last job I was in, we tried that, and it was very successful – it cut absenteeism by about ten per cent.'

8 'Well, that may be all right for you but just imagine how my lot are going to react to that. It's always the same, you never think about the ones who actually have to implement your great ideas.'

9 'So, it looks as if our only problem is finding the space to put the machine until it can be properly installed. Perhaps we could persuade Jim to shift those crates in B warehouse. That's near the unloading bay and reasonably near where it will finally be used, so transporting it shouldn't be too difficult. What do you think?'

10 'Now that's a great idea. I hadn't thought of that.'

ANSWERS

1 Seeking opinion and/or gatekeeping.
2 Summarizing.
3 Expressing group feeling.
4 Probably an example of 'blocking', but if it is followed up with reasons it could be an example of 'evaluating'.
5 Standard setting.
6 Competing.
7 Giving information.
8 Seeking sympathy.
9 'Diagnosing' but also 'initiating activity' and 'seeking opinion'.
10 'Giving opinion' but worded the way it is, it is likely to serve an 'encouraging' function as well.

6 | Leading and participating in meetings

We have already discussed the three major styles of leadership and examined the ways in which people contribute to meetings. In this chapter let's look briefly at the responsibilities of group leaders and at the requirements for effective participation in small group discussions, together with the requirements of conducting and recording fairly formal meetings.

 Self-check

 From what you now know about the nature of groups, what do you think the responsibilities of the chairman are?

Responsibilities of leader/chairman

The role of a chairman or leader at a meeting or conference requires that he should preside, maintain order and ensure that his group does a constructive job of work. He needs to bear constantly in mind two things: the task to be done, and the kind of group he is dealing with. A sense of purpose needs to be quickly created. This can be achieved if he starts the meeting on time and provides the group with its terms of reference for the meeting – in other words, spelling out the order of the business and the plan of campaign.

The objectives should provide the leader with a basis of control and the rest of the group with a sense of direction. Well-defined objectives, stemming from a carefully prepared and clearly expressed agenda, will provide a good foundation for teamwork. Ideally a group should identify themselves with the objectives so that they realize they have a responsibility and a real part to play. Remember that most people work better when they know what a job is about, that they have a useful part to play and can have a hand in making decisions. If a group's function is an advisory one it is best to let them know. It may prevent frustration later.

Controlling the meeting

The reason for the meeting should indicate the type of control and structure most appropriate, as we have seen. Control should be exercised with a view to setting standards of performance. Results should be checked against these standards and where necessary corrective action should be taken. The leader must accept the responsibility for ensuring that this is done because it is he alone who must accept the ultimate responsibility for the group's performance.

To be effective a chairman should use the following basic principles:

- Decide the item of business to be discussed.
- Define the limits of discussion.
- Keep people to the point and ensure that one person speaks at a time.
- Try to be as impartial as possible and at all costs avoid arguing with members.
- Make sure the rest of the group understand what is going on.

Guiding

However much the chairman intends to limit his own contributions, he will be obliged to start things off and make sure topics and problems are discussed in the right order. Members have an unfortunate habit of jumping in with solutions before they have understood exactly what the problem is, for example.

Introducing an item of business

When considering a subject there are four basic stages:

Identify the subject/problem – this should be stated clearly and if necessary repeated at intervals.

Exchange and develop ideas – get the evidence and interpret it *before* getting ideas for the solution to the problem.

Evaluate the alternatives – identify the range of choices available, predict the consequences of each (time, cost, resources, political considerations).

Select a course of action – preferably by consensus. Decide 'who?', 'where?', 'when?', 'how?', and make sure everyone knows what their responsibilities are.

The chairman should make sure that members stick to this order of events and he may have to intervene in order to suggest new ideas, clarify previous statements, summarize and draw attention to possible consequences.

Stimulating discussion

We have already discussed 'brainstorming' as a technique for encouraging ideas and encouraging quieter members, but 'brainstorming' is not always appropriate.

However, the chairman should from time to time stimulate members by asking appropriate questions. The types of question discussed on pp. 70–8 can be used in discussions as well as interviews. The use of questions helps not only to stimulate members but also to control the discussion. This may require interrupting a too-talkative member and calling on the more retiring members for their thoughts. This can be achieved by commenting as you interrupt the too-talkative member: 'Now there's an interesting point. What do you think about that, Tony?'

- Phrase questions to avoid 'yes' or 'no' answers.
- Keep questions brief and straightforward.
- Use simple words.
- Use questions directly related to the topic.
- Use questions which cover a single point.

Coping with the hidden agenda

The chairman should also try to keep the discussion on an ideas level, rather than allowing it to slip into a conflict of personalities among members. Hidden agendas, competition among members and emotion-laden statements made by group members must be dealt with properly or else social and emotional concerns will become the major focus of the group, at the expense of task considerations. Asking members to give *examples* of sweeping generalizations is a good technique for encouraging members to keep to facts and ideas but you may need help with this task of 'maintaining the group'. Research has indicated that the socio-emotional leader may often be someone other than the officially designated leader.

Reaching a decision

So far as reaching a decision is concerned, in the absence of formal voting methods, the chairman should either adopt the consensus method or, if appropriate, decide himself which conclusion is the most suitable as an answer to the problem. The nature of the work and the composition of the group should produce a procedure most suited to the situation.

Self-check

What are the main methods a group can use to make decisions? What are the advantages and disadvantages of each?

Decision-making methods available to meetings

1 Decision by authority
- Chairman makes the decision.
- Efficient and fast.
- *But* members may not be committed or agree.

2 Decision by majority rule/voting
- Generally recognized as fair.
- Timing of the vote is crucial.
- May divide the group members.
- Minority will not agree and therefore may not be committed.

3 Decision by consensus
- Decision 'emerges' as the general feeling of the group.
- Members highly committed.
- Lengthy – necessary for all members to have their 'say' even if they do not eventually get their 'way'.
- Preferable but not always possible.

4 Decision by unanimity
● Everyone genuinely and wholeheartedly agrees.
● Difficult to achieve, and usually not necessary anyway.

No way is the best way, since all have advantages and disadvantages, but if possible the group should agree to the method adopted. In any event, whichever method is chosen, it is vital that the group should know what the final decision is, and the chairman should make sure it is recorded.

Finally, once the meeting is over the chairman is responsible for ensuring that minutes of the meeting are prepared and any action agreed during the meeting is followed up. This may involve writing a report or monitoring the progress of any action.

Review

Name two techniques a chairman can use to stimulate discussion.

ANSWER

Brainstorming is a good way to encourage ideas but the question technique encourages quieter members and controls the more talkative members.

Responsibilities of participants

Self-check

What are the responsibilities of participants at meetings?

One of your first responsibilities as a participant is to develop a healthy attitude to meetings – one of openmindedness and consideration for others.

You should resist negative feelings about meetings. They are an essential tool of management and supervision, and they can have positive value for you.

Self-check

How can you benefit from meetings and other small group discussions?

Meetings can provide you with opportunities for:

- benefiting from the knowledge and opinions of others
- gaining maximum information from the backgrounds and experiences of your colleagues
- feeling a part of a policy or decision under which you will be working
- developing a better understanding and appreciation of your colleagues and the teamwork that can be developed among you
- expressing and communicating your own thoughts to others
- evaluating your own opinions, beliefs and attitudes in the light of other people's

If you are a student, you might also like to consider that most of these benefits can also be derived from small dicussion or tutorial groups.

Your second responsibility is to ensure that you are properly prepared and informed on the topic. This may require considerable time and effort, but the quality of a meeting can rise no higher than the quality of information possessed by the group members. (Again, students should take note of this responsibility.)

As far as the meeting itself is concerned, knowledge of 'group process' and how groups function will both help you to develop the right attitude and make you a better participant. You should know the basic steps in problem-solving. You should be aware of the problems and responsibilities of the leader, so that you can be more understanding of his methods of leadership and also be helpful in contributing positively towards helping him achieve the meeting goals.

Leadership is a dynamic phenomenon. During a two-hour meeting various leaders (you may be one) may emerge from time to time, even though the same person remains as the official leader.

You should realize that every other member sitting around the table with you is an individual who is different from you. He has his own personal problems, his own self-centredness (which all of us should try to avoid in favour of being more 'you-centred') and his own way of thinking, which may be different from yours.

The goal of your development as a good meeting participant should include a constant study of other people, including a consideration of their basic drives, prejudices, emotions and thinking processes.

Your own actual participation depends on how good a communicator you are and the recognized characteristics of an effective participant include therefore:

- a consideration of the other people involved
- a recognition that the interaction process must be two-way, flexible and tolerant
- an awareness of communication barriers and a desire to overcome them
- an ability to think logically and analytically
- an ability and desire to speak clearly, to the point and in a language adapted to others
- a sense of proper timing both in terms of when and how to speak, and consideration for the setting and place of the meeting
- a desire to cooperate and conciliate in order to achieve group goals
- an understanding of the need for attentive listening

Self-check

When should you participate in a meeting?

The answer should be: when you have something to say. You should never talk just for the sake of talking, but nor should you be too diffident. Be ready to get involved on the spur of the moment. Contribute your ideas at the moment that group interest in your contribution will be strong. Don't sit back patiently until everyone else has had his say. There is some indication that members who contribute early in a discussion gain the initial respect of the whole group, and are perceived as credible sources as the meeting progresses. Another psychologically good moment to make perhaps another contribution is at the end of a section of discussion. It will of course depend on the subject and the group, but if you have a good argument to put with sound evidence, it can come at a very persuasive moment just as everyone else is drying up.

It is also wise to talk a number of times, rather than to try to say all you have on your mind at one time. Speak only to the point at hand, and do not fall into the pitfall of becoming a 'chain' talker, whose one thought leads to another and who doesn't know when to stop. Remarks of about one minute in length are usually sufficient at one time, or perhaps up to two minutes at most.

You may find that several people want to speak as soon as the present speaker has finished, so you must come in with split-second timing. The slow and less alert member may want to say something but finds himself going all the way through a meeting saying nothing because he doesn't maintain constant alertness.

Of course, this does not mean that the group does not need attentive listeners. An animated, alert listener contributes a great deal. But listening alone will keep within you valuable information or opinion that should be offered so that the group can consider your contributions.

The table below provides a useful reminder of the essential duties of the officers and members of meetings.

OFFICERS AND MEMBERS OF A MEETING: ESSENTIAL DUTIES

Before meeting	*During meeting*	*After meeting*
Chairman		
1 Establish and understand the items of business to be transacted.	1 Start on time.	1 Verify draft copy of minutes prepared by secretary or minute writer.
	2 Introduce topics clearly.	
	3 Obtain valid contributions.	
2 Agree a draft agenda.		2 Monitor progress.
3 Ensure members are notified of time, place, purpose of meeting and issue agenda if possible.	4 Maintain order.	
	5 Get decisions effectively.	
4 Ensure the room is properly arranged – seating arrangements, papers, water, ashtrays, etc.		

Before meeting	During meeting	After meeting
Secretary or minute writer		
1 Obtain the material from previous minutes or new sources.	1 Attend before time.	1 Draft minutes
2 Draft agenda to a logical order of priorities.	2 Get the room ready.	2 Agree with chairman.
3 Agree with chairman.	3 Have all necessary papers available.	3 Distribute to members within two days of meeting.
4 Circulate notice of meeting and agenda.	4 Take note of the proceedings.	4 Issue instructions arising from minutes and monitor if necessary.
	5 Do not allow unclear discussion and decisions to pass.	
	6 Assist the chairman.	
Members		
1 Notify secretary/ chairman of items for agenda.	1 Attend on time.	1 Read and verify minutes.
2 Read all papers.	2 Make disciplined contributions.	2 Carry out any action required and if necessary report back.
3 Prepare, if appropriate, own supporting papers.	3 Take note of decisions made and action required.	
4 Clear any points of correction with secretary.		

NB If there is no appointed secretary, the chairman is responsible for ensuring that the secretary's duties are performed by someone, if not himself.

The agenda

An agenda for a meeting should indicate the order in which items of business will be discussed. When appropriate, these items may have been obtained from contributors. Some care should be taken to ensure consideration of items in the most logical order. Another feature of agenda planning is the ability to appreciate what can be achieved in a given period of time. As a general rule, very routine items are placed at the beginning of an agenda followed by business arising from the last meeting. This information is then succeeded by new items requiring consideration. Where there are several fairly brief and/or urgent items on the agenda, attend to those first, allowing the rest of the meeting to be concentrated on more time-consuming matters. Remember the warnings on p. 116 about mixing different kinds of task on one agenda.

It is a mistake to compress major items from the previous meeting under the heading of 'matters arising'. These are far better placed under individual headings, but high on the agenda. This provides the chairman and participants with a more realistic idea of the work that has to be done.

Don't be tempted to overload the agenda. This inevitably leads to overrunning time, which in turn leads to inefficiency (hastily agreed decisions, for example) because members quite reasonably want to get away.

Order of agenda This is a comprehensive list of the most usual order of items at a formal meeting, but obviously not all these items will always appear.

1 Election of chairman and officers (as necessary).
2 Notice of meeting – read by secretary (usually only at a very formal meeting).
3 Minutes of previous meeting – taken as read (or read by secretary) and then signed by chairman.
4 Matters arising from minutes.
5 Correspondence received – read by secretary.
6 Chairman's opening remarks.
7 Matters adjourned from previous meeting (if any).
8 Financial matters (treasurer's report, circulation of accounts, etc).
9 Reports by committees and working parties.
10 Motions showing wording where possible and names of proposer and seconder.
11 Any further items of business previously notified and listed on the agenda.
12 Date of next meeting.
13 Any other business. (Sometimes referred to as AOB. Only minor points should be permitted; significant items should

have been previously notified and should therefore be held over to the next meeting.)
14 Vote of thanks to the chairman (not usually proposed at regularly held meetings).
15 Reply by chairman (see above).
16 Meeting declared closed by chairman.

Each item on the agenda should be numbered. If for any reason the sequence of items then needs to be altered, the chairman should clearly give the reasons at the start of the meeting. This is important because members interested in other items may feel aggrieved if their business is deferred or even postponed.

When an item is continued from a previous meeting it is helpful to quote the minute number and date of the meeting. Cross-referencing is useful because it allows the history of an item to be traced and thus may prevent wrong decisions being made. This method is also helpful to new members who do not know what has gone before.

Another useful practice is to make a reference to essential supporting papers, either against the relevant item of business, or in the form of a short checklist at the end of the agenda.

In preparing the agenda for a meeting, you may want to remember that questions stimulate a greater variety of responses than do plain statements. This is particularly true if care is taken to structure questions in an open and unbiased manner. Your agenda, then, could consist of a carefully thought out series of questions.

Finally, the agenda should provide a reminder to fix the date, time and place of the next meeting. If a meeting is likely to be recurrent, it is helpful if a calendar can be agreed on.

Activity

Using this section on the agenda, produce a checklist for planning an agenda which you could use to remind you of the important things to cover and in the order you would do them, if you had to produce an agenda for any meeting.

Steps in agenda planning
1   Establish what is outstanding from previous meeting.

2 Identify new items of business through anticipating current developments and contacting meeting participants.
3 Select significant items.
4 Avoid overloading 'matters arising' (show significant items separately, high on the agenda).
5 Place routine items early on the agenda.
6 Arrange significant items in logical sequence (see p. 137).
7 Relate these items to time available and people attending.
8 Number items consecutively.
9 Cross-reference items from previous meetings.
10 Ensure details of next meeting are asked for by placing 'date of next meeting' at the end of the agenda.
11 Specify what additional papers are required or included with agenda.
12 Discuss and agree agenda with chairman (if appropriate).
13 Submit draft agenda for typing.
14 Proof-read typed agenda.
15 Link to minutes of previous meeting and circulate both documents and any relevant papers.

The minutes

Any meeting which makes decisions should certainly record how the decision came about, what final decision was reached and who is responsible for any action. But most meetings whatever their purpose benefit from recording the nature of their business. Minutes provide a useful reference on the history of a committee's business, reducing the possibility of disagreement over what exactly was discussed and decided when and by whom. For this reason properly constituted meetings and legally based organizations are required to keep minutes.

Normally, taking minutes is the responsibility of the secretary, but whether or not you are ever prepared to take on this role officially, it is always possible that it will fall to you to record the minutes of a meeting, in the absence of anyone else either authorized or willing to do so.

Minute writing is not an easy task but there are some basic do's and don'ts which, if you can bear them in mind, will make the task that much easier.

MINUTES OF A BOARD MEETING HELD AT THE REGISTERED OFFICE OF REES AND
GREENWOOD LIMITED ON WEDNESDAY, 10 DECEMBER 1981 AT 10.30.

PRESENT: Mr S. Ashley (in the Chair)
           Mrs B. Coultate
           Mr T. A. Thorne
           Mr S. R. Gilbey
           Mr N. W. Langham
           Mr R. G. Sheddon (Secretary)

Apologies for absence were received from Mr P. Green and Miss S. Shelton.

162   MINUTES OF THE LAST MEETING

> Minutes of the meeting held on 13 November 1981 were taken as read
> and signed by the Chairman.

163   MATTERS ARISING FROM THE MINUTES

> 163.1   Minute 159.2
>
> > Mr Thorne reported that all supervisors had been issued with
> > leaflets outlining the details of the Harmonisation Programme.*
> > They had been asked to ensure that all employees receive a
> > leaflet, and to explain the programme to all members of their
> > section.   This should be completed by 15 January as requested
> > by the Board.
>
> 163.2   Minute 160
>
> > Mr Sheddon reported that all the necessary alterations had
> > been made to the Pension Scheme and that each employee would
> > be seen personally by the Personnel Department.   These
> > interviews were scheduled to start on 16 January 1982.

164   REACTION TO THE HARMONISATION PROGRAMME

> 164.1   Noted that the only real opposition received had been submitted
> by employees absent from work during the week that the
> consultative meetings had been held.
>
> 164.2   Resolved that these employees should be seen personally by
> their Department Managers, if this had not already been done.

165   CANTEEN ALTERATIONS

> 165.1   Noted that building work on the two canteens would begin on
> 31 January and was expected to be completed by the middle of
> February.
>
> Resolved that both canteens should be redecorated, in view of
> the architect's report.   Redecoration would begin immediately
> the building work was completed.

166   TIME CLOCKS

> 166.1   Mr Gilbey reported that all the time clocks had now been
> repaired except one, which was considered to be beyond repair.

166.2 <u>Resolved</u> that two new clocks should be rented rather than bought. One clock would replace the one that could not be repaired and the other would be sited in the annexe of the new office block.

blk

167 PRESS COVER

167.1 <u>Resolved</u> that the Public Relations Officer should draft a press release in time for the next Board meeting. The decision about the date of the press release would be considered at that meeting.

167.2 <u>Resolved</u> that should the press wish to, they should be invited to interview any employee, who was agreeable, on the subject of the Harmonisation Programme once the press release had been issued.

168 DATE OF THE NEXT MEETING

The date of the next meeting of the board of directors would be Wednesday 15 January 1982.

In the absence of any other business, the meeting closed at 11.45.

Signed:

S. Ashley
Managing Director

15 January 1982

*
Harmonisation is the term used to describe the process of giving all employees the same conditions of work — the same canteen facilities, the same hours of work, the same holiday entitlement, etc.

Before the meeting
1   Seek guidance and instruction on how to do the job. Check with the chairman if there is a particular house style, but anyway, familiarize yourself with the basic pattern of minutes. (See the example above.)

During the meeting
2   Record the date, time and place of the meeting.
3   Record who has attended and from whom 'apologies for absence' have been received.
4   Identify topics of discussion. If suitable, use the agenda as your guide.

5   Follow the convention of dealing with routine items first –
     minutes of the last meeting read and signed, matters arising
     from the minutes, correspondence received.
6   Plan your minute-taking on the basis of a short title which
     summarises the topic, a *brief* summary of the discussion,
     decision taken and action required, by when and by whom.
7   Give each minute a consecutive reference number.
8   Keep up with the thinking of the meeting.
9   Clear up outstanding or ambiguous points before it is too
     late.
10   Discriminate between fact and opinion.
11   Write in note-fashion, and unless required avoid verbatim
     recording.
12   Use short clear sentences and paragraphs.

After the meeting
13   Draft the minutes clearly and neatly immediately after the
     meeting.
14   Check them through with another person – preferably the
     chairman.
15   Submit them for typing with clear instructions on layout,
     etc.
16   Proof-read the typed minutes.
17   Have them completed and typed within two days of the
     meeting.
18   Circulate the minutes to all who were or should have been
     at the meeting and to anyone else who needs to know what
     took place. Send out edited versions if necessary.
19   File the minutes carefully. There may be a minute book into
     which the minutes are pasted onto numbered pages. This is
     for security reasons – to prevent pages being removed.
20   Check that any action is monitored and followed-up.

Do not
• try to chair the meeting *and* take minutes; appoint someone
  else to take the minutes
• allow the pace of discussion to overtake you and so prevent
  accurate note-taking
• allow your own personal bias or point of view to creep into
  your interpretation of what has been said

- insert too many names of people into the minutes
- include unexplained abbreviations and jargon unfamiliar to potential readers
- delay the drafting of the minutes – you won't remember what took place
- be over-influenced by status of members; just because your boss is there doesn't mean you have to record diligently every word he utters
- forget to ensure that the date, time and place of the next meeting is agreed

Activity

Volunteer to act as secretary next time you get the chance.

Review

Which of the following statements are true, and which are false?

1 Authoritarian leadership is a type of leadership in which the leader plays a 'permissive' role sharing the functions of leadership with the members of the group by encouraging their participation in goal setting, and in planning and directing the activities of the group.

2 Participation involves a willingness to assume some leadership functions and a willingness to contribute your comments spontaneously.

3 Items of business requiring very little discussion should be placed last on the agenda, in case time runs out and there isn't a chance to discuss everything.

4 Solutions to a problem should be invited immediately the chairman has introduced the subject for discussion.

5 In knowing how to participate at meetings, your best advice is to follow the basic principles of effective communication.

ANSWERS

1 False. This is a definition of democratic leadership. A definition of authoritarian leadership might be: where the leader plays a strong directive role in setting group goals and in

planning and directing the activities of the group, delegating few of the functions of leadership to the group.

2   True. Effective participation means that you at least are aware of the responsibilities and functions of the leader and are willing to carry out some of those functions if the leadership style invites it, particularly those concerned with group maintenance. An effective participant will also not sit silently through a meeting depriving the group of the chance to consider his ideas and benefit from his knowledge and experience, but will be alert to the moments when his contribution will be most usefully received.

3   False. Routine items and items requiring little discussion should be placed high on the agenda, but the amount of time allowed for their discussion should be carefully controlled by the chairman to allow sufficient time for discussion of more lengthy items.

4   False. Solutions should only be invited after the problem has been carefully identified and diagnosed, otherwise there is a danger of solving the wrong problem.

5   True. All the basic principles of good communication concerning purpose, audience, timing, two-way communication, listening, etc. apply to participating in meetings.

Activity

1   Attend a local council meeting, or a staff meeting, or some other meeting of a small group.

Who are the high participators? Do they include the leader? Who are the low participators? Does participation change during the meeting?

Which members are high in influence? (That is, when they talk, other seem to listen attentively.) Which members are low in influence? (Others do not listen to or follow them.) Does the influence pattern change during the meeting?

Is there any rivalry, competition, conflict in the group? How is it dealt with? Is there a struggle for leadership? Is there a willingness on everyone's part to share leadership functions?

Are the task functions and maintenance functions shared by all? Or do some concentrate on the task and others on the group?

Characterize each member of the group as predominantly self-oriented, group-oriented or task-oriented.

What were the major successes of the meeting? Failures? What factors seemed to account for these?

2 Examine carefully the cynical statements about committees and meetings at the beginning of the previous chapter. Suggest the breakdown or problem which probably prompted each of those statements.

Formal procedure

In very large meetings, over about twenty members, it is often customary to adopt a fairly formal method of dealing with the items on the agenda and controlling the conduct of the meeting. This formal procedure, sometimes called parliamentary procedure, is intended to help maintain a degree of order in what might otherwise be an unruly, unmanageable shouting match. However, as you will realize, any restriction on the interaction of participants is bound to affect the quality of discussion and decision-making. It is therefore advisable to keep the degree of formality to the minimum compatible with conducting the business.

However, many bodies are required by law to conduct their meetings according to established conventions, and these are usually indicated in the rules of the association, and are referred to as 'standing orders'. Even if you do not agree that meetings should be run on very rigid lines, it is nevertheless advisable to be familiar with this formal procedure or you may feel inhibited from speaking at all at such a meeting, purely because you don't 'know the ropes'. The danger of this is that the few people who seem to make a hobby of learning and then pompously adhering to these standing orders are able to take advantage of everyone else's ignorance.

Another danger of being rather ignorant of the formal conventions and procedures is that 'a little knowledge can be a dangerous thing' in that it is possible for the formal procedure to end up confusing the issue rather than facilitating the discussion.

There is not space enough to deal with all the details of formal procedure in this book and anyway the subject has been eminently well covered in various books on the law and procedures of meetings. However, I would warmly recommend you to a book by Lord Citrine called *The ABC of Chairmanship*.*

However, to whet your appetite, I shall end this chapter with an amusing example of what can result when formal procedure is used in a rather half-hearted way in a meeting, by people who are not too clear about the meaning and implications of some of the terminology, nor about quite how to manage a meeting.

Activity

Read through the extract from *The Ragged Trousered Philanthropists* below and try to define the terms which are in italics. You could then use these as a basis for your first dip into *The ABC of Chairmanship* to check your answers.

The Ragged Trousered Philanthropists, by Robert Tressall,† is a very readable novel about the 'reality of the subjection and destitution of working class life in "the good old days" of the Edwardian age – an age when everyone knew his place and because of it was supposed to be content'. It revolves around the lives and experiences of a group of housepainters, and the inspiration of a newcomer to arouse them from their acceptance of their lot.

This extract describes the events of 'The Beano Meeting' – a meeting called to decide if, when and where the annual outing – the Beano – should take place.

The Beano

1   It was just about this time that Crass, after due consultation with several of the others, decided to call a meeting of the hands for the purpose of considering the advisability of holding the usual beano later on in the summer. The meeting was held in the carpenter's shop down at the yard one evening at six o'clock, which allowed time for those interested to attend after leaving work.

2   When all those who were expected to turn up had arrived, Payne, the foreman carpenter – the man who made the coffins – was *voted to the chair on the proposition of Crass, seconded by Philpot*, and then a solemn silence ensued, which was broken at last by the chairman, who, in a

* NCLC Publishing Society, 1952.
† Lawrence & Wishart, 1955; Panther, 1965.

lengthy speech, explained the object of the meeting. Possibly, with a laudable desire that there should be no mistake about it, he took the trouble to explain several times, going over the same ground and repeating the same words over and over again, whilst the audience waited in a miserable and deathlike silence for him to leave off. Payne, however, did not appear to have any intention of leaving off, for he continued, like a man in a trance, to repeat what he had said before, seeming to be under the impression that he had to make a separate explanation to each individual member of the audience. At last the crowd could stand it no longer, and began to shout 'Hear, hear!' and to bang bits of wood and hammers on the floor and the benches; and then, after a final repetition of the statement that the object of the meeting was to consider the advisability of holding an outing, or beanfeast, the chairman collapsed on to the carpenter's stool and wiped the sweat from his forehead.

3   Crass then reminded the meeting that the last year's beano had been an unqualified success, and for his part he would be very sorry if they did not have one this year. Last year they had four brakes, and they went to Tubberton Village. It was true that there was nothing much to see at Tubberton, but there was one thing they could rely on getting there that they could not be sure of getting for the same money anywhere else, and that was – a good feed. (Applause.) Just for the sake of getting on with the business, *he would propose* that they decide to go to Tubberton, and that a committee be appointed to make arrangements – about the dinner – with the landlord of the 'Queen Elizabeth's Head' at that place.

4   Philpot *seconded the motion* and Payne was about *to call for a show of hands* when Harlow *rose to a point of order*. It appeared to him they were getting on a bit too fast. The proper way to do this business was first *to take the feeling of the meeting* as to whether they wished to have a beano at all, and then, if the meeting was in favour of it, they could decide where to go, and whether they would have a whole day or only half a day.

5   The semi-drunk said that he didn't care a dreadful expression where they went: he was willing to abide by the decision of the majority. (Applause.)

6   Easton suggested that a special saloon carriage might be engaged, and they could go and visit Madame Tussaud's

waxworks. He had never been to that place and had often wished to see it. But Philpot objected that if they went there, Madame Tussaud's might not be willing to let them out again.

7   The chairman then began rambling on again at considerable length. Having thus made another start, Payne found it very difficult to leave off, and was proceeding to relate further details of the last beano when Harlow again rose up from his heap of shavings and said he wished *to call the chairman to order*. (Hear, hear!) What was the use of all this discussion before they had even decided to have a beano at all! Was the meeting in favour of a beano or not? That was the question.

8   A prolonged and awkward silence followed. Everybody was very uncomfortable, looking stolidly on the ground or staring straight in front of them.

9   At last Easton broke the silence by suggesting that it would not be a bad plan if someone was to make a motion that a beano be held. This was greeted with a general murmur of 'Hear, hear' followed by another awkward pause, and then the chairman asked Easton if he would *move a resolution* to that effect. After some hesitation, Easton agreed, and *formally moved*: 'That this meeting is in favour of a beano.'

10   The semi-drunk said that, in order to get on with the business, he would *second the resolution*. But meantime, several arguments had broken out between the advocates of different places, and several men began to relate anecdotes of previous beanos. Nearly everyone was speaking at once, and it was some time before the chairman was able to *put the resolution*. Finding it impossible to make his voice heard above the uproar, he began to hammer on the bench with a wooden mallet. Some of them looked at him curiously and wondered what was the matter with him, but the majority were so interested in their own arguments that they did not notice him at all.

11   Whilst the chairman was trying to get the attention of the meeting in order to put the question, Bundy had become involved in an argument with several of the new hands who claimed to know of an even better place than the 'Queen Elizabeth', the 'New Found Out'. He went there last year with Pushem and Driver's crowd, and they had roast beef, goose, jam tarts, mince pies, sardines, blancmange, calves' foot jelly, and one pint for each man was

included in the cost of the dinner. In the middle of the discussion, they noticed that most of the others were holding up their hands, so to show there was no ill-feeling they held up theirs also and then the *chairman declared it was carried unanimously*.

12   Bundy said he would like to ask the chairman to read out the resolution which had just been passed, as he had not caught the words.

13   The chairman replied that there was *no written resolution*. The motion was just to express the feeling of this meeting as to whether there was to be an outing or not.

14   Bundy said he was only asking a civil question, *a point of information*: all he wanted to know was, what were the terms of the resolution? Were they in favour of the beano or not?

15   The chairman responded that the meeting was unanimously in favour. (Applause.)

16   Harlow said that the next thing to be done was to decide upon the date. Crass suggested the last Saturday in August. That would give them plenty of time to pay in.

17   Sawkins asked whether it was proposed to have a day or only half a day. He himself was in favour of the whole day. It would only mean losing a morning's work. It was hardly worth going at all if they only had half the day.

18   Harlow proposed that they decide to go to the 'Queen Elizabeth' the same as last year, and that they have a half a day.

19   Philpot said that, in order to get on with the business, he would *second the resolution*.

20   Bundy suggested – *as an amendment* – that it should be a whole day, starting from the 'Cricketers' at nine in the morning, and Sawkins said that, in order to get on with the business, he would *second the amendment*.

21   One of the new hands said he wished to move another amendment. He proposed to strike out the 'Queen Elizabeth' and substitute the 'Three Loggerheads'.

(For three more pages of the novel from which this extract is taken, the meeting rambles on through various motions, amendments, counter-amendments, heated arguments, quarrels, jeers and cheers, until they eventually agree to the original motion that they go to the 'Queen Elizabeth's Head'.)

Review

1   What do you deduce from paragraph 1 about the principles governing where and when a meeting should take place?
2   What mistakes did Payne make in carrying out his role as chairman?
3   In paragraph 3, Crass makes a proposal. What was his reason for doing so? Is the reason justified?
4   Crass and his colleagues were obviously not sure about the difference between a proposition, a motion and a resolution. What is the difference?
5   What are the accepted rules for speaking at a formal meeting?
6   There seemed to be a fair amount of confused uttering of meeting terminology. Did the members understand the terms they were using? Do you know what the following terms mean?
   a   a point of order
   b   call the chairman to order
   c   a point of information
   d   rule the point out of order
   e   an amendment
7   Which points should the chairman be aware of in conducting a vote?

ANSWERS

1   A meeting should be held at a time and in a place convenient to as many members as possible.
2   Payne started off well by explaining 'the object of the meeting', but in trying to stimulate discussion he was guilty of talking too much rather than asking questions, and being too ready to express his own very detailed opinions and experiences.
3   'Just for the sake of getting on with the business', Crass makes a proposal. This is as good a reason as any, and might have prompted a proposal earlier if Payne had realized he should invite proposals.
4   A 'proposition' is a suggestion, a call for action or an opinion,

put forward by a member of the meeting.

As soon as it is seconded and submitted for discussion and vote it is called a 'motion'.

If and when the motion is agreed upon by a majority of those present, it becomes a 'resolution'.

In practice, the term 'proposition' is not used very often since most propositions have been seconded and therefore become motions before the meeting discusses the matter. However, if a proposition is put forward but fails to gain a seconder it is dropped.

A motion should be very clearly and positively worded and many committees insist that a motion is submitted in writing, preferably before the meeting starts. In any event, it should be clearly recorded by the secretary and should be repeated by the chairman from time to time so that everyone is quite clear what they are discussing. Positive wording is advised because when the voting takes place, it may be confusing for a member who is in favour of something, e.g. the reintroduction of capital punishment, to find that in order to vote in favour of that idea, he must actually vote against the negatively worded motion, 'That capital punishment should not be reintroduced'.

5 Rules for speaking are indicated in the standing orders of a committee or organization but will usually include:

- Members of the meeting may only speak by permission of the chairman, one at a time. 'Catching the chairman's eye' is therefore a skill worth developing.
- Anyone who speaks must be standing. The speaker then 'has the floor'.
- A speaker must address his remarks to the chair and not to any individual member of the meeting, hence the frequent use of 'Mr Chairman'.

6 Other terms which relate to the standing orders are:
a and d A 'point of order' must deal with the *conduct* or *procedure* of the debate, e.g. an objection raised by another member of the meeting that the speaker is departing from the subject, that the standing orders concerning the rules of debate are not being operated, or that offensive language is being used. Harlow 'rose to a point of order' justifiably, I

think, since the meeting needed to be reminded that they should not decide where the Beano was to take place without first deciding *if* the Beano should take place. However, it is up to the chairman to rule an objection 'in' or 'out of order' and he therefore needs to know the standing orders.

b 'call the chairman to order' – strictly speaking, there are only two ways you can object to the chairman's chairmanship: (i) challenge the chairman's ruling, and (ii) propose a motion of 'no confidence in the chair'. However, in practice the chairman's ruling is normally regarded as final, other than in exceptional circumstances.

c and d   A 'point of information' is made by a member of the meeting rising either to ask the speaker's permission to correct a misrepresentation or to give or ask for information. Again, since this is often used as a device for taking the floor out of turn, the chairman is empowered to 'rule it out of order'.

e   An 'amendment' is a proposition to change the wording of a motion either by deleting or adding words. The amendment must also be seconded before it can be discussed, and it must be voted on before discussion of the main motion is resumed.

7 The chairman should repeat the motion clearly to make sure that everyone understands the motion they are voting on. He should also be aware of the different methods of voting – ballot, show of hands, etc. – and the advantages and disadvantages of each method.

Activity

1   Write the notice and agenda for the Beano meeting, which Crass might have distributed before the meeting took place.

2   Write a brief set of minutes of this part of the Beano meeting.

3   Check Lord Citrine's definitions and explanations of the terms given above and then find out what a quorum is, and what 'putting the question' and 'the previous question' mean.

7 | Giving a talk

Diana had worked for the personnel department of Hossack Construction Ltd for three years and during this time she had learned a lot and was gradually being given more responsibility. The company had expanded recently and had won several large contracts. Each new contract involved recruiting hundreds of construction workers. The personnel department was beginning to feel the strain of taking on all these people.

Little by little, Diana realized that her responsibilities were changing. She was being asked to speak on company induction and training courses. She had never minded talking to people on a one-to-one basis, but when faced with large groups, she became terribly nervous, her stomach churned, her mouth went dry and her voice either dwindled to an inaudible murmur, or became shrill and breathless . . . and she forgot what she had intended to say. She had always hated this sort of thing, even at school, and had managed to avoid reading or reciting in class.

Eventually, she decided she couldn't cope with the job any more. Fortunately, she was able to find another position with another company as a personnel clerk and at a salary level considerably below what she had received at Hossack. In two minds whether to take the new job, she had decided to keep looking for a while, when her boss called her into his office.

'Good news, Diana, we've just won the Glenfrome contract but we've got to get 200 extra men within the month. The personnel director has decided to try TV and local radio in the North-East to see if we can attract enough men that way. Second piece of good news – we'd like you to be the one to make the radio and television announcements.'

Diana went back to her office and wrote two letters – one resigning from Hossack and the other accepting the new job.

Activity

How would you have felt in Diana's position?

Feeling the way she did, did she take the right action?

Is it fair to ask people who may be very good at their job in other ways to take on the responsibility of talking to large groups?

It is true that unless you become a politician, an actor, a teacher, a television personality, or similar public figure, you may not be called upon to talk formally very often during your working life, especially early on. However, perhaps because we are living in an era when oral and visual communication are very common, many people prefer listening to messages rather than reading them; and because organizations are realizing the advantages of face-to-face communication, the number of occasions when you might be called upon to talk to a reasonably large group of people is increasing. For these reasons it may be difficult to avoid this task without jeopardizing your reputation and the chances of promotion.

This chapter should help you tackle the task with more confidence – confidence born of knowing what you are going to do, when you are going to do it and how you are going to do it. It will provide you with practical suggestions on how to approach different kinds of talk, open and close the talk, design good-looking visual aids even if you aren't a graphic artist, and organize your 'stage' on the day so that you feel as confident as possible to meet an audience, who after all is said and done want you to succeed.

Knowledge, after all, may be useless unless it is communicated to others. In the case above, Diana clearly knew her company's business, especially her responsibilities in the personnel department. She could communicate this to her supervisor and to others in very small groups. But she became nervous and hesitant when talking to larger groups. The thought of going on television and radio with an audience of thousands looking at her and listening to her terrified her, so she left her job – a job with responsibility, variety, a good salary and probably the chances of promotion.

What she obviously did not realize is that it is quite normal to be nervous before talking to large groups. Famous politicians, whose job consists largely of speaking in public, have confessed to feeling literally sick with nerves before making a speech. Lloyd George, who is considered by many to have been the best orator and debater this country has seen, was said to have been like a cat on hot bricks before he had to speak in the House of Commons.

Perhaps, if Diana had talked to her boss about her fears, she might well have discovered that she had performed much better on those occasions when she had had to do it than she realized. We are often far more critical of our performance than others are. Perhaps because we know how we feel inside – and they don't.

Her boss might also have suggested that she attend a training course to help her gain the necessary confidence. Few people are born speakers. It is an acquired skill, and everyone is able to acquire it to some degree. Diana didn't give herself a chance – a chance to discover that skill and confidence come from two things: hard work and practice.

Even if your job does not involve talking to large groups of people, the day may come sooner than you think when you will have to. How well you can do this will affect your job success.

> All the great speakers were bad speakers once.
> Emerson, *The Conduct of Life*, 1860

So how do you go about the hard work and practice? Let's deal with the practice first.

It is true that no amount of reading about and learning techniques from a book will turn you into a competent, confident speaker. Radio recordings spanning the long careers of famous speakers reveal that the practice they gained over the years perfected their art. Early recordings of Lloyd George have none of the power and oratory that he later developed and in the early days Aneurin Bevan was greatly hampered by a stammer. But over the years, although he never mastered it completely (which perhaps proves that even difficulties like this do not prevent someone from being a successful public speaker), Aneurin Bevan developed an enviably wide command of language which allowed him to avoid almost completely the words which he couldn't pronounce fluently.

Although political speaking is perhaps a very specialized form of public speaking and you may feel that it is irrelevant to the demands that speaking for business or social purposes may make of you, we can learn a lot and gain confidence from appreciating the effect of carefully mastered techniques and the rewards to be gained from practice.

'But how can I get practice?' you may say. Think back over your life. There are almost bound to have been occasions when you avoided the chance to practise. Have there been occasions when you asked someone else to give a vote of thanks, or just 'stand up and say something!' when the occasion seemed to demand it? Have there been occasions when perhaps someone else has tentatively asked you if you would say a few words to open a meeting perhaps, or thank a visiting speaker and you have hastily declined, saying, 'No! I'm really no good at that sort of thing, ask so-and-so, they've got the gift of the gab.' Have you sat through a public meeting on something you felt strongly about, dying to put your point of view, but resisting the urge to get to your feet? Well, these are the occasions which can provide you with practice. From now on, take every opportunity you get to 'say a few words'. Not only will you gain in confidence, but you will also find out what are your own particular strengths and weaknesses, and like Aneurin Bevan learn to exploit your strengths and avoid your weaknesses.

However, there are techniques which we can also learn from experienced speakers – and the most essential of these, as with every other form of communication transmission, is *preparation*.

In one biography of Lloyd George* we learn that he prepared his speeches very thoroughly with the help of *Roget's Thesaurus* and often wrote them out beforehand and learned them by heart. But all the work that went into his speeches paid dividends. He was renowned as a brilliant phrase-maker. He once described the people of Monmouthshire as 'suffering from morbid footbal-lism'. The House of Lords was simply '500 men chosen accident-ally from the unemployed'. To that skill with the language it is true he added a dramatic talent and the voice to demand atten-

* By John Grigg (Methuen, 1978).

tion for the product of all that hard work. Aneurin Bevan too had the essential talent of making his speeches sound informal. It seemed as though he was thinking on his feet but the work had been done long before he reached the platform.

Your platform may not be the House of Commons or the political rally but you would do well to learn from these speakers the need for thorough preparation until your talk is so polished that you can deliver it with the enthusiasm and vitality that suggests it is impromptu.

Preparation

First questions

Yes, as with any other communication, it's back to Why? Who? What? When? Where? and How? Let's look at how they might apply to giving a talk, speech or presentation. When you are first asked to give the talk there should automatically be some questions to which you should seek an answer, then and there:

When will it take place? Be sure you have adequate preparation time – for both written material and visual aids.

How long are you to speak for? Is the time adequate for your subject?

Remember that, contrary to what may seem the case, the less time you have to speak, the more carefully planned your talk must be, or as one speaker said:

If you want me to speak for five minutes – I need two weeks to prepare.
If you want me to speak for an hour – I need a week to prepare.
If you don't mind how long I speak, I'll get up and do it now.

Where is it to take place? In surroundings familiar to your audience? Familiar to you? If not, try to visit the venue before you speak and in any case check beforehand the type and size of the room, tiered seating or flat floor, acoustics, lighting, equipment available (projector, OHP, blackboard), etc. Don't be frightened to ask if particular arrangements are possible.

Who are to be present? Number, age and type of people, male or female, intellectual level, their current knowledge of the subject, their reasons for attending and their attitudes (possible objections to what you have to say, for example). These will, of course, influence the ideas and the language you use.

Why me? What special knowledge or position have you? What will the audience expect from you? This is not the moment to be falsely modest, but honestly realistic. If you have been asked to speak as a newcomer to the organization, perhaps to give your impressions or reactions to something, then no one will expect you to behave like a managing director with thirty years' experience.

How? Are you expected to give a formal speech or lecture, or an introductory talk to provoke a discussion? Will there be a question session? If there is to be a discussion or question session, you might like to leave some things unsaid, so that you leave your audience with some questions to ask and yourself with something fresh to say in answer to them.

Adjust to circumstances

Of course, some of these points you may have control over, or you may be the one who has suggested the occasion, in which case you can regard it like a performance with you as the producer, able to determine the most suitable room, the ideal size of audience, whether there will be questions or not, and so on.

But in either case there is likely to be a conflict between the *desired* circumstances and the *given* circumstances, since they usually don't match. In this case, some modification or compromise is necessary.

For example, you decide that the audience should be fairly small – perhaps a maximum of twenty people – because a high level of interaction between you and members of the audience is essential if you are to achieve your goal. But your boss, or perhaps someone else of high status even though unconnected directly with the proceedings, wants at least sixty to attend. Should you modify what you want to achieve, or offer to give the same talk three times? Supposing you want to keep the audience to twenty. What arguments would you use in persuading your boss that this is the ideal number?

Take another example. You have decided that you need at

least forty minutes to do the job adequately but the organizer can allow you only thirty minutes. Will you modify your objective or convey parts of your subject matter by means of audio-visuals?

> *Activity*
>
> Choose one of the subjects below. Imagine your audience and the circumstances in which you might be called upon to talk on that subject. Write down a description of the audience and the circumstances. Use this framework and your chosen subject to apply the suggestions which follow in this chapter.
>
> The place of humour in your life.
> The advantages of foreign travel.
> A speech to make on leaving your job.
> On wanting to work.
> Economic self-sufficiency.
> The case for the three-day week.
> The freedom of the press.

Having adjusted to your circumstances you are now ready to consider the question 'why?' carefully.

What do you plan to achieve with this particular group on this particular occasion? *Be as precise as you can.*

What do you want to do to your audience?

What do you want them to do/feel at the end?

OBJECTIVE

To inform or describe
• Describing observations, background against which something happened, facts and details.

APPROACH

Know their current level of knowledge, use appropriate language – if jargon is necessary and they are unfamiliar with it, you must explain the meaning of the words.

Use anecdotes, examples and illustrations to give life and colour. Use deductive, chronological or spatial order and carefully chosen words to describe things precisely.

To instruct or explain
- Explanations, directions, instructions.
- You are concerned with explaining *how* things work, *how* processes or procedures are carried out, *how* actions are performed. You may also want to include an explanation of *why* things are the way they are, *why* certain steps are taken in a process.

You should concentrate on *showing*, either by means of diagrams, pictures or demonstrations. In the last resort, your words must be chosen to produce clear visual images that the audience can grasp. Analogy can be helpful here. 'This process is rather like . . .' (describing something they are all familiar with).

Usually, deductive, chronological or spatial order is most suitable but if you are concentrating on *why* a procedure is necessary, or is the way it is, inductive order might be appropriate.

To persuade, convince or inspire
- Usually changing beliefs, attitudes or behaviour.
- Presenting a case, or an argument in favour or against.

Recognize how difficult a task this is. You must appeal to the heart and the head by quoting audience benefits and evidence to back up your arguments – statistics, authoritative opinion, experience of others, but these must be accurate and relevant.

Avoid generalizing and exaggerating, 'emotive' and 'coloured' language. If you base your arguments on assumptions, explain those assumptions. Avoid, or at least admit, your prejudices.

Give some reference to the other side of the story, or your case will be weakened.

Your structure must be *very* logical – and inductive order can be very persuasive.

Above all, (a) you must get the audience's attention, (b) find out what the audience's needs and interests are, (c) show how you can satisfy those needs, (d) ask for an appropriate reaction or approval.

To entertain or amuse ● Vote of thanks, 'after dinner'.	This kind of speaking is, more than any, an art to which some people seem born. However, since we all have to do it some time, it is worth learning. The general guidelines are: be brief; ration the humour (quotations, i.e. other people's humour, can be very useful here); relate your speech to the audience's interests and to the occasion – be personal and particular.

Developing the material

Start by breaking the main theme/objectives down into key ideas and work out how these might best be presented, illustrated and put together. This process can take place over quite a long period of time. It is a process of incubation when the ideas can be developed in your mind, in different ways and along different routes.

Stage one – think
You have selected your subject, now give the talk time to grow.

● Take time to gather and arrange your thoughts.
● Think about the talk at any convenient moment. A good time often presents itself when you are doing some other, usually manual job, like digging the garden, or decorating your flat, or perhaps travelling to work or college.
● Discuss the theme with colleagues and friends.

- Carry a note book or card, on which to note ideas as they occur to you.

Stage two – read
Read as much as time permits. Gather more material than you can possibly use, not only on the subject itself but also, for example, possible quotations. (*The Penguin Book of Quotations* and *The Penguin Book of Modern Quotations* are both very useful sources which can provide not only quotations but ideas for ways to tackle your theme.) Collect anecdotes and stories from newspapers and magazines.

Stage three – construct your outline
As with any carefully presented message, it will require an *introduction* and a *conclusion* and a simple outline might look like this:

    Introduction
    Presentation of one main point ⎫
      – illustrations   ⎪
      – reasons   ⎬   repeated as necessary
      – dealing with objections   ⎭
    Conclusion (appeal for action?)

But it should be logical and systematic. (Look back at pp. 22–3 at the beginning of this book or at Chapter 11 in *What Do You Mean, 'Communication'?*

Ideally write each main point and its development on a card. You can then shuffle them around to get the best order, as with writing a report, but this method has the added advantage in speech-making that, once you are really familiar with what you are going to say, you may be able to use these cards and their headings as keyword notes during the delivery of your talk.

A famous piece of advice that has an element of truth in it is: 'Look after the beginning and the end . . . and the middle will take care of itself.' Of course, the middle needs to be well structured if you are to achieve your goal, and another saying runs: 'Men perish because they cannot join the beginning with the end.'

But you need not worry so much about the actual words; whereas how to start and how to finish usually hold the most terrors for the beginner – justifiably so, perhaps, since a good speech can be made or marred by its opening and its close.

Activity

Before we look at some suggested ways of coping with these essential parts of a talk, think back to talks, speeches and lectures you have listened to. If you can't remember any in sufficient detail, break off at this point and spend the week listening carefully to radio and television lectures and talks – the Open University programmes are a good source of material for this sort of observation, or you might go to a public lecture or meeting.

What does the speaker say and do which makes the beginning and ending successful or unsuccessful for you/for the audience as a whole?

Make a note of the opening and closing remarks and then analyse them in the light of the comments that follow in this chapter.

Opening the talk

For three reasons, it is crucial to be absolutely sure in your own mind exactly what you are going to say and do in the first few minutes:

- You may have to follow a speaker who, through the attractiveness or strength of his personality or by reason of his subject, has achieved great acceptance by the audience; or you may have to follow some other activity which has been extremely entertaining, or the high-spot of the occasion.
- You may be the first or only speaker on that occasion and you have to cut the ice, so to speak; make the audience feel immediately that their attendance is worthwhile.
- You may, like most other people, feel far more nervous during the first few minutes.

For any of these reasons, you have to create an impression and gain the attention and interest of your audience at once, and to do these things you need to know exactly what you're going to say.

General guidelines

- Remember, your preparation is only complete once the talk begins. Arrange the 'stage' on which you are to perform. Take a little time before you start speaking to position your notes and visual aids so that you can use them comfortably. Make sure you have room to move between the table or lectern and the blackboard or OHP, that your notes are high enough for you to see without continually dropping your head.
- Don't hesitate; start as soon as the audience is settled, but take a few seconds to survey the audience and let them take stock of you.
- Don't open with clichés or hackneyed expressions, e.g. 'It gives me great pleasure . . .' You may want to thank your audience, or express pleasure in the occasion, but do this a little later, or even towards the end of your talk.
- Don't apologize. You may not feel that your knowledge, subject, ability or even presence is up to the occasion but the audience will be confident, if *you* start with the confidence that stems from being well prepared.
- The opening must be something original and interesting enough to make them want to hear what you have to say.
- Avoid too early a climax – interest will fall if the high standard of the opening cannot be sustained.
- Remember it is only an opening – an introduction. Don't make it too long. Keep it in proportion to the total length of the talk.

A dozen ways to start

- *Statement of subject or title* – not very inspiring. They probably know your subject anyway.
- *Statement of your objective and the plan of your talk* – a good safe way to start if you have adopted a deductive sequence (see p. 20) but if you are trying to persuade you don't want to give the game away too early. Even where it is appropriate to include the objective and structure of your talk in the introduction, don't make this your opening remark – try one of the more interesting ideas which follow.
- *Informal* – for informal occasions. 'Only a few days ago Mr Brown and I were discussing the problem of . . .' Mr Brown is on your side at once, and you have avoided giving the

impression of 'making a speech'.

- *Question* – anticipate the sort of questions your audience might want answered in connection with your subject: 'Are the days of a *Great* Britain finished for ever?' 'Must we sacrifice the essential quality of life if we are to take full advantage of the benefits that high technology can bestow?'

  The audience instinctively tries to arrive at the answer and you can go on to give yours.

- *Mind-reading* – similar to the use of the question. Anticipate the audience's preconceived ideas; bring these into the open and correct them if necessary. 'If I were a member of the audience tonight, I might be expecting just another "pep-talk" on safety at work. But this evening I have something more valuable to propose . . .'

- *Anecdote* – must be well told, relevant to the subject, brief and, if possible, personal (the willingness to laugh at yourself will usually win an audience).

- *Joke* – if your experience tells you that you can do this well, then it may be worth risking it. But people's sense of humour differs radically, and if the joke falls flat you are worse off than before. Again, it must be well told, relevant and brief.

- *Local colour* – can often be very effective. Use it sincerely: 'I always love coming back to the mills and chimneys of Bradford' may sound like empty flattery unless they know that perhaps you were born in Bradford. But 'I never cease to be heartened by the way in which the people of . . . have tackled the problems of . . .' is a sincere use of local colour.

- *Facts and statistics* – used sparingly they can get the audience to rise to the occasion. Most business or technical subjects offer many facts which will interest and inform your audience. Choose them carefully, make sure they are accurate and keep them simple. Contrasting facts can be particularly interesting: 'Annually, the average number of working days lost through strikes is six million, yet the average number lost through industrial accidents and sickness is *300* million.' Don't be too specific – no audience can take in numbers like 6,454,100, without plenty of time and reinforcement from visual aids. Even then rounded figures and percentages are easier to grasp.

- *Quotation* – perhaps the easiest method to use and often most effective. The quotation should be from a well-known person or author known to the audience, and strictly relevant to your subject.
- *Shock* – not just the gimmicky opening, firing revolvers or letting off explosions, which can often go wrong and are always difficult to sustain. Shock can be created through the effective use of words: 'Training is a waste of time and money . . .' pause to allow the shock to take effect, then: 'unless, of course, it is aimed at developing the team rather than the individual.'
- *Topical story* – as opposed to the humorous story. Everyone likes a story – but only if it is skilfully chosen and told. Ideally it should have an intriguing twist and must lead into the subject.

Choosing an opening to a talk will depend, of course, on your personality but be flexible and imaginative. Polish the opening until you have got it off to perfection and are sure what you are going to say and how it will flow into the main body of the talk.

> *Activity*
>
> Now keeping your imagined audience and objective firmly in mind, write out openings for your talk using each of the twelve suggestions above, if they are at all appropriate. Use your imagination and actually carry out any research that is required, e.g. for quotations, statistics and so on.

Closing the talk

Just as you need to attract the interest of your audience at the beginning of a talk, so you must finish on a high note. The effect of a speech which is otherwise good can be damaged by its close. Before looking at ways of strengthening the ending, let's see what are the pitfalls to avoid.

- Avoid 'wandering' towards the end. End on a high note which is relevant to all that has gone before.
- Don't make a 'second speech'. Even if you suddenly think of something else which is relevant don't be tempted. It is very

easy, as the tension relaxes, to start developing a new line of thought which was not developed in the body of the talk.

- Avoid repetition. In summing up the main points you have made, don't repeat details or labour over points again. If you have finished before your allotted finishing time – sit down. Don't pad it out.

- Don't give too many closing signals, e.g. 'and finally', 'in conclusion, then', 'one other thing before I finish'. In fact, it is probably best to avoid a closing signal altogether. Your closing remarks should round off your talk and therefore by implication your audience will know that your talk is complete.

- Avoid having to rely on your notes for your final remarks. Learn your closing words so that you can look at your audience as you reach your climax.

Ten ways to stop To avoid these pitfalls, you need to have a closing plan which is an integral part of the development of your whole speech. In this way you won't get lost at the end of your presentation. Here are several suggestions for rounding off your presentation.

- *Summary* – a fairly standard way to finish but nevertheless effective. A brief review of the important points leaves no doubt in the mind of your audience.

- *Question* – send the audience away to think of an answer. 'This then is what we have to do. The question now is, how can we best achieve it?'

- *Story or anecdote* – should be brief and to the point. A story can illustrate how your ideas have worked out in practice.

- *Quotation* – as with the opening, a quotation can indicate wide knowledge, and can therefore lend credibility to your performance. The quotation must be relevant and not just tacked on for its own sake.

- *Alternative* – offer a choice of alternatives, or different solutions. The one you want accepted should be obvious from the way you have constructed your presentation and you can give this one more weight than the others in your summary.

- *Dramatic* – if you can carry it off by dramatic use of your voice, or dramatic content, this method can certainly end things on a high note.

- *Action* – you want action *now* – not later. So ask for it. Many of your audience will respond.
- *Incentive* – if you can suggest ways in which the audience can benefit, some sort of reward or incentive, they are even more likely to respond. An audience is less likely to forget your message, if you offer a reason for taking action.
- *Fear* – use of fear to gain action is risky because it can alienate the audience. But since it is often difficult to provoke the audience to action, you may be justified in introducing an element of fear if the end result is worthwhile. 'You must act – now! Before it is too late!'
- *Conscience-pricking* – this can have the same effect as fear, but it is less risky. By appealing to their honesty, you may make your audience realize that they have been lazy, apathetic, too busy, or ostrich-like in the past, to do what they *know* they should do.

Whichever way seems appropriate, above all *don't go on*! Remember the old adage on effective public speaking: *stand up*, *speak up*, *shut up*.

Activity

Carry out the exercise on p. 166 only this time dealing with the close of the talk.

Stage four – visual aids

You don't have to be a graphic artist but it helps! At this stage you might like to look at Chapters 8 and 13 for guidance on the use of visual aids, but bear in mind the following points:

- Handouts and/or visual aids during the talk?
- Use pre-prepared visuals for:
  * complex interrelated ideas;
  * persuasive communication.
- Words alone are *not* visuals – where you do use words make them provide visual impact by means of graphic devices:
  * underlining and boxes or circles;
  * bullets and asterisks (as in this example);

* careful layout;
* use of space.

- Don't use overcomplicated visuals – everybody in the audience must understand every aid you use by the time you have finished with it.
- Visuals must complement what you say.
- You should have a visual for everything you want your audience to remember.
- Don't have a visual aid which you don't need.
- Make sure there are no spelling mistakes.
- You don't have to be a professional to produce good visuals:
  * OHP transparencies allow you to write using guide lines underneath and to trace shapes, cartoon figures, even letters.
  * Don't write letters too small (they won't be seen) or too big (your hand will wobble).
  * Use a stencil, or press-on letters, if you can't write neatly.
  * Achieve a good balanced layout.
  * Use colour – coloured chalks or felt-tip pens – but use bold colours not wishy-washy ones. Don't use too many colours on one visual, and let them reinforce the verbal message (e.g. red for danger, stop, debit, problem; green for go, credit, favourable).

Mark on the outline of your talk where you are going to use visual aids and which ones.

At this stage, if you are unsure of yourself, then it is probably advisable to write out your talk in full so that you can become really familiar with it, but write in spoken English not written English, and don't rely on using this script on the day.

Use of Notes

Why use notes? Even the best and most confident speakers use notes because:
- Memories are faulty.
- They guard against omissions.
- They help to develop a complicated close-knit argument.
- They prevent loss of sequence.

Written and read Even if you have written out your talk you should not use it as a script on the day, because a 'written and read' speech, by any but the most experienced speakers, produces a normally dull and stilted speech which lacks vitality and prevents you looking at your audience.

Exceptions: If the speech is highly technical, liable to be quoted or concerned with policy matters, it should be typed and double-spaced and marked for stress and pauses.

Written and memorized Lloyd George learned to do it as though he was speaking impromptu but for the rest of us it has pitfalls – it produces the effect of a 'canned speech' and forgetfulness in a supposedly memorized speech spells disaster.

Summary headings or keyword notes Cards or sheets (numbered or fastened with a tag) containing main points and key arguments and illustrations. This is the best method providing you are really familiar with your material.

Tip: if your nerves show through shaking hands, use cards rather than paper notes, and preferably place your notes on a lectern (or a pile of books if there is no lectern handy).

Practising the talk

Two activities can keep 'butterflies' within reasonable bounds:

- thorough preparation
- plenty of practice

So practise the whole talk

- out loud
- in a similar sized room
- using a tape recorder
- checking the timing

Mark on your notes how much speaking time should have elapsed by the end of each key area in the talk.

Consider a 'dry run', with an audience of colleagues – if you can bear it, and if it is a very important occasion.

Remember you may well feel more self-conscious and less

relaxed because of the artificiality of a rehearsal.

Room and platform layout

Room

Examine it at leisure, when empty. Consider: *seating plan* – audience more responsive when close together. Semi-circle better than a 'classroom' layout; *windows* – balance need for fresh air with the need to avoid draughts! Check blackout arrangements; *lighting* – know the position of the switches. Avoid lights behind the speaker.

Visual aid apparatus

Overhead projector – plugged in; on/off switch; acetate pen; how to focus; spare bulb.

Blackboard/whiteboard – check chalk/pens (amount and colours) and rubber/duster.

Platform layout

- room to move (but not too far!)
- supply of clean, covered water and glass
- microphone?
- will you sit or stand?
- will you obscure the screen/blackboard?

Delivery of the talk

Be yourself! And look at your audience!

For every book on the do's and don'ts of delivery techniques, there is a very successful speaker who breaks the rules.

So if you are at the beginning of your career as a public speaker, you should concentrate on thorough preparation, the basic skills of speaking outlined at the beginning of this part and the qualities listed below.

Maintaining interest

You can break almost every rule in the book, but don't break this one. The audience will listen with interest if you have these four qualities:

Conviction/sincerity The audience wants facts (and they must be accurate) but more than that, they want to know your attitude towards those facts. They need to feel that you have a sincere belief in what you are saying and a sincere interest in them – the audience.

Enthusiasm Real conviction breeds enthusiasm. If you are listless and half-hearted, so will they be. If you are enthusiastic, they will catch your enthusiasm.

Power of speech Speak with controlled power. Be positive – avoid weak phrases like 'in my humble opinion', 'please bear with me', 'forgive me'.

Use the power of the words and the emphasis and punctuation of speech (stress, pauses, variety in pitch, pace and volume) to reinforce important words and phrases.

Simplicity Speakers frequently do not recognize the complexity of the idea that they are expressing and falsely assume that it is clear to their audience. They are suffering from what is known as the 'COIK' fallacy – 'clear only if known'.

We can make the unknown clearer by expressing it in terms of the known (familiar ideas and familiar language).

In fact, these four qualities are the basic ingredients of all effective communication.

8 | Chalk and talk . . . or slides and films?

John had been asked to give a five-minute talk on one of the company's products, to a group of new employees as part of their induction course. Aware that even a five-minute talk requires careful preparation, he had been hard at work, on and off all week, writing his notes and getting his material together and now he was as confident as you can be when you have to stand on your feet and keep the show going on your own, even for five minutes.

His subject was 'the nose-cone of a satellite' – well, I think it was, but then I can't really remember, because for the next five minutes we, the audience, worked extremely hard. In the space of the next five minutes, as well as talking at breakneck speed, he showed us eight overhead projector transparencies all beautifully drawn in minute detail (which we couldn't have seen from the back of the room, even if he had given us time to look at them); he also directed our attention to two wall posters, both of which looked, from where I was sitting, like aerial views of London taken from the moon; and while all this was going on he circulated six photographs which we were expected to pass round the room.

Any speaker faced with the task of giving a talk or presentation is nowadays spoilt for choice. He can select from an impressive array of imaginative and technologically sophisticated devices, as well as the more traditional methods for providing his audience with visual aids. It doesn't seem surprising then that many people, like John, will go overboard trying to use as many of them as possible or, bewildered by possible methods which they don't really know how to use, will rely entirely on the spoken word, as if they didn't even know the blackboard had been invented.

So what exactly is available? What are they each particularly suitable for? What are the advantages and disadvantages? And how can you best use them so that they 'aid' you as well as your audience? This chapter is intended to take you on a guided tour of the 'hardware' of visual aid methods currently available, providing some tips on how to use them effectively, but above all pointing out what can go wrong, how to avoid the more obvious traps and what to do when things do go wrong. Whether or not you have ever given a presentation, talk or lecture, you will no doubt have experienced different methods of visual aids and been aware of what some of the problems are. At the very least, you will inevitably have suffered at the hands of the schoolmaster who spent the entire lesson scribbling furiously in illegible handwriting on the blackboard and only turned to face his audience as he left the room.

> ### Activity
>
> List as many different kinds of visual aid as you can think of, together with the problems for the speaker or the audience, associated with the use of each one.

Obviously the number of aids available is enormous, and your list may well contain examples that I've missed. My list includes:

- static boards – blackboards and whiteboards
- flip charts
- magnetic boards and other 'build-up' visuals
- physical objects
- models and experiments
- overhead projector
- slide projector
- films
- closed-circuit TV and video-tape

Let's go on to look at these in more detail – but first some general principles.

General principles

The most important thing to remember is that visual aids should be just that: *visual* and *aids* – visual, in that they make use of the most effective channel of communication of all, the sense of sight, not just by providing the audience with something to look at, but wherever possible providing them with pictures rather than words to look at; and aids, in that they should help, not hinder, the speaker in getting his message across and help, not hinder, the audience in receiving and understanding the speaker's message.

All too often, audiences are subjected to a never-ending stream of what Antony Jay in his thoroughly practical book *Effective Presentation** calls 'visible verbals'; in other words, blackboards or slides covered in words, and fairly indigestible words at that: 'costs', 'benefits', 'advantages', 'disadvantages', 'reliability', 'creativity'. However, whereas some authorities would argue that visual aids should very rarely contain words, there is a danger that in an attempt to find a pictorial or graphical representation of everything, many speakers would find it so difficult that they would give up altogether and not use any kind of visual aid at all. As with most things, it is a question of judgement and compromise. Certainly, speakers in planning their visual aids should aim for pictures of some kind or another, and even abstract concepts can be turned into pictures of sorts – diagrams, charts, cartoons and so on – with a little imagination. However, visual aids can use words very successfully to reinforce the speaker's message, and to remind the audience of the key ideas being presented, but they need to be *designed* not just written out in untidy writing as if the speaker had merely jotted down a few of his thoughts, while awaiting his turn to speak.

As far as serving as aids is concerned, many speakers give the impression that the visual aid equipment they are using provides more of an obstacle race than anything else; and the visual aids themselves are 'designed' to cloud the issue rather than help communicate the message. Using two media of communication is almost always more effective than one, but *only* if the two are complementary.

Visual aids used badly are time-wasting, distracting, expensive, inflexible, at best confusing, at worst catastrophic and humiliating!

Visual aids used well are time-saving, essential, interesting, entertaining, memorable, and invaluable.

* British Institute of Management, 1974.

So if you are to avoid the traps and make them work for you, rather than against you, you need to know what is available, what are the problems, what are the most suitable applications and how to manage them effectively.

Static boards

These include the traditional blackboard, or chalkboard, and its more modern descendant, the whiteboard or marker board, which is usually a plasticized laminate surface on which you can write with felt-tipped pens. Whiteboards are cleaner to use, allow a more varied use of colour and tend to show up visuals more clearly than blackboards, but they can reflect the light and sometimes retain traces of the pen colours. In every other respect black and white boards have the same applications, advantages and disadvantages.

Useful for
- Building up a fairly simple visual message.
- Spontaneous use with small informal groups.
- Display of permanent background information.

How to manage
- Always have a spare piece of chalk or pen in case either gives up.
- Check beforehand that chalk works, board isn't greasy and is not reflecting the light.
- Plan in advance what you are going to write or draw.
- Keep drawings bold and simple (if a drawing is complex, trace it faintly on the board beforehand using dotted lines).
- Restrict writing to key words or short, memorable sentences.
- Practise writing clearly, quickly and in straight lines.
- Use capital letters, unless your handwriting is very clear and beautiful.
- Don't talk to the board. Stand aside, face the audience with the board on your left if you are right-handed. Try to write or draw in short bursts and then turn to talk to your audience.
- When referring to the board, try to use a pointer.

Advantages
- Usually available – although being replaced by the overhead projector.

Disadvantages
- The blackboard is rather dirty – chalk dust on clothes and hands.
- Temptation to play with chalk or pen.
- Reminds audience of being at school.
- Temptation to use board as a scribbling pad. Result – illegible hieroglyphics.
- Tedious for audience to watch speaker laboriously spell (or misspell!) words he has just spoken.
- Interrupts eye contact/rapport with audience.

Flip charts

These are usually pre-prepared on large sheets of paper or card and then used either singly or in sequence, to present information to small groups of people. The term is also used to describe the large sheets of paper, clipped together on a stand, used to write up information provided by the audience which can then be referred to later, or removed and stuck up on the walls for reference purposes. However, because the effect can be rather untidy, the speaker should try to obey the rules for black and white boards.

Useful for
- Providing background information during a presentation when used singly.
- Building up an increasing amount of information or revealing the successive stages of a story, when used in sequence.

How to manage
- Keep lettering and diagrams simple, bold and colourful.
- If you are using a single chart and want to reveal information gradually, use hinged flaps of card or paper to mask parts of it.
- A flip-chart sequence can be very effective but needs a lot of

preparation – it might be better to use an overhead projector.
- As with other visual aids, a picture left up after it is finished with can be very distracting. The answer is to have a plain sheet after every picture or sequence of pictures.
- You need to be very familiar with each of the charts and the order they are in, so that you know what to expect.

Advantages
- Colours are much more effective on a white background.
- Useful way of preparing a complete presentation which is to be repeated.
- Visuals are not rubbed off each time as with black and white boards, so they can be kept for future reference.

Disadvantages
- Whatever the mechanism for clipping the sheets together at the top, there is a problem with folding each sheet back: they are liable to start falling back after about the sixth sheet, so you need to be familiar with the particular flip chart you will be using and you should rehearse the sequence right through.
- Temptation to make drawings and lettering too small for audience to see detail.
- Cumbersome to use: you need some method of propping up the charts, either your own home-made version or the conventional stand but either can topple over easily.
- If you are using a flip chart as a 'blackboard' you can't erase each drawing so you need to get rid of the previous sheet each time. Either you have the fold-back problem, or you can tear off each sheet and drop them, but this may leave the stage looking rather like a football stand after the match is over. Either have a cardboard box for the purpose, or have an assistant who can retrieve the sheets unostentatiously.

Build-up visuals

These include magnetic boards, slot boards, pin boards and felt or flannel boards where you can build up a picture as you go along and add things and take things away at will. This adds movement to your presentation which is not possible with black and white boards or flip charts.

Slot boards are not very common but can be made by cutting slots into a board where you will need them and then making words or pictures on card with a tag at the top or bottom which can be fitted into the slots.

Pin boards are usually made of cork or fibreboard on to which you can then pin cards with drawing pins, although ordinary sewing pins can be used and are less obvious to the audience.

Magnetic boards are often available as modern chalkboards have a metal backing but if not, you can always use the back of a metal filing cabinet or cupboard. All kinds of display items can be used by glueing them to a flat magnet or a piece cut from plasticized magnetic strip which can be obtained from do-it-yourself or hobbies shops.

Although felt or flannel boards are sometimes available, perhaps the simplest way of providing a flannel board is to throw a blanket over a blackboard. Cards are backed by almost anything which will adhere to the blanket – felt or similar cloth to the board, flock-paper or sandpaper and nowadays Velcro is a very effective and secure method, but is obviously fairly expensive. Staple the backing to the items; glue is messy.

Useful for
- Building up a simple visual presentation.
- Moving display items about the board.
- Complex visual presentations: better on a magnetic board than a flannel board, because items can be moved more easily.
- Achieving a dramatic effect, e.g. the Navy uses magnetic boards for demonstrating ship movements and changing formations.

How to manage
- For a demonstration of how to manage a magnetic board, watch the weathermen on TV.
- Limit the range of items or the number of items in each range, otherwise you will get confused trying to hunt through too many items to find the one you want.
- Make display items large and colourful.
- Unless you are absolutely sure that you will always be able to use a magnetic board, it is not worth going to the trouble and

expense of making magnetic items; use cards with sandpaper
backing and take a blanket with you.

- One way of avoiding the confusion of lots of items to sort
through each time you add something to the board, is to
reverse the process (the revelation board): prepare the board
in advance with all the items in the right places; then, cover
the items with blank cards, which you can then remove during
the presentation. This will obviously not work with magnetic
boards, and does restrict the movement of pieces across the
board.

Advantages
- Allows movement and dramatic effect.
- Pieces, once prepared, can be used over and over again.
- Less conventional visual aid, so immediately interests the
audience.

Disadvantages
- Confusion over pieces to be added.
- Takes time and effort to prepare well.
- More expensive than static boards and flip charts.
- Magnetic board would be heavy to carry around, especially if
it is used for a complex display.
- Using the subtraction method (or revealing the pieces as you
go along) can be slow and tedious for the audience who can
see how much further you have to go. One speaker's suggestion for overcoming this problem is to use the stripper's
technique of removing the first few covers fairly quickly to
capture the interest of the audience! Then you can afford to
slow down to keep up the suspense.

Physical objects

Real examples of what you are talking about can be extremely
effective in capturing the interest of the audience and turning an
abstract word or concept into something concrete and easily
understood, but it is a method which tends to be under-used.
This may be because it is all too easy when you are speaking
about something with which you are extremely familiar, to

assume that your audience is, too.

Small objects produced at the right moment from your pocket or even larger ones hidden under the desk or in a bag can turn a fairly conventional lecture into an entertaining and dramatic presentation.

Useful for
- Providing an example of a product or concept which the audience has heard of, but never seen, e.g. not perhaps so much now, but several years ago, many people had never seen a silicon chip.
- Providing an everyday example of the more unfamiliar and complex process you are talking about.

How to manage
- Picking the right moment to produce the item needs careful judgement and some rehearsal; the climax of a statement or at the end of an introductory section can be quite successful. If you leave it until the very end of your presentation, it must be good or it will produce an anticlimactic effect.
- If you have enough to pass round the audience, this is ideal but in that case, allow enough time for everyone to receive their example or it will cause distraction as everyone watches the box being passed from hand to hand.
- If you have only one example it must be big enough for everyone to see, or alternatively you must keep it back until the end and then invite people to come up and look at it when you have finished. If you produce it too early with an invitation to look at it at the end, people will be frustrated and distracted by their curiosity.

Advantages
- Introduces interest and vitality.
- Provides real examples of what you are talking about.

Disadvantages
- Can create frustration if people can't see what you are showing, or have to wait until the end to satisfy their curiosity.

- Fumbling around in your pocket or struggling to get something out of a bag may create the opposite effect from the one you intended.

Models and experiments

These, if they work and are really relevant to the presentation, can be absolutely captivating and the high spot of any presentation. But if they are not really relevant, the audience may feel they have been conned by showmanship; and if they don't work, they are almost always a complete disaster so beware!

Useful for
- Explaining abstract or scientific concepts and processes, where they are almost essential despite the dangers.
- Transforming a potentially dry subject into an involving and fascinating demonstration.

How to manage
- It is absolutely essential to know exactly where the model or experiment is to be used and to check for space, table height, power supply, ventilation and possibly even fire regulations and measures to control fire, should the need arise.
- Make sure you have everything you need, to do the experiment or make the model work – remember, water is not usually on tap in the ordinary lecture room: you may have to bring your own supply.
- Practise. Everyone involved in an experiment should practise over and over again until they can play their part without thinking.
- Don't be put off from using models and experiments by the potential problems – just prepare extremely carefully and rehearse very conscientiously. The value of a successful demonstration is worth the risk of disaster! But if the success of your whole talk rests on a working model or experiment, either have a standby or a prepared diagram or visual which would do instead.

Review

So far we have looked at mainly non-mechanical aids. Before we go on to look at the group of aids which might be classified as 'projected' aids, try these questions:

1 As office manager you are responsible for office organization which includes deciding who occupies which office, the efficient location of furniture and people and the best use of space generally. A new extension to the office block is about to become available and you have called a meeting of thirty staff representatives to discuss the way in which the old and new offices should be reorganized. You have several alternative plans which you intend to present at the start of the meeting before opening it up to discussion and you recognize that people may have their own ideas as well. Which visual aid method would you choose to support the presentation of your suggestions if money and effort were no object? Why?

2 When you are using a blackboard or flip chart, on which side of it should you stand and why?

3 Can you think of two reasons why producing some physical object during a presentation might be useful?

4 You have been asked to give a talk which will require a detailed explanation, based on a rather large complicated visual aid, of a piece of equipment. Which visual aid, would you use and what would you need to bear in mind when preparing it?

5 You have been asked to conduct a discussion on a subject about which you know quite a bit, but about which the audience will also be able to contribute quite a lot. The main points of the discussion are to be reported in the organization's newspaper. Which visual aid would you use and why?

ANSWERS

1 Probably some kind of build-up board, ideally a magnetic board but a makeshift flannel board would serve as well. This

would allow you to move pieces representing furniture, people and department names around the board as you put forward your alternative office layouts. It would also provide the facility for building up pictures of alternative suggestions from the meeting, so that everyone could see what is being suggested.

However, the problem with using build-up boards for presenting distinct alternatives is that you also need a permanent record of each alternative for reference purposes when you get to the point of comparing them. You might therefore consider supporting your initial presentation with separate charts for each alternative which can be distributed to everyone present for reference purposes both during and after the meeting. Large charts at the front of the room may possibly be difficult to see in a group as large as thirty, so individual handouts would be better, but this is where judgement of the particular circumstances comes in. It would depend on the actual room, the seating arrangements and the degree of detail which you want everyone present to see.

Handouts The idea of reproducing your visual aids as individual handouts is always worth considering. The timing of the issue of these handouts is crucial: produced early in a presentation they can provide your audience with individual copies of detailed material to refer to, but they draw attention away from you, the speaker, and can be distracting; produced late in the presentation or at the end they can cause frustration because people often take notes from visuals which they then discover they don't need. The solution is to tell your audience either at the beginning of your presentation or at appropriate points as you speak, which visuals they will receive at the end as handouts.

2 If you are right-handed you should stand on the left of a board or flip chart; if you are left-handed you should stand on the right. This will obviously affect where you position a free-standing board, so that you can reach your notes and move around easily.

3 To provide an example of something the audience may not have actually seen before.

   To provide an everyday example as an analogy of some

more complex process you are talking about.

To provide interest, vitality and reality.

4 If you will be able to gain access to the room where you will give your talk well before the session begins, you would probably be advised to draw the diagram carefully on the board but very faintly. In this way you will be able to draw in each part of the piece of equipment as you explain it and following the faint guidelines which only you can see. This method will prevent you frightening your audience to death by revealing a large complex visual aid right at the start.

To be successful you will have to make sure that you can get into the room sufficiently early to be able to draw the diagram very carefully. You should also make sure that you will be able to draw it sufficiently large for the back row of the audience to see it.

If you will be unable to get into the room beforehand, then a large wall chart might serve as well. In this case you might consider sticking lift-up flaps over sections of the drawing, so that you can reveal the diagram fairly gradually as you go along.

5 The most appropriate form of visual aid for recording a discussion is probably a flip-chart board with lots of paper. The audience's contributions can be written up and the torn-off sheets can be fixed to the wall as they are completed. These can then serve as the basis of the report for the newspaper. You would also be able to produce your own prepared visual aids on flip charts as and when they seemed appropriate in the context of the discussion. An alternative to flip charts might be overhead projector transparencies or a roll of OHP film which could be used in the same way as the flip charts, but cannot be hung up on the walls. With this possibility, let's move on to look at the advantages and disadvantages of overhead projectors – that is, if you have not already been exposed to them.

Overhead projector

Known as OHP for short, this is becoming more and more common and beginning to take over from the chalkboard, so if you don't know what it is or what it does, now is the time to find out.

The OHP is a device for projecting prepared transparencies, or writing and drawing done at the time of the presentation, on to a screen which is above and behind the speaker. A light is projected up through a horizontal transparent plate on which the speaker places his prepared transparencies. Alternatively, he can write or draw on blank acetate film which is rolled over the plate. The resulting image is transmitted to the screen by an optical system erected over the plate.

The OHP is intended to remove the problem of subjecting the audience to a view of the back of the speaker as he writes on a board or flip chart. He can face the audience throughout his presentation, even while pointing to the visual as he should point on the transparency rather than on the screen.

In theory, it has all the advantages and flexibility of many other methods and in the hands of an experienced speaker it is effective and easily controlled; but in practice it has numerous traps which await the inexperienced amateur. However, practice will pay dividends in that you will inevitably have to use it sooner or later because it has become so popular, and familiarity will enable you to take advantage of its possibilities and operate it in a confident and controlled manner.

Useful for
- Almost everything that can be portrayed on transparent film.
- Complex visuals: quite complicated effects can be created with the use of coloured acetate film stuck on to the basic transparency; and by means of masks – paper sheets which are placed on top of the transparency and then removed to reveal additional parts of the picture – and overlays, which are additional transparencies which can be laid one after another on top of the original transparency to produce a changing picture.

How to manage
- Start off with simple transparencies until you can use the machine with ease and confidence.
- Position yourself in such a way that you can reach the machine

naturally as well as your notes, without standing in the audience's line of sight to the screen. Apart from obliterating your picture, you are likely to find yourself dazzled by the light shining full in your face. In practice some speakers seem to get so bemused with concentrating on operating the machine that they are totally unaware that the light is shining in their face and that furthermore, much to the amusement of the audience, their head is silhouetted on the screen.

- Your transparencies should be carefully prepared beforehand (see 'Visual aids', pp. 168–9). Arrange them carefully in the right order, preferably with blank sheets of paper in between, so that you can see them clearly as you pick them up. Tip: place each one between the folds of computer print-out paper.

- Don't get into a panic about which way round they should be in order to be projected properly – OHP slides are not like 35mm photographic slides which have to be put into the machine in almost any way other than the one you would have expected. Simply pick a transparency up and if it looks the right way up to you, put it down like that on to the plate. Somehow, by the miracles of optical science, it will appear on the screen as it appears to you, looking down at the machine.

- Glance once at the screen just to check that the whole of your transparency is being projected and that it is straight – a crooked picture with bits cut off can be very distracting to the audience and you will wonder why they are fidgeting or sniggering.

- Some authorities suggest that you should not switch the light on until your transparency is in position and then switch it off before the transparency is moved away. However if you are using quite a lot of slides, the effect of the light going on and off continually can be more distracting than watching the slide positioned while the light is left on. Again, it is a case for practice and judgement.

- Point to the transparency with a pencil if you want to refer to a detail on the screen. A pointer is better than a finger because just as the machine magnifies your picture so it will magnify your finger . . . and your hand. And if you are shaking because you are nervous try to avoid pointing at all.

- Follow the rules for chalkboards if you want to write or draw on the blank acetate film. It is possible to prepare a roll of this film beforehand, with all the visuals you need for the whole presentation but, of course, this gives you no flexibility and you are stuck with the order of visuals on the roll.

Advantages
- Allows complete control and great flexibility by the speaker.
- The speaker can face his audience throughout the presentation.
- Although it is a projector, it can be used in normal lighting.
- Provided the screen is properly positioned, nothing can obscure it.
- Adds vitality and movement – allows considerable variety, through use of masks and overlays, and changes in sequence of slides.

Disadvantages
- Difficult to use expertly and casually – this can be overcome by practice.
- Many rooms have permanent screens which are poorly positioned making it almost inevitable that the speaker will obscure part of the screen for part of the audience.
- Most projectors are fairly heavy and bulky, though portable 'briefcase' ones are now available.
- Many speakers use the acetate film roll as a scribbling pad.
- Most speakers do not take enough care in producing their transparencies, although it is possible to get good results without using the services of professional graphic artists.

Slide projector

Very commonly used and frequently misused. It can be used on its own or in conjunction with a tape recorder, where the slides are either changed by means of a remote control button controlled by the speaker or an assistant, or automatically by means of a synchronized sound tape which has been electronically pulsed. Commercially produced tape/slide presentations can be bought ready-made but the speaker can, of course, use his own slides.

Useful for
- Showing real photographs (35mm) of people, places or objects.
- Showing visuals of diagrams, plans or charts which would be too complicated to produce on chalkboards or be seen on flip charts or an OHP screen.

How to manage
- Always use a magazine-loaded projector, if possible. You can then load the slides beforehand and ensure that they are in the right sequence and up the right way.
- Since slides are usually only worth the expense and trouble of making them if they will be used more than once, store them carefully, preferably in their own magazine, so that you don't have to load and unload them every time.
- Never use poor quality slides however relevant or interesting you think they are. There is nothing worse than being subjected to a series of shadowy, unrecognizable photographs, or pictures of people or things with bits cut off by poor photography, which is accompanied by repeated apologies from the speaker. If you feel you need to apologize for a slide – don't use it.
- Either use a synchronized tape/slide presentation which you have checked and double-checked to make sure it is synchronized correctly or, if you are providing the commentary, use a remote control lead which you control. Never let someone else change the slides unless it is absolutely necessary, which it may be if you are showing slides in a large room because the throw of projectors which you can operate yourself will be too short. In this case, you will need a projectionist who knows as as much about your presentation as you do, who is willing to work to your script and cues, who is quick-thinking and intelligent; you must agree the sequence and cues with him and then stick to them – never change the order or make cuts once you have had the final rehearsal – and you must agree a breakdown procedure, for example what to do if a slide sticks.
- Arrange cues for raising and dimming the houselights.
- Prepare a commentary which links the slides so that the continuity is smooth and fluent. There is nothing worse than a

presentation in which virtually all the speaker says is 'And this is a picture of. . .'

- Know your projector – they tend to be extremely temperamental, prone to breaking down, overheating, changing focus, etc. In fact they are probably the most potentially disastrous of all visual aids.
- Be hypercritical in preparing or selecting your slides. Antony Jay lists seven main faults of slides: They are – too verbal; too comprehensive; too complex; too crowded; too colourless; held too long; not explained.
- Bear these potential faults in mind when you are preparing your slides and then get someone to sit through the rehearsal and criticize them frankly and honestly.

Advantages

- Slides provide the clearest and most colourful reproduction of any projected aid.
- They add reality to your presentation.
- If you are good at photography the slides are fairly cheap and easy to make compared with using film, for instance.
- They can magnify details which is impossible with non-projected aids and the OHP.

Disadvantages

- The potential problems are almost too numerous to mention.
- Normally the room has to be darkened or blacked out – so unless you're prepared to give your whole presentation in a darkened room, you need to arrange to show slides in fairly large batches rather than scattered throughout.
- If you want to point to a detail on a slide, you have to point to the screen, and you will therefore be in danger of obscuring it.
- Slides are easily damaged or lost.
- Unless you are using a preloaded magazine, it is very easy to get slides the wrong way round or upside down (of the eight possible ways of inserting a slide, only one is right!)

16mm film projector

Making and using film is an area worthy of a book on its own, so if you are interested in going deeply into this subject start with your local library. Most pcoplc will only be concerned with the problems of hiring ready-made films and operating the projector.

Most films used for presentational purposes are 16mm (cinema films are usually shown on a 35mm gauge projector and home movies are 8mm) so you will almost certainly have to arrange for a 16mm projector to be available. If you just say you want 'a projector' without mentioning the gauge, you are likely to end up with a slide projector.

Most projectors nowadays are portable (though heavy) and self-threading which makes operating them reasonably easy.

Films can be hired from film distributors, whose addresses can be found in the library, but some addresses of those distributors which produce films suitable for business and training purposes are included at the end of this chapter.

Useful for
- Bringing the real living world into your presentation.
- Providing an entertaining as well as instructive dimension to your presentation.
- Showing processes which would be impossible to reproduce by means of any other visual aid.

How to manage
- Preferably use a projectionist unless you are showing a film in a small informal group. Give him very clear instructions about how and when you want to use the film with cues for raising and dimming houselights, stopping and starting the film and so on.
- If you are operating the projector yourself, allow enough time before you start your presentation to find out how to thread the projector and how to operate it. You may well find that you have been provided with a projector which is not self-threading, in which case threading the film is quite difficult and you will need advice and practice. Some projectors also have a separate loudspeaker which has to be plugged into the projector. The most intelligent of us can be reduced to an incompetent clueless idiot by the sight of a film projector, so beware.

- Select your film carefully. Preview as many films as possible and measure each against your objective. Can you use one film complete or should you use only parts of it?
- Run through the film several times until you are completely familiar with it. It often helps to write notes on the main sections and the sequence of events so that you have something to refer to during any discussion afterwards.
- If you only want to use selected sequences, stop the film at the beginning and end of each sequence and on each occasion insert a piece of paper into the film where it joins the take-up reel. These slips will act as cues either for you or the projectionist.
- Have a contingency plan ready, in case you find the distributor has put the wrong film in the box – or in case the film breaks.
- If, when the lights go up, you find you have 500 feet of film on the floor don't touch it! Wait until after the presentation and then, still not touching the pile of film, take the end and wind it, by hand, on to an empty reel. If the gods are with you, you may be lucky and it will wind out of its tangle without breaking.

Closed circuit television and video-tape

At the moment we are living through a technological revolution which means that the speaker will have access to an increasingly sophisticated range of television recording apparatus. Just as the range and sophistication is increasing, so the expense of this equipment is tumbling and before long it will be common practice for even individuals to be able to make their own video-tapes comparatively easily and cheaply, just as most people now have access to television.

Since the rate of change in price and choice of equipment is so fast it is difficult to be very specific about exactly what is available and how best to use it. However, in principle, using a video recorder to play back either television film you have made yourself or tapes which you have hired or bought, is now as simple as using a tape recorder. Similarly, video cameras are much simpler to operate than film cameras because they allow instant control of picture and lighting for instance, as you can see the picture you are filming while you are filming it. In addition, you can check instantly how successful you have been (cf. waiting for film to be developed) and therefore do a retake immediately if necessary.

Moral If you can get access to a video recorder and/or a video camera, use them. Experiment with them; they are a lot easier to use than they look. It is all too understandable to be put off by the apparent complexity and mystique which surrounds the 'video and television business' and it is certainly true that you will need quite a lot of practice and advice to produce really good films yourself, but, and this is my real message, *you can cope with the mechanics* and you can really only discover the pitfalls and secrets of success if you are prepared to have a go.

Points to remember

1 *The audience can't do two completely unrelated things at once.* They can't read your visual aid while you talk about something else; and they certainly can't look at your visual, listen to you and pass things round and look at them, all at the same time.

2 *Don't use too many different types of aid.* If you try to include use of an overhead projector, a slide projector and show some film, you will find it very difficult, if not impossible, to schedule it all smoothly enough so that each piece of equipment is ready at the right time and in the right place. The result is more likely to be a complete shambles.

3 *Decide in advance exactly what aids and equipment you are going to use.* Check that equipment, e.g. projectors and screens, is available before you start working on the visuals themselves. Don't assume anything – there may not even be a blackboard, let alone a projector of the type you want. If a piece of equipment you need is not normally in the room you will be speaking in, it is really safer to take care of the arrangements for booking it and actually collecting it yourself. There is nothing worse for your confidence or your reputation, than to turn up having based the whole of your presentation around a film, only to discover that something has gone wrong with the arrangements and there is no projector.

4 *Organize the layout of your 'stage' yourself.* First, find the
   time and the opportunity to get into the room and familiarize
   yourself with the position of everything you're likely to need.
   Is that table going to be big enough to get all your notes and
   material on, without your having to stack things in piles? Is
   that screen in such a position that you won't obscure it when
   you're talking? If not, can it be moved? If not, plan your
   presentation accordingly – perhaps it would be better not to
   use the overhead projector at all, for example. Secondly, get
   into the room at least a quarter of an hour before you are due
   to speak; work out how you want the area you will be working
   in arranged so that you will be able to move easily and
   naturally in the space provided; and then move the furniture
   so that it feels right for you. Obviously, you should do this
   tactfully, but don't feel that you must use the room in the
   way it happens to be laid out. It may have been set out that
   way for a previous speaker who had different needs, it may
   have been set out by the organizer working purely on intelligent guesswork – it may even have ended up that way because
   that was the way the cleaner left it! So check that the film or
   slide projector is correctly positioned; that the flip chart will
   be on your left when you face the audience if you are right-
   handed or on your right if you are left-handed; that the table
   or lectern is near enough to the OHP so that you won't have
   to keep skipping about between them to look at your notes;
   that there isn't an electric cable stretching right across the
   area in which you will want to move; that you know how to
   operate the blinds quickly and smoothly when you need to;
   that you know how to operate that particular machine and
   that it works.

5 *Visuals should not be too detailed.* First, because your audience will probably not be able to assimilate the information
   quickly enough, and even if you vow to allow enough time, in
   the heat of the moment you are almost bound to forget; and
   second, because you will either have to plough through detail
   by detail and they will get bored, or worse, you will probably
   get yourself confused.

6 *Visuals should be big enough for 'everyone' to see.* The film
   must occupy the whole of the screen; the slides must be clear

enough and big enough for the man in the back right-hand
corner to see; prepared slides, flip charts, blackboard work
or transparencies always seem big enough to you, when
you're up close, preparing them – they have an unfortunate
habit of 'shrinking' to the illegible or even invisible when
viewed by your audience, even in a fairly small room.

7 *Be careful using pointers.* While it is always better to use
some kind of pointer than just your hand or finger, they do
tend to accentuate any movement in your hand, so if you are
nervous it may show more. An old telescopic radio aerial is
ideal as a pointer since it can be extended to reach quite large
distances and then contracted when you don't need it but if
you are nervous the end will tend to flutter.

8 *Don't leave visuals up too long.* Visuals left up after they have
ceased to be relevant to what you are talking about are
distracting.

9 *Always be prepared for disaster.* However well prepared you
are, things can, and frequently do, go wrong. What will you
do when the OHP bulb blows, half-way through the second
of your ten essential transparencies? When the film breaks?
When you open the box and they've sent the wrong film?
When your sandpaper cards won't stick to their flannel
board? When the experiment on which the whole of your
lecture depends doesn't work? When the felt-tip pen dries
up?

Think now about all the disasters that you've seen happen
to other people, recall how they dealt with them. Then, let
your imagination run riot and think of worse things still.
Now, don't panic. Instead, spend your mental energy on
thinking up a contingency plan for every possible disaster, or
ways in which you could deal with them. A good speaker
always anticipates the problems, then minimizes the chances
of them happening by thorough preparation, but above all,
when they do happen (and they do – to the best of speakers)
he thinks very quickly and copes . . . somehow!

Review

1 If you want to show a film, which kind of projector
should you ask for?

2 You have decided to limit yourself to two kinds of visual aid. Which ones would you try to avoid using together in the same presentation because the 'stage management' might present problems?

3 You want to explain a complex process which involves various machines and complicated operations. Which visual aid(s) would be ideal for the purpose?

4 Through the gloom, you suddenly realize that the film is winding gently into a wriggling heap on the floor, instead of on to the take-up reel. What should you do?

5 The overhead projector bulb suddenly blows – and you've only just started. What do you do?

ANSWERS

1 You should ask for a 16mm (known as '16 mill') film projector.

2 You might try to avoid using more than one aid which requires a screen, since you would have to move the overhead projector to prevent it getting in the way of the film or slides, and you would have to move the slide projector in order to position a film projector and vice versa. There are various other 'unhappy bedfellows' but the overall principle is to be able to arrange as much as possible beforehand, and cut any movement of equipment or general fiddling-about down to a minimum once the presentation has started. However, a tea break in the middle of the proceedings might allow you to rearrange things if you want to.

3 Any process which depends on movement is obviously best shown on film – either cine-film or video-film. If you can't get hold of a commercially produced film of the operation you want, you should seriously think about the possibility of making your own, especially if it is likely to be of use again in the future.

4 You should forget it and enjoy the film. Let the film and your presentation run right through, and only then try to sort it out in the way suggested on p. 192.

5 Know how to replace it with the one you've brought along in case. Failing that, give a prearranged signal to someone in the audience who will seek out the technician while you carry

on talking. Failing that, abandon the slides because you thought about this eventuality beforehand and have arranged your presentation so that you can do without them – at a push. As an absolutely last resort, if the visual aids are vital and if the audience is quite small and fairly close to you, and if the walls are plain, you might just get away with holding them up against the wall.

General information

Advice on visual aids

The National Audio-Visual Aids Centre
254/256 Belsize Road
London NW6 4BT
Tel 01 624 3312/4

Rank Audio Visual Ltd
Great West Road
Brentford
Middlesex

The Scottish Film Council
16/17 Woodside Terrace
Glasgow C3
Tel 041 332 5413

Advice on films

The Industrial and Scientific Film Association
Watergate House
1 Watergate
London EC4Y OJH
Tel 01 353 2805

British Institute of Management
Management House
Parker Street
London WC2B 5PT
(Publishes an annual guide called *Films for Managers*)
Tel 01 405 3456

Film hire

Central Film Library
Government Building
Bromyard Avenue
Acton
London W3 7JB
Tel 01 743 5555

Rank Film Library
PO Box 70
Great West Road
Brentford
Middlesex
Tel 01 560 0762/3

Guild Sound and Vision Ltd
269 Kingston Road
London SW19 3NR

Video Arts Ltd
205 Wardour Street
London W1V 3FA
Tel 01 734 7671/7918

Shell Film Library (wide range and free)

Materials

Mathews, Drew and Shelbourne Ltd
The Visual Aid Centre
78 High Holborn
London WC1
(For flock paper, magnets and a wide range of visual aid material)
Tel 01 242 6631

Further reading

Jay, Antony, *Effective Presentation*, London: British Institute of Management, 1973 (particularly 'Commissioning a Film' and 'Writing Film Commentary')

Part 2:
The business of writing

For many people, apart from the more stressful occasions of interviews and public speaking, the business of speaking presents few of the horrors that rise up at the thought of having to put pen to paper. There seems to be something so permanent and irretrievable about the written word – and yet, it is of course this very permanence that makes written communication such an essential medium for conveying ideas in business. Because it is so permanent and useful for recording anything which may need to be considered carefully or referred to later, it is all the more essential to spend time and effort in getting the message right and reducing the chances of being misunderstood.

Bearing in mind the general principles of preparing and planning any message, described earlier in the book, let's now go on to look at the business of writing and in particular the techniques which can help us to write more effective letters, reports, memos, questionnaires and so on. You will also find in Part 2 a chapter on applying for a job which deals with the whole application process from thinking about your own likes and dislikes, skills and abilities to matching these with the requirements of the employer and making an effective application which will stand you a good chance of getting that all important interview. The final chapter then looks at the way in which we can use visual communication to complement the written (or spoken) message.

9 | Business letter writing

Apart from using the products and services of a business organization and reading advertisements, the only direct and individual communication contact many people have with a company is a business letter. You as the writer of a business letter have a tremendous opportunity to help your organization meet its objectives and help a customer or client while at the same time building goodwill.

This chapter looks at how you can write letters which achieve their purpose – to convey your message and maintain goodwill. It then goes on to examine the mechanics of letter writing and letter layout so that the finished product will complement your message, and at the end of the chapter you will find some tips on dictating.

Self-check

Which is cheaper: a letter or a telephone call?

Cost

One county council calculated that if every employee whose job involved writing letters made only one mistake a week which either required the letter to be rewritten or retyped, or made an extra letter necessary, the total annual cost would be about £750,000.

A local authority exists to provide a service at the lowest possible cost. A business organization depends on making a profit. Communication costs are a part of the total expense of doing business or providing services. So what is the cost of a business letter? A piece of paper, an envelope and a postage stamp? How did the council mentioned above arrive at the astronomical cost of £750,000 then?

The real cost of a letter involves not only the stationery and postage, but the costs of handling the letter through the internal post system, filing time, filing equipment and space, and the biggest item of all – the salaries of the letter writer and the typist. It follows then that the higher these salaries, the higher will be the cost of their letters.

Some organizations estimate the cost of a business letter at about £5. Knowing this, you may discover that it is cheaper to make a telephone call, and in some very delicate and/or important matters requiring face-to-face communication, it may be cheaper to travel (even fly!) across the country and deal with things personally. You are better able to make this decision if you know some of the advantages and disadvantages of the business letter.

Self-check

List the advantages and disadvantages of written and oral communication.

Now compare your list with the chart below.

WRITTEN OR ORAL COMMUNICATION

Written	*Oral*
Advantages	
• Better for facts and opinions. • Better for difficult or complicated messages. Can be reviewed. • Useful when a written record is required for reference purposes. • Can be both written and read when individuals are 'in the right mood'. • Can be carefully planned and considered before transmission. • Errors can be removed before transmission.	• Better for feelings and emotions. • More personal and individual. • Provides far greater interaction and feedback. • Can make more impact. • Generally less costly. • Allows for correction and adjustment of message in the light of feedback and non-verbal cues.

Written	Oral
Disadvantages	
• More time-consuming. • Feedback is either non-existent or delayed. • Lacks non-verbal cues which help interpretation. • Some people can't or don't like to read. • You can never be sure the message is read. • Lacks warmth and individuality.	• More difficult to think as you speak. • Something once said cannot be erased. • People may look as though they're listening but may not be receiving you – difficult to check with a large audience.

One disadvantage of a letter stems from the fact that many people either do not communicate well in writing or think they do not communicate well in writing.

If you feel that you fall into this category, I hope that the general principles of communication outlined in *What Do You Mean, 'Communication'?* and the particular suggestions which this chapter covers will prove helpful in giving you justified confidence in your ability to write a 'good letter'.

Planning the letter

Letters that get results do not just 'happen'. Like every other form of effective communication they have been thought about: *why? who? where? when?*, etc.

To plan your letter well you will need to review the background that has led to the need for a letter. This will often mean reviewing previous correspondence, and it is helpful to underline key points in incoming correspondence and make notes in the margins which will ensure you cover everything necessary in your own letter.

As you review the background, the reader and the reason for writing, the nature of the problem you have to solve will become apparent. You can then determine the type of letter you must write in order to solve the problem. For instance, if you have received a letter from a customer claiming some reparation for what he sees as a fault on your part ('claim' or 'adjustment letter') and you are unable to satisfy his claim ('adjustment refusal') a certain type of letter, with a certain type of structure, will be indicated. If your purpose in another letter is to send a credit note or refund cheque, another type of letter will be suggested.

Most of the letters that you have to write will fall into certain categories:

Purpose	Letter Classification	Area
To seek information, opinion, confirmation	Query	General
To give information, opinion, confirmation	Acknowledgement, information	,,
To seek reparation for some fault or deficiency	Complaint/claim	,,
To accept the claim, provide reparation	Adjustment	,,
To place an order for goods or services	Order	Ordering and estimating
To confirm acceptance of an order	Confirmation of order	,,
To give an estimate of price, time, etc.	Estimate	,,
To give a final price, time, etc. (contractual)	Tender	,,
To sell goods or services	Sales letter	Sales and advertising
To remind of sales offers	Follow-up sales letter	,,
To advertise goods or services	Non-solicited sales letter	,,
To authorize advance of credit	Letter of credit	Financial, and credit management
To check or comment on credit worthiness or rating	Credit reference inquiry/ reply	,,
To obtain payment of a debt	Collection (various stages – usually 1, 2 and 3)	,,

In all these letters you are acting as an ambassador for your organization, trying to maintain or build goodwill. In some of these letters, this task will be easy, in others, more difficult, depending on the *anticipated reader reaction*. It is this which you should keep clearly in your mind, as it will help you to determine how to write the letter.

Favourable You agree to do something: send goods, services, money, will speak at a meeting, etc. Fairly easy to write.

Neutral Neutral messages are neither favourable nor unfavourable. Many business letters fall into this category, e.g. writing a letter of recommendation for a former employee or providing a credit reference.

Unfavourable You have to refuse to do something. Difficult to write because saying 'no' runs the risk of losing goodwill. Your letter must therefore use every possible method of softening the blow and building goodwill in other ways.

Persuasive You have to sell an idea or a product, turn the reader from being disinterested, or even uninterested, to being interested enough to do what you want – accept your position or proposal, buy your product or service.

Your analysis of your reader's reaction and the type of letter you must write will suggest the approach you should adopt and the most appropriate organization or structure of your material.

Activity

For which of these types of letter (favourable, neutral, unfavourable, persuasive) would you consider using deductive sequence? For which would you consider inductive sequence? (See pp. 20–1 for an explanation of deductive and inductive sequence.)

Obviously there is no hard and fast rule, and many letters defy classification since their subject matter and purpose often cut across the boundaries between different types of letters. How-

206 The business of writing

ever, the table below may give you some help in tackling a particular letter.

Broad type of letter	Particular type of letter	Suggested approach	Structure
Favourable	Order, confirmation of order	Deductive	I Pleasant idea in yes letter or main idea in routine neutral letter
	Acknowledgment Information Claim (expecting yes)		II Details or explanations
	Adjustment Credit offer, acceptance		III Closing thought
Neutral	Credit reference Personal reference Letter of credit Estimate Tender Resignation		
Unfavourable	Adjustment refusal Credit refusal Order refusal Favour refusal Information refusal Solicitor's letters	Inductive	I Neutral statement that leads to reasons II Facts, analysis, reasons
Persuasive	All sales letters Claim (expecting no) Collection letters Application Estimate Tender		III Unpleasant message or unsolicited suggestion IV Related idea that takes emphasis away from the unpleasant or asks for action

Self-check

In each of the cases below consider what kind of letter you would have to write, given the likely reaction of the reader to the basic message you have to convey.

Now consider how you *want* the reader to react. What therefore is your real purpose? What do you want him to do/feel/believe? How then are you going to structure your letter? What are you going to say and how are you going to say it?

1 Your department of Floridan Airlines is responsible for dealing with customer complaints. You have received a letter from a woman who reports that she was served a live frog in her meal on a flight from Nassau to Mexico. She realizes that there is nothing you can do about it now, since the event is in the past, but she does feel that you should know about it and avoid this sort of thing happening again. How would you reply?

2 You work for a rather traditional firm in the credit control department and have received a routine request for a credit reference on behalf of a small company with which your firm has never had any debt collection problems. How would you reply to the company requiring the reference?

3 Your boss has been asked to speak at a company communications seminar but will be unable to do so as he will be involved in his annual visit to regional offices to discuss plans for the coming year. He has to be away from the office today and asks you to draft a letter for him to see on his return. As he leaves the office he mumbles something about 'perhaps I could get old Wainright to do it for them'.

4 You have so far failed to pay £10 for a Green Card (insurance confirmation necessary for travelling abroad) which was issued several months ago. You have felt disinclined to offer payment until the insurance brokers asked for the money and intend now to offer only £5, since you were put to considerable inconvenience by the insurance company (for whom the

brokers act). They were extremely inefficient, failing to produce the card on time despite adequate notice, and only supplying one eventually at the eleventh hour after you had made several telephone calls and personal visits. What sort of covering letter would you send with the cheque?

Now look at the suggestions below. They are all genuine letters (even the first one!) with only the names changed.

1 Favourable letter

Dear Madam,

Our Catering Superintendent for Southern Stations, Mr Taylor, has reported that a live frog was served with your meal tray on the flight between Nassau and Mexico on 19 June. I hope you will accept our sincere apologies for this, which I very much hope has not lost us a valued customer.

Needless to say, this kind of thing is taken up very seriously with the Stations concerned and their contractors, but despite every effort to ensure that this type of incident will not occur, very occasionally we must admit to a failing in our very stringent quality procedures.

We greatly appreciate your liberal approach to the incident, but hope not to trespass on your goodwill in the same way again on a Floridan Airways flight. Thank you for flying with us.

Yours sincerely,

S. Temple-Combe
Customer Relations Manager

Part 1 Opens with positive reaction to complaint and reference to 'you' as a 'valued customer'.
Part 2 Gives explanation of action taken by the company.
Part 3 Ends with a note of goodwill.

2 Neutral letter

Dear Sirs,

In reply to your letter of 4th July, we have always regarded Rees and Greenwood Ltd of Winterdown as a firm of high repute.

For many years we have had the privilege of supplying them with our goods. As a matter of fact, many of the orders we have received have been greatly in excess of the amount you state so that we feel there should be little danger in granting them credit for the sum mentioned.

If you should need any specific details, please do not hesitate to contact us.

Yours faithfully,

M. Wisbech
Credit Control Manager

Part 1 Identifies the subject quickly and offers some information about the firm immediately.

Part 2 Gives further details (length of time over which business has been transacted) and justifies confidence in the subject (many orders in excess of sum mentioned).

Part 3 Ends on a helpful note – confirming goodwill.

3 Unfavourable letter

Dear

I was very interested to hear of your plans for a Company Communication Seminar – an initiative which I'm sure will be welcomed by the impressive number of firms taking part.

Spring is always a hectic time of the year for me because I make my annual visit to each of our regional offices to discuss plans for the coming financial year. As you can imagine, it is quite a task fitting all these visits in and, having made the arrangements so far ahead, I must stick to the time-table. Unfortunately, on the date you have asked me to speak, I shall be in Scotland.

However, can I suggest my colleague Mr David Wainwright, who would make an ideal alternative speaker. He has ten years' experience in Industrial Relations and Employee Communications during which time he has himself initiated several successful ventures and would, I am sure, be happy to speak on 'Tell or Listen?' if he is free. Let me know if you find this an acceptable suggestion and I will ask him to contact you.

Best wishes for a successful seminar.

Yours sincerely,

R. Sharp.

210   *The business of writing*

Part 1 Using inductive order (see pp. 20–1), the letter leaves
the unpleasant element until later, and opens with a pleasant and
sincere comment on the idea of the seminar.

Parts 2 and 3 Present explanation and reasons for being unable
to say 'yes' without saying 'no' bluntly or directly.

Part 4 Offers an alternative and then ends with a goodwill
idea.

4 Persuasive letter

Insurance and Mortgage Brokers Ltd
Sharp Hill
Sheffield S37 4BS

Dear Sirs,

Thank you for the statement indicating that I still owe you £10 for the
Green Card issued at Easter. I seem unable to trace an invoice for
£10. However, I accept that as yet I have not settled the bill.

You will probably recall the considerable problems I encountered
trying to extract this card from Sure-All Insurance in time for my
departure. Despite having given the required notice for the issue of a
Green Card, I had still not received it 24 hours before my expected
departure. I was therefore obliged to make two special trips into
town to fetch the card, both without success, although I had been
told it would be ready on both occasions; two phone calls to you and
one to the ferry company to inquire about my position if I sailed
without it; and finally another trip into town to fetch a specially issued
card – all at my expense in terms of money, time and unnecessary
anxiety.

Since I regard £10 as an excessive charge for the work involved in
issuing a certificate to demonstrate that I am already insured, and
since I incurred considerable expense in trying to obtain the card, I
am therefore enclosing a cheque for £5.

Unless you advise me otherwise I shall assume that Sure-All agree
with me that under the circumstances £5 is more than adequate.

Yours faithfully,

Helena Smailes (Miss)

The main idea of this letter is that the writer is sending a cheque
for only £5 in settlement of a bill for £10, but by careful use of

inductive order for both paragraph sequence and the sentence structure of the last but one paragraph, she only presents the reader with the unfavourable idea at the end of paragraph 3 – very near the end of the letter. This is achieved by presenting the reasons for not paying any more, in paragraph 2, without actually saying so directly.

Part 1 Neutral idea first – agreeing that the bill is not yet settled despite not having received an invoice before.

Part 2 This main paragraph leads up to the idea of the writer's expense (inductive order).

Part 3 Introduces a further justification for thinking £10 too much, and summarizes main justification (inconvenience and expenses) before announcing unfavourable message.

Part 4 Related idea that takes emphasis away from the unpleasant idea, assumes success of the persuasion, and puts the onus on the recipient to do something if he has not been persuaded.

Each of those letters began by clearly *identifying the subject* of the letter in the first paragraph and ended by *suggesting what happens next* so that the reader is quite clear whether he has to do something next, or whether the writer has to do something else or whether the matter is now complete. In between the introduction and the conclusion goes the detail which should be set out in paragraphs – one main idea to each paragraph. Within this basic framework you can use your skill at choosing words to create goodwill whatever the nature of your message.

Review

1 Why is a letter not a cheap method of communication?
2 What is the purpose of each of these letters:

- Adjustment
- Credit reference inquiry
- Collection

3 Letters can be classified in many ways, but most letters fall into four main categories depending on how their message will be viewed by the reader. What are the four main categories?

4 What is the psychological effect on the reader of a business letter when negative elements are introduced early in the letter? How does proper organization help the writer to deal with his problem?

5 What are the advantages of using a question as a technique for beginning a letter?

6 Can you think of four ways to end a letter effectively?

ANSWERS

1 The cost of a letter includes internal handling costs, filing time, filing equipment and space, cost of writer's and typist's time as well as stationery and postage – estimated by some companies at a total of £5 per letter on average.

2 An 'adjustment letter' seeks to satisfy a complaint, make reparation for a fault or deficiency.

A 'credit reference inquiry' is written to check on someone's credit worthiness.

A 'collection letter' is written at periodic intervals in the process of trying to obtain payment of a debt. Different letters are written at different stages in the process.

3 Letters fall into four main categories:

Favourable

Neutral

Unfavourable

Persuasive

4 When a letter introduces the negative elements too early the reader may switch off and not be prepared to be convinced by any reasons or justification which follow.

Negative elements can be made to seem less important if they are subordinated through positive word choice, careful sentence structure and positioning in the letter. Since the first and last sentences in a letter should be reserved for views you want to emphasize, negative elements should not be put in the first or last sentences.

By using inductive word order, which presents the reasons and details first and then introduces the negative idea, the reader may be persuaded to accept it.

5 Questions (or exclamations) are very acceptable beginnings for letters of a sales or persuasive nature. They may be used to start any letter in which your objective is to gain the reader's attention quickly. A question involves the reader quickly and provides a bit of mystery and suspense to keep him reading until you can explain where he fits into the picture. A question can also be flattering to the reader by asking for his opinion.

6   Favourable elements: it is always desirable to end a letter with a favourable element, a positive tone, to leave the reader in a good frame of mind.

Goodwill: without overdoing it, you should take every opportunity to build goodwill in a letter. Pleasant sounding words throughout the letter are always welcome but endings which include 'Thank you', 'Good luck', 'Best wishes', are especially useful for ending letters which have contained disappointing news.

Resale: sometimes it is appropriate to end a letter by reassuring the reader that the purchased product is right for the customer, or that the company the customer is dealing with is the one that can do the best job for him, but this should not be done too blatantly.

Action: this is perhaps the most useful way to end any letter in which some action is required by the reader or writer. Specify near the end of the lettter exactly what is going to happen next: 'I will let you know as soon as I have the information you need', 'Please ring me on ext. 252 to let me know whether you will be able to attend', 'Please reply on the enclosed reply-paid card.'

Activity

Collect examples of different business letters, perhaps ones sent to you personally as a consumer or householder from firms or public organizations you deal with.

Classify each one: was it a favourable, neutral, unfavourable or persuasive letter for the writer to tackle?

Did he assess the reader reaction correctly and organize the letter accordingly?

What structure did the writer use?

What techniques for beginning and ending the letter have been used?

What metacommunications elements are present in the letter?

What reaction did you have to the letter? Was it the one intended by the writer, do you think?

Letter layout and letter style

A letter begins its job as an ambassador of the organization immediately it arrives, and however well the message has been planned and written, the reader cannot help but be affected by the overall appearance of the letter (and even the envelope).

Most organizations, appreciative of the significance of conveying the right 'corporate image' and creating a favourable impression from the first moment, devote considerable effort to the design of their packaging and advertising material, and this attention to design is reflected in the printed stationery and the appearance and layout of the typescript. Consequently, you will probably find that your organization has a particular 'house style' which all secretaries and typists follow.

Activity

Find out whether your organization has a house style.

Does your department or section follow this house style or does it have its own?

What are the rules for laying out a letter or memo and the envelope?

What impression does it create:

● reliable? efficient? modern?
● old-fashioned? traditional?
● uncaring? untidy?

What factors contribute to this impression?

Do you like the layout? Why?

You should not ignore these aspects of letter writing, even if you feel they are the preserve of the typing and secretarial staff, for the following reasons:

- You may one day, if not now, be in a position to influence or help create a house style.
- You will probably have to write or type letters for yourself, and a poorly laid-out letter, whether typed or handwritten, will convey metacommunications – 'I'm not really interested in what impression I create', 'I am untidy and careless', 'I am not concerned with details', 'I am not sensitive to the many ways in which "messages" can be conveyed'.

Remember then:

- The neat appearance of the type or handwriting is important.
- Careful use of space, balanced paragraphing and positioning of the various parts of the letter can create a visually pleasing effect.

Shape

You will probably have come across the layout style known as 'fully indented' (see p. 216).

Both addresses and the close and signature are progressively indented, each paragraph is indented and the heading is centred. But this layout is now very uncommon. Can you think of two reasons why this layout is no longer preferred?

Take a ruler and, placing it vertically down the page at the beginning of each new line on the page, draw a pencilled vertical line. How many have you got? I calculate that there are about a dozen different vertical lines. Any typist typing out this letter would have to calculate where to centre the heading and the close and signature ('subscription'), use a tabulator key to line up the paragraphs, and calculate how many back spaces are required to make the sender's address and date fit into the top right-hand corner without overflowing into the margin. This all takes time. One reason for abandoning full indentation layout, therefore, is efficiency. But a second reason is that all those imaginary vertical lines produce a cluttery effect. For these reasons the layouts on p. 217 are currently preferred.

RUNAWAY   AND   BOLT,   LTD.

Thorn Mills,

BRADFORD,

BD3 7RS

3rd May, 19..   ② Date (in full)

① Letterheading

③ Ref. No.

Our ref:

Your ref:

④ Recipients name, position and address

The Chief Accountant,
    Messrs. Rees & Greenwood,
        Winterdown Road,
            SHEFFIELD.

Salutation ⑤

Dear Sir,

<u>Alan Francis Lines</u>   ⑥ Subject heading

    Replying to your letter of 30 April,
we are pleased to inform you that
Mr. Alan Lines has served this firm faithfully and well for the last five years.

    He is a thoroughly efficient, honest
and capable member of our staff. If he
considers leaving us, we shall indeed be sorry
to lose him, even though we realise his
qualifications and experience must enable
him to gain promotion.

⑧ Body of the letter

    We have therefore no hesitation in
recommending him to you and wish him well at
the interview.

        Yours faithfully,

⑤ Complimentary Close

        Edward Q. Bolt,
        Company Secretary

and Signature ⑦

A Fully blocked

B Semi-blocked

Fully blocked Everything starts at the left-hand margin – one vertical line.

Advantages – efficient, very modern.

Disadvantages – it has a rather lopsided look which would be even worse if the sender's address had to be written on the left above everything else (when non-headed paper is used).

Semi-indented Like semi-blocked but the paragraphs are indented.

Advantages – slightly less cluttery and easier for the typist than fully indented – but not much.

Semi-blocked The date and the subscription are on the right, the heading is centred and everything else starts at the left-hand margin. Paragraphs, etc. are blocked.

Advantages – fairly efficient, and produces a more balanced look.

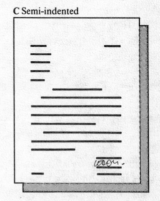

C Semi-indented

Activity

Which of these do you prefer? Which would suit a hand-written letter?

You will probably come across other variations of these three basic models and the one you choose will depend on (a) your organization's house style or (b) your personal preference. But whichever you adopt, be consistent. For example, don't block some paragraphs and not others.

Open punctuation

This is the practice of omitting punctuation marks from everything in the letter *except the main body of the message*. It is perfectly acceptable and is being increasingly adopted – again because it makes the typist's life easier. It does not necessarily have to be used with fully blocked layout. However, use it with care. Again, be consistent and pay particular attention when writing the initials of names to leave sufficient space, so as not to produce absurd or incomprehensible 'words', e.g. PEAGREEN Esq, Mr ITIsis (people with names like that probably have enough problems already!).

Stationery sizes

Decisions concerning the design of the letterhead and choice of layout will depend on the size of paper used.

Paper The most popular sizes of paper currently in use are:
A4 – 297mm × 210mm
A5 – 210mm × 148mm (half the size of A4)
A short single-spaced letter on A5 paper would look better than double-spacing on A4.

Envelopes There are various envelope sizes available. The Post Office Guide gives those that the Post Office prefers, but choose an envelope which will not force you to fold the letter more than twice.

When window envelopes are used, care should be taken to type the recipient's address in exactly the right place on the letter so that it can be seen clearly through the window. The *post code* should always be visible and *last* in the address, either on its own or alongside the county. In the case of cities or large conurbations, the county can be omitted.

The parts of a letter

A business letter normally consists of eight parts (see p. 216).

1 Heading or letterhead

On business letters the name and address of the sender are printed: the name usually in much bolder type. The letterhead usually spans the whole page approximately two to three inches deep, or is positioned in the top right-hand corner. It usually includes the company's trading name, address, post code, telephone and telex numbers, and telegram address. As a result of the Companies Act 1948 and the European Communities Act 1972 it *must* include certain other information.

Statutory requirements
Company's trading name
Its status as a limited company (if appropriate)
List of company directors if founded after 23 November 1916 (showing nationality in certain instances)
Address of its registered office
Registration number of company
Location of registration

} Usually placed at the bottom of the page

Logo More and more organizations are using logos in the design of their stationery and packaging. A logo is a visual symbol or identification mark which is usually directly related to the firm, its products, or its services; or simply a design that has become associated with the firm over time. The logo is closely linked with the image the firm wishes to convey and so some marks are updated while others remain the same over the years.

The sender's address On non-business letters, the sender's address (which should not include the name) is usually placed in the top right-hand corner

2 Date

This is usually typed two or three spaces under the last line of the address. Ideally it should finish flush with the right-hand margin.

The recommended method of writing the date is day, month, year. Increasingly the 'th', 'st' and 'nd' are omitted as is the comma between the month and the year.

	20 February 19. . ⎱	European practice
or	20th February, 19. . ⎰	
but	February 20th, 19. .	United States practice

3 References

So that letters can easily be filed and traced for reference purposes, it is advisable to provide a reference code: 'Our ref: NL/JM CF2'. When replying to a letter which itself includes its own reference, both references are typed:

Our ref: NL/JM CF2 (outgoing letter)
Your ref: SB/sjt (incoming letter)

References are usually entered level with the date on the left-hand side and are composed of:

- first: initials of letter-writer (in capitals)
- second: initials of typist (sometimes in lower case)
- if relevant, third: reference to a particular file ('Conference File 2')

In all cases, they should be quoted when replying to a letter.

4 Recipient's name, position and address

Usually typed two or three spaces below the reference(s) either blocked or indented (see p. 217) with open or closed punctuation:

Mr R A Jones	S. Stevens, Esq.,
British Engineering Company Ltd	Personnel Director,
20–27 Wansdyke Road	ABCA Engineering Co., Ltd.,
SHIPLEY	206, Mile Road,
Yorks SY3 1QS	MANCHESTER, M12 3DQ.
Blocked and open punctuation	*Indented and closed punctuation*

Where possible the address should be confined to three or four lines to avoid starting the body of the letter too far down the page.

The name and address should never be omitted from a business letter as without it the copy preserved for reference would be useless.

Names and forms of address How do you address a knight? When should you use 'Mr' and when 'Esq.'? How do you write to a company if you don't have a person's name to use? How do you address a woman if you don't know whether she's married or single?

These and similar questions have caused untold problems for letter writers and secretaries, and justified the writing of countless books on 'etiquette' over the years – and it is still difficult to remember the rules.

Self-check

Try to work out the rules from the following examples. If all the following forms of address are correct, what are the rules governing:

a 'Mr' or 'Esq'?
b Women?
c People with titles?
d People with degrees, diplomas, decorations, orders and membership of professional bodies?
e Companies and partnerships?

1   Mr R. Smith
2   John Smith Esq.
3   John Smith Esq. VC MA MIPM
4   Rev. S. Martin, Llb.
5   Miss V. Ryan MSc.
6   Mrs S. Taylor BA Dip Ed.
7   Ms Lisa Thompson BEM AMIMech.E
8   Lady Abigail Smythe
9   Lord Chalstead
10 Sir Alex Groves
11 Dame Anna Smailes
12 Messrs Hamlyn and Cook
13 Sir Matthew Dunn & Sons
14 The Company Secretary, Marsdyke Shipping Co. Ltd
15 Sir Frederick Tinsdale Ltd

a 'Mr' or 'Esq' 1, 2 and 3. Originally the term 'esquire' was only given to people of high rank in society; in more recent times it has been used instead of 'Mr' for members of the professions – solicitors, doctors, engineers, architects, etc, while 'Mr' has been used for aldermen, councillors, tradespeople and others of lower rank! However, lately the 'Mr' prefix has become more popular and can now be used when addressing everyone but those of higher rank in society.

Note: the two should never be used together; if 'Mr' is used 'Esq'. should be omitted.

The christian name is given in full when 'Esq.' is used, but initials are sufficient when 'Mr' is used.

b Forms of address for women 5, 6, 7, 8 and 11. The most commonly used styles are: Miss, Mrs, Ms, Lady, Dame. Women in business are tending to use 'Ms' since many regard it as irrelevant to their job whether they are married or single. If you do not know which style is preferred (or indeed which is appropriate) you have to take a chance between Miss and Ms, but since many women are rather sensitive about the implication associated with both, you probably can't win!

In the case of titles the christian name is used for wives of knights (Sir Reginald and Lady Abigail Smythe) and for Dames, but not for wives of lords (Lord and Lady Chalstead).

c Titles 8, 9 and 10. Note that the christian name is used with 'Sir' but not with 'Lord'. Other titles currently in use are 'Dr' which is used both for a medical doctor and someone who has been awarded a doctorate of philosophy (Ph.D) – a medical consultant and a dentist are both addressed 'Mr' or 'Esq.' and 'Reverend' is abbreviated to 'Rev.'. Just as 'Esq.' is omitted when 'Mr' is used, so it is when any other title is used.

d Letters and qualifications after the name 3, 4, 5, 6 and 7. Many people who have earned academic degrees, military decorations and membership of professional bodies are understandably proud of their achievements. They may therefore be gratified if these letters are used as part of their style of address (some may even be offended if you don't). The problem of writing them correctly and in the right order is not always as difficult as it may seem. The simple rule is that they should appear in the following order:

1 decorations (military and civil)
2 degrees and diplomas
3 membership of professional bodies

If in doubt, you will probably have access to a letter or other document from which you can copy. Failing that, a phone call to the secretary or another official in the organization will probably provide the information you need.

e **Companies and partnerships** 12, 13, 14 and 15. Writing to organizations does not normally cause a problem as the correct title usually appears on their stationery. However, one word does appear to cause problems and in fact has been used inaccurately (perhaps through ignorance) by many companies.

'*Messrs*' The word is derived from the French word *messieurs* meaning 'gentlemen'. It is correctly used when writing to an *unlimited company* or *partnership*, unless another title (e.g. 'Sir') is already included, or the partnership is registered under another name. However, it should never be used before the name of a *limited company*.

Letters to a limited company are normally addressed to the Secretary, or some other official. *Example:*

Messrs Hamlyn and Cook
Messrs John Fielding & Sons   }   Unlimited
Sir Robert Dunn & Sons   companies or
'Just Boats' Hire Company   partnerships

Sir Frederick Tinsdale Ltd   Limited
The Secretary, Marsdyke Shipping Co. Ltd   }   companies

How well did you work out the rules? It is possible here to deal with only the most general rules and the most common problems, and you would be well advised to check in a reference book whenever you are in doubt. (See 'Guide to reference material', p. 197, *What do you mean 'Communication'?* Chapter 11.)

5 *Salutations and complimentary closes*

These refer to the formal opening and closing of the letter's message and there are certain conventions which should be followed. With the increasing relaxation of formal business-writing style, it may seem odd that these rules of propriety still exist, but exist they do and many people still feel so strongly about these conventions that they are provoked into writing to *The Times* about the frequently found mistakes in this matter, particularly incorrect pairings of salutation and complimentary close.

Self-check

Which of these is right and which is wrong?

a	Dear Sir	Yours sincerely
b	Dear Mr Brown	Yours sincerely
c	Dear Miss Jones	Yours faithfully
d	Dear Madam	Yours faithfully
e	Gentlemen	Yours faithfully

Check your answers against the list below.

Salutation   *Complimentary close*

Dear Sir
Dear Sirs
Gentlemen   }   **Yours faithfully**
Dear Madam
Dear Mesdames

Dear Mr Smith
Dear Miss Jones
Dear Mrs Bennett
Dear Reverend Cavendish
Dear Dr Smythe   **Yours sincerely**
Dear Sir Lionel
Dear Lady Julia
Dear Lord Chalstead
Dear Lady Chalstead

Dear Jane   Sincerely
Dear Robert   Kind regards

Note particularly that where the name is *not* used 'Yours faithfully' is the only correct complimentary close ('Yours truly' as an alternative to 'Yours faithfully' is really unacceptable now), and note also that 'faithfully' and 'sincerely' both start with *lowercase* letters when written after 'Yours' which starts with a capital letter.

The conventional linking of a salutation with a particular complimentary close is based on the degree of relationship between the writer and recipient:

Dear Sir	Yours faithfully (writer and recipient have not met, name of recipient is not known, relationship is fairly formal)
Dear Mr Brown	Yours sincerely (more friendly, name known – commonly used in business even where correspondents have not met)

Other than these two particular conventions, the rules are becoming more relaxed and where the relationship is fairly familiar, writers can choose what seems the most appropriate to them and the circumstances. *Examples*:

Dear Charles/Dear Susan/My dear Charles/My dear Susan/My dear Brown, etc.

with

Sincerely/Kind regards/Best wishes/Yours affectionately/Affectionately, etc.

6 Subject Heading

Strictly speaking every business letter should deal with one subject (it makes filing easier) and it should therefore be possible to sum up the subject of the letter in a brief but helpful heading which assists the reader in knowing immediately what the letter is about. It should be placed *between* the salutation and the body of the letter and is either centred over the type area (semi-blocked and indented layout) or started at the left-hand margin (blocked layout)

Self-check

Devise clear brief headings for each of the letters on pp.
208-10.

7 Signature

The practice of typing the name of the organization immediately
under 'Yours faithfully' has almost disappeared:

> Yours faithfully,
> ARNOLD J. BROWN & CO.,
>
> *S Stevens*
>
> S. Stevens
> Company Secretary.

but it is good practice to type the name in lower case letters (or
handwrite the name in capital letters) in case the signature is
illegible, and most people's are. The designation of the writer is
then written immediately below the name:

> Yours faithfully,
>
> *S. Stevens*
>
> S. Stevens (Mrs)
> Company Secretary.

8 The body of the letter

If you have already read *What Do You Mean, 'Communication'?*
you will have worked through material concerned with conveying your message effectively, and earlier in this chapter you will
have found techniques for writing typical business letters. However, you should remember that the body of the letter should be
written in clear and concise English with correct paragraphing
and punctuation.

Paragraphing Each paragraph should express a separate item in
the letter and may therefore consist of only one sentence; but
too many short paragraphs can spoil the appearance of the letter.
   Subheadings If the message can usefully be divided into sec-

tions, do not hesitate to use subheadings (within reason).

Lists Similarly if a paragraph contains points which could usefully be presented in list form, do so.

Punctuation Even where open punctuation is chosen for the addresses and so on, the body of the letter must still be punctuated.

Punctuation should be used to help understanding. Too many commas liberally sprinkled about a letter are not necessarily helpful to the reader and usually suggest that the writer is really not too clear about the purpose of the various punctuation marks (see Appendix A).

Remember:

- reference to previous correspondence where necessary
- the rules for word division (see Appendix D)
- indentation or spacing for paragraphs (see p. 217)
- punctuation to help understanding
- the use of subheadings where helpful

Moral: anything that helps the reader to understand the message quickly and easily, and improves the visual appearance of the letter, is usually permissible.

Margins Typists will have received training in appropriate margin widths. However, the most important guide is visual appearance. Generally a margin of about one inch on both sides of the sheet looks good but it will of course depend on the length of the letter and the position of the letterhead.

Spacing Nearly every business letter is typed in single spacing with a double space between paragraphs. Some organizations, however, prefer that very short letters (up to say ten lines) be typed in double spacing with wider margins. The recipient's address (and the sender's address, if it is not already printed) should always be typed in single spacing.

Enclosures The fact that a letter contains enclosures is indicated by the letters 'Enc.' or 'Encs 3' at the foot of the letter, or by '/' placed in the margin alongside the reference to the enclosure in the text.

Follow-on sheets or continuation sheets These are used where the letter extends beyond one page, but you should avoid using them if fewer than two lines of the letter would appear on the sheet and you should never use a continuation sheet which would only contain the complimentary close and signature. The printed letter heading is not required, but the continuation sheet should bear the name of the recipient, the page number, and date:

G. Mainwaring & Co. Ltd.   –2–   22 February 19. .

Copy(ies) When a copy of the letter is to be sent to a third party, this is indicated by: 'copy to', 'copies to', or 'c.c', usually written near the bottom of the letter.

Warnings If the contents of a letter are confidential, private or personal, this should be indicated prominently on the letter (usually above the recipient's name and address) and on the envelope, e.g.

CONFIDENTIAL or PRIVATE AND CONFIDENTIAL
PERSONAL or PERSONAL AND CONFIDENTIAL

Note: if a letter is marked 'Personal' it will only be opened by the person to whom it is addressed.

Another method of ensuring that a particular person in a company deals with your letter is to write the words:

For the attention of:
The Personnel Manager
Rees Engineering Co.
Greenwood
Bucks

Dictating

Until recently you might have considered it fairly unlikely that you would be called upon to dictate messages into a machine until you were fairly advanced in your career; only senior managers and people who were required to work away from base would have to grapple with the apparently difficult task of thinking through the creation of a letter out loud. Certainly many people who have access to both shorthand typists and dictating machines still go to great lengths to avoid dictating where possible.

In the future we shall all find our roles increasingly affected as more efficient methods of communication are introduced, and we will need to be familiar with the modern electronic information-processing equipment which is now increasingly available.

Amongst the many new skills which will be required, more and more emphasis will be placed on the specific skills in oral communication which are essential when using modern equipment, where clarity in enunciation and precision and unambiguity of expression will be particularly important.

So whether or not you have occasion to dictate material to a shorthand typist or a tape recorder at the moment, practice in the skills involved will stand you in good stead for the future.

Preparation for dictation

Good dictation is only good writing out loud; and good writing is only good thinking well expressed. In other words, so long as you give your messages preparation time, and plan in advance what you are going to say, it should make very little difference whether the final draft is handwritten on to paper, dictated to a shorthand typist or dictated into a tape recorder. The fear that dictating holds for many people results either from unwillingness to plan the message carefully before they start or simply from fear of the unfamiliar; so as usual it is a case of practising. Practise at home using a small cassette recorder, if you have one, until you have the knack of stopping and starting.

1 *Prepare yourself* Forget everything else. Clear your mind and your desk – concentrate. Clear your mouth – pencils, cigarettes, anything in your mouth interferes with speech.
2 *Prepare your material* in just the same way as you would if you were going to *write* the draft, i.e. as far as the skeleton outline stage.
3 *Prepare your priorities* If you have more than one letter to dictate, list them by priority. You may be interrupted.
4 *Prepare your typist* Brief the typist fully, whether face-to-face or on the tape recorder. Tell her

- who the letter is to
- who the letter is from

If you need to keep copies for filing tell her

- the reference
- how many copies you need
- who the copies are to

If you need the typist to see letters to you, for addresses, etc., tell her clearly which original goes with which letter.

Dictating practice

1 Say it simply – in brief sentences – one idea to a paragraph.
2 Punctuate as you dictate. Say: 'paragraph' (new paragraph), 'stop', 'comma', 'indent', 'list', etc. Natural pauses when speaking are a good clue to the need for punctuation marks, but don't go overboard.
3 Concentrate on speaking clearly and more slowly than usual. Mumbling is expensive – it leads to mistakes and frustration for the typist. But don't speak too slowly – this will disrupt your natural fluency and the typist's natural speed.
4 Spell names of people, roads, towns and technical terms when they are not obviously simple.
5 If you dry up – stop. It happens to everyone and it doesn't matter, but it would be unwise to try. What does matter is trying to plough on when you've lost your thread.
6 Play it back, collect your thoughts and then carry on.
7 When you've finished, check. Have you been clear, correct, complete and concise?
8 Every so often, listen back to your dictated material. Although it may be a painful experience, it will help you to improve.

Remember: most shorthand and audio-typists type what you say

- not what you think you say
- not what they think you wanted to say

Activity

Bearing in mind the principles covered in this chapter on

organizing a letter – creating the appropriate tone, and laying out the letter well – write a letter suitable for sending to the unsuccessful applicants for a position of personnel manager with your company.

Remember that as well as needing to convey your message you will also want to maintain goodwill – that is, leave the disappointed applicants with a good impression of your company and with their self-respect intact.

Before you write the final draft, try dictating the letter into a tape recorder.

Then write out the letter and compare your written letter with your dictated letter.

Now look at the letter below, written with the same objective as yours. It is an example from real life which particularly impressed me. What do you think of it? Why? How does it compare with yours? Which do you like best? Which would you prefer to receive?

Dear Mr Thompson,

Personnel Manager – HOU 163X
This letter is to let you know the latest position regarding the above appointment.

I am about to see some candidates whose overall background and experience appear very close to our requirements. In view of this I do not suggest you come for interview at this stage; but should the position alter, I shall write to you immediately.

However, if I am not able to take matters further on this occasion, I hope that you will let us know if one of our future advertisements appeals to you.

Yours sincerely,

G. B. England
Personnel Director

10 | Applying for a job

One of the most important letters you are ever likely to write is the one applying for a job, but sometimes in the excitement or desperation of the moment it is easy to grab a pen and paper and start writing without giving the matter too much thought and without realizing that writing the letter is only one part of the whole process – a process which although it is pretty demanding can actually be rather interesting because it is like a detective hunt for clues – clues to help you find out what kind of job you really want and clues to help you work out what kind of person they really want.

The intention of this chapter is to help you find out what sort of job suits you, what is available and what they are looking for. In addition it should provide you with some tips on how to complete application forms, write application letters and generally increase your chances of getting an interview, which is really the first major objective of the application process.

It will obviously only be useful if you are looking for a job at the moment or about to start the process, so if you are happily settled and not thinking of moving for a while you might prefer to skip this chapter and return to it another time when it is more immediately useful. However, remember to refer to it well in advance – the process of applying for a job is not one to be hurried, as we shall see.

More haste – less speed You may have seen an advertisement and simply want to apply; you may be trying to get promotion; you may be at college in the final year of your course and in the unenviable position of needing to write to organizations 'cold' (i.e. inquiring from many organizations whether they have any vacancies, rather than applying for a particular job that has been advertised). These are at least three of the possibilities which exist and which will require special treatment appropriate to the circumstances.

Whichever position you find yourself in, and even if you are desperate, don't be in too much of a hurry at first. The process of getting a job can be a long drawn-out and sometimes exhausting business and you should certainly start to think about beginning the process in plenty of time, rather than optimistically leaving it until the last minute. If you are at school or college you should certainly not leave it until the last year; if you are already working then you should already have given some thought to the matter of your career; but if you have never stopped to think about it too deeply before, then now is better than never. However, don't be in too much of a hurry to put pen to paper. As with most things to do with communication, some careful thinking and planning will avoid costly mistakes, disappointment and frustrating time-wasting.

Deciding what sort of job you want

With the unemployment figures now well over two million, it may seem tactless to suggest that you should start out being choosy, and it is true that it is very often the employer who can afford to be choosy, not you, the applicant. But for two very good reasons, however desperate you may feel, you should think carefully about what sort of job you want:

- The situation may change. By the time you apply for a job, the picture may be looking slightly less bleak, and however bad employment prospects are generally, there will always be some areas where the situation is reversed; where it is a seller's market and the employers are crying out for applicants.
- Unless you think carefully about the sort of job you want and are qualified to do, you are likely to apply too hastily for jobs for which you are not suited, and will probably therefore be unsuccessful. Even if, more by luck than judgement, you happen to succeed in getting a job, then you may well turn out to be not very good at it, in which case you may eventually start the process all over again.

So, first of all – *what sort of a person are you*?

In order to find out what sort of a job would ideally suit you, you need to think about what kind of a person you are, what your particular likes and dislikes are, what sort of things worry you, where and how you like working and so on.

In doing this, you should not necessarily be prejudiced by the kind of job you are doing now or the particular course of studies you are taking. First of all, you may be in the wrong job, or on the wrong course. Secondly, it is easy to be over-influenced by the nature of your present or previous jobs or courses into believing that you must search for a job in that perhaps rather limited field. For example, if you are taking a business studies course at the moment you should not feel restricted to the traditional areas of business and industry, for you should remember that these are not the only places where you can make good use of the skills and knowledge you are acquiring. Doing office work can mean anything from working quietly on your own doing a tidy routine job, to working as part of a large team where one day is never like the next; from working in a large commercial firm doing a specific job like wages clerk or accounts clerk, to being a jack-of-all-trades in a farm office or for a football team, for example.

At this stage you should *think imaginatively*. It is true we cannot all land the exciting glamorous jobs and you may not be lucky enough to find exactly the sort of thing which would suit you immediately, but it is all too easy to limit the scope unnecessarily.

Of course, you may feel you are in the opposite position – aware that there are so many jobs in existence that you don't know where to start. In either case you need to think carefully first of all about yourself.

Activity

Here are some questions to ask yourself, but don't be limited to these; try to think of some of your own:

- Do you like working with people, or animals, or things?
- Do you like being part of a team, or working on your own?

- Do you prefer being indoors, or outdoors; in the town or the country?
- Do you welcome responsibility, however modest, or do you feel happier if someone else 'carries the can'?
- Do you like solving problems? What sort of problems: Practical? Theoretical? Numerical? Mechanical? Intellectual? People problems?
- Are you creative or practical?
- Do you like working under pressure, or do you do your best work when you can set your own more leisurely pace?
- Do you like to be closely supervised, or do you prefer to be left to get on and sort things out for yourself?
- Are you self-disciplined, or do you need to feel there is someone driving you on?
- Do you want a quiet sedentary job, or an energetic job that takes you out and about?
- Do you like jobs that involve marshalling facts, juggling figures, a lot of writing?
- Do you prefer talking to people, selling your ideas, persuading people?
- Does it matter where you work? Near your home, friends and family?
- Would you be prepared to move?
- Would anyone else be affected adversely if you did move? Husband, wife, parents, children? What are their views?
- Could you settle down easily, make new friends quickly if you moved to a new area?
- What matters most to you? Pay? Conditions of work? Job satisfaction? The people you work with?
- Would you be prepared to undergo more training?

Note: don't answer these questions too quickly. Think about things you have done in the past and work out why you liked or disliked them and why. Ask other people what they like doing and why. Keep your answers for future reference.

Personality tests and vocational guidance tests There are tests available which can help you to discover what sort of person you are and what your real interests, likes and dislikes are. Ask the careers officer at your local careers office or college.

Activity

Now armed with your answers to these questions and any others you have thought of, think about how strongly you feel about these things and which of them are absolutely essential in any job you apply for. These will form your *criteria* against which you will then be able to measure the suitability of any job.

Produce three lists headed 'Musts', 'Wants' and 'Would be nice'. Example:

Musts	*Wants*	*Would be nice*
Working with people	Training opportunities	Good pay

This might be the beginning of the list if you have decided you would be miserable working on your own; want to get further training but would be prepared to get more training/qualifications in your own time, e.g. evening classes, if the job itself does not provide training opportunities; and are prepared to settle for low pay while you are getting further qualifications or training.

Thinking about questions like these will:

- help you to narrow the field
- help you to apply for suitable jobs rather than waste time going up blind alleys
- provide you with material both for your application letter/form and for the interview stage, so keep your answers to these last two tasks for future reference

Activity

Now, using this information, try to analyse the sort of job you want. How many different jobs would measure up to your criteria? Which would you prefer? Have you got the necessary qualifications or will the organization help you get them?

To help you think of possibilities, get a copy of the local daily/evening paper and one of the quality national papers and go through every advertisement thinking about each carefully in relation to your criteria. Put a cross against each one which really does not measure up and a tick against each one that you would be prepared to consider (even if you would never have thought of it as a possibility before).

Now list all the jobs you have ticked. How many have you got?

More than you thought possible? In this case, subject them to really careful examination. Have you been realistic? Have you aimed too high, been optimistic about your own ability to do the job, included jobs which you might be able to do in a few years' time with a bit more experience but which may be outside your reach for the moment? Even if you exclude these, you should still be left with quite a few which are in areas you might never have thought of before.

On the other hand you may have set your sights too low, causing you to include jobs for which you are really overqualified. Although there are some employers who seem unwilling to take on people with more qualifications than the job needs, it may not be a bad thing, at this stage, to be prepared to consider starting right at the bottom if necessary. For some occupations it may be the only way in and if you have talent and enthusiasm for whatever you do, you should not find it difficult to be promoted fairly quickly. There are more than a few managing directors who started out as office juniors.

If, however, your list is disappointingly short, again think carefully about the reasons. Have you been rather narrow-minded in considering possibilities? Are you short of qualifications in your chosen field? Are you being too demanding in what you expect from a job? You may of course have been too modest about what you have to offer, in which case you may not have aimed high enough or considered a wide enough range of possibilities.

So be realistic but don't go in for false modesty. If you don't have faith in yourself, no one else will. Know what you are aiming for and be prepared to do what is necessary to get it.

Finding out what is available and what they are looking for

You should by now have a fairly good idea of the sort of job you are looking for. I say 'sort of' because at this stage, you should not be too specific, but considering as wide a range of jobs as possible. Now begins the real search for vacancies: *keep your eyes and ears open*. You need to explore every possible source of information and be constantly on the alert for job opportunities. Likely sources of information will obviously depend on the type and level of job you are seeking but here are some suggestions you should explore energetically. Unless you have a guardian angel, the jobs will not come to you. You will have to go out and search for them.

> *Self-check*
>
> Where can you find out about job vacancies? List all the sources you can think of.

Newspapers The obvious source of job vacancies, but because they are so obvious and a comparatively easy source they reach a very wide readership, and there will be a large number of applicants for most jobs, so you will have to move fast and be prepared to follow up other sources.

Local newspapers are a useful source if you want to stay in a particular area, but if you are happy to move then national newspapers may provide a greater choice. Most of the quality newspapers tend to run special features from time to time on particular areas of employment and some devote space to particular areas of employment on the same day each week, so get to know your newspapers. If one particular newspaper looks like being a particularly good bet, it is probably worth buying it every day, but you must also make it a daily routine to visit the local public or college library, otherwise you will be in danger of missing advertisements which may be in for only one day.

If you want to move to a particular area elsewhere in the country, then you will increase your chances by getting hold of the local newspaper for that area. If you do not know anyone who can send you copies regularly, then write to the newspaper office asking for copies to be sent to you daily until further notice. If you do not know the name of the newspaper, address your inquiry to 'The Local Paper' followed by the name of the town.

Finally, read the advertisements of an appropriate weekly paper like *New Society* or *New Statesman* or specialist papers like *Dataweek*, the newspaper of the computing industry, or *Marketing Weekly*; the Sunday papers; and lastly do not forget the professional journals which usually appear monthly.

Careers office Visit your local careers office or Department of Employment office (address in the phone book). Some people often assume that careers officers are only there to help school leavers, but careers counselling is now a well-established profession which requires extensive training in helping all manner of people with all sorts of problems: from getting a first job to changing jobs and careers; from helping people deal with the problem of redundancy to advising people on how and where to obtain further training or qualifications. So whatever your particular problem, it can do no harm to visit a careers officer – they are paid to help.

If you are at college, you will almost certainly find that there is some form of careers advisory service or appointments board within the college. Get to know it, preferably during the first year of your course.

If you are already working but feel that perhaps you are not in quite the right job for you and would like a change, then don't forget your own company's personnel department. There may be possibilities for change, not necessarily promotion, within your own organization. The personnel officer cannot be expected to guess that you would welcome a change unless you approach him to discuss your ideas and inclinations.

Job centres and employment agencies Most towns now have Job Centres which act as a clearing house for vacancies existing in an area and can therefore link employers with applicants.

However, now that Job Centres are so well known, you will

have to move fast if you find a vacancy which you like the look of, as there will be plenty of competition for most of them. In addition to these government agencies, there are also plenty of private agencies which specialize in finding applicants for office and clerical jobs.

Attack on all fronts Above all, it is important once you get to this stage to follow up as many possibilities as you can at once. Don't just apply for one job and then sit back and wait to see what happens. You may be unlucky, in which case you will have wasted valuable time when you could have been applying for other jobs. So explore all the sources mentioned above and apply for as many jobs as possible, and keep at it. Most people have to make many applications, sometimes hundreds, before they are offered the right job.

What are they looking for?

It is very tempting and unfortunately quite common to skim through a newspaper, catch sight of the kind of occupation which applies to you and pick up your pen and start writing: so long as the job is the kind you are looking for and the advertisement mentions a few other things that seem relevant to you, like pay, area, the level of the job and so on, then why not apply? Well, look at the two advertisements on page 241. They are for the same kind of job – or are they?

Both the advertisements seem to be looking for the same sort of person with the same sort of qualifications and experience to do apparently the same sort of job. But if you look carefully you will see that there are some clues in the advertisements which suggest that the jobs may actually be rather different and that the two companies are looking for two rather different people.

Self-check

Underline the words in both the advertisements which seem to you to be key words which communicate rather different messages.

ASSISTANT ACCOUNTANT

required by old-established city firm, to assist the company accountant in the preparation of accounts to trial balance stage.

Candidates should have an ONC in Business Studies or similar. Preference will be given to candidates with some general experience.

The company may be prepared to offer the facility for day-release to complete accountancy training.

Please reply in writing to The Company Accountant at the address below, giving full details of qualifications and career to date.

ASSISTANT ACCOUNTANT

A rapidly expanding local company seeks a young ambitious student to assist the Chief Accountant in the preparation of accounts and the operation of an in-house mini computer.

Ideally you will have completed a course of further study, hold the ONC in business studies and have two or three years' practical experience of accountancy and/or office routine.

In return we will offer you a competitive starting salary, attractive working conditions, and encouragement with further studies — probably involving part day-release.

Please telephone for an application form, quoting

Ref. 48991/NAP

In the first advertisement, words like 'old-established city firm' and 'the facility for day-release' seem to conjure up an image of rather staid, old-world respectability and the advertisement itself is fairly straightforward and unspectacular both in its layout and style and the information it conveys. The second advertisement conveys a rather more modern and exciting image not only in the style and layout of the advertisement but also through adjectives like 'rapidly expanding', 'young ambitious', 'competitive', and 'attractive'. The younger, more progressive image of the company is also conveyed by the fact that it offers rather more than the basic information about the job, and goes so far as to mention that it has a mini computer. The first company may also have a computer, but if so, it is less eager to advertise it than the second which is able to reinforce its go-ahead image by the very mention of it. Look too at the way that the two companies deal with the issue of further training opportunities. The second company provides 'encouragement' whereas the first 'may' offer the facility for day-release. There is another important difference between the two advertisements. The first is written in the third person – 'candidates should have . . . the company may be prepared . . .' while the second manages to create a much more lively personal relationship between the company and the reader (its potential employee?) by using the personal pronouns 'you' and 'we', and reinforcing the idea of an equal relationship by balancing what it requires of the candidate by what it will offer 'in return'.

How many differences did you spot? It is important to be alert to these quite subtle clues not just because they may tell you quite a lot more about a company than would at first seem possible in a small number of words, but because they can tell you a lot more about the kind of person they are really looking for. At first sight we decided that the two advertisements seemed to be looking for fairly similar people. Now, however, we must reconsider that first impression. If the second company conveys an image of a young, modern go-ahead company then it is more than likely it is looking for someone with a personality that will fit. Similarly, the first company is consciously or unconsciously asking for someone who is solid, dependable and perhaps less demanding, who would be happy working in a rather quieter, less ambitious environment. Of course, we should not take these conjectures too far, for conjectures are all that they can be without any more evidence. However, at this stage of the application process this is all we have to go on and our impressions do seem to be based on reasonable evidence, whether the companies intended to convey these impressions or not. The advertisements may, of course, only be telling you something about the companies' advertising agencies.

Having carried out this kind of analysis, you should then compare the result with the personal analysis which you did on p. 234 to see whether either of these jobs would suit you and, perhaps more importantly, whether you would suit either of these companies. You might then feel that it would be better to apply to one and not the other. Whichever you choose, you must bear carefully in mind what you have learned from looking at the advertisement, when you come to write your application. How are you going to prove that you will fit into an 'old-established city firm' or that you are 'ambitious' and just what a 'rapidly expanding' company is looking for?

But perhaps you feel that you would be happy working in either firm and that bits of your personality would adapt well to the image of both. In that case you must still bear in mind the two very different personalities of the companies because you will need to write two very different letters and, if you get that far, adapt your behaviour appropriately for each interview.

The application itself

Now at last we come to the application letter. Did you notice another difference between the two advertisements? The first asked for an application in writing giving full details, but the second asked the applicant to telephone for an application form. Many organizations still ask applicants to write a letter setting out their qualifications and experience, as this provides the company not only with this essential information but also with a chance to see how the applicant writes; how he sets out and orders the facts about himself; and even what his handwriting is like, something which some firms consider so important that they employ the services of a handwriting expert to give them additional information about a candidate's personality. This kind of application obviously poses more problems for the candidate as he is left to decide exactly what the company wants to know and how best to set it out. So let's deal with the method employed by the second company first. More and more companies, particularly the larger ones, ask applicants to complete an application form, as it ensures that they get all the information they need in a standard layout to which they can refer easily.

'Please apply for application form to . . .' If the advertisement merely says *'Please apply'* you can choose whether to write or telephone to ask for the form.

'Write for application form to . . .' In this case it is not necessary to write a long letter giving all your qualifications and experience with your reasons for applying for the job. A brief letter referring to the advertisement and the post for which you are applying is all that is required, e.g.

Name and/or position of person to whom application is to be made	Your address
Company name and address	Date

Dear Sir (or name if given in the advert)

> *Job title and Ref. no.* (if given in the advert)

Please send me details of the job (or appointment or vacancy) advertised in the *Sunday Era* of 23 May 19 . ., together with an application form.

> Yours faithfully,
>
> JANET BROWN (Miss or Mrs as appropriate)

Even though this letter seems to be a mere formality, it should be written neatly and correctly, as it will be put on your file and will therefore contribute to the total picture that the company has of you.

'Please telephone for application form.' Although this may seem the simplest way to apply, you should be on your guard. When you telephone, you cannot be absolutely sure how much influence the person you speak to has, and if you are vague or discourteous or unfriendly or even too familiar, this might well be reported to the person who is responsible for selecting the person who is to get the job. So remember your best telephone

technique – be prepared; be clear about what you want, and about what they will need to know in order to help you (e.g. title of the job vacancy and reference number if there is one); speak clearly, especially when giving your name and address; and be friendly and courteous without being overfamiliar or presumptuous.

Application form

Remember that even though you should send a covering letter with your form, the application form will be the main thing on which the company will base its decision whether to invite you for interview, and if they do interview you, it will form the basis of the interview. So *never start filling in an application form before you*

- Read the whole form through very carefully so that you are clear exactly what information it asks for and where you are required to put it.
- Make sure that you have plenty of time to complete the form carefully and completely.
- Make a rough draft of your answers to the questions so that you can ensure that you can get the information into the spaces provided and that you don't make any mistakes on the real form. Tip: if possible, make a photocopy of the blank form before you start. Use this to make your rough copy and then you can be sure that the final version is laid out as neatly as possible.

Hints on completing an application form:

- Dates become increasingly difficult to remember as you get older and there are more of them. Start keeping a file now which includes dates of school, exams, jobs and courses attended plus copies of any certificates and testimonials you may have.

  (A testimonial is an open (as opposed to confidential) letter given to you to pass on to anyone you like. Because you are able to see what is said the comments tend to be rather general and complimentary and are therefore not valued very highly by employers, who usually prefer to ask for names of referees

.... COMPANY LTD.	APPLICATION FOR: (state position applied for)

SURNAME (BLOCK CAPITALS)	FIRST NAMES

ADDRESS	TELEPHONE NUMBER HOME WORK

AGE	DATE OF BIRTH	PLACE OF BIRTH	MARITAL STATUS

NUMBER, AGE AND SEX OF CHILDREN

EDUCATION AND TRAINING (schools and colleges attended since the age of 11)

QUALIFICATIONS (in chronological order)

EXPERIENCE (all employment and military service in chronological order,
          Include positions held and reasons for leaving.)

(Use additional sheets if necessary)

ADDITIONAL INFORMATION you would like to give about yourself or
                    your experience.

(Use additional sheets if necessary)

HEALTH (Give details of any physical disabilities or serious illnesses.)

PRESENT SALARY

REFEREES (Give the names and addresses of two people from whom we may
        seek references.)

If selected when could you start?

Signed: Date:

from whom they can seek a confidential assessment of you.)
- Presentation must be faultless. You should write with dark ink, as the form may later be photocopied, and avoid a pen which runs even slightly on the particular quality of paper on which the form is printed. A ballpoint pen may therefore be safer than a felt-tip pen but a very careful experiment in one corner on the back should be enough to tell you which to use.
- Obey the instructions. If the form says BLOCK CAPITALS write in BLOCK CAPITALS, if it says write in ballpoint pen then do as you are told. The company will have good reasons for their instructions even if you don't appreciate them.

Some forms are very specific about the information required, providing subheadings and columns, for instance, under main headings so that you know where to include dates of exams or the responsibilities of the jobs you have done. However, some forms are much more general, merely including main headings (like the form shown here). In this case you must think carefully about which details to include under each heading and present your information under your own subheadings and in columns if it will look clearer, e.g.

Education Give the names and addresses of schools you have attended together with the dates.

Qualifications Give the subject, grade *and date* of examinations – fifteen 'O' levels taken on five different occasions is not as impressive as eight taken and passed at one sitting, and one 'A' level taken and passed while you were working may be more impressive than two taken over two years while at school. Don't include short courses under this heading unless they resulted in some kind of terminal examination, or unless there is nowhere else on the form to put them. (Another reason why it is important to read through the form carefully *before* you start writing.)

Experience Unless the form says otherwise, list any jobs you have had, starting with the most recent and then going backwards in time (chronological order in reverse). Include the title of the job, the name and address of the company, and the dates you were employed as accurately as possible. If there is room, you should also add a brief description of the *main* responsibilities involved in each job. If in doubt about what to include, concentrate on those things which are relevant to the job for which you are applying. But remember that previously insignificant parts of jobs can take on new importance if you think hard and realize their relevance. No experience? If you have just left school or are still at college, the section headed 'experience' can present some problems because you probably feel you haven't any. However, if you have done any part-time or holiday jobs or if you held any positions of responsibility at school and have not put them anywhere else on the form, then use this space to give brief details – it can't do any harm, and although you may think that your holiday job is unimportant or irrelevant, the employer will at least be able to see what you have done with your time.

Present salary Don't forget to include any fringe benefits like luncheon vouchers or a company car.

Referees You will usually be asked to give the names of at least two people who would be prepared to supply a reference. If you are still at school or college then one referee should be from education and the other can be either someone who has known you privately for several years or preferably someone for whom you have worked if only for a short time. If you are already working then it is essential to give names of people for whom you have worked. Remember that although you will obviously want to choose someone who will speak well of you, it is also important that your referees are themselves able to communicate effectively, so think carefully before you put down the first names that come to mind.

Note: it is courteous to ask your referees for their permission before giving their names. Apart from giving them rather a surprise when they suddenly receive a request for a reference, they may find the task difficult if you have not given them some idea in advance of the nature of the job for which you are applying. If you do not want your referees approached before you have been offered the job, you should indicate this on the form. This is an understandable request and will usually be quite acceptable.

Supporting statement Most application forms will include a space headed 'Supporting statement' or 'Other relevant information' or some other form of words inviting you to give additional information not covered elsewhere on the form. *Never leave this space blank*. Apart from the fact that it represents an opportunity to add to your case for being considered, it is often regarded by the employer as the most significant section on the form, for it is here that you give some indication of what kind of person you are, not by bald statements claiming that you are 'energetic, ambitious, hardworking and reliable, etc.' but by the way in which you deal with this section, select what to include and express yourself in continuous prose.

So always use the space but *plan* what you are going to say very carefully. Occasionally you will find that under the main heading of this section there is some additional guidance, e.g. 'You should use this space to describe your leisure activities and any other activities which you feel are relevant to your application', or 'Please give your reasons for applying for this position'. Where guidance is given, stick to it and don't go off the point. However, sometimes the heading is vague and no guidance is provided. Probably the best advice in this dilemma is to provide a short autobiography. This should not be a repetition in prose of the facts given on the previous pages but rather additional information which, taken with the facts, provides a fuller picture of you as a person and a personality. For instance, you could explain why your career to date has taken the course it has, mentioning things which have influenced you; the main interests you have developed; the achievements you particularly remember and your ideas and ambitions for the future, if you have any. Above all, it should be written in continuous prose, not notes, and in correct and clear English. This section more than any other must be drafted in rough so that you can work out how best to use the space provided.

How much should you write? As much and no more to fill the space provided. Although you may be invited to add another page if necessary, you should bear in mind that the company may have provided what they consider to be enough space. If you need more, it may be because you are not writing concisely enough and are tending to ramble on at great length on things which are not relevant. So work out what you want to say and then edit it and rewrite it, over and over again if necessary, until you have found the precise wording to say what you want to fluently but concisely. Only as a last resort when you judge it absolutely essential should you add an additional sheet.

If there is no space provided or if this section asks for specific information and still leaves you with things unsaid which you believe support your application, then you should include them in the covering letter to send with the application form.

- Photocopy the form once you have completed it and take this copy to the interview. It is surprisingly easy to forget exactly what you said on the form several weeks before.

Activity

1 Using the basic application form on p. 246, design a more detailed one which will ensure the company gets the information it wants under suitable headings, and which will help the applicant complete it clearly, by dividing the sections into subsections with suitable sub-headings. (It will probably have to be larger than the one illustrated.)

2 Using your own data, complete the form as if you were applying for the job advertised in the second advertisement on p. 241. (Keep this completed form, as it will provide you with a useful reference copy and checklist when you come to apply for a job. It will also be useful as a record of your data when we come to the problem of writing an application letter when no application form is provided.)

3 What problems did you have in redesigning the form? See 'Designing forms and questionnaires' in Chapter 12.

4 What problems did you have in completing the form? Make a brief note of these problems to remind you of the difficulties when you come to do the real thing.

The full application letter

'Please reply in writing to . . . giving full details of your qualifications and career to date.' Although issuing application forms is becoming increasingly common, many companies will still prefer to ask for details in writing for the following reasons:

* Application forms are standard and although this has advantages for the employer as we have seen, it has disadvantages too: each candidate is different and what may be enough space under one heading for one candidate will not be enough for another and vice versa. Similarly either a form must be designed to allow for every possibility in which case it will probably be far too long and for many applicants will end up full of blank spaces; or alternatively, as in the simple version illustrated on p. 246, it will probably not be detailed enough.
* In controlling the way the applicant presents the information, the employer does not really get a chance to see how the applicant can select and order information for himself – a skill which is in itself an essential prerequisite for many jobs.
* Following on from the last point, if the applicant is given no real guidance about what information to include, then he must use his judgement and in doing so will tell the employer a great deal about his judgement and his personality.

Activity

Look at the following examples taken from letters replying to a request for details in writing. What would they tell you about the applicant if you were the employer?

Examples from application letters

a

Dear Sir,

I am writting about the job in your advertisment. I have ten years experiance in buisness as well as the qualifications you want, so I would be glad if you would consider me.

Yours Sincerely

Beginnings

b

Please will you consider me for the job of accounts clerk I am afraid I don't have any formal qualifications but I do have some experience and I need the job very badly as my wife and I are expecting our first baby next month, and at the moment I am unemployed following an accident . . .

c

I noted with interest your advertisement for a Production Assistant in today's Daily Times . . .

d

Further to your advertisement for a computer operator in last week's 'Dataweek'.

e

My name is Jacqueline Matthews and I am 19. I left school last year and since then I have been working for J. G. Telford and Sons. I am very hard-working and quick with numbers so I am sure I would be able to do the job to your satisfaction . . .

f

With reference to your advertisement for a management trainee advertised in yesterday's paper I would like to apply for the position as I have a National Diploma in Business Studies and one year's experience as a sales clerk and am now taking a course leading to the HNC in Business Studies which amongst other things includes Accounting, Statistics and Production Methods all of which you mentioned in your advertisement . . .

Middles

g

I am 32 years of age, and I am currently working as a Production Control Assistant. Before this I worked as a Progress Chaser at Bellings Ltd and then I got a similar job with Selco Fittings. I am responsible for making sure that the right components are being produced at the right time, which means that I have a lot of experience of organizing and planning. I have just got married and I went to Chillingworth Comprehensive School which is on the outskirts of Manchester near Bletchton. I enjoyed art and woodwork but I was not very good at games. I have a clean driving licence and I am in good health. If you need any more information I shall obviously be happy to provide it. Also I have 5 'O' levels and would be available for interview at any time.

h

You will see from the attached curriculum vitae that I have five years' experience of various aspects of office work. In particular, my last job gave me the opportunity to gain some valuable practice interviewing and the chance to discover that I should like to specialize in personnel work.

i

I enjoyed my course very much. It was very good and we studied all the business subjects so I have the qualifications which you are asking for.

j

I am very ambitious and for a long time now I have been looking for the right job which will use my talents to the full. I am not prepared to do a monotonous or routine job and feel that perhaps the job you are advertising is the one for me.

k

I want to work for your company because I have checked up and found that you are a very successful company. You produce a wide range of products and have a good export record.

Endings
l

Thanking you in anticipation.
Yours faithfully,

m

If you consider that my qualifications are suitable I should be available for interview at any time.

n

I would be grateful if you could let me know as soon as possible as I have a lot of applications in progress at the moment.

COMMENTS ON EXAMPLES

a Far too short and uninformative in answer to a request for details in writing. This together with the poor spelling (wri*t*ing, advertis*e*ment, b*us*iness, experi*e*nce) and careless presentation would not help his application for any job which involved writing and would be likely to prejudice his chances even for a manual job unless he were the only applicant. 'Dear Sir' should be followed by 'Yours faithfully'; 'Dear Mr Smith' should be followed by 'Yours sincerely'. Note: both 'faithfully' and 'sincerely' start with small letters.

b The tone of this letter is inappropriate. It is far too humble and pleading. An application letter is not the right place to seek sympathy.

c 'Noted with interest' is a good way to make the first, rather ordinary sentence in an application letter sound a little different and attract the attention of the reader. In addition the sentence states clearly exactly which job is being applied for and where the advertisement was seen. Apart from wanting to know which job is being referred to, the employer will be interested to know which of perhaps several advertisements is attracting applicants.

d This opening contains the very common error of an incomplete sentence (see p. 389).

e No mention of which job is being applied for nor of the advertisement or publication. The employer may never have heard of J. G. Telford and Sons and even if he has he is still none the wiser about what sort of work the applicant did while she was there. The applicant also fails to give any evidence to support her assertions that she is hard-working, etc. It is not enough to state that you are sure that you can do the job; the employer needs reasons.

f One long sentence! The reader will have forgotten what the first bit of the sentence said by the time he gets to the end.

g This long paragraph, which contains far too many ideas in a confusing jumble, is not guaranteed to convince the reader that the applicant is good at organizing and planning, as he claims to be. The paragraph moves backwards and forwards in time and deals with qualifications, experience and personal details all mixed up together. Much of the information appears to be irrelevant and any sentence which starts with 'also' is likely to sound like an afterthought, which in this case it is. The applicant has obviously just picked up his pen and started writing without any attempt to group related information or plan the sequence of his letter.

h A curriculum vitae is a good way to communicate the facts about yourself in a clear easy-to-refer-to manner. Where a curriculum vitae is sent, it should be accompanied by a covering letter which does not just repeat the facts but explains and interprets them, as in this example. The employer reading this letter is likely to be impressed by the applicant's method of presentation which in turn implies a tidy, well-organized mind. The letter also allows the applicant to explain why he wants the job and how his experience relates to the requirements of the vacancy.

i Apart from possibly implying that the applicant likes studying, this letter tells the employer very little else. What does 'very good' mean and which business subjects did he study? How can the employer tell that the applicant has the right qualifications? The applicant's assurance is not enough.

j The tone of this letter is likely to put off the most tolerant of employers. It sounds arrogant and overconfident, and therefore implies that the applicant is also far too sure of himself. He sounds very demanding and unlikely to be willing to do anything he does not want to. In other words he has succeeded in reversing the traditional relationship of the employer and the applicant, leaving the employer with an uneasy feeling that *he* is being selected rather than the other way round.

k This letter also conveys an idea of overconfidence by using the words 'checked up'. While most employers would be impressed by an applicant who has taken the trouble to find out something about the company, this is not the way to communicate it. Furthermore the applicant seems to have discovered very little of apparent relevance and has merely succeeded in telling the employer what he presumably knows already.

l Just as it is easy to use a hackneyed expression to open a letter (see **d**) and leave the sentence incomplete, so the same trap awaits the unwary at the end of the letter. 'Thanking you in anticipation' has no main verb. It is therefore a phrase, not a complete sentence (see p. 389). The crime is made worse by the tone of this phrase, which either implies creeping humility or sounds oversure that the application will be successful.

m This is quite a neat ending. It hints at the possibility of an interview without sounding overconfident.

n Again this ending sounds rather too demanding. Unfortunately it is the applicant who must wait patiently for a reply because in the application process it is the employer who is in control. Furthermore, even though most employers will be fully aware that this is not one's only application, it is hardly a good idea to communicate one's desperation, nor state the truth of the situation quite so bluntly.

Now that you have had the chance to 'be the employer' you should be well aware of the reasons why some employers prefer the unstructured request for information and of what they will be looking for. You should keep this constantly in mind when writing your own application letters.

So what is the best way to present your information? We have seen from examining the application form the basic information which you must include in any application letter:

Surname	Education and
First names	training
Address	Qualifications
Telephone number (home and work, if	Employment
relevant)	experience
Marital status (married, single, divorced,	General interests
separated)	

Alternative 1: The long letter
You could write a rather long letter incorporating all this information but this method has disadvantages:

● Being written in continuous prose without headings and so

on, the essential information will be hidden and difficult for the employer to pick out.
- This method presents problems of style for the writer. It is difficult to avoid a rather monotonous catalogue of 'I did this . . . and then I did that . . . and then I did that.' Notice the number of times the word 'I' is used in the examples.

Alternative 2: The short covering letter and curriculum vitae

With this method you list all the facts on a separate sheet of paper (see example on p. 260). In effect, you invent your own application form, more or less. This list of qualifications and experience is traditionally known as a 'curriculum vitae' which literally means 'the course of one's life' and is usually headed CURRICULUM VITAE. Make sure you spell it correctly. This method of combining a businesslike list with a covering letter has the advantages of the application form without the disadvantages, and above all gives you, the applicant, the chance to show that you are neat and well organized without being prompted by the employer's application form.

Method Order: the information should be set down in the same order as the application form; personal details first, then education and experience, then other interests like spare-time activities, membership of clubs, part in school, college and community life, and so on, finishing up with names of referees.

Presentation: each piece of information should be written under appropriate headings, with subheadings and columns where necessary. The appearance should be neat and systematic and well spaced out. Don't overcrowd the page.

Style: it is not necessary to write in complete sentences, but be consistent.

Advantages
- The information set out under headings and in columns is easy to pick out.
- Providing it is set out clearly and neatly in straight lines and columns, it will convey an impression of efficiency and attention to detail.
- It will avoid the problems of style noted above.

The covering letter You will still need to include a short letter with your CV which should include

- a formal application for the position (including the job title, reference number, and source of the advertisement, e.g. the name and date of the newspaper or magazine)
- your reasons for wanting the job
- your reasons for feeling you are qualified and competent to do the job

Self-check

In connection with the last point, which of the following ways of proving competence would you find the more convincing?

'I am good at supervising people and feel sure that I would be able to manage the department successfully.'

'While in my last job, I was promoted to section head in charge of the three other clerks. This responsibility gave me the opportunity to discover the problems of managing people and to gain some experience of allocating work fairly, motivating people, and dealing quickly with problems.'

The first example is merely an assertion. The reader has no real evidence for accepting that the writer's confidence in himself as a successful supervisor is justified. However, in the second example the writer manages, without explicitly saying so, to imply that he is quite likely to be successful. He does this by (a) quoting real evidence – he was promoted in his last job, so someone must have had confidence in him; (b) revealing that he is at least aware that managing people can have problems; (c) showing that he recognizes the opportunity he was given; (d) using the word 'some' to describe his experience, which does not overstate the case and shows an appealing humility by subtly recognizing that he has still something to learn; and (e) demonstrating that he knows something of what being a supervisor involves – quite a lot packed into two sentences. Try always to justify your opinions and provide some evidence for your reasons.

Finally a covering letter provides you with the opportunity to show that you can write well, to emphasize those aspects of your experience which are particularly relevant to the job for which you are applying, and to demonstrate an understanding of and an enthusiasm for the responsibilities of the job.

To type or not to type? Probably the best advice is a combination of the two. Type the CV but handwrite the covering letter. This will allow you to present a neat businesslike approach while allowing the employer to see a sample of your handwriting. But if you can't type well, write it by hand or get someone else to type it, and if your handwriting is appalling and you can't do anything about it, then type both the CV and the letter.

Tip: once your CV is typed, get several copies made. Then each time you apply for a job, all you have to do is compose an appropriate covering letter and attach a copy of your CV. This will reduce the time spent on applications and also the tedium caused by having to do the same thing over and over again.

Review

Indicate whether each of the following is true or false.

1 The first stage in looking for a job involves replying to as many advertisements as possible.

2 In replying to newspaper advertisements, promptness is a key factor.

3 You should not 'read between the lines' when looking at advertisements.

4 You should take as much care with a telephone call asking for an application form, as with writing a complete application letter.

5 If you can't think of anything to say under the heading 'Other relevant information' or 'Supporting statement' on an application form, you should leave it blank.

6 Instead of two separate sheets, it is better to combine all the factual information in your letter of application. It is easier to write and the employer does not have so much to read.

7 When you are applying for an office-type job, you

CURRICULUM VITAE

Name: Scott Ashley NASH

Address: 34 Pike Street, Handsworth, Birmingham BM10 43W

Tel. No.   (0981) 307062 – Home   (0981) 234937 – Work

Age: 31   Date of Birth: 29 August 1950

Married with two children: boy (8) girl (1)

EDUCATION

Fairlawn Comprehensive School, Bristol	Sept. 1961 – July 1966
Brindley Technical College, Bristol	Sept. 1968 – June 1970
Lanchester Polytechnic (part-time)	Nov. 1970 – July 1972

QUALIFICATIONS

*C.S.E.	Maths, English, Physics, Technical Drawing, Woodwork, Geography	1966
*G.C.E.'O' Level	Technical Drawing	1966
H.N.C.	Mechanical Engineering	1970

EXPERIENCE

Technician Apprentice	Sealco Ltd	Coventry	1970 – 1974
Junior Welding Engineer	Sealco Ltd	Wolverhampton	1974 – 1975
Welding Engineer	Worldwide Engineering Services Ltd	London	1975 – 1979
Welding Superintendent	Minichip Modules Ltd	Birmingham	1979 – 1981

Experienced in engineering work planning, troubleshooting, quality control, commissioning of new plant including EBW and friction welding, as well as argon arc and electric and gas welding. Recent direct experience of man management.

OTHER ACTIVITIES

Pianist with local jazz group.
Plays regular club football.

REFEREES

Mr B.J. Cameron	Mr James McKechnie	Mr John Patel
Personnel Manager	Welding Engineer	Company Director
Minichip Modules Ltd	Sealco Ltd	38 Pike Street
6-9 Brigstock Road	14 Ryecroft Street	Handsworth
Birmingham BM3 9QZ	Coventry CY6 1DS	Birmingham BM10 4EW

September 1981

* Note: the applicant whose curriculum vitae is shown has not given his CSE and 'O' level grades. At his age and with other experience behind him, these grades cease to be very significant. However, if you are looking for your first job after school or college, or if you are applying for a course of study, it is advisable to show the grades you obtained, so that an employer or college can see which CSEs are equivalent to 'O' level and can distinguish 'O' level passes from failures.

should omit from the CV any experience which involved manual work, since it is irrelevant.

8 If the traditional headings like 'Education' or 'Qualifications' in CVs seem too general to indicate the particular relevance of your education and qualifications to the job you are seeking, you should produce your own headings as appropriate.

9 The covering letter represents the chance to express in good fluent prose what is contained in note form in the CV.

10 Typical errors made by applicants include: copying a letter written by some other person; using the present employer's stationery to write the application letter; and making negative remarks about the present employer.

ANSWERS

1 False. The first stage in applying for a job is deciding what sort of a person you are and what sort of a job would suit you. The second stage involves finding the vacancies and discovering exactly what the advertisers are looking for. Only then should you think about actually replying to advertisements.

2 True. More people will see newspaper advertisements (especially those in national newspapers) than those publicized anywhere else, so there are likely to be more applicants. The first letters received may get more careful attention. Furthermore, the quality of promptness is a personal virtue that employers may consider a business virtue.

3 False. Careful consideration of the style of the advertisement, the tone of the wording, what is omitted and what is included can often tell you more about what the company wants, than the obvious statements of qualifications and experience required.

4 True. Any contact you have with the prospective employer, however informal, can help or hinder your application, and therefore deserves thought and preparation.

5 False. You *must* think of something to say. Most employers will give you a black mark if you cannot write a short coherent

statement in this section and seem to be content to limit your application to the straightforward factual questions in the rest of the form.

6 False. Two sheets are preferred – one that gives the facts in easy-to-locate summary form (the curriculum vitae) and another that states clearly which job is being applied for, interprets the CV information, and gives reasons for applying (the covering letter). This method is actually easier for you. It avoids problems of style and, if you are applying for lots of similar jobs, it allows you to reproduce copies of the facts for use as and when you need them.

7 False. The duties and attributes required for certain manual jobs may be required also for the office-type jobs you are seeking. For example, if you have worked in a shop-floor manual job this may provide evidence of such qualities as initiative, reliability, cooperativeness and punctuality, as well as a willingness to 'dirty your hands', mix well with all sorts of people, or 'try anything once'. Even a temporary or holiday job may display evidence of wanting to gain experience, earn your own living or provide the means of achieving some other goal, all qualities which would count in your favour.

8 True. If two headings 'General education' and 'Business education', or 'Technical qualifications' and 'Other qualifications', allow you to link some of your qualifications and experience more closely to the job you are seeking, then you should use whichever headings you feel are appropriate.

9 False. While the covering letter does serve the invaluable purpose of showing how well you can express yourself, it should never merely repeat the facts in the CV. It represents a chance to expand on some of the bare facts, draw out and pull together those that are significant, emphasize what responsibilities and opportunities certain jobs have given you, explain why you want the job. Above all, in doing all this you should be able to *imply* those qualities which you possess and recognize as significant for the job.

10 True. Copying someone else's letter will at best cause you to commit inadvertent inaccuracies (between the CV and the letter, for example) and at worst will cause you to be 'caught

out' if you do get an interview. As for using your present employer's stationery or making negative comments about him – both would reveal a disloyalty, a lack of good manners and an underhandedness, undesirable qualities in themselves but hardly likely to recommend you as a prospective employee. Other common errors made by applicants which should be avoided are:

Writing as if the letter were an autobiography
Overworking 'I', 'me', and 'my'
Sounding unduly humble
Begging or pleading
Asking for sympathy
Sounding too flippant or casual
Seeming to lecture the reader
Seeming to brag about accomplishments
Making assertions about your qualities and qualifications without giving evidence to support the statement
Writing about educational qualifications as if they were the only things needed
Using vague, general terms
Repeating instead of interpreting CV information
Using colloquial or hackneyed expressions

Activity

Try replying to the first advertisement on p. 241.

Now try writing a curriculum vitae and covering letter which would be suitable for the company in the second advertisement.

Compare the two letters. Are there any differences? If so, what?

How did you convey the impression that you were capable of fitting into an old-established city firm, for the first letter, and young and ambitious, eager to join the rapidly expanding second company?

11 | Writing reports

by Schulz

Panel 1: THIS IS MY REPORT... I SAT UP ALL NIGHT WORKING ON IT

Panel 2: WELL, ACTUALLY, I DIDN'T SIT UP ALL NIGHT WORKING ON IT...

Panel 3: WHAT I DID WAS, I SAT UP ALL NIGHT WORRYING ABOUT IT

Panel 4: THERE'S A BIG DIFFERENCE!

'Write a report' – the very sound fills people with horror. Reports seem to be the things people dread writing more than anything else. If you feel like this, then you are in good company.

This chapter will introduce you to the structure of a report and the essential elements of any report long or short. It will also provide you with a step-by-step guide to preparing and writing reports and some tips on how to cope with the mechanics of producing the final document. Even if you feel that it is unlikely you will need to write a report as such in the very near future you should still find the following pages useful, since the structure of a good report is very similar to the structure of any fairly long piece of writing – an essay, or an article, for example; reports come in many shapes and sizes as we shall see.

But first, let's go back to the dread and horror which writing a report seems to produce for even the most capable writers.

Self-check

Write down your reactions to being asked to write a report? What feeling do you experience at the very idea? What exactly is it about reports which engenders this feeling?

Perhaps it is because reports seem less common forms of communication. Writing letters, going to meetings, talking to people in all sorts of informal situations are more common activities for most people, and therefore seem less frightening. We don't have to write reports very often and so when we do have to, we aren't very practised at it and we don't know how to go about it.

Perhaps another reason for dislike of report writing is that 'reports' seem to be so large and unmanageable. We conjure up a vision of many sheets of closely printed words in a rather official looking binder and the prospect of producing something like that seems very daunting. But let's look at the facts.

First of all we have discovered that even to perform the apparently simple communication activities efficiently and effectively we need to do a lot more thinking and planning than we realized.

Secondly, the principles we have explored in relation to communication in general and writing in particular apply in exactly the same way to writing a report as they do to letter writing. Armed with those principles and techniques you should be in a position now to write a very effective report, even if there are a few special techniques to bear in mind which you may not yet be aware of and which this chapter is designed to cover.

Thirdly, the problem of size: not all reports are long, complicated affairs as we shall see. Without realizing it, you probably produce reports on all sorts of things in the course of a day, because reports come in countless shapes and sizes. Furthermore, the long, complicated report has basically the same elements as the short simple report – it is just a question of scale, and coping with a large-scale project is only a question of disciplining yourself to stick to the steps in the procedure and above all having the courage to start.

What is a report?

A report is a written communication of information or advice, from a person who has collected and studied the facts, to a person who has asked for the report because he needs it for a specific purpose. Often the ultimate function of a report is to provide a basis for decision and action.

> *Self-check*
>
> Using this definition of a report, think back over the last

|| week and make a list of all the 'reports' that you have produced, or helped to produce.

If you have accepted the wider implications of this definition, you will have realized that you have produced 'reports' on all sorts of things during the week. For example:

- a report on a film for someone who was deciding whether to see that particular film or not
- a report of what happened in a lecture or meeting for someone who didn't attend
- a report of your knowledge of the facts or of your opinions on a particular situation or issue at work for your boss to help him in arriving at a decision, or taking some action or other
- a report of some figures or facts on a form which when completed goes elsewhere in the organization to enable someone else to take action or make a decision
- a report in the form of a letter or memo telling someone what you know about something, or giving them advice about what to do

In other words, there are probably as many different types of reports – written, oral and visual – as there are occasions which call for a report, from a casual conversation to a two-inch-thick government report which would act as a good door-stopper.

Unsolicited reports

Strictly speaking the name 'report' is only given to those documents which are commissioned by someone else other than the writer. When an individual chooses on his own initiative to comment on an aspect of the business – make a suggestion or put forward new proposals – the document used is usually termed a 'memorandum'. The word is always written in full (not abbreviated to 'memo') when used in this sense, and is usually written across the top of the first page of the document, e.g.

MEMORANDUM

To:
From:
Subject:
Date:

Types of reports

Reports can be transmitted in the form of:

- conversations
- demonstrations
- letters
- memos
- fill-in forms
- many-page documents

They can be classified according to:

- length (short/long)
- tone (informal/semi-formal/formal)
- subject matter (engineering/financial/marketing/accident)
- timing (daily/weekly/monthly; interim/progress/final)
- importance (routine/special/urgent)
- style (narrative/descriptive/expository/pictorial/statistical)
- distribution (inter-office/company/public/private)

It follows then that the report whatever form it takes must always be planned and communicated in a way which suits the receiver (reader or listener) and his purpose. Consequently some reports will require very little planning, others will require more; some reports will be spoken, others written; some will be short, others will be longer.

Since this chapter is intended to encourage you to tackle what may seem to be the more difficult report – the written report – we will concentrate on this viewpoint, but you might like occasionally to consider how the principles and techniques suggested in this chapter can apply, with appropriate modification, to any reporting.

Essentials of a good report

- The report should be unified. It should contain nothing that the reader does not need, nothing that is off the subject.
- It should be complete. It should exclude nothing that the reader *does* need.
- All the information should be accurate and all the reasoning from the facts must be valid.

- It should present the subject matter according to a plan based on a logical analysis and classification of the material.
- The manner of presentation should make the plan clear, so that the reader is never in doubt as to where he is in the report and why he is there.
- The report should be written in a simple, concise style that is easy to read and impossible to misunderstand.
- The report should be readily intelligible to all who are likely to read it even though they may not be specially versed in the technical and other details of the subject.

Terms of reference

It is essential to make sure when you are asked to write a report that you know exactly what you are supposed to be covering and why. These instructions, often called 'terms of reference', should define the scope and limitations of your investigation. They should be clear and agreed before you start as they will provide you with your *public objective* and guide you in carrying out your investigation and writing your report. Frequently, as in the case of committee inquiries, the terms of reference are quoted at the beginning of the report. If you are given formal written instructions which, as they stand, are suitably worded, they can be written into your introduction. If your instructions are clear but rather long winded you may have to make them more concise before including them in your report.

Example of formal terms of reference (the terms of reference of the Robbins Committee on Higher Education in 1960):

> To review the pattern of full-time higher education in Great Britain and in the light of national needs and resources to advise Her Majesty's Government on what principles its long-term development should be based. In particular, to advise, in the light of these principles, whether there should be any changes in that pattern, whether any new types of institution are desirable and whether any modifications should be made in the present arrangements for planning and coordinating the development of the various types of institution.

It is also useful to refer to the person or body who commissioned the report – the *authority*. In its simplest form this is often

expressed by the words 'On the instruction of'. In more important reports, typical authorizations may be letters of authorization, or resolutions of committees.

Fundamental structure

Any report has three main 'parts' which must include four
(sometimes five) essential elements:

Parts	*Elements*
Introduction	{ Terms of reference or objective Procedure
Body of the report	Findings
Terminal section	{ Conclusions (Recommendations if asked for)

This structure must be evident in any report, however short. A
longer report might contain in addition to these essential elements what might be called 'accessories', as we shall see.

> *Self-check*
>
> List what you think the introduction of a report should
> include.

The introduction

The function of the introduction is to prepare the reader for the
report proper – the body of the report. The structure generally
follows a standard plan which has been found in practice to be
the best way of avoiding incoherent, badly proportioned and
wrongly emphasized openings:

(a) a clear unambiguous statement of the real subject
(b) an indication of the purpose, together with any background
     information necessary to the clear understanding of that
     purpose
(c) a brief description of the methods used to obtain the
     information
(d) a summary of the conclusions, findings and recommen-
     dations, etc. in their briefest form

(e)   an announcement of the plan on which the body of the
      report is arranged

Within this structure the introduction should have these
characteristics:

(a)   it should be as brief as is consistent with clarity
(b)   it should correctly focus the reader's attention on your real
      theme and purpose
(c)   it should harmonize with what follows, i.e. it should prom-
      ise nothing that is not done later in the report and it should
      not appear in any way inconsistent with the terminal
      section

The body of the report

The body of the report is the report proper, i.e. the several
sections that lie between the introduction and the terminal
section. In it are set out all the facts (e.g. the character of the
investigation, a detailed explanation of the methodology used,
the procedure followed, the results obtained), and an analysis of
these facts leading to such conclusions and recommendations as
may appear to be warranted.

The terminal section

The function of the terminal section is to present briefly, clearly
and finally the conclusions reached, the recommendations to be
made, or whatever is the logical conclusion of the matter in
hand. The characteristics of a good terminal section are:

(a)   it introduces nothing new
(b)   it harmonizes with the introduction and with the body of
      the report
(c)   it leaves the reader with the final impression that you want
      to make

Making the structure clear

Good arrangement alone is not sufficient. The subject matter is
often heavy going when compared with other kinds of reading,

and the inherent design must be made immediately apparent to the reader. There are two main ways of helping to make the structure clear:

Sectional headings

Headings are an aid to the eye and hence to the understanding. There is no one right system and you may often be forced to follow the system adopted in your organization or department, but here are some principles to guide you.

- The typography and spacing of the heading should reflect the inherent order of the report.
- Fussiness should be avoided: headings should help, not irritate, the reader.
- The text should remain independent of the headings. They are additional to, not part of, the text.
- Headings are useless if they are not illuminating and self-explanatory.
- They should consist of words or phrases, never of sentences.

HEADINGS IN TYPEWRITTEN REPORTS
_____

CAPITAL LETTERS UNDERLINED

CAPITAL LETTERS UNDERLINED

First line should be indented 5 spaces

Small letters underlined

First line should be indented 5 spaces

Small letters underlined, with a full-stop. The text begins immediately after it on the same line.

These are the four main methods of indicating a heading. However, there are other variations, e.g.

Spaced Headings

These are not underlined, but stand out because there is a wider space both above and below them. NB However, try to limit the number of different levels of headings, or it will become confusing for the reader.
_____

Coherence The aim of all paragraphing and sectionalizing is to separate and yet at the same time to bind together the elements of the whole. A logical arrangement is the primary means to coherence. But it is often necessary to help the reader to pass smoothly from section to section by the use of *linking words and phrases* and *reference back and forth*.

Similar in purpose, on a larger scale are 'functional' paragraphs. These are short paragraphs which do not add information but introduce, conclude and effect transition between sections.

Reference numbering

Numbering of headings is a matter of taste. If the appearance of the headings is clear enough, then numbering is not necessary. However, some writers prefer the level of importance of the headings to be reinforced by a numbering system which repeats the visual effect of the varied headings. It is based on an *alternation of numbers and letters* in descending order of importance:

I, II, III; A, B, C; 1, 2, 3; (a), (b), (c); etc.

Similar is the so-called 'decimal' system:

1.
   1.1
   1.2
2.
   2.1
   2.2
      2.2.1
      2.2.2

This system can be particularly useful where the report is to be discussed at meetings. Reference to individual sections is made easier by the decimal system, e.g. 'point 3.2.1' is easier to find quickly than 'point 1 in subsection B of section III'.

However, if your plan is sound and the headings clear, an alternative system which aids ready reference is simply to *number each paragraph sequentially* throughout the report, whether it forms part of a major or minor section, e.g. '1, 2, 3, 4, 5 . . . 25', etc.

For more detailed guidance on sectioning and numbering, see Chapter 11 of *What Do You Mean, 'Communication'?*.

Self-check

What elements should be included in a report, however short, and in whatever form?

What would be the minimum number of sections required?

To check your answers, see the letter report reproduced on p. 274.

Format of reports

Reports, as we have seen, can come in a variety of formats, but providing that the report does not have to be written on to a form, or to a particular style, you will have a choice of layout.

Letter/memo format

Perhaps the simplest form of short report is the one written in the form of a letter or memo. The essential elements are there though they are not headed as such (see the letter report on p. 274).

Schematic format

This report could have been presented as a short separate report with a covering letter. The report would use sections and headings but would still contain the essential elements.

Activity

Using the information contained in the 'letter report' write a short report using 'schematic format', i.e. sections and headings.

Now compare your report with the example on pp. 275–6.

The Managing Director,
Bolton and Foster Ltd,
31 Merrydown Lane,
BRISTOL BS17 2BT

Dear Sir,

① Introduction

In accordance with the instructions of the Board
I have visited the Coldharbour Trading Estate
with a view to the Company's acquiring a site
for a factory there, and now have pleasure in
submitting my provisional report.

← Terms of reference
← Procedure
Subject

② Body of the report

The Trading Estate is a government-sponsored
enterprise situated about ten miles from the
port of Speymouth, with which it has excellent
road communication. Water, light and power
supplies on the estate are adequate and the
rate charges compare favourably with those in
similar industrial areas elsewhere in the
country.

The particular site offered to the Company is
well drained, is adjacent to the main road
which passes through the estate, and within
$\frac{1}{2}$ mile of the M94.

I have interviewed a number of building contractors in the district and there would appear
to be no difficulty in getting the building
work carried out locally. The necessary planning permission should be readily obtainable
since the Government have scheduled this as a
'development area'.

Supplies of skilled and semi-skilled labour
are fairly plentiful and the local office of
the Department of Employment welcomes the
establishment of a factory, employing 200 men
and 400 women. It would, however, be necessary for the Company to bring in a number of
skilled operatives and technicians. The
accommodation of these key-workers would
present a serious problem, as the housing
shortage in the area remains acute. It would
be possible to build temporary hostel accommodation on a site available near the factory,
as an interim solution to this problem.

Findings in
paragraphs

③ Terminal section

Despite this problem, the site at Coldharbour
in all other respects appears to suit the
Company's requirements ideally, and in my
opinion, the Company should accept the site
and proceed with the building of the factory
without delay.

Conclusions

Recommendations

Yours faithfully,

J. Longman
Development Manager.

REPORT ON PROPOSED NEW FACTORY SITE

I. TERMS OF REFERENCE

In accordance with the instructions of the board, to report on the possibility of acquiring a site for a new factory on the Coldharbour Trading Estate and make recommendations as appropriate.

II. PROCEDURE

This report was compiled following a visit to the Coldharbour Trading Estate and interviews with the Estate Manager, local building firms and the local office of the Department of Employment.

III. COLDHARBOUR TRADING ESTATE

A. Location and Facilities

The trading estate is a government-sponsored enterprise situated ten miles from the port of Speymouth, with which it has excellent road communication. Water, light and power supplies on the estate are adequate and the rate charges compare favourably with those in similar industrial areas eleswhere in the country.

B. Proposed Site

The particular site offered to the Company is well drained, is adjacent to the main road which passes through the Estate, and within ½ mile of the M94.

C. Building and Planning Permission

1. There would appear to be no difficulty in getting the building work carried out locally.

2. The necessary planning permission should be readily obtainable since the Government have scheduled this as a "development area".

D. Labour

1. Skilled and Semi-Skilled

Supplies of skilled and semi-skilled labour are fairly plentiful and the local office of the Department of Employment welcomes the establishment of a factory employing 200 men and 400 women.

2. Skilled/Technician Labour

It would be necessary for the Company
to bring in a number of skilled operatives and technicians.

3. Accommodation

The accommodation of these key-
workers would present a serious
problem, as the housing shortage in
the area remains acute. It would be
possible to build temporary hostel
accommodation on a site available
near the factory, as an interim solution to this problem.

IV. CONCLUSIONS

The site has:

- good access to roads and motorways
- adequate facilities
- competitive rate charges
- local supply of skilled and semi-skilled
  labour
- ready availability of building contractors
- no planning problems

Despite the problem of accommodation, the site
appears to suit the Company's requirements in
all other respects.

V. RECOMMENDATIONS

That the Company accept the site and proceed
with the building of the factory without
delay.

Signed: *J. Longman.*

Development
Manager

Date: 9 March 19..

You may feel that this is a case of taking a mallet to crack a hazelnut, but it does demonstrate how the same information can be presented in different formats. Schematic format does help the reader to find the information he needs at a glance but, of course, the headings should not normally outweigh the subject matter (as perhaps they do in this case).

Mixed format

Of course, a compromise between these two formats might be a letter, but with a few simple headings for the body of the letter/ report: 'Trading estate', 'Proposed site', 'Labour', etc. This is called 'mixed format' and is very common in practice, since it follows good practice for setting out a letter of any length, i.e. subheadings if they are helpful.

Long formal reports

A typical structure of a long formal report might look like this, but bear in mind that you may modify and adapt the following components to virtually any type or length of report.

a *Preliminaries*
 1 Title page
 2 Letters of authorization, transmittal and approval (terms of reference)
 3 Table of contents
 4 List of tables and figures (if appropriate)
 5 Foreword/preface
 6 Acknowledgements
 7 Synopsis (or abstract)

b *Main report*
 1 Introduction
 2 Findings and discussion
 3 Conclusions (and, when appropriate, recommendations)

c *Supplements*
 1 References and bibliography
 2 Appendices
 3 Index

Preliminaries

The title page The title page is the reader's first contact with the report and its layout is worth taking some trouble over.

It answers questions in the mind of someone who might be going through a pile of reports looking for a particular one and those questions would probably be:

What is it about?	(Subject of report)
Who wrote it?	(Author(s))
For whom?	(Name of person or group for whom it was prepared)
From where?	(Full postal address of organization on whose behalf it was written)
When?	(Date, including month, when report was completed)

An example of a title page is given opposite. Although the title should be short enough to be read almost at a glance, it should still be definite. *The title should be centred in the middle of the page.* If the title runs into two or more lines, significant words should be grouped together in centred lines. The end of a line should never break a significant group of important words. Avoid:

> The Incidence of Bark
>   Infestation in Apple
>   Trees in the Channel
>   Islands

Better:

> The Incidence of Bark Infestation
>   in Apple Trees
>   in the Channel Islands

Letters of authorization, transmittal and approval These are normally only required for a very formal report being presented to or written within a public body, and may often be excluded from the report and presented separately.

In business reports the authorization and instructions are usually run together in summary form under a title such as 'Terms of reference', as we have seen.

Bolton and Foster Limited

Report on Proposed New Factory Site

Coldharbour Trading Estate

For: The Board of Directors,   By: John Longman, M.Sc.
      Bolton and Foster Ltd,   Development Manager
      3 Merrydown Lane,
      BRISTOL BS17 2BT.

      Tel. No: Bristol 732210   9 March 19..

Table of contents This not only aids reference, and makes possible selective reading by those who are interested in only parts of the report, but by bringing all the headings and subheadings together it shows even more clearly the logical structure of the report. A few moments' study of the contents page by the reader helps rapid understanding, provided the layout really does show the structure clearly, and if the titles and subtitles are concise and explanatory and identical with those used in the text. For an example, look at the Table of Contents of this book.

It should also include the page numbers and should therefore be typed last of all, when the final page numbers are known.

List of tables and figures This list not only aids the reader, but also helps to provide a valuable check against inaccurate collating (assembly) before stapling or binding.

Foreword or preface This may be found in a large general report perhaps issued for a whole profession or for the general public rather than a particular body. It briefly explains why the writer or his employers wanted to carry out the investigation or to write a report about it, or to explain why the report was produced in the way it was.

Acknowledgements It is customary to thank by name those who have helped in the investigation and compiling of the report, both within your own organization and in other organizations. This does not mean listing every single person who had anything to do with it, only those of particular significance: 'The Managing Director, Mr . . . , and his staff', 'my colleagues and in particular Mr . . . and Miss . . .'.

Where money has been provided from outside funds, this must be mentioned but without any indication of the actual sums involved. Help by secretarial staff and technicians should equally be mentioned.

Synopsis or abstract The synopsis or abstract is a highly compressed paragraph summarizing the purpose of the report and the general character of its conclusions or recommendations. Its function is to give the busy reader quickly a good idea of what he may expect to find in the report even before he has read the probably much longer introduction. The synopsis has not been a common feature of reports in industry in this country, but its wider use is recommended. Where a synopsis is not included its function is often fulfilled by means of placing the conclusions and recommendations sections early on in the report instead of at the end – their more usual position.

For guidance on summary-writing look at the section on 'Summarizing' in *What Do You Mean, 'Communication'?* or have a look at the diagram on p. 345 of this book.

Supplements

References and bibliography If you have used other people's work or writing to compile your report, you should acknowledge this in the text and then list the references at the back of the report.

You should strictly observe these five rules:

- *All items which are not your own original work should be clearly shown as such.* This should prevent allegations of plagiarism (copying without acknowledgement).
- *Put any quotation within quotation marks.* Even a single word might have to be treated in this way if it expressed a major aspect of another writer's opinion.
- *Every reference in the text and illustrations to other work should appear in the list of references.*
- *Every item in the list of references must be referred to in the text (or a figure).* It is good practice for the text to make some mention of any reference quoted or a figure as a source of data.
- *Every figure and photographic plate must be referred to in the text.*

Normally the numbering of references should correspond to the order of mention in the text and should give the author, the title of the book or work, the publisher and the date of publication. Example:

Gowers, Sir Ernest, *Complete Plain Words* (Pelican edn, Penguin Books 1973).

A *bibliography* is optional. It provides a guide to suitable background reading around the subject of the report.

Appendices An appendix (plural – appendices) should be used whenever statistical data or lengthy quoted material (e.g. passages from books, other reports, letters) would congest the main text, hold up the argument or otherwise hinder the reader. The main text itself must make quite clear the exact part played by the information given in the appendix. It is not sufficient to say simply 'see Appendix A', and hope that all will be clear from a first glance at the appendix. If an appendix is constantly referred to at many places in the text, it could be made to open out for easy reference. Mounted photographs or other flat examples should be placed in a pocket of the back cover.

Index An index is really only necessary for very long detailed reports. Key topics are listed alphabetically providing easy reference for the busy reader who wants to find a particular point. See the index of this book for an example.

Report writing method

We have already explored in some detail the preparation and planning stages of creating any message, be it a letter, an essay, a report or a talk and so on. If you are actually in the throes of tackling a report now, you might like to refer to Chapters 10 and 11 in *What Do You Mean, 'Communication'?* for detailed guidance on how to prepare and plan a message. However, it might be useful to have a checklist for quick reference.

> *Self-check*
>
> Before reading on, try designing your own checklist or points to remember under these four headings:
> *Stage 1* Assembling the material.
> *Stage 2* Planning the report.
> *Stage 3* Writing the first draft.
> *Stage 4* Editing the report (criticisms and review of first draft).

Use this chapter as a basis but you may also like to skim back through Chapters 10, 11, 12, 13 (and 14?) of *What Do You Mean, 'Communication'?*.

Write the checklist for stages 1, 2 and 3 in the form of points to remember and stage 4 in the form of questions to ask about your first draft.

Assembling the material (period of synthesis)

1 Collect all relevant material in the form of notes, documents, etc.
2 Check details:
   - determine the relative value of details
   - eliminate the obviously irrelevant
   - add details that are lacking
3 Consider the purpose of the report:
   - who will read it?
   - why does he want it?
   - what does he require of it?
   - how will he use it?
4 Draft a 'thesis sentence' which states your main objectives and the most important point of emphasis.

Planning the report (period of analysis and classification)

1 List on cards or pieces of paper, one for each item, the topics that it appears from the study of your material you will have to cover.
2 Check these topics against your objective or 'thesis sentence', paying particular attention to the purpose and the limitations of your report.
3 Look for the natural main divisions of your whole subject, or for some principle of division from which they can be derived.
4 Arrange your topic cards under these main groupings (the floor is a good place to work at this stage). The main groupings will be the main sections in your finished report.
5 Organize the material within each of these main groupings in a logical order – possibly into second order and even third order grouping.

6 Arrange these main organized groups in the best logical and psychological sequence.
7 Draft on a separate sheet of paper a working plan – this will form the basis of your table of contents. Use all the devices of lettering and spacing, to indicate what are main and what are subordinate and 'sub-subordinate' headings.
8 Decide which areas of your report may need visual aids. (For guidance on the use of visual aids and the visual presentation of information see Chapters 8 and 13.)

Writing the first draft

This is the period in which the first draft is written. Forget that blank white sheet of paper – start writing! If you are really 'hung up' about starting, make yourself write something – anything – it doesn't matter at this stage and it will get you going.

Produce the first draft as quickly as possible, the whole or at least the whole of one section at one sitting. Don't worry about style or expression or about the details of construction. Leave these until the final critical stage.

Ideally this first draft, whether handwritten or typed, should be laid out in double spacing on one side only of the paper. It is essential to leave plenty of room for such things as your after-thoughts, comments for the typist and editorial corrections for later reproduction.

1 *Write the introduction*
• State the subject; stress its value, or other important features to arouse your reader's interest.
• Indicate the purpose of the report, with any explanatory background information which may be necessary.
• Summarize briefly the results or findings, the conclusions and recommendations.
• Announce the plan of the report (not necessary in a short report).

Note: some people prefer to write the introduction *after* they have written the body of the report and the terminal section. Even though it will appear first in the report it is often easier to write it when you know what the report has covered.

But there is a danger in doing this, of twisting your report away from your real purpose and then having to modify your objective. This may be justified but it will depend on your terms of reference, so at least be aware of the danger.

2 *Write the body of the report*
- Describe the sources and methods of your investigation.
- Explain what procedures you followed.
- Analyse and interpret the results and indicate the inferences to be drawn from them.

3 *Write the terminal section*
- Summarize the discussion, drawing out the main points of the report and presenting a considered judgement of them. Only draw conclusions which are justified by the evidence and the facts contained in the body.
- Make recommendations based on your discussion and conclusions.
- Don't introduce any new material or line of argument.
- Close with emphasis on the final impression you want to leave with your reader.

Now if your report is a long, detailed one prepare the 'accessories'.

4 *Write the synopsis or abstract*
- Summarize the entire report into a substantial paragraph.
- Check it against your 'thesis sentence' to see that you have adhered strictly to your original conception and intention.
- Check it against your introduction.

5 *Prepare the table of contents, appendices, etc. as appropriate.*
Now leave the report for a day or two and then come back to it to criticize it ruthlessly and objectively.

Editing the report

1 *Take a general look at your draft as a whole*
  Is the design of the report obvious?

Is your system of headings consistent with your purpose?
Are there any causes of confusion?
Is the balance and proportion of the facts appropriate?

2 *Consider the title, table of contents, introduction and conclusion in relation to one another*
Do they harmonize and agree with one another?
Do your headings agree with your table of contents?
Have you carried out your working plan?
Have you emphasized the correct points?
Have you stated your subject, purpose and plan?

3 *Examine the text*
Have you provided clear transitions from one topic/section to another?
Are paragraphs too long? Too short?
Is the sentence structure of *every* sentence clear and grammatical?
Is the average sentence length reasonably short?
Is the choice of words effective? Too many long words? Unnecessary technical terms?
Are there any spelling or punctuation errors?

4 *Read the text aloud to yourself or, even better, to someone else*
Does it read easily and smoothly?
Can your listener follow you?
Are there any 'echo' effects – repeated words, repeated ideas which are unnecessary?
Have you left anything out? Or failed to mention something early enough to ensure understanding?

5 *Check your visual aids*
Does each convey its message clearly enough?
Have you linked illustrations with the text clearly enough?
Have you taken advantage of visual aids to avoid long-winded explanations?
Have you given each visual aid a caption or title?
Are the captions precise and informative?

For guidance on visual communication and the use of visual aids look at Chapters 8 and 13.

6 *Finally, and if possible, get someone qualified to give constructive criticism, to look through the report.*

Change anything that needs changing – your reputation is at stake!

Producing your report

Whether your report is to be printed or not, it will have to be typed and you should always allow yourself plenty of time from the moment when your final draft is completed to the moment when your report is required, to allow for typing, proof-reading and correcting.

Decide how many copies of your report you will need and how you will produce them. Look at the table below for guidance on the advantages and disadvantages of the different methods.

COMPARISON CHART OF DUPLICATING, PHOTOCOPYING AND PRINTING

	Advantages	Disadvantages	Cost
Carbons	Ready immediately	Poor appearance especially after first two or three copies	Very cheap
Typed Banda	Banda master is easy to type Coloured masters can be used to create different effects	Appearance – not very professional at all	Cheapest method up to about 10 copies
Photocopying	Copies are reproduced quickly, cleanly and accurately Easy to correct	Appearance generally very good but depends on quality of original	Expensive but gets slightly cheaper on a long run

Typed stencils	Cut well, stencils produce copies which are legible, clear and can look as good as photocopies or printing especially if 'electronic stencils' are used	Not popular with typists Badly cut stencils produce messy illegible copies Good stencils are difficult to produce and difficult to correct	Relatively cheap after about 10 copies Good for large numbers of short documents
Offset-litho printing	Clean and professional-looking copies produced from any original	Appearance depends on quality of original	Cheapest method after about 10 copies Suitable for large numbers of long documents
Typeset printing	The most professional appearance Almost any design possible (only worth considering in exceptional cases – seek advice from a printer)	Reproduction time much slower	Expensive

Typewritten and carbon copies

Always submit the top copy of a report, not a carbon. If there are any mistakes which have slipped through the process such as corrections, alterations or insertions, these should be made very neatly in ink. It is better to submit a report with one or two handwritten alterations than to risk giving offence by leaving spelling and other mistakes uncorrected. However, with the aid of Tippex or Snopake, a white fluid which can be painted over handwritten and typed letters, it is possible to make these alterations so that that they do not spoil the overall appearance

Typing and printing

There is a difference between the repertoire of a printer and that of a typist.

The print compositor can choose between different shapes, weights and sizes of type (called 'founts'). You can show headings and emphasis by means of bold lettering (bold face), capital letters (upper case), small letters (lower case) as used for these words, small capitals (capitals of the same height as the normal a, e, i, o, u of lower case, sloping letters (italics) and so on.

By comparison, the typewriter is limited but since all reports have to be typed at one stage or another the following comments are mainly concerned with what is possible on general typewriters. However, many modern electric typewriters have a changeable type-face, which gives you more of a range to choose from than used to be the case.

Talk to the typist (and the printer, if appropriate) before you complete your final draft so that you can design the headings and layout in the light of all the possibilities and limitations. The typists will also explain how you should indicate your special requests without confusing them with the text.

Overall spacing and appearance

Most typewriters (apart from those with a 'golfball' changeable typeface facility) are limited to either Pica size – ten letters to the inch – or Elite size – twelve letters to the inch, and have spacing ability to allow three, four or six lines to the inch. See the diagram on p. 290 for examples of the two type sizes.

Single spacing is not normally used for reports as it is hard to read.

Conclusion Line-and-a-half (Pica) or double (Elite) spacing is better for theses or projects which have to be marked as it looks good but leaves room for examiners to insert notes, comments, corrections, etc. Line-and-a-half spacing is probably the best compromise for reports.

Correcting the typed draft

Check with your typist what symbols she would prefer you to use to indicate corrections. The following list represents a suggested selection, but *Symbols for Proof Correction* (HMSO Code 10-16-0) should always be used for making amendments on work which is to be printed.

The marginal mark usually goes in the *nearest* margin. Make all corrections very clearly.

These three lines are typed with double spacing in Pica size type.

These three lines are typed with double spacing in Pica size type.

These three lines are typed with double spacing in Pica size type.

This is line-and-a-half spacing in Pica size type.

These three lines are typed with single spacing in Pica size type.
These three lines are typed with single spacing in Pica size type.
These three lines are typed with single spacing in Pica size type.

Because Elite type has 12 letters to the inch, the letters are smaller

and therefore do not look very good with this double spacing, as the

type and space are not in good proportion.

This line-and-a-half spacing is probably the best for Elite type, although

Elite should be avoided for theses and academic projects or other lengthy

work, as it is more tiring to read for long periods even with wider line spacing.

Elite type single spaced gets many words into a small space, but looks poor.

Examples of two type sizes and different spacing effects

Review

1 What is an unsolicited report usually called?
2 What are the main elements of any report?
3 What is the minimum number of sections a report should contain?
4 What is a synopsis? What purpose does it serve?
5 What is a 'functional' paragraph in a report?
6 What are the four main stages in writing a report?

ANSWERS

1 An unsolicited report is usually called a memorandum.
2 The main elements of any report are: terms of reference (including the objective or statement of the subject, and the authorization, if appropriate); procedure; findings; conclusions and recommendations (if asked for).
3 Any report should contain three main sections: introduction; body of the report; and terminal section.
4 A synopsis (sometimes called an abstract or a summary) is a summary of the whole report, usually placed very near the beginning of the report, and providing the busy reader with a quick idea of the scope and objective together with a brief version of the conclusions and recommendations of the report.
5 A 'functional' paragraph does not add information, but is used to introduce, conclude or link sections of the report.
6 The four main stages of writing a report are: assembling the material; planning the report; writing the first draft; and editing the report.

List of correction marks

Instruction	Marginal Mark	Mark in the text
Delete (take out)	*♂*	Cross through thus /
Leave as it was before alteration	stet.	. . . under words or letters to remain.
Change to italic	ital.	_____ under words or letters to be altered
Change to capital letters (upper case)	caps	_____ under words or letters to be altered
Change to bold (heavy) type	bold	∿∿∿∿ under words or letters to be altered
Underline word or words	underline	_____ under words affected

Change to lower case	l.c.	
Change to roman type	rom	
Wrong fount, replace by letter of correct fount	w.f.	Encircle letters or words to be altered
Changed damaged character(s) or make clearer	x	
Close up — delete space between letters/words	⌒	⌒ linking letters or words
Insert space between lines or paragraphs	#〉	Indicate space required
Make equal spacing between words	eq #	/ between words
Reduce space between words	less #	
No new paragraph	run on	∾ between paragraphs
Begin a new paragraph	n.p.	[before first word of new paragraph
Transpose	trs	⊔⊓ between letters or words
Place in centre of line	centre	⌐ ¬ indicate words to be centred
Move to the right	⊏	⊏ at left side of group to be moved
Move to the left	⊐	⊐ at right side of group to be moved
Raise lines	⤒	⊤ over lines to be moved
Lower lines	⤓	⊥ under lines to be moved
Spell out abbreviation or figure in full	Spell out	Encircle words or figures to be altered
Substitute or insert:		
full stop	⊙	
comma	⸌	
semi-colon	⸵	/ through character
colon	·	⋏ or where required
question mark	?/	
exclamation mark	!/	
Insert: parenthesis	(/)/	⋏ or ⋏
Square brackets	[/]/	
dash	⊢	
apostrophe	⸝	⋏
space	#	
quotation marks	⸜ ⸝	
Correct vertical alignment	‖	‖

12 | Other writing tasks

'Geoff's out today. Write him a note and let him know tomorrow's meeting's off, but we'll still need his figures first thing . . .'

'Can you send a memo to the purchasing department confirming our order for three new filing cabinets? I have phoned him so he knows all about them.'

'Draft a circular about the new catalogue, to go out to all our current customers. Oh, and include some sort of reply-paid card to go with it, so that they can let us know if they want one.'

'There's no other way of contacting him. You'd better send a telex.'

'Can you have a go at devising a questionnaire. . .'

'Apparently Sue's gone home ill. Can you take the minutes. . .'

Letter writing and report writing tend to get a great deal of attention in most books on business communication – the one because it's such a common activity both in and outside the workplace, and the other because it is regarded as a fairly onerous job by most people. However, the barrage of instructions above is fairly typical of the many other writing tasks which you might very easily be called upon to tackle. Do you know how a memo differs from a letter? Have you ever sent a telex? Could you devise an effective questionnaire which doesn't create badwill rather than goodwill?

 In this chapter we will look at these other writing tasks – writing short notes and briefing notes, writing memos which serve their purpose, devising reply cards, composing telex messages, and designing forms and questionnaires. You will find some guidance on writing minutes of meetings in Chapter 6.

Notes

Perhaps the least formal kind of written business communication is a brief note to convey information that does not need to be permanently recorded. Although informal, such notes are common and important to in-company communication. They may be typed or handwritten (legibly!). They may be written on printed forms that the sender merely completes. For guidance on how to avoid the pitfalls which exist even in this simple form of communication, turn to the section on telephone messages in Chapter 2.

Another kind of note often required in business is the 'briefing note' or 'briefing report'. This, as its name suggests, is designed to provide someone with the background, or a short analysis, of a particular problem to enable him to attend a meeting, perhaps, clearly *briefed* on the nature of the problem. It usually consists of a summary of events, data, people concerned and any other information considered essential in understanding what the matter is all about. It can be written in note form providing that you are absolutely certain that the reader will be able to understand the points which are mentioned. In fact, this brings us to the essential principle of briefing notes: to serve their purpose they depend on some very careful thought about the level of knowledge and technical jargon possessed by the reader, and an appreciation of why the reader needs the information. He doesn't want to be burdened by a lot of irrelevant detail, nor does he want to find at the meeting or during the interview that you have omitted to tell him about a crucial point. Should you have to write briefing notes in the course of your job, you would do well to practise the art of summarizing, the art of reporting and, above all, the art of distinguishing the relevant from the irrelevant on the basis of a careful analysis of the needs of the reader – all basic skills in the process of communicating effectively.

Activity

Think of a matter about which you know quite a lot. Now think of someone who knows very little, or even nothing about the matter – your boss, perhaps, or a friend. Write him a briefing note, giving him all the information he would need in order to discuss the matter intelligently.

Now, if possible, test its effectiveness by showing it to the other person and asking him whether it would serve its purpose, whether you have got the level of detail right, whether you have written it in a comprehensible manner, whether, in fact, he would feel confident to attend a meeting at which the matter was to be discussed, simply on the basis of your briefing note.

Internal memoranda (memos)

Originally the word 'memorandum' came from the Latin *memorare* – to remember, and meant literally 'a thing to be remembered'. However, memos now have a rather wider use in business than simply a memory aid, as they have become the main method of internal communication together with the telephone. Their use, instead of a telephone call, retains the idea of a memory aid, in that they do, of course, have the advantage of written communication in providing a written record. They are used to communicate information, inquiries and instructions and in a longer form (memorandum) can serve the function of a report. (See 'Writing reports', p. 265.)

In other words, memoranda (or memorandums – both are acceptable) are the internal equivalents of letters. However, because they are *internal* letters there are one or two minor differences:

- The salutation and the complimentary close can be dispensed with, since normal politeness is assumed. It is also not necessary to sign a memo, although longer memorandums often are signed.
- The memo message should be kept as short as possible and should usually deal with only one item.

296 The business of writing

- Most organizations provide memo pads of headed message
  forms, but whether a headed form is used or not, a memo
  usually has a four-part heading: 'To' (the recipient's name),
  'From' (the sender's name), 'Date' (day, month and year and
  sometimes time, if appropriate), and 'Subject' (a brief summary phrase). Sometimes it also includes the sender's office
  number or department and telephone number.

A typical memo would therefore look like this:

```
                    M e m o r a n d u m

    To:       N. Bromhead
              Personnel Director

    From:     W. Taylor
              Training Manager

    Subject:  Induction Training Programme.  Date:  11 March 19..


    I am enclosing a draft programme of the proposed course,
    as you requested.

    You will see that the M.D. is down for the Wednesday after-
    noon.  Since I ought to get the whole thing buttoned up
    by Friday, can you check with him that Wednesday will be
    O.K. and also let me have any comments you may have
    before then.


    ada.
```

Self-check

What do you think of the style of this message? What does
it tell you about the relationship between the sender and
the recipient?

Style

There can be no fixed rules about the style of language which is appropriate for an internal memorandum. It will depend on several factors.

Nature of the message Information, inquiry, request, reprimand, congratulations, etc.

Context of the message Potential reaction of the reader, what has gone before, how much the recipient knows already, urgency of the situation and priority of any action required – routine, emergency, crisis, follow-up instructions to all staff. etc.

Status and personality of the recipient Position in the organization, known tastes and attitudes on written style and methods of working, technical/practical background, education level, etc.

Relationship between sender and recipient Friendly, distant, informal, formal, etc. (A neutral tone may be necessary where there will be several recipients.)

Activity

Supposing you had to write to the managing director about the induction training programme because he had asked to see a copy of the draft programme. Using the same information, write the memo required.

The style of memoranda will obviously vary a great deal. Directives and instructions from a very senior executive to all personnel may well be written in rather formal, impersonal language whereas a hastily written message scribbled on a memo pad to a colleague may be written in extremely conversational English complete with 'in jokes' and slang expressions. Memos written *up* the organization ladder will possibly be more cautious in style than those written *down*. You therefore need to be extremely sensitive to people's likes and dislikes, their attitudes to things like status and position, and to your position and relationship *vis-à-vis* the people you communicate with. Always be alert to clues, but cautious in their interpretation. A very senior manager may write chatty, familiar memos to you, but he might be quite offended if you felt free, following his example, to do the same.

If your position in the organization was fairly low compared with the managing director's and you had never met him personally, or perhaps only on very formal occasions, your memo might look like this:

To: Managing Director.
From: A. Bloggs, Training Manager.
Subject: Induction Training Programme.   *Date*: 11 March 19. .

Following your secretary's telephone call, I am enclosing a draft programme for the Induction Course we are proposing to hold from 15 April to 20 April.

You will see that following your agreement to speak to the new staff, I have provisionally arranged your session to start at 2.00 p.m. on Wednesday 17 April.

I would like to be able to finalize the arrangements fairly soon and would therefore be grateful if you could confirm that Wednesday is still convenient for you, and let me have your comments on the programme by Friday of this week if possible.

The tone and style are more dignified but without being pompous or subservient.

Specific dates are mentioned in case he is unsure of when exactly 'this training course' is taking place, and to enable him to confirm his availability.

You might argue that since you occupy a lower position in the hierarchy you should not give him a 'reply by' date. However, since the memo has been organized on an inductive basis with the call for action at the end, after presentation of the reasons for some urgency, it would seem reasonable to give him some idea of when you need his answer. The apparent demand for action 'by Friday' is somewhat softened by ending with 'if possible'. This hints that you are aware of the other more important demands on his time, but without leaving the matter completely open.

Postcards and reply cards

Since postcards and reply cards are relatively fast and inexpensive methods of sending business messages they are worth bearing in mind. They save the cost and time of writing an unnecessarily long message, of folding, sealing and stamping a message.

They are usually pre-printed to suit standard situations – acknowledgement of receipt of a letter, order, etc. – or, in the case of reply cards, to encourage the recipient to respond by doing the work for him (see the two examples below). The postage on reply cards is often paid by the originator, which further increases the incentive to reply.

Dear Mr. Luty,

I am interested in the proposal contained in your letter and would like your department to contact me. I understand you reserve your right of choice and I am under no obligation.

NAME ....

ADDRESS ....

....

TEL. HOME .... TEL. BUSINESS ....

SUNUSER ^B
Solar System

POST TODAY!

Pre-printed postcard

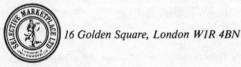

16 Golden Square, London W1R 4BN

Date as postmark

Dear Customer

ACKNOWLEDGEMENT OF ORDER

Thank you for your recent order which has been safely received and is now being processed.

If at any time you have any queries regarding your order please contact us quoting the reference number printed in the bottom left hand corner, on the reverse of this card. Knowing the reference number will enable us to help you without delay.

Yours faithfully,
SELECTIVE MARKETPLACE LTD.

Reply-paid postcard

The heading and the salutation both appear on the message side of the card. The recipient's address can be omitted as the address on the stamped side is sufficient.

The message needs to be fairly neutral in tone since it will go to a variety of recipients, but it needs to be courteous and friendly to compensate for the fact that it is a standard message and the recipient knows this.

Telex messages

The telephone and fast train and air travel have cut the problems of distance so dramatically for today's businessman. However, where the recipient cannot be spoken to personally by telephone, the telex message, which can be transmitted fast to the person concerned, may still prove invaluable in extremely urgent situations where immediate action is required.

Telex messages present the communicator with his greatest test in conveying a clear unambiguous message in the minimum number of words.

Wording a telex

> #### Self-check
>
> You have been asked to attend a meeting in Exeter. Overnight accommodation was booked but subsequently cancelled (you think!) when you said that, for family reasons, it was extremely unlikely you would be able to attend. However, you now find you are able to attend but cannot contact the hotel ('Lines to Exeter are engaged. Please try later'). If you are to arrive in time, you must leave immediately to catch the train. The organizer of the meeting has already started his journey and will arrive before you, but you want him to make sure you have a room for the night either at the hotel in question or somewhere else convenient to the meeting. You expect to arrive at 6.15 p.m. Send a telex to await his arrival at the hotel.

Your first task is to extract from all the available material only that which is absolutely essential and relevant, in order to get the receiver to perform the necessary action.

Having reduced the content of your message to the absolute minimum, you now have to find a way of conveying the idea in the *shortest message possible*. This usually requires some ingenious juggling with words and the removal of all unnecessary minor words such as personal pronouns, indefinite and definite articles, and prepositions. It is also advisable to ignore all normal sentence division and punctuation (although a full stop can be inserted, between sentences). However, all this must be done while at the same time anticipating any possible misunderstandings which might arise from the words which are left.

In wording the telex above, the stages might therefore look like this:

Stage 1

> I can attend the meeting after all but I need a room for the night. Can you please ensure I have one. I shall arrive at 6.15 p.m.

Stage 2

> CAN ATTEND MEETING.
> NEED ROOM. PLEASE BOOK.
> ARRIVING 6.15

– 9 words. At first sight, this looks pretty good. All the unnecessary words seem to have been removed and it seems to make sense. Is it now possible by judicious use of words to reduce it still further? Is it really necessary to say 'can attend meeting' if you are also saying you need a room and are arrivng at 6.15 p.m.? These surely imply that you are obviously able to attend the meeting. Furthermore, is it not possible to combine 'need room' and 'please book' and reduce the words? And supposing the room originally booked was never actually cancelled? Do you want him to book another one? Will he work it out for himself?

This version perhaps answers some of those questions:

> ARRIVING MEETING 6.15 PLEASE ENSURE ROOM

– 6 words. 'Ensure' covers the idea of confirming the original room or booking a new one and the message is reduced to only six words, but it could be argued that 'meeting' is not really

necessary since you are unlikely to arrive for any other reason.
'Please', on the other hand, should not be dropped. You are
causing inconvenience and should always be polite even when
economizing with words. The last dilemma is perhaps 'room'.
You might argue that this is too vague and does not convey the
precise idea. 'Accommodation' might be better. However, since
telex messages are charged on the basis of time, it is better to use
the shorter word, 'room', so the final message might be:

ARRIVE 6.15. PLEASE ENSURE ROOM (5 words).

Designing forms and questionnaires

Perhaps you think, like many people, that we have too many
forms; that hardly any situation can occur without someone
designing a form which we have to complete to get what we
need, or do what we want, or merely help someone else do their
job. Your frustration may be justified, but forms do have their
uses, and very frequently the cause of our irritation is not so
much the need to complete a form, as the form itself – its design.

Self-check

Can you think of four good reasons for using a form to gain
information?

1 It enables you to get the *same information* from different
people.
2 It enables you to get that information in the *same way*
3 This means that it is easier to *compare information*.
4 It also makes it easier to get and refer to *specific bits of
information*.

Forms, in fact, provide a vehicle for asking for particular information in a way that ensures that you get the information you
need and exclude the information you don't need. The problems
arise for all the parties who use a form, when it has been badly
designed.

Activity

Think back to forms you may have filled in recently, e.g.

application forms for jobs, for money, for services perhaps, or to questionnaires you may have been asked to complete, and to forms which perhaps you use at work. What were the problems with these forms? Make a list.

The problems with forms . . . !

1 The form is too long and asks for too much information. Result: people get bored or irritated, give incomplete answers or even fail to answer some questions at all.
2 The form tries to cover too many possibilities. Result: the form is confusing to follow and difficult to complete correctly. It is unclear in its purpose, or even has too many purposes so it fails to do any job properly.
3 The form is badly designed. Result: the language and the form itself are complicated and ambiguous, the instructions only add to the confusion and the form contains contradictions, or apparent contradictions, e.g.
    1 Do you have any children?
    2 Do you intend to have any children?
   (The first question must presumably have been expecting the answer 'no', otherwise the second question is nonsensical. But worded as it is, what happens if the answer is 'yes'? This may seem an absurd example, but it is typical of the kind of nonsense which can end up in a badly designed form or questionnaire.)
4 The form is badly laid out. Result: it provides too much space for some answers and not enough for others.
5 The form asks the wrong questions. Result: even if information is obtained, it's the wrong information or information which is produced in an unusable way.

Designing forms

Designing forms is quite an art and certainly not something to be undertaken lightly. With the increased use of computerized data processing, the task can be one requiring special training. However, it is more than possible that you may be called upon to 'have a go at designing a form' or at least help someone else with the task, or you may find that your experiences of using a form at work bring to light its deficiencies and prompt you to try designing a better one. Bear in mind the following brief essentials, but the section on questionnaire design which follows contains principles which apply just as much to form design.

Layout
- Make it as attractive as you can.
- Make it as brief as you can.
- Ensure that it is functional:
  * provides the information you actually need
  * provides sufficient space for each answer
  * can be filled in as easily as possible

Arrangement
- Arrange your questions and instructions in a logical order.
- Avoid cross references and explanatory notes where possible.
- Beware of internal contradictions or apparent contradictions.

Style
- Direct questions and instructions are generally better than headings.
- Use simple, clear and direct English.

Activity

1 Design a form suitable for your organization's (or college's) suggestion scheme, on which people can submit their suggestion. In the instructions section give them some ideas on what kind of suggestion might be acceptable, how to submit their suggestion, and what will happen next.

2 Start a collection of different forms. Try filling them in and note any problems or difficulties you experience.

   Keep the forms – you never know when they may come in handy as examples of layout, question planning, instructions, etc.

Questionnaires

A questionnaire survey is a formal way of getting first-hand information. It is commonly used for research but recently it has become the subject of a fair amount of criticism, mainly because it imposes on people: taking up time and asking difficult questions that may not be easily answered. Questionnaires are also frequently criticized for asking vague questions or asking people to commit themselves on issues where perhaps they do not feel it is possible to be definite one way or the other without considerable qualification, or for asking them to commit themselves in a permanent way on paper.

Certainly as a method of obtaining information there is much to commend the questionnaire but indiscriminate use by amateur research workers tends to bring a great deal of discredit on the method, and to the validity of the results under certain conditions.

If, therefore, you do want to use a questionnaire, you should ideally seek expert advice, and in any case construct it with considerable care. Here are a few suggestions:

- Make sure that the questionnaire is the best method for getting the information you are seeking.
- Frame the questions in a neutral fashion so that you will not influence the answers.
- Write short questions. Avoid long, complicated questions.
- Be sure that your questions are direct. Avoid ambiguity.
- Be specific in the information you are seeking. Consider how you intend to collect, analyse and present the information received.
- Frame your questions as far as possible, so that only simple ticking of yes/no answers will get the information. Make the answers you receive easy to work with.
- Arrange your questions on the questionnaire in a logical manner.
- Select your 'sample' – those to whom you are going to send the questionnaire – with care and attention to recognized sampling techniques. See the sections on sampling in Peter Clarke, *Using Statistics in Business*, also in Pan Breakthrough Books.

- Test your questions on a pilot group (a small group of people similar to those you are going to question but who are not to be included in your actual survey). This is an *essential* step in form and questionnaire design. However well you have anticipated the respondents' answers you are almost bound to have missed something and what seems clear to you may seem confusing to someone else.
- Use an attractive but straightforward layout so that your questions can easily be read, answered and returned.

Activity

You have been asked to carry out some research and prepare a report which will require you to write letters requesting information from several organizations in your locality. You have had no previous contact with these organizations and will therefore have to write 'cold' letters. In other words your letter will arrive 'out of the blue' and, in effect, will be asking busy people to work for you free of charge or reward, in order to supply you with the information you need in answer to several questions.

You will have to consider the tone and style of the letter very carefully, so that it will create a favourable impression and persuade the recipient to provide you with the information you need, willingly. You will have to make it easy for the recipient to answer your questions, arouse interest in the problem and motivate him to a positive action on your behalf.

1 Consider this situation very carefully and then write a list of the 'don'ts' which you will have to bear in mind as you plan and draft the letter.
2 Invent a reasonably realistic research project (a real one would be even better, if you have one in progress at the moment); decide which organizations you would write to, and then draft the letter, bearing in mind the letter-writing techniques of Chapter 9 and the specific 'don'ts' governing the writing of request-for-information letters, which you have just listed.

When you have finished the letter and would be absolutely happy to send it, criticize it against the list of 'dont's' suggested below.

When writing 'request-for-information' letters, DON'T:

- ask for information that might be confidential
- make your letter hard to understand
- send your letter to the wrong person (i.e. someone who can't or won't help you)
- ask too many questions
- make your questions too involved or complicated
- ask the person to do 'research' work for you (i.e. don't ask him for information he cannot easily give you)
- expect the person to drop everything just to answer your questionnaire
- expect anything! Be grateful for what you do receive, and if possible, be prepared to write back thanking them (goodwill)
- make a pest of yourself by writing again asking for explanations of their answers. To the best of your ability, work out what they mean
- try to kill too many birds at once. Narrow down your range of questions

13 | Graphs and charts and things

In the companion volume *What Do You Mean, 'Communication'?* the importance of non-verbal communication was highlighted in considering the principles of communicating and receiving messages. In this book we have touched on the need to consider the presentation of a message – letter layout and appearance, report format and presentation and so on. We need now to look at the way in which we can use visual communication – graphs, charts, pictures and symbols – to help us to communicate more effectively.

While it is true that there are occasions when pictures can stand alone, it is perhaps safer to regard visual communication as a complement to verbal communication. In this chapter we will look at the way we can use pictures of one kind or another to reinforce our message, make it easier to take in and understand, or simply to make the receiver's task easier by providing variety.

Look at the following extract from a written report.

Ten newsagent shops in the Bristol area were selected to test the effectiveness of two different display stands in generating sales. For the purposes of the survey the shops were designated with the letters A–J (see Appendix for the address of each shop).

During the period 15 March to 20 March the total sales for three items were recorded:

Two different stands were used to display these items for sale. Five of the stands were the traditional sloping top 5 ft wide stand made of Formica with Perspex divisions while the other five were the metal revolving type, 2ft in diameter. Shops A, C, D, G, I used the traditional stand and shops B, E, F, H, J used the revolving stand.

Total sales of the items during the six day test period (Monday to Saturday inclusive) were as follows: shops A, B, C, and D sold 175, 410, 220 and 187 respectively. Shops E, F, G, H showed sales of 435, 475, 286 and 575 cards and Shop I 275 with Shop J at 525.

There is an obvious correlation between sales and type of display stand. This correlation is reflected in similar studies carried out in Manchester and Aberdeen . . .

This material is taken from a survey report. How well have you been able to assimilate the information? Was the correlation between the sales and the type of display stand quite as 'obvious' as the author suggests?

║ *Self-Check*

║ Draw the most effective visual aid to represent the data before reading on.

Much of the business of communication in organizations is concerned with presenting facts in order to enable decisions to be made. Many of these facts are in the form of numbers or statistics, and yet as we saw at the start of this chapter, these statistics are frequently presented in a way which appears to be designed to confuse rather than clarify the facts.

The function of this statistical information may be historical – to show what has happened in the past; 'comparative' – to enable comparisons to be made between different things or between different periods of time; or 'predictive' – to forecast and predict what may happen in the future. In other words the statistical information has to be used, but to be used it needs to be understood and it is the function of the communicator to present this information in such a way that the person who needs the information is able to abstract from it the most pertinent ideas and concepts which it contains. In order to serve its purpose, then, the oral or written report must give the receiver its information quickly, clearly and completely.

Someone once calculated that:

1 Of each £10 spent on voluntary reading for employees, £3 was wasted.
2 Of each £10 spent on copy for customers and the public, £4 was wasted.
3 Of each £10 spent on writing to shareholders, £4 was wasted.
4 Of each £10 spent on required reading for management, £8 was wasted.

Although this may be a rather exaggerated guess, there is a very real danger that much of the material presented, particularly for reading, is never used in the way it was intended, and that the cost involved in producing the material outweighs the value of the information conveyed.

This is particularly true of organizations which, through the introduction of data-processing equipment, may be tempted to produce such a mass of information that the user is unable to 'see the wood for the trees'.

For this reason, it is up to the producer of the information – the report writer or speaker – to show the crucial relationships between various bits of information, and to pick out from all the information available only that which is critical to the person who will use it.

In this chapter we shall look at the different methods of presenting statistical and other data, so that you can choose the method which is best suited for any particular purpose. In addition, it may be useful to examine ways in which it is possible to distort the message conveyed, by presenting it in a particular way, so that, as a communicator, you can avoid misleading your reader, and as a receiver, you will be alert to the possibility that other people might be misleading you.

Using graphic and visual aids

Graphic aids are the names we give to charts and other illustrations which are used for presenting data. Used effectively they can simplify and speed up the communication or instruction. However, used to present statistical data they cannot usually totally replace words but they can considerably reduce the number of words necessary. Graphic aids, *plus* a brief commentary in words, can make an invaluable combination to help you communicate, even if it is not strictly speaking true that 'a picture is worth a thousand words'.

Graphic aids are, therefore, excellent supplements to the written or spoken word. Your reader or listener may find it difficult or at least hard work to take in the relationships when reading or, worse, hearing that 'sales rose 5 per cent during 1979, 10 per cent during 1980 and 2 per cent during 1981'. However, if that same data can be seen in a graph, a better and stronger mental image of the events is received than from words alone. Look at the simple graph below, for example:

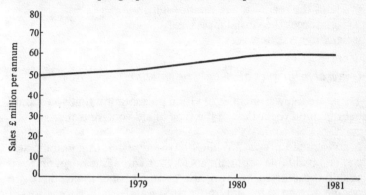

Simple graph

Certainly some people who are not particularly word-oriented will probably find graphic aids essential, but almost everyone can benefit from having words reinforced with some form of graphic or pictorial presentation. Remember that meanings are in people and not in words. By quantifying information and presenting it in graphic form, you can help to reinforce the meaning of the words in your reports. Charts, graphs and tables are tools that help you make this presentation of quantitative data more efficiently by enabling your reader to compare and contrast data. Diagrams and pictures help still further to produce concrete mental images out of abstract and often ambiguous concepts. Your reader or listener will thank you for absolving him from the effort of understanding, and the consequences of misunderstanding.

Advantages of visual presentation

- Gains attention if well done and pleasing to the eye.
- Provides the maximum amount of information as quickly as possible.
- Speeds comprehension if not unduly complex.
- Relieves the monotony of solid text.

- Conveys easily and quickly impression of overall trends and tendencies.
- Helps the reader to pick out specific figures.
- Helps the reader to see relationships.
- Reinforces the verbal message.
- Highlights differences.

General principles of visual presentation

There are a few principles of visual presentation that you should bear in mind regardless of the type of aid you are using.

Is a visual aid needed? While I have suggested that graphic aids can be invaluable supplements to your verbal message, and you should therefore never forget to *consider* using them, there are people who go to the opposite extreme and produce some sort of visual aid for practically everything they want to say on a subject which is not particularly technical, quantitative or complex.

A visual aid should be incorporated only when there is a clear purpose for it – a *need*. Aids should be included only when they will produce advantages like those listed above.

Visual aids should not be used simply to impress your receiver or make your presentation look more 'professional', or to 'make it look pretty'.

What type should be used? Ask yourself: 'Which visual aid will best tell my story?' It is easy to get into the habit of always using a certain table for one type of representation, a certain chart for another, merely adapting them to suit every situation. This sort of habit runs the risk of not stretching your imagination enough to see if there might not be another, better way of presenting the data or the idea.

The most appropriate method to use in a particular circumstance will vary according to the reader, the type of information (statistical or non-statistical) and the purpose (to contrast specific figures, to show trends, to explain a procedure, etc.).

Designing the content You must not only choose the best type of visual aid, but also decide how complex or simple it should be in reference to the data and the receiver. One reader may be comfortable with five different graph lines on one chart (e.g. solid, broken, dotted, dashed and dot-dash). Another reader would require five different charts because he doesn't have sufficient ability, interest or motivation to analyse a single complex visual aid.

Prepare the reader Always prepare your reader or listener for a visual aid. A visual aid forces your reader to pause in order to work out its purpose and this delay reduces the readability of the text. So introduce the visual aid. This does not have to be a lengthy business. Just mention it as you call attention to a particular piece of data. For example; 'In the table below (fig. 6) you will see that wages increased by 10 per cent while sales only increased by 5 per cent.'

Explain the visual aid Never assume that your readers will read and study a particular visual aid, and even if they do you can't assume that they will interpret it in the way you intended. It is therefore not enough to say: 'Table 6 is on p. 9' or 'Look at this graph' with no further comment. You must explain what you intend the graph or the table to convey. Remember, visual aids are *aids*, that is, they should supplement the text not replace it.

Presentation of statistical data

Textual presentation

Most people cannot take in strings of facts and figures presented in the text and are therefore unable to recognize the significance of the information being presented or even pick out a specific figure which has particular importance or relevance.

However, you can *direct attention* or *emphasize certain figures* even in this type of presentation, and can *call attention to comparisons* which seem important. Consider this example:

Average earnings last October of full-time men manual workers in the United Kingdom, in the industries covered by the regular annual inquiry conducted by the Department of Employment, were £59.58 per week, an increase of £10.95, or 22.5 per cent on a year earlier. Their weekly hours worked were 43.6 and their hourly earnings 136.7p. For full-time women manual workers average earnings were £34.19 per week, an increase of £7.18 or 26.6 per cent on a year earlier. Their weekly hours worked were 37.0 and their hourly earnings 92.4p.

At least this has presumably extracted the important figures and comparison, but it is still fairly indigestible and would be impossible to take in if presented orally. However, as a commentary to a visual presentation of all the figures it would be very useful in helping to highlight significant figures and comparisons between the years.

As an alternative to the textual presentation of information in this way, the most common types of graphic aid available to choose from are tables, graphs and charts. However, numerous variations and combinations of these basic types are possible.

Types of graphic aid

TABLES

Strictly speaking tables are not graphic aids, but they are usually discussed in connection with visual aids because they do have a visually different effect compared with expressing the same information in the text, as we have just seen.

They are the simplest form of visual aid and consist of an orderly arrangement of figures in columns and horizontal lines, enabling the receiver to grasp the significance of the figures presented and at the same time to discard from consideration those figures which are irrelevant.

By arranging in tabular form the figures that were presented in the verbal statement above, it is now possible to include all the other figures and still see how much more readily comparisons can be made.

Average earnings and hours of full-time manual men and women: October 1973, 1974, 1975. (a) all industries covered by the inquiry (b) all manufacturing industries. (United Kingdom)

	October 1973	October 1974	October 1975	Percentage increase 1973-4	1974-5
All industries covered					
Average weekly earnings					
men	£40.92	£48.63	£59.58	18.8	22.5
women	£21.16	£27.01	£34.19	27.6	26.6
Average hours worked					
men	45.6	45.1	43.6	—	—
women	37.7	37.4	37.0	—	—
Average hourly earnings					
men	89.74p	107.83p	136.65p	20.2	26.7
women	56.13p	72.22p	92.41p	28.7	28.0
Manufacturing industries					
Average weekly earnings					
men	£41.52	£49.12	£59.74	18.3	21.6
women	£21.15	£27.05	£34.23	27.9	26.5
Average hours worked					
men	44.7	44.0	42.7	—	—
women	37.5	37.2	36.8	—	—
Average hourly earnings					
men	92.88p	111.64p	139.91p	20.2	25.3
women	56.40p	72.72p	93.02p	28.9	27.9

The addition of two columns to the right, showing the percentage increase from year to year, further helps the receiver to make comparisons and find specific figures of relevance to him.

Uses
- Convenient devices for displaying large amounts of data in a relatively small space.
- Useful for reference – comparisons and contrasts can be seen easily and *specific figures* picked out.

Remember
- Each vertical column should be headed clearly and concisely.
- Data to be compared should be placed in the same horizontal plane from left to right.
- Decimals rather than fractions should be used.
- Tables should be laid out very carefully with careful ruling and plenty of white space.

GRAPHS AND CHARTS

Continuous and discrete information When deciding whether to use charts or graphs one important judgement has to be made. Is the information 'continuous' in that every point on the line of graph is valid, e.g. speed, acceleration, population growth, resource usage, sales, plotted against time; or conversion graphs like °C to °F, or £s to $? Or is the information 'discrete' in that it is not directly related to other items of information being plotted: it occurs in distinct steps, e.g. children per family, population in one country at a particular moment in time compared with population in other countries at the same moment. Look at these two examples to see the difference:

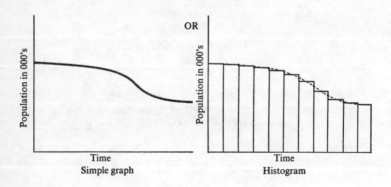

Presenting continuous information

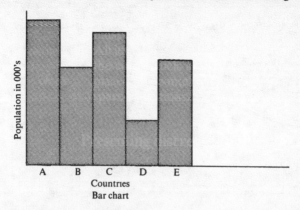

Countries
Bar chart

Presenting discrete information

Generally speaking 'continuous' information is best displayed on some sort of line graph whereas 'discrete' information is best shown on a chart. However, sometimes a line graph can be constructed by plotting vertical bars. This is called a histogram and must not be confused with a conventional bar chart.

Presenting continuous information

Graphs

Graphs are useful for showing *trends* in *continuous* information over periods of time. They are easy to make and most people are familiar with them from maths and science classes at school.

Simple graph A graph is an aid in which points on a scale are connected with a line in order to show increases and decreases. The degree of slope to the line provides a better impression of the *intensity* of activity as well as a picture of the *trend* over a given period of time. See the graph on page 316.

Multiple graph Sometimes it is useful to show trends of more than one thing as a basis for comparison. This is possible by the use of solid, dotted and broken lines where there would be any confusion as the lines cross.

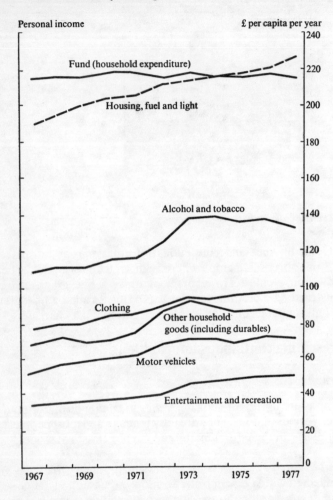

Personal income   £ per capita per year

Fund (household expenditure)

Housing, fuel and light

Alcohol and tobacco

Clothing

Other household
goods (including durables)

Motor vehicles

Entertainment and recreation

1967   1969   1971   1973   1975   1977

Multiple graph (Facts in Focus, *Penguin/HMSO, 1980*)

Divided (compound) graph This shows the value of both the
total and its parts by a series of lines on the graph. In order to
distinguish it from a *multiple* graph, the area between each
successive line should be coloured or shaded distinctively and
shown in a key or labelled clearly.

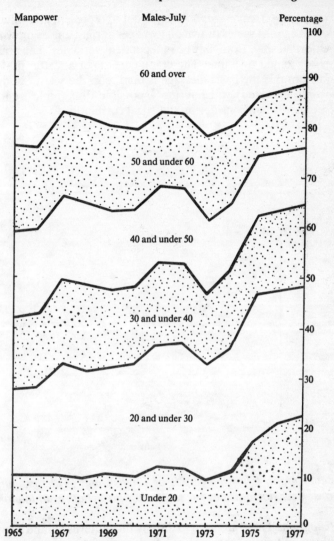

Divided (compound) graph (Facts in Focus, *Penguin/HMSO,* *1980)*

Scatter graph (scattergram) A single dot to represent one value is plotted against scales drawn on two axes at right angles drawn in the normal way. Both may be independent variables. The points are not joined by a line. The graph consists of a scatter of dots and from this the basic message is read, e.g. the scatter of dots (loosely enclosed) will indicate a possible discernible trend – often used when considering statistical correlations.

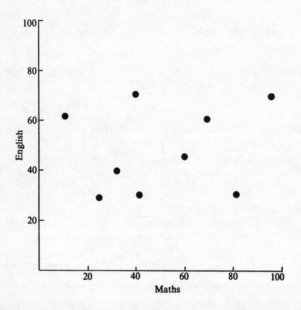

Scatter graph (showing results of English and Maths examinations. Each dot indicates one student's score in both examinations)

Histograms These are used to display the patterns behind a large volume of figures, e.g. income of a large number of employees. The information is divided into 'intervals' and the vertical measurement represents 'frequency'. Columns need not have the same widths since this is a measure of the intervals used – they need not be uniform.

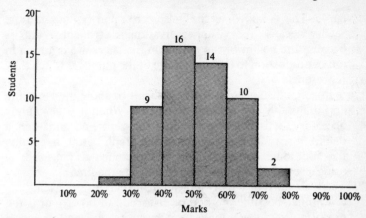

Histogram (showing the frequency of distribution of examination marks of 52 students in 10% intervals)

However, where the intervals are uniform then a line may be used to join the tops of the columns and the profile of the graph becomes a curve. The area below the line can be shaded so that a section of the curve may now represent 'frequency' on the histogram.

Beware! A histogram looks like a vertical bar chart but the bars are not separated and their width as well as their height is significant.

Rules for producing graphs (and warnings when reading graphs!)

1 Always include a zero line on the vertical scale.
2 Emphasize the zero line by making it heavier than any other lines.

Beware the 'false zero'. When high figures which vary very little need to be plotted, there would be a large amount of space between the zero and the graph line or curve. Sometimes to save space the bottom part of the graph is removed, so that the vertical axis now no longer starts at zero. Those who want to make rather small variations in figures look more impressive not only cut away the bottom of the graph but draw the horizontal axis across only just below the lowest point on the curve. This is known as the 'false zero', and can mislead the reader because the visual impression is erroneous. This is because the height of the points on the curve are not then in direct proportion to the magnitude of the numbers which they represent.

In some instances, it seems difficult to show the zero line and the graph line without doing this. When it is absolutely necessary, it is possible to show the zero line and then a definite break all the way across the graph before beginning the additional numbers. This is sometimes emphasized by using a serrated or jagged line to indicate the break.

3 The scale must be clearly indicated and carefully chosen.

Another possible method of distortion to beware of is the use of a scale which makes a comparatively small variation between the figures look large. This can be easily done once the constructor of the graph has adopted a 'false zero' and can mislead the inexperienced reader who is not conscious of dangers like these. But it can also be achieved by elongating or condensing the values on the horizontal axis. Look at the two graphs below. They both represent the same statistical data but the visual impression is very different. Both as a constructor and reader of graphs, you should be aware of the implications of selecting a particular scale.

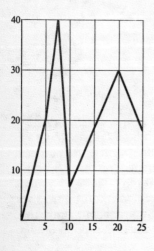
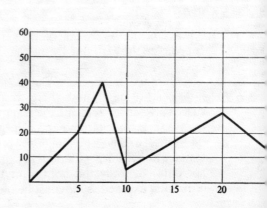

4 The nature of the information and the units used on both axes must be clearly stated.
5 All lettering – the scale labels, the values, the key (or legend), the curve labels and any other words and figures – should be placed horizontally unless absolutely impossible because of space limitations.

Presenting discrete or non-continuous information

Bar charts

Bar charts are used to convey discrete or non-continuous information about different kinds of things (e.g. ownership of cars or washing machines, mortality rates in different places), sometimes at different moments of time.

They are particularly useful for conveying a quick *comparison* of quantities (e.g. tons of coal mined in different areas) or sums of money (e.g. gross national product in different countries) where exact figures are not so important. However, where items are plotted at various time intervals they can also depict *trends*.

They are drawn by showing a series of values plotted against two axes, but instead of being formed by a line the values are represented by vertical or horizontal bars or columns. Vertical charts are used when chronological data or other quantitative data is presented. Horizontal charts are generally used when making comparisons of data which is classified qualitatively or geographically (see simple bar chart overleaf).

Each bar is usually kept separate from its neighbour to emphasize that the information is discrete, not continous as in a histogram. No attempt should be made to join the tops of the bars to form a curve.

Divided (component) bar charts Each bar may be divided into any number of parts to compare the constituents as well as the total value (e.g. population broken into different age groups or percentages). Each part is shaded differently and must be indicated by a key or labelled (see example overleaf).

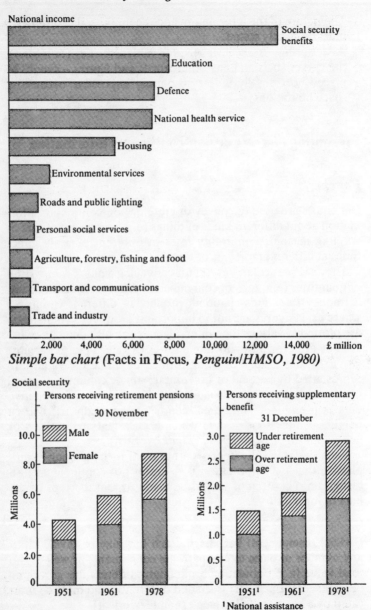

Simple bar chart (Facts in Focus, *Penguin/HMSO, 1980*)

Divided (component) bar chart (Facts in Focus, *Penguin/HMSO*)

Component bar charts can be confusing, since they can also be used to compare two sets of data, as in the chart below.

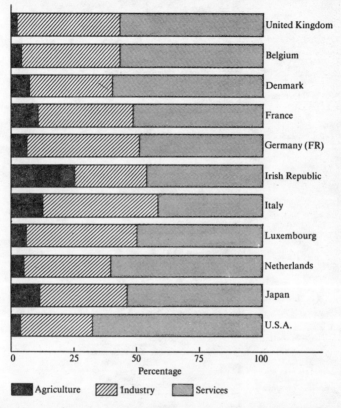

*Component bar chart (*Facts in Focus, *Penguin/HMSO, 1980)*

When looking at component bar charts you should be sure that you know the difference between these two methods of using a component bar chart. The information in the chart immediately above would be less ambiguously represented in a multiple bar chart.

Multiple bar charts Bar charts can be used to compare any number of different items by producing a bar for each item and setting them in groups.

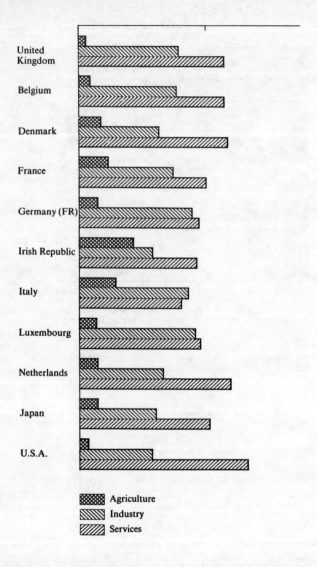

*Multiple bar chart (showing civilian employment by sector)
(Source of statistics: HMSO)*

Population pyramid This allows the representation of both the age and sex structure of population, by building up the age groups, male on one side and female on the other. The ages can be grouped every one, five or ten years and the information can be read, apart from the length of the bar, by comparing the shape of the pyramid with another.

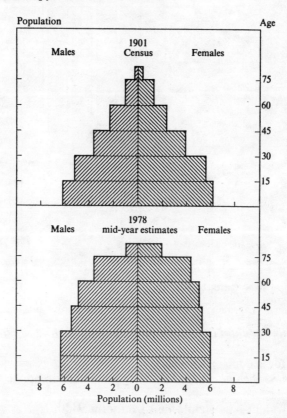

*Population pyramid (*Facts in Focus, *Penguin/HMSO, 1980)*

Floating bar charts The bar 'floats' either in the area of the graph or above and below a zero line from which a value runs down as well as up, e.g. for plotting variations in a quantity.

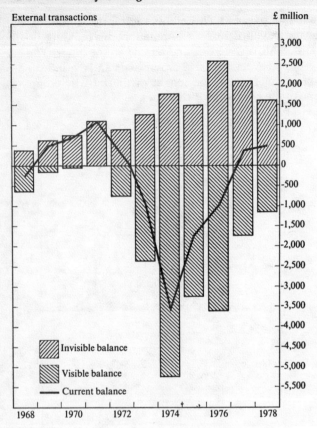

Floating bar chart (Facts in Focus, Penguin/HMSO, 1980)

Rules for producing bar charts

1 Always include a zero line. The same caution applies as for graphs.
2 Individual bars should be of uniform width (for a word of warning see 'Rules for producing pictorial charts').
3 Individual bars should neither be very short and wide, nor very long and narrow.
4 The bars should be separated by spaces which are not less than one half nor greater than the width of the bar.

5 A scale is generally useful. It should be about one quarter the width of the bar from the top bar or from the left bar if the bars are vertical.

Pie or circle charts

The 'pie' or circle chart is one of the most common visual aids used. It is easy to interpret, does not require extensive art work and communicates its basic message with clarity and simplicity. Although each segment represents a different percentage, the total comes to 100 per cent. Each section is proportional to the value it represents, e.g. division of expenditure between different areas.

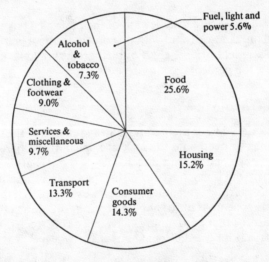

Pie chart (showing average division of weekly household expenditure)

Pictograms

The pie chart can be presented in a variety of ways. Some firms use a picture of their product to represent their 'pie' and divide it into appropriate segments to represent cost of materials, salaries, depreciation, etc. This can lead to distortion if the various segments are out of proportion.

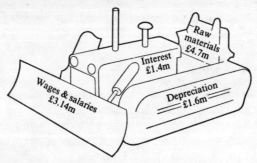

Pictogram (misleading because segments are not in proportion to figures)

The reader should also beware of the pie which has segments labelled only in words but with no percentage figures.

Each segment in a pie chart or pictogram should be identified and show the percentage it represents.

Pictorial chart

The pictorial chart or pictograph is an adaptation of the bar chart but it aims to overcome the lack of appeal of the bar chart by actually representing the subject. The pictorial chart is ideal for the reader who is in a hurry or disinclined to interpret a conventional bar chart. He can quickly see, for example, that the cost of living has gone up if little shopping baskets are shown marching up a chart, or that more houses have been constructed this year than last year if five additional houses are shown.

The symbols, such as people, homes, aeroplanes or £ signs, should all be of uniform appearance and size. Each should represent the same quantity and dimension (which should be shown in a key). For this reason, they are rather more difficult for the amateur to produce accurately. The symbols should be simple and so easily recognizable that it would be almost impossible for two readers to interpret them differently.

Only a limited amount of information can be presented in a

= 100 new homes

1978   1979   1980

Pictorial chart (showing rise in number of houses completed)

pictorial chart. For data which has several facets and requires thoughtful interpretation, other visual aids are preferable.

Rules and warnings
1 Symbols should be self-explanatory.
2 Pictorial charts should give an overall picture, not minute details.
3 They make comparisons between things, not flat statements about things.
4 Changes in numbers are shown by more or fewer symbols, not by larger or smaller ones.

Activity

Look at this chart.

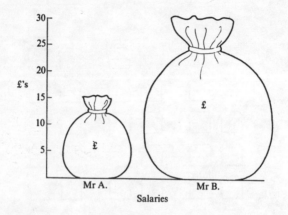

Does Mr B earn twice as much as Mr A?

This example is adapted from an unputdownable book, *How to Lie with Statistics*,* which I strongly advise you to read in order to discover how other people may mislead you, and how you may unwittingly mislead others. Darrell Huff, the author, goes on to explain how easily we can be tricked by a pictorial chart like this, which breaks rule 4:

> The catch, of course, is this. Because the second bag is twice as high as the first, it is also twice as wide. It occupies not twice but four times as much area on the page. The numbers still say two to one, but the visual impression, which is the dominating one most of the time, says the ratio is four to one. Or worse, since these are pictures of objects having in reality three dimensions, the second must also be twice as thick as the first. As your geometry book put it, the volumes of similar solids vary as the cube of any like dimension. Two times two times two is eight. If one money bag holds £15, the other, having eight times the volume, must hold not only £30, but £120.

* By D. Huff (Penguin Books, 1963).

Statistical maps

Statistical maps are a particular kind of graphic device for
showing quantitative information geographically. They consist
of representations of geographic areas shown either shaded,
hatched or coloured.

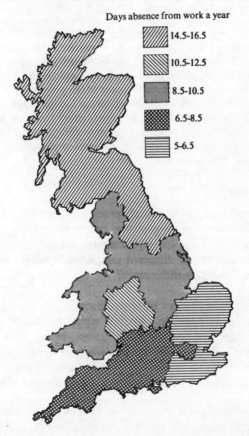

Days absence from work a year

14.5-16.5

10.5-12.5

8.5-10.5

6.5-8.5

5-6.5

*Statistical map (showing annual average days of incapacity per
person – males aged 16–44)**

* The map above is taken from *Complete Atlas of the British Isles* published by
The Reader's Digest Association Limited.

334   *The business of writing*

Statistical maps sometimes also include dot or pin maps, the frequency of the dots indicating the relative density of the statistic being shown. Sometimes the size of the dots is varied as the magnitude of the data being presented varies. The drawing above shows an example of a statistical map.

Another word of warning from Darrell Huff in *How to Lie with Statistics*:

> A map shows what proportion of the American income is now being taken, and spent, by the federal government. It does this by shading the areas of the states west of the Mississippi (excepting Louisiana, Arkansas, and a part of Missouri) to indicate that federal spending has become equal to the total incomes of the people of those states.
>
> The deception lies in choosing states having large areas, but, because of sparse population, relatively small incomes. With equal honesty (and equal dishonesty) the map maker might have started shading New York or New England and come out with a vastly smaller and less impressive shadow.

Activity

Now go back to the visual presentation which you made of the data concerning greetings cards and display stands. On the basis of what you now know about the advantages and disadvantages of different charts and graphs, would you present the data differently?

Let's examine the choices we would have in presenting that data as effectively as possible. At first sight, we have to choose whether to present specific sales figures, or trends in sales, a combination of the two, or a picture of the information (pictogram).

The information to be represented is discrete: the sales in each newsagent shop is distinct and separate from the others and since we are given no information on time of sales, there is apparently no trend to present, so a graph is not appropriate, and little is to be gained from showing a lot of little pictures of display stands. We are also told that the importance of the data is in the *comparisons* of sales using the two different stands, not in which shop or shops had the highest sales.

From this we can deduce that a table or bar chart is the best visual aid to use, as they will convey specific data and allow comparisons to be seen *if* we organize the data sensibly.

Look at the eight examples below. The tables in 1, 2, 3 and 4 show specific data and the bar charts give a visual reinforcement of the message. However, 1, 5 and 6 are confusing as they do not emphasize the comparison between the two types of display stand, whereas when the data is grouped by display stand it is easier to see what is important straight away.

Examples 4 (table) and 8 (chart) show the data the most effectively. Which of the two would you prefer? Would it depend on your purpose and/or your audience?

SALES OF GREETINGS CARDS 15–20 MARCH

Example 1

Shop	Total sales
A	175
B	410
C	220
D	187
E	435
F	475
G	286
H	575
I	275
J	525

Shows specific data, but not very effectively.

Example 2

Shop	Traditional stand	Revolving stand
A	175	
B		410
C	220	
D	187	
E		435
F		475
G	286	
H		575
I	275	
J		525

Shows specific data.

Example 3

Shop	Traditional stand	Revolving stand
A	175	
C	220	
D	187	
G	286	
I	275	
B		410
E		435
F		475
H		575
J		525

Example 4

Traditional stands		*Revolving stands*	
Shop	*Traditional*	*Shop*	*Revolving*
A	175	B	410
C	220	E	435
D	187	F	475
G	286	H	575
I	275	J	525

Shows specific data; well organized.

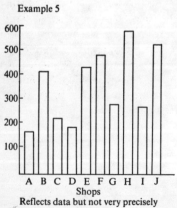

Example 5

Reflects data but not very precisely
and difficult to assimilate

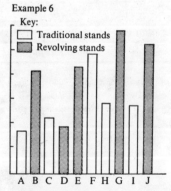

Example 6

Key:
☐ Traditional stands
▨ Revolving stands

Reflects data, attempts to show
comparison but effect is confusing.

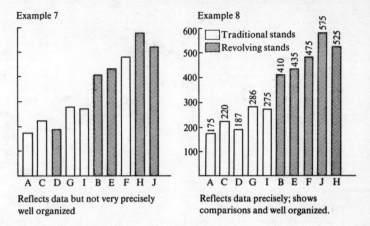

Example 7

A C D G I B E F H J

Reflects data but not very precisely
well organized

Example 8

☐ Traditional stands
▨ Revolving stands

175 220 187 286 275 410 435 475 575 525

A C D G I B E F J H

Reflects data precisely; shows
comparisons and well organized.

A final word of warning

'There are three kinds of lies: lies, damned lies and statistics,'
said Mark Twain, and statistics in the hands of the ignorant, the
inexperienced or the downright dishonest can be made to mislead the reader. A writer has to select facts for a chart, graph or
table and omit others. The facts he does present may be accurate,
but the impression they create may be misleading. Look at the
following bar chart for an example of selective omission. The
casual reader might simply *assume* that sales rose steadily from
1973 to 1981. However, if we look at the section of the chart
which has been removed, ostensibly to save space, the picture is
rather different. Sales have *not* gone up consistently. The chart
showing a broken line to indicate the missing years 1976, 1977
and 1978 would be accurate, but misleading.

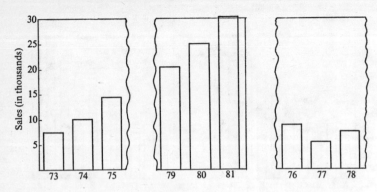

Example of selective omission

The moral, therefore, is that when we read charts, graphs and illustrations, or interpret statements which quote statistics, we must do so very critically. Are the ideas accurate and complete? And when we transmit ideas through graphic aids or statistics we must continually ask ourselves whether we are being complete and honest in our intentions.

Review

1 List five advantages of visual presentation.
2 List the specific factors which should influence you in your choice of visual aid.
3 What specific advantages do tables have that make them particularly useful for presenting large quantities of statistical data?
4 If you wanted to present 'continuous' information would you use line graphs or bar charts?
5 List at least five ways in which someone presenting statistical data could intentionally mislead the reader.

ANSWERS

1 Turn back to p. 311, 'Advantages of visual presentation', to check your answers. But here is a quick checklist:

● gains attention
● provides information quickly

- speeds comprehension
- relieves monotony
- conveys trends and tendencies
- highlights specific figures
- shows relationships
- reinforces the words
- highlights differences

2 In choosing a visual aid, your first consideration will be, Is a visual aid needed? Will it produce some of the advantages above? Then you should consider:

- What exactly are you trying to 'say'?
- The complexity of the information.
- The ability and motivation of the reader.
- Whether you want to highlight specific figures, show trends, or compare and contrast differences.

3 Tables are particularly useful for:

- displaying large amounts of data in a relatively small space
- providing an easy reference device from which specific figures can be picked out
- making comparisons between and among statistics
- conveying quantitative data in a more comprehensible form than submerged in the body of the text

4 Generally speaking line graphs are used to present 'continuous' information and bar charts to present 'discrete' information. However, histograms, which look like bar charts but should not be confused with them, can be used to present 'continuous' information.

5 Graphic presentation can mislead by:

- Omitting a zero line.
- Starting a graph just below the lowest point on the graph line.
- Condensing or extending the scale on the two axes in relation to one another.
- Omitting percentages and producing disproportionate wedges on a pie chart.

340 The business of writing

- Showing increase in number by showing wider bars or bigger symbols on bar charts or pictorial charts.
- Choosing to shade particular areas rather than others on a statistical map.
- Selective omission: omitting certain facts which if they were included would tell a rather different story!

Activity

Get a copy of Darrell Huff's *How to Lie with Statistics* and start by reading as far as the end of the chapter called 'The Well-Chosen Average' (Chapter 2 in my copy). Find out how easy it is to be misled (and to mislead) by using the common expression 'on average'.

Using this knowledge what particular cautions would you recommend to the reader if the following figures were presented as (a) mean, (b) modal, and (c) median averages?

Salaries of directors

Mrs Simmonds	£15,000
Mr Clough	£70,000
Mr Langham	£16,000
Mr Green	£13,000
Mr Shaw	£14,000
Mr Beg	£60,000

Incidentally, Darrell Huff's book will not only amuse and horrify you with its examples of how easy it is to lie with statistics, but it will also teach you quite a lot about statistics.

If, however, the prospect of 'number-crunching' at all tends to frighten you, try working through *Using Statistics in Business* by Peter Clark, also in Pan Breakthrough Books.

Presenting non-statistical information effectively

It is not just statistical information which can benefit from being presented visually. A chart showing the steps in a process, or a diagram showing the constituent parts of a piece of equipment, can save thousands of words, and reduce the likelihood of misunderstanding. Sometimes, reducing the number of words can be not only time-saving, but the only way to communicate where the message is aimed at such a large audience of different people from different backgrounds and with different abilities that a verbal message may be in the wrong language and incomprehensible to many, including those who are unable to read.

Public and directional information

Geographical maps are probably the most obvious form of visual aid in this category, but in offices, shops, public places and work places, signs, symbols and cartoons may be used to direct and inform visitors, the public and the workforce. In our western society, the use of symbols is now quite widespread and assumes a fairly sophisticated level of 'visual literacy' (the ability to 'read' pictures) on the part of the whole population. The well-known ambiguity of road signs may cause much amusement but could have serious consequences in failing to communicate the intended message:

Parachute
dropping area?

Danger: Man opening
umbrella?

Danger: Woman
lying in road?

Do you know what these signs are really conveying? The first one signifies: 'hazard'; the second: 'roadworks', and the third: 'uneven road'. Some road signs are considerably more difficult to understand immediately. However, the words would take up more space, take longer to read and would probably still be ambiguous, if not incomprehensible to some, e.g. 'heavy plant crossing' may conjure up something from *The Day of the Triffids*! Where language barriers may cause problems in interpreting written or spoken words, e.g. between different ethnic workers on the same workforce, the use of signs and symbols allied with a touch of humour may be a very effective method of presenting information.

Instructional or problem-solving information

Flow or process chart Flow charts are very useful in representing in graphic form all the steps in a process. They begin at the very beginning and take the reader, or trainee perhaps, through a logical sequence of steps to the completion of the operation. In some cases this will involve assembling the materials or ingredients, processing them, and then channelling them in all directions to other user groups. In other cases, it may be a very simple operation. Represented visually, the flow chart needs no special symbols. A sequence of written statements, linked by arrows to indicate the line of reasoning, is enough. However, method study officers, systems analysts, training officers and others who analyse jobs and processes tend to use a series of simple symbols to represent the various kinds of activity involved:

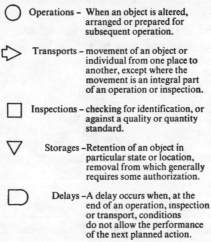

Operations – When an object is altered, arranged or prepared for subsequent operation.

Transports – movement of an object or individual from one place to another, except where the movement is an integral part of an operation or inspection.

Inspections – checking for identification, or against a quality or quantity standard.

Storages –Retention of an object in particular state or location, removal from which generally requires some authorization.

Delays –A delay occurs when, at the end of an operation, inspection or transport, conditions do not allow the performance of the next planned action.

Activity

Using these symbols if possible, or a simpler system of your own, draw a flow chart showing the process of an operative preparing a cup of instant coffee. Start with 'operative seated on chair in lounge' and end with 'operative seated on chair with coffee'. There are approximately twenty-five stages in the process. Assume the operative is using an electric kettle. Then see the suggested version opposite.

FLOW PROCESS CHART FOR PREPARATION OF CUP OF INSTANT COFFEE

Seated on chair

Stand up

Walk to kitchen work top

Pick up kettle

Walk to sink

Fill kettle

Walk to work top

Put kettle down, plug in and switch on

Walk to cupboard

Remove cup and saucer

Walk to work top

Place cup and saucer on work top

Remove teaspoon from drawer

Remove coffee and sugar from cupboard over work top

Add coffee and sugar to cup

Replace coffee and sugar in cupboard

Carry cup and saucer to kettle

Wait for kettle to boil

Switch off kettle, unplug and pour water into cup

Carry cup and saucer to refrigerator

Remove milk from refrigerator

Add milk to cup

Return milk to refrigerator

Walk to lounge with cup of coffee

Sit down on chair

Seated on chair with coffee.

It is useful to be able to break down a job or process into stages in this way. It is easier to explain it to someone learning the job and it enables processes and jobs to be made quicker, easier and generally more efficient by working out where there may be wastage of time or energy (unnecessary movement, for example) and where unnecessary or avoidable delays occur.

Algorithms An algorithm is a set of instructions and decisions which will always give an answer, provided the procedure is followed correctly. Algorithms are very similar to flow charts in their function, but they also include a breakdown of the decision-making element. At any point in the system where a decision has to be made, the chart can show the alternative choices open to the operative and the subsequent route he must take depending on the particular decision made. For this reason, they are sometimes called 'decision-trees' and the chart resembles a tree with various branches showing all the possible routes and the re-entries back into the main route.

Again, although simple boxes and arrows are perfectly adequate the representation is helped by a set of standard symbols:

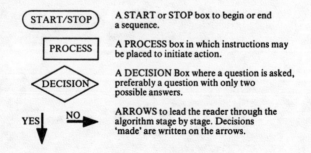

START/STOP   A START or STOP box to begin or end a sequence.

PROCESS   A PROCESS box in which instructions may be placed to initiate action.

DECISION   A DECISION Box where a question is asked, preferably a question with only two possible answers.

YES   NO   ARROWS to lead the reader through the algorithm stage by stage. Decisions 'made' are written on the arrows.

The example of an algorithm given opposite shows how to write a summary.

HOW TO WRITE A SUMMARY

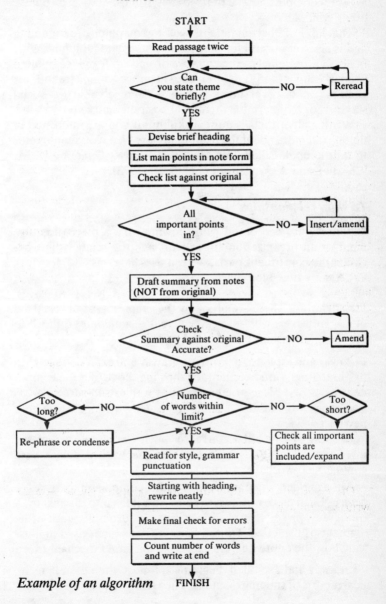

START

Read passage twice

Can you state theme briefly? —NO→ Reread

YES

Devise brief heading

List main points in note form

Check list against original

All important points in? —NO→ Insert/amend

YES

Draft summary from notes (NOT from original)

Check Summary against original Accurate? —NO→ Amend

YES

Too long? ←NO— Number of words within limit? —NO→ Too short?

Re-phrase or condense

Check all important points are included/expand

YES

Read for style, grammar punctuation

Starting with heading, rewrite neatly

Make final check for errors

Count number of words and write at end

Example of an algorithm   FINISH

More complex and extended algorithms may incorporate other symbols.

This kind of charting adapts well to computer programming and is also very useful for diagnostic testing and fault finding. It is also an extremely efficient way of getting forms completed properly and is therefore often used in public administration, for example to discover quickly if people are eligible for social services, or to determine their legal position, and so on.

Writing algorithms is quite a skill but if you are interested in finding out more about the techniques involved, you should refer to a little book called *The Algorithm Writer's Guide* by D. M. Wheatley and A. W. Unwin (Longman, 1972).

To show relationships

Where we are concerned with showing what a piece of equipment or an organization consists of, and the relationships between the constituent parts, we can use diagrams and drawings and 'family tree' type charts.

Line drawings These are probably the simplest type of visual aid of all. However, without perspective it is sometimes difficult to see the relationships between the parts.

Cutaway and exploded drawings Cutaway and exploded sketches or photographs are excellent for showing the reader the component parts of a piece of equipment as well as sub-surface areas ('what goes on inside'). They are usually arranged to give a perspective view.

A cutaway can often convey a much clearer picture of the interior working parts of a complex mechanical device than could a 5000-word description.

An exploded diagram presents the component parts of a device. Each piece is drawn to show how it fits into, or next to, a contiguous piece. If it is a piece part, for example, each of its segments is exploded. Dotted lines are sometimes used to illustrate how the entire unit is attached to the larger mechanism.

Cutaway and exploded diagrams are most often used in technical reports or training manuals. They really require the services

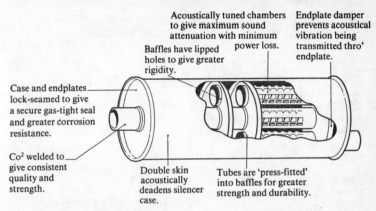

Acoustically tuned chambers to give maximum sound attenuation with minimum power loss.

Endplate damper prevents acoustical vibration being transmitted thro' endplate.

Baffles have lipped holes to give greater rigidity.

Case and endplates lock-seamed to give a secure gas-tight seal and greater corrosion resistance.

CO^2 welded to give consistent quality and strength.

Double skin acoustically deadens silencer case.

Tubes are 'press-fitted' into baffles for greater strength and durability.

Cutaway diagram (showing the inside of a car exhaust silencer)

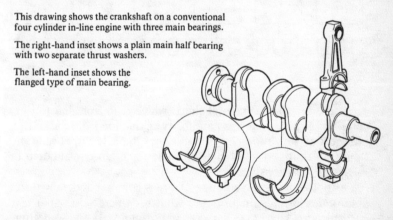

This drawing shows the crankshaft on a conventional four cylinder in-line engine with three main bearings.

The right-hand inset shows a plain main half bearing with two separate thrust washers.

The left-hand inset shows the flanged type of main bearing.

Exploded diagram

of an artist who can draw with care and precision, and can also use his imagination, but if you have a little talent for drawing you could always be prepared to have a go.

FAMILY TREE CHARTS

Organization charts Modern organizations are so complex that it is often difficult to have a clear understanding of who reports to whom and how exactly you fit in. Every employee usually feels more comfortable when he knows precisely where he stands within a company, who is his boss, who is his boss's boss, and so on.

There are several kinds of organization chart, but probably the most common is the vertical chart like the one shown below which reads from top to bottom.

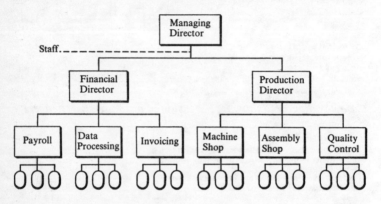

Example of a vertical organization chart

There are also horizontal charts which read from left to right and circle charts that show authority emanating from the centre. In most organization charts, solid lines indicate direct relationships and broken lines indicate indirect, often consultative or advisory, relationships.

Although authority and the chain of command usually differ between the real situation and what is depicted on paper, the organization chart does serve an important purpose. Something is needed to give an appreciation of the structure of the company and nothing does it so quickly and easily as an organization chart. At the same time, it is well to remember that the actual centres of authority in an organization usually differ from what is shown on the chart, and the lines of communication do not always follow the lines on an organization chart.

Information trees If the set of information which you want to present or need to consider can be classified into subsets, it can be displayed in the form of 'trees' rather like a family tree. However, unlike the algorithm, this method of representation is not problem-solving or instructional in the sense of being prescriptive. It merely gives a historic view of the 'problem' showing all related facets and leaves the reader to interpret the relationships and draw conclusions.

It is, incidentally, a useful method of taking notes (see p. 350).

Information mapping or charting A variation on the idea of information trees, this system allows you to show all the information on one subject on a single piece of paper, chart or transparency. It doesn't necessarily rely on the existence of subsets or close relationships, but it does allow you to see at a glance all the items which make up your subject, and you may find that having written down your information in boxes placed almost at random on the paper, you will detect relationships between one 'box' and another. These relationships can be shown by arrows, or by cross-links in the form of ●——●, as in the diagram on p. 351, which represents a quick information chart which formed the basis of this book and its companion volume, *What do you mean, 'Communication'?*.

Overlays

When the visual aid is to be part of an oral presentation, a useful method of presenting statistical information is the use of transparent overlays. All the graphic aids mentioned can be used in this way. A base chart gives the scale, grid, title and so on, and comparatively simple data is gradually superimposed through the use of different transparent overlays made with different coloured transparencies. This combination could be used as a line graph, a bar chart or even a statistical map.

Obviously, all the same rules apply but it is a very effective

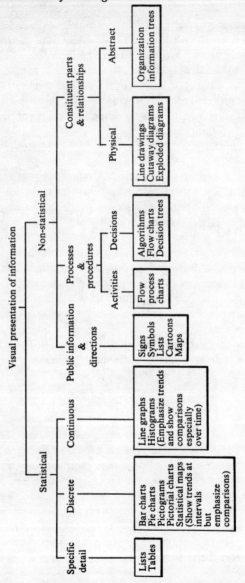

Example of an information tree based on the contents of this chapter

WHAT DO YOU MEAN 'COMMUNICATION'?/THE BUSINESS OF
COMMUNICATING

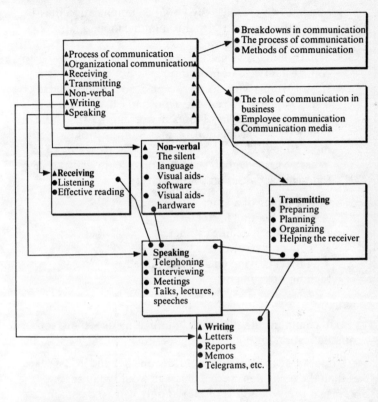

Example of an information chart

method of presentation in that a specific comparison can be
made and then removed. In other words, whereas on a chart of
a single dimension, once all the information is on the chart it is
difficult for the reader to eliminate some of the information,
when overlays are used, the reader can be shown only those
overlays that he is particularly interested in. Another advantage
is that overlays allow the presenter to show the cumulative effect
of different numerical data.

The same advantages, of course, apply to building up complex
diagrams and charts of non-statistical information.

Review

1 Suggest two reasons why visual communication may be more effective than verbal communication.
2 What is 'visual literacy'?
3 What kinds of visual aid might you consider using to convey a process or procedure?
4 If you were trying to devise an instruction manual or leaflet which would enable a mechanic to discover why a washing-machine has stopped working so that he can repair it, which method of presentation would be the most effective?
5 What visual symbols would you use to indicate the following activities on a flow chart?

Check typing of a letter.
A worker waiting for materials.
Papers filed in a filing cabinet.
Picking up a screwdriver.
An object moving on a conveyor belt.
Signing a document.

ANSWERS

1 Visual communication can be more effective than verbal communication for the following reasons:

● Visual aids can often communicate quicker and in less space than the equivalent verbal message would require.
● Visual presentation is often the only way to communicate where language and literacy barriers would make a verbal message incomprehensible.

2 'Visual literacy' is the ability to 'read' pictures, signs, symbols, charts, etc. Although visual communication can be very effective, and we are generally used to receiving messages visually since we are said to gain 83 per cent of our information in this way, nevertheless some people are 'visually illiterate': they find interpreting visual communication more difficult than reading words. For this reason, messages should perhaps

be communicated by both verbal and visual media, wherever possible, as in this message in a lift:

3 Flow charts, algorithms and decision trees are all variations of plotting visually the steps in a process or procedure.
4 An algorithm. Algorithms are particularly useful for diagnosing faults and problem-solving, since they should provide an answer to every possible question, providing the procedure is followed correctly *and* the algorithm has been designed logically.
5 Checking typing of a letter – *inspection*: □

A worker waiting for materials – *delay*: ⃞

Papers filed in a filing cabinet – *storage*: ▽

Picking up a screwdriver – *operation*: ○

An object moving on a conveyor belt – *transport*: ⇨

Signing a document – *operation*: ○

Activity

1 Draw a cutaway diagram of any simple object, e.g. a fountain pen, a cigarette lighter.
2 Try to draw a flow chart tracing the process of application for your course or your job. You will probably need to interview people concerned with admissions, or recruitment and selection to find out what pieces of paper are involved and what happens to them.

   Do you think from examining the steps in the procedure that the process could be made any simpler? More efficient?

Part 3:
The bricks and mortar
of English

If you suspect that your knowledge of basic
English either has been rather neglected in the
past, or has become rather rusty over the years
since you left school, you may find it helpful to
work through both Chapter 14 which explains
briefly some of the basic elements of the English
language and the way it is constructed, and
Chapter 15 which covers some of the more
common problems we are likely to encounter
when trying to write correctly and grammatically.

If, on the other hand, you feel fairly confident
that consciously or instinctively you usually
manage to write quite easily without committing
the errors which other people seem to make, then
you may prefer to use these two chapters merely
as a quick reference section to check your
knowledge on those occasions when you have a
nagging doubt about what is generally acceptable.

In either case, I would suggest that you have a
go at the self-check on page 359 as this will help
you to know just how well you use the language
and will indicate which areas or problems you
need to look at in more detail. You can then go
on to look at the relevant section in Chapter 15.

Finally you will find at the back of the book
seven appendices intended to provide quick
reference information on punctuation, writing
numbers and using capitals, dividing words at the
end of lines, words which are commonly misused
and confused, and last – but not least – spelling.

14 | What is a verb then?

You may not know what a verb is, or for that matter what a noun, or a preposition, or an adverbial clause, is. Furthermore, you may feel that it is not necessary to know. Perhaps you feel that these things are the stuff of English lessons, English teachers and dusty grammar books. Or perhaps you feel that these words are just another kind of jargon: useful for the specialists in the field of English but unnecessary double-dutch to everyone else. And you may be right!

Many people speak and write English quite correctly without knowing very much about the rules and conventions of the English language. They automatically apply them without thinking or realizing that they are doing so. Most of us, because we have been brought up to speak English as our mother tongue, are able for the most part to put down words in the right order; that is, in a way that other people expect, and understand fairly easily. Most of us, for example, would recognize that to write: 'I haven't never been their' is wrong – wrong in that 'their' is used when we are indicating possession of something – 'their coats', 'their children' – but is not spelled like that when we are referring to a place; and that two negatives cancel one another out – 'I haven't never' = 'I have not never' = 'I have', which is presumably the exact opposite of what the speaker meant to say.

The problem is that all of us, to a greater or lesser extent, make mistakes through either ignorance or carelessness and these mistakes can lead to misunderstandings, confusion and sometimes failure to communicate in the way we intended.

As we saw in the earlier chapters, we communicate by means of previously agreed symbols, but if we don't use the correct symbols, or if we don't use them in the way other people expect, they will have difficulty understanding what we mean. If we break the rules of the code they will at worst not be able to understand, and at best be irritated at being obliged to make what they consider to be an unnecessary effort to work out what we mean.

Another reason for trying to use good English is that otherwise, rightly or wrongly, others may judge us ignorant, ill-educated, lazy or careless – all characteristics which are not very desirable in our society. As we have seen, it is unfortunately often the case that the unintended non-verbal communication – in this context, poor spelling, or bad grammar or awkward sentence structure – will have a greater impact on the receiver than the real *content* of what we are trying to say.

But, you may say, while all this may be true, and acceptable justification for learning and obeying the generally accepted rules and conventions of the English language, why is it necessary to know the names of the various parts of a sentence or the functions of the parts of speech? The reason is simple if you think about it. It is almost impossible to explain to someone where and why he is making mistakes, how he is breaking the rules of the code or even what those rules are, unless he knows the names of the things you are talking about. Imagine trying to explain to someone else how to do your job or some part of your hobby perhaps, without first describing what things are called and how they relate to one another. For example, it would be very difficult to teach someone to drive a car unless he knew the names of the various pedals and switches and so on. It might just be possible, if you and the learner were both sitting in the car, to get by with instructions like 'Unless you move this like this and that like that while moving your foot like this and gradually putting your other foot on that, the car won't move!' but it would make understanding what to do much more difficult and would depend on a practical visual demonstration in the car. Similarly, any explanation of accepted English language practice depends on knowing at least some of the terminology.

In this and the following chapter we shall briefly be looking at the way in which our language is constructed and the way in which we should use it in order to reduce the chances of our being misunderstood, or of causing unnecessary irritation in our receivers. Above all, these chapters will concentrate on the more common problems and errors in using the language and will therefore cover only the bare essentials of English grammar and usage necessary to solve the problems and avoid the more common errors. If you find that you need more detailed explanation than is possible here, or that you become hooked on what can really be a fascinating study and want to go further, you will find some suggestions for further reading as you progress through the chapters.

Self-check

Let's start by finding out what you know already. Look at the following sentences and decide whether in your opinion they are correct or contain errors. Make any corrections you think are necessary – there may be more than one error in a sentence and some sentences may have no errors. Unless you need to rewrite the whole sentence in order to correct it, you need rewrite only the word or words which are wrong.

1 Thanking you for your letter of 6 Febuary in which you complained about the control mechanism.
2 Furnished accomodation is required by young lady about to be married for one year.
3 Each of the new members are to be introduced seperately.
4 The office needs redecorating, but its carpet is in good condition.
5 The manager, together with his assistants, is working on the project now.
6 Toys, which are dangerous, should not be given to children.
7 She is one of the students who is taking the examination.
8 He found the job very different to what he had expected.
9 Please book the seats for my wife and I.
10 He is the man who we expect to be the next chairman.
11 Looking at it the next morning, the task seemed easier.
12 We complained about them having taken the notice off the board.

13 She cannot type as quickly as I.
14 Its the type of product that we need in order to be competitive.
15 She does not remember the incident as well as me.
16 He is the only one who you could ask.
17 Nothing succeeds like success.
18 I do not remember him having told me about the meeting.
19 Although they were dissapointed they had only theirselves to blame.
20 The power of his arguements, which were very persuasive, were not enough.
21 A cue of people stretched along the pavement, which was getting longer.
22 Our trading had not only increased beyond our expectations but also our hopes.
23 There was less paper than was needed to do the job.
24 Neither of the rooms were laid out like he had requested.
25 This is the letter from the file, which he wrote last week.
26 It looks like he will succeed.
27 In my opinion he never has, and never will be, a success.
28 He swims like a fish, but runs like an elephant.
29 They ordered an extra a hundred boxes for the new season.
30 Due to become the next president, he was hurt not to have been invited.
31 They finished there work before going home.
32 Due to the strike, production was severely delayed.
33 The two company's were not only in competition but also at risk.
34 He asked me to carefully correct the errors before giving it back.
35 He is the tallest of the two brothers.
36 There were less papers in this year's exams.
37 Surprisingly, he did not deny that he was not guilty.
38 Entering the office, he saw the secretary already typing the report.

39 He writes reports as well, if not better than, his boss.
40 He survived the scandal without hardly a dent to his reputation.
41 The report will take me some time to read.
42 These kind of problems are very difficult to solve.
43 Due to shortage of supplies, we are unable to dispatch the goods today.
44 Cycling along the lane, the bull suddenly charged out in front of me.
45 Less problems might have meant success instead of failure.
46 If I was you I would go to the meeting.
47 Going into the office, the secretary could be seen already typing the memo.
48 Having opened the meeting, there was no way of avoiding the issue.
49 Having stolen the cash, the manager had no option but to sack me.
50 There was fewer people and less questions than had been expected.

ANSWERS

Altogether there were fifty mistakes in the sentences. How many did you recognize? Check your answers carefully with the correct sentences below. The number of mistakes in the original sentence is indicated by the number in brackets.

refer to page

389   1 Thank you for your letter of 6 February in which you complained about the control mechanism. (2)
400   2 Furnished accommodation is required for one year by young lady about to be married. (2)
378   3 Each of the new members is to be introduced separately. (2)
406   4 The office needs redecorating, but its carpet is in good condition. (√)
378   5 The manager, together with his assistants, is working on the project now. (√)

410 **6** Toys that are dangerous should not be given to children. (1)

378 **7** She is one of the students who are taking the examination. (1)

417 **8** He found the job very different from what he had expected. (1)

404 **9** Please book the seats for my wife and me. (1)

405 **10** He is the man whom we expect to be the next chairman. (1)

385 **11** When we (he/she, etc.) looked at it the next morning, the task seemed easier. (1)

389 **12** We complained about their having taken the notice off the board. (1)

404 **13** She cannot type as quickly as I. (√)

406 **14** It's the type of product that we need in order to be competitive. (2)

404 **15** She does not remember the incident as well as I. (1)

405 **16** He is the only one whom you could ask. (1)

417 **17** Nothing succeeds like success. (√)

389 **18** I do not remember his having told me about the meeting. (1)

402 **19** Although they were disappointed, they had only themselves to blame. (2)

378 **20** The power of his arguments, which were very persuasive, was not enough. (2)

401 **21** A queue of people, which was getting longer, stretched along the pavement. (2)

417 **22** Our trading had increased not only beyond our expectations but also beyond our hopes. (1)

398 **23** There was less paper than was needed to do the job. (√)

378 **24** Neither of the rooms was laid out as he had requested. (2)

401 **25** This is the letter, which he wrote last week, from the file. (1)

418 **26** It looks as if he will succeed. (1)

419 **27** In my opinion he never has been, and never will be, a success. (1)

418 **28** He swims like a fish, but runs like an elephant. (√)

397 **29** They ordered an extra hundred boxes for the new season. (1)

397 **30** Due to become the next president, he was hurt not to have been invited. (√)

407 **31** They finished their work before going home. (1)

397 **32** Owing to the strike, production was severely delayed. (1)

406 **33** The two companies were not only in competition but also at risk. (1)

382 **34** He asked me to correct the errors carefully before giving it back. (1)

397 **35** He is the taller of the two brothers. (1)

398 **36** There were fewer papers in this year's exams. (1)

421 **37** Surprisingly, he did not deny that he was guilty. (1)

385 **38** Entering the office, he saw the secretary already typing the report. (√)

419 **39** He writes reports as well as, if not better than, his boss. (1)

421 **40** He survived the scandal with hardly a dent to his reputation. (1)

400 **41** The report will take me some time to read (√)

378 **42** This kind of problem is difficult to solve. (1)

397 **43** Owing to shortage of supplies, we are unable to dispatch the goods today. (1)

385 **44** As I was cycling along the lane, the bull suddenly charged out in front of me. (1)

398 **45** Fewer problems might have meant success instead of failure. (1)

391 **46** If I were you, I would go to the meeting. (1)

385 **47** As I entered the office, the secretary could be seen already typing the memo. (1)

389 **48** Having opened the meeting, I (we/they) had no way of avoiding the issue. (1)

385 **49** Since I stole the cash, the manager had no option but to sack me. (1)

379 **50** There were fewer people and fewer questions than had been expected. (2)

The numbers in the left-hand margin refer to the numbers of the pages in the next chapter, where you will find an explanation of the errors in the test sentences.

How did you score? If you spotted fewer than 30 errors you would do well to read through the whole of this and the next chapter carefully. If you spotted 30 to 45 errors, look particularly at the relevant sections in the next chapter, but you obviously write fairly correct English (even if you are not always sure of the rules). 45+ Congratulations!

Self-check

Before we discuss the reasons why some of those sentences were incorrect and why some of them which perhaps you thought were incorrect, are strictly speaking correct, see what you can remember about the eight main parts of speech by describing what each of them does and providing some examples of each.

Part of speech   Function   Examples

Noun
Pronoun
Adjective
Verb
Adverb
Preposition
Conjunction
Interjection

The parts of speech in brief

Every word in an English sentence belongs to one or another of the eight parts of speech, according to the work it is doing in that sentence. Some words can belong to more than one part of speech – but we will come to that later. These parts of speech are as follows:

Nouns are words which *name* persons, places or things, e.g. 'man', 'Peter', 'Bristol', 'book', 'anger'.

Pronouns are words which are used *instead of nouns* in order to save repeating the noun several times in the sentence, e.g. 'The manager met *his* assistant and *they* went to the meeting.'

Adjectives tell us more about nouns and pronouns. They *qualify* or describe persons, places and things, e.g. 'This *beautiful* picture is the *finest* in *this* collection.'

Verbs are the '*doing words*'. They are the words around which the whole sentence turns, for they show what happens, e.g. 'The factory *closes* for three weeks', i.e. what is done. 'She *gave* him the letter', i.e. what is said to be. 'He *is* the brother of my friend', i.e. what is.

Adverbs are to verbs what adjectives are to nouns and pronouns. They *modify the verb* or, in other words, describe the circumstances (how, when, where, why, etc.) in which the action represented by the verb is done, e.g. 'He writes *slowly* but types *quickly*.'

Prepositions are words (usually) placed before a noun or pronoun to show its *connection* or relation with the other words in the sentence, e.g. 'She came *into* the room.' The preposition 'into' shows the connection between her coming and the room. If we change the preposition to 'from', that connection is altered.

Conjunctions are used to *connect* words, phrases or clauses in the sentence, e.g. 'Matthew *and* his partner have arrived.' 'The company has the same name, *but* is owned by his brother.'

Interjections are used to show emotion or draw attention and do not strictly speaking form part of the sentence. They are not normally used in business writing, e.g. 'Hallo!' 'Indeed?'

Self-check

Now look back at your list and assess how well you did. You may still be uncertain about some of your answers because parts of speech are not always as simple to distinguish as this brief explanation may suggest, but it should provide you with a quick reference list.

Self-check

Now try this exercise. Give the different parts of speech that each of the following represents:

arm	maroon
as	rough
base	second
best	set
desolate	where
error	why
fish	wrong

To check your answers, look up each word in the dictionary. As you will realize, often a word is used as more than one part of speech. The different ways a word can be used are indicated in the dictionary by the abbreviations n. (noun), adv. (adverb), v.t. (verb transitive) and so on. So, in this sentence: 'She bruised her arm', the word 'arm' is being used as a noun, and in this sentence: 'The soldiers picked up their arms and marched on', although the meaning of the word 'arm' is different from the first sentence, it is still being used as a noun. However, when we say: 'They were armed with shovels and pickaxes', we are using 'arm' as a verb – in this case, as part of the past tense of the verb 'to arm'.

In looking up these words you may have come across abbreviations which you didn't understand. If so, you will probably find somewhere near the front of the dictionary a list of the abbreviations used in the dictionary together with their meanings. However, this may still pose problems. Perhaps you are none the wiser when you find that a word can be used as a 'verb transitive' and its 'past participle' is such and such. In this case, you could first try looking up the word itself in the dictionary. For example, you will find the word 'transitive' under 'transit n.'. Look it up now. Found it? You will probably find something like this: 'adj. transitive,' (i.e.' transitive' is the adjective formed from the noun, 'transit') 'passing over: having the power of passing: taking a direct object (gram.).' From this we discover the meaning of the word and, in particular, that in *grammatical* terms it means 'taking an object,' so a transitive verb is a verb which takes an object, or in other words, 'passes over' an idea from the subject to object, from the *doer* to the *receiver*. Put another way, a transitive verb needs an object to complete its meaning, e.g. 'She *hit* the tree.' Without 'the tree' we would be left asking: She hit *what*?

Activity

What, then, do you think an 'intransitive' verb is? Now look it up to check that you have guessed correctly. Can you think of five examples of intransitive verbs?

Now look them up in the dictionary to see whether they are transitive (v.t.) or intransitive (v.i.).

Perhaps you found that some could be used as both, or that with one meaning the verb is transitive, but with another meaning it is intransitive. Let's look at an example of a verb which can be both transitive and intransitive.

'She manages.' In this sentence the verb 'manage' must mean 'get by' or 'cope' because there is no object and yet the verb is complete – it makes sense. So 'manage' used like this is intransitive. Now look at this sentence: 'She manages the company.' Here 'manage' means 'handle', 'conduct' or 'control' and needs the object 'the company' to complete it, so 'manage' used this way is transitive.

Most of the time you will probably not need to know the difference between transitive and intransitive verbs because you will naturally use them correctly without thinking twice. However, it is important to know the difference because some of the more unusual verbs are frequently used incorrectly; e.g. 'require' when it means 'need' is a transitive verb which requires an object, and should not be used intransitively as in 'A special programme requires to be arranged for their visit.' A correct version might be 'A special programme needs to be. . .' or 'A special programme will have to be. . .'

Self-check

Can you see anything wrong with this sentence?

The report which you wanted was laying on the table.

If you can't, look up the verbs 'to lay' and 'to lie' in the dictionary.

'To lay' is transitive and must therefore have an object: 'Hens lay eggs.' (Present.) 'I laid the report on the desk.' (Past.) 'They were laying the table.' (Past continuous.)

'To lie' is intransitive: 'I lie down to go to sleep.' (Present.) 'I lay on the bed.' (Past.) 'They were lying on the floor.' (Past continuous.)

Notice the difference between the past versions of the two verbs. These are frequently confused. 'The report was laying next to the typewriter.' 'Was laying' is the past tense of the verb 'to lay' which is transitive and must therefore have an object, but there is no object in the sentence. If we want to say what the report was doing we must make sure we use the correct verb in the correct form: 'The report . . . was *lying* next to the typewriter.' Without care the same confusion can occur in the present tense: 'They are *laying* the table' (transitive) but 'The books are *lying* on the desk' (intransitive).

Joining the parts together – the sentence

The sentence

A sentence is the expression in words of a complete thought. In other words, it is complete in itself and does not leave the reader or listener with a sense of something unfinished.

Subject and predicate

Every sentence must have a 'subject' – the person or thing under discussion; and every sentence must have a 'predicate' – what is said about the subject. Example:

Subject	Predicate
The manager +	has interviewed all the candidates

The subject is usually a noun or pronoun; the predicate must have a verb, since it is the verb that tells us what is done or said to be.

Where there is another person or thing directly affected by the verb, this is called the 'object'. Example:

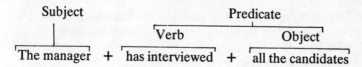

It is possible to go on dividing the parts of a sentence into twos in this way and this process of breaking down the structure of a sentence, called 'binary analysis', can be quite a useful way of making the structure of a sentence clearer, like this:

The manager has interviewed all the candidates.

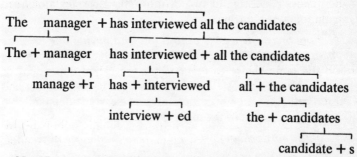

Now I am not suggesting that every time you write or utter a sentence you should go through this process. Fortunately most of the time we are able to speak and write quite fluently and work out, without thinking, how to structure our sentences. But, sometimes things go wrong: we get stuck in the middle of a sentence and are not sure how to finish it grammatically; or we reread a sentence and it sounds wrong and we are not sure why. Sometimes in these circumstances it is helpful to be able to work out the architecture of the sentence in order to solve the problem. Try it out next time you need help in constructing a sentence. In the meantime, it may be worth bearing it in mind as we go on to look at more complicated sentences and the parts of speech in more detail.

More complicated sentences

We do not usually write in a series of short sentences like the one above; we link two or three sentences together. This can be done by:

- *Joining them with conjunctions* (In this case we call the 'sentences' which combine to make the main sentence, 'main clauses' – they each have a subject and a verb and without the conjunction could stand alone.) Example:

sentence

main (or independent) clause	*main (or independent) clause*
The manager has interviewed all the candidates,	*but* he has not made a decision.
(The manager has interviewed all the candidates.	He has not made a decision.)

Sentences consisting of two or more main clauses are called 'compound sentences'.

- *Making one sentence the central one and having one or more others depending on it* (The 'sentences' which are depending on the main clause to make sense are called dependent or 'subordinate clauses'. Although they too have a subject and predicate, they are not completely and clearly understandable without reference to the main clause.) Example:

main clause	*subordinate clause*
He has seen all the candidates	who have applied for the job.

'Who have applied for the job' is a subordinate or dependent clause because it depends for its meaning on the main clause. Another example:

subordinate clause	*main clause*
Although he has seen all the candidates,	he has not made a decision.

Or:

main clause	*subordinate clause*
He has seen all the candidates,	although he has not made a decision.

Note: 'although' is a conjunction but it cannot join main clauses because it is a subordinate conjunction, not a 'pure' conjunction. See 'Conjunctions', p. 411–18

Sentences consisting of a main clause and at least one subordinate clause are called 'complex sentences.'

● *Turning the less important sentences into 'phrases' or even single words and adding these to the central sentence* (A 'phrase' is a group of related words, *without* a subject and a predicate, used as a part of speech, so a phrase could be called an adverbial phrase if it functions like an adverb in the sentence.)

In the following example, mark the main clause, the subordinate clause and the adverbial phrase.

Although he has interviewed all the candidates with great care, he has not made a decision.

subordinate clause

Although he has interviewed all the candidates with great care,

main clause
he has not made a decision.

phrase
(adverbial)

'With great care' is a phrase because it does not have a subject and a predicate and it certainly cannot stand alone. It acts in this sentence as an adverb in that it describes how the interviewing was done.

It is useful to be able to recognize phrases, clauses and sentences because, as we shall see, you will be better equipped to avoid grammatical and punctuation errors. In addition, you should be able to combine them in different ways to serve different purposes and create different effects.

See what you think of the following passage.

We have decided to modernize the dockyards at Devonport and Portsmouth. The improvements will be the most radical in their history. We will bring them up to date for the first time this century, We expect to spend about £76 million. The work will be completed in the early 1980s. The main features are as follows.

As one writer said: 'The human mind welcomes variety and a change of pace. It craves the freshness of different kinds of

372   *The bricks and mortar of English*

sentences. It does not want them to come marching out all the same, like so many cartridge boxes off the end of an assembly line.' The sentences in the passage above are all simple sentences and the effect on the reader is likely to be very similar to that produced by watching identical boxes falling off the end of an assembly line.

> *Self-check*
>
> Try rewriting the passage using a variety of sentence struc-
> tures – simple, compound and complex.

Without too much overhaul, it would be possible to produce something like this:

> We have decided to modernize the dockyards at Devonport and
> Portsmouth. The improvements, which will be the most radical in
> their history, will bring them up to date for the first time this century.
> We expect to spend about £76 million and to complete the work in
> the early 1980s. The main features are as follows.

The effect is still direct and clear. None of the sentences is too long for the reader to cope with and yet the passage flows more smoothly and provides a variety of pace which should keep the reader's interest.

However, in trying to avoid a series of simple, staccato-like sentences, there is always a danger of going to the other extreme. You might be amused (or bemused!) to read the original version of this passage which is borrowed from the first paragraph of a parliamentary statement on the modernization of the Royal Naval Dockyards.

> The following are the main features of the most far-reaching plans to
> modernize the dockyards at Devonport and Portsmouth in their
> history at a total estimated cost of £76 million which we hope to
> complete by the early 1980s, giving these two dockyards their first
> facelift of the century.

There can't be many readers who would be able to keep up with that sentence and still fewer who, when they got to the full-stop, would remember that the *first words* said: 'The following are the main features. . .' although they have had to wait until the beginning of the *next* paragraph before finding them!

So, as with many aspects of communication, there are no hard and fast rules. Constructing sentences which are varied and flowing but at the same time, clear and easy to read, requires thought and judgement.

15 | Common problems with English

You should now be aware of the basic framework of the English language and of some of the basic terms used to describe the various parts of speech and their functions. We now need to look at these in rather more detail in order to discover some of the typical problems which arise from not sticking to the accepted rules and conventions. It is not simply a case of obeying the rules for the sake of obeying rules. It is more a case of trying to obey the rules in order to avoid being unclear and ambiguous when we are communicating.

1 Subject–verb agreement

A verb must agree in number with its subject, so we say, 'The man *catches* the ball' but 'the men *catch* the train'. We make the verb 'to catch' plural because its subject, 'the men', is plural. That is fairly straightforward and in most simple cases the majority of people don't have too much difficulty. The problems arise when the sentence becomes complicated and it is difficult to be sure exactly which word or words represent the subject of the sentence.

(a) Multiple subjects

(i) 'and'. When two subjects are joined together by 'and', the verb must be plural rather than singular:

right	The man catches the train.
right	The man *and* his son catch the train.
wrong	In the garden there *was* a fountain and a swimming pool.
right	In the garden there *were* a fountain and a swimming pool.

But when two singular nouns represent one subject they are followed by a singular verb: 'The chairman and the founder of the company *are* (both) to be invited', *but* 'The chairman and founder of the company *is* to be invited.' (In the latter case, the chairman is the founder of the company, i.e. one person. Note also that in this case the definite article 'the' is only used once.)

Similarly, when the two words connected by 'and' represent one idea or are closely connected in thought, e.g. whisky and soda, fish and chips, they take a singular verb: 'The bread and butter *was* piled high on the plate.'

(ii) 'With', 'together with', 'as well as' are also prepositions which can join two subjects. However, they have the effect of making one subject subordinate to the other so that the verb in this case is singular not plural:

The man, with his son, *catches* the train.
The boy, as well as his sister, *goes* to that school.

Other prepositions which have this effect are 'in addition to' and 'including'.

(b) Collective nouns

Some nouns are called collective nouns. It is important to recognize them because they affect the use of verbs. Traditionally, a collective noun, e.g. 'army', 'committee', 'audience', 'class', is treated as singular and therefore takes a singular verb and a singular pronoun:

An army *fights* on *its* stomach.
The audience *was* most impressed by the speaker.

However, this rather inflexible rule has been relaxed in recent years so that the verb can now be either singular or plural according to whether our attention is directed to the group as a single unit or to the individuals composing the group:

The audience *was* too large for the room.
The audience *were* talking quietly among themselves.

Beware! Whether singular or plural is selected as the more appropriate, it is important to be consistent; you cannot change from singular to plural in the same sentence, as in this confusing example:

> The committee was not unanimous because some of them felt that it had not had enough time to discuss all the issues.

Either 'the committee were' and 'they had' or 'some of the members felt' would make the sentence consistent and therefore acceptable.

But when a collective noun is followed by 'of' plus a plural noun as in: 'a committee of women', 'a team of engineers', 'a collection of stamps', a common mistake is to treat it as a plural subject:

> *wrong*   A committee of women were formed.
> *right*   A committee of women was formed.

As in the last example the problem of uncertainty often arises when the subject is separated from the verb by a number of other words: 'The reasons for the move to the new building *were* explained.' By the time you get to the verb it is easy to forget which of the nouns is the real subject. This is probably the main reason for the errors described in the next three sections.

(c) 'Kind', 'sort' and 'type'

These are all singular nouns:

> *wrong*   These kinds of problems are the most difficult.
> *right*   This kind of problem is the most difficult.

It is true that 'these kind' and 'those sort' are often heard in conversations, but whereas this might be acceptable in informal spoken English, in formal writing it is wiser to use the correct form. In practice the error is usually made even worse by non-agreement of the demonstrative adjective ('this', 'that', 'these' and 'those') as well!

> *very wrong*   These kind of problems are the most difficult.

In this example, neither does the verb agree with its subject ('kind') nor the demonstrative adjective agree with its noun, so we end up with this muddle:

pl.   s.   pl.   pl.
These kind of problems are . . .

To conclude this very confusing area with some advice, it is probably wiser to make sure *all* the constituent parts of the subject and verb are kept in the singular whenever possible and then the rule is simpler to obey.

(d) 'Each', 'every', 'everyone', 'everybody', 'anyone' and 'anybody'

These, too, are all singulars. While it is easy to attribute the idea of a lot of people to words which include 'every' and 'any', perhaps it would be helpful to think always of the idea of 'one' which is either expressed or understood in these words, so:

each = each (one)
everybody = every*one*
anybody = any*one*
wrong   All the students have a book. (Only one book between them all?)
right   Each of the students has a book.

(e) 'Either', 'neither'

Both 'either' and 'neither' are also singular: 'Neither of the secretaries *knows* when the meeting starts.'

The use of 'either . . . or' and 'neither . . . nor' can present a few problems though. The rule is that the verb agrees with the nearer of the subjects. However, while 'Neither my husband nor I am able to drive' is correct it sounds rather odd. In cases like this it is better to try to find another way to express it: 'Neither my husband nor I can drive' replaces the verb with another which sounds the same in the singular and plural. Where this is not possible it may be necessary to recast the sentence completely: 'My husband and I are unable to drive.'

Work out carefully the exact subject in the sentence and check that the verb agrees. Don't be misled by elements that fall between the subject and the verb, or by the fact that the normal word order – subject, verb, predicate – is reversed.

Self-check

Now check your answers to numbers **3**, **5**, **7**, **20**, **24**, **42** and **50** in the test.

ANSWERS

3 Wrong. The subject is 'each' which takes the singular, so 'are' should be 'is'. There is also a spelling mistake in this sentence – 'seperately' should be 'separately'. This is a very common spelling mistake. If you didn't spot the spelling error, learn the correct spelling now.

5 Right. 'Together with' has the effect of making 'his assistants' subordinate to 'the manager', so, although they are both subjects, the verb must agree with 'the manager' which is singular.

7 Wrong. 'who is taking the examination' is a subordinate clause in which 'who' is the subject, but 'who' is a relative pronoun referring back to 'the students'. It is the students who are taking the examination, so the verb 'to be' must agree with the students and must therefore be plural – 'are taking'.

20 In this sentence 'the power' is the real subject of the verb 'to be', so the sentence should read: 'The power of his arguments, which were very persuasive, *was* not enough.'

Did you also notice that 'arguments' was spelled incorrectly in the original sentence? The verb 'argue' drops its 'e' when it is turned into the noun 'argument'.

24 Wrong. 'Neither' is the real subject of the sentence, and as we have seen 'neither' is singular and must therefore take a singular verb, so the sentence should read: 'Neither of the rooms *was* laid out . . .' There is another mistake in this sentence, but we will come to that when we look at problems associated with the use of 'like' and 'as'.

42 Wrong. There are several pitfalls in this sentence. Did you sort them out? The real subject is 'kind' which as we have seen is usually better left singular, so its verb should be singular – 'is' (very difficult). But if 'kind' is singular then its adjective (in this case a demonstrative adjective) should also be singular – '*This* kind' – and 'problems' should also be singular: 'This kind of problem is very difficult to solve.' If you at least managed to get everything to agree – '*These* kind*s* of problem *are* very difficult to solve' – then you deserve half marks; but as we have seen, the whole phrase is better when it is all singular.

50 Wrong. Here the subject of the sentence is 'people and questions' so the verb must be plural – 'were' instead of 'was'.

There are also some problems in this sentence concerned with 'less' and 'fewer' but we will look more closely at these when we come to problems with the correct use of adjectives (see section 3, p. 398).

2 Problems with verbs

(a) Main and subordinate verbs

The verb, as we have seen, indicates what is said or done, and is the key word in the sentence, since without a main verb you cannot have a sentence. But what is a main verb?

> *Self-check*
>
> Try to pick out the main verbs in the following sentences.
>
> **1** He answered the letter.
> **2** He read out the minutes of the meeting and then signed them.
> **3** While he was signing them someone began to speak.
> **4** While he was signing them, someone began to speak, although the discussion had not officially begun.

In the first sentence 'answered' must of course be the main verb because it is a simple sentence and a simple sentence has only one main verb. The second sentence consists of two simple sentences joined by 'and' to make a compound sentence, so there are two main verbs – 'read out' and 'signed'. When we come to number **3** things become more difficult because this is a complex sentence consisting of one main clause and one subordinate sentence, so the main verb is the one in the main clause, i.e. 'began'. Number 4 is again more difficult because this too is a complex sentence but this time with a main clause and *two* subordinate clauses. The main verb is therefore the verb in the main clause – 'began'.

It is important to be able to recognize the main verb because, as we shall see, several common errors arise from not being able to recognize which is the main verb, which is the subordinate verb, or which is just a part of a verb – like a participle – which sometimes behaves more like a noun than a verb.

(b) Active and passive voice

When you want to show that the subject of the sentence is performing the action, you should use a verb in the *active* voice:

The auditor approved the accounts.

But when the subject of the sentence is being acted upon, having something done to it by something or someone else, you should use a verb in the *passive* voice:

The accounts were approved by the auditor.

It is important to be able to recognize the difference between the active and the passive voice because it is sometimes useful to draw attention away from the person who did the action and concentrate the reader's attention on the thing that was acted upon:

The management shut the factory for three weeks every year.
The factory was shut for three weeks every year.

If the person who does the action is not as important as the thing that is acted upon, then the passive voice is a useful mechanism for focusing on what is important.

However, traditionally there has been a tendency to use the passive voice too much in business writing, particularly in reports. This habit has probably been encouraged by the need for 'objectivity' and the consequent removal of 'people' with their subjective opinions from formal factual reporting. This has led to a style of writing which is therefore very cold, lifeless and lacking in vitality.

Self-check

Which of the following do you prefer?

The consent of the Secretary of State to the transfer of the issued share capital of the Company to the National Enterprise Board was given with effect from 25th February.

The Secretary of State has consented to the transfer of the issued share capital of the Company to the National Enterprise Board with effect from 25th February.

Neither of the sentences is particularly readable but in the first sentence we have to wait until almost the end of the sentence before we discover what happened to the 'consent'. In the second sentence at least the style is more direct and the main 'idea' of the sentence is brought nearer the beginning of the sentence.

In order to encourage business writing to be more straightforward and lively there is now a trend towards using the active voice wherever possible and appropriate. In particular you should try to avoid the 'impersonal passive' such as 'It is felt that . . .' for 'We feel that . . .' or 'It is regretted that . . .' for 'We (or I) regret that . . .'

In letters, too, the use of the impersonal passive gives the reader the impression that he is dealing with robots rather than human beings. Active verbs make for an active style which is easier to read and gives an impression of liveliness and action.

(c) Infinitives

Infinitives are verb forms that indicate in a general way an action, or a state of being. They are identified by 'to' which is either expressed or just understood. Infinitives can be used as nouns, adverbs or adjectives:

noun (subject)   To err is human.
noun (predicate)   His intention is to work.
adjective   Here are the letters to be signed.
adverb   He has gone to get the report.

After some verbs – 'make', 'hear', 'bid', 'let', 'help', 'dare', 'feel', 'see' – the sign of the infinitive 'to' is, or can be, omitted:

He heard him shout out.
They watched her start the conveyor belt.

Beware the split infinitive! If an adverb is placed between 'to' and the main stem of the verb – 'to carefully follow', 'to quickly discover' – we call it splitting the infinitive and it is regarded by many people as incorrect. In fact, it is probably one of the best known rules of grammar. However, in colloquial English people do split infinitives all the time – 'You're not going to actually rewrite it all?' or 'We will have to completely reconsider the decision.' Despite the objections of the purists, successful modern writers occasionally use the split infinitive for the sake of clarity or emphasis.

As with other matters of style it is a question of judgement.

There are two things to consider: first your reader. If you know you are writing to someone who will react badly to a split infinitive, then make sure the adverb is placed before or after the infinitive.

split   We therefore ask you to carefully consider this proposal.
normal order   We therefore ask you to consider this proposal carefully.

Your second consideration should be one of style. In the majority of cases a split infinitive just sounds awkward and should therefore be avoided on those grounds alone. However, very occasionally, it may sound more awkward *not* to split the infinitive. In this case, if your reader would be offended both by a split infinitive and by the awkward style arising from avoiding it, it is probably wiser to recast the phrase or sentence completely. (Not, you notice, 'wiser to completely recast the phrase or sentence'.)

Self-check

Now, look back at number **34** and see how you could correct it.

Yes; it contains a split infinitive and should read: '. . . to correct carefully . . .' not ' . . . to carefully correct . . .' or better still put 'carefully' after 'the errors'.

(d) Participles

The present participle is the form of the verb ending in 'ing' and denotes action in progress, e.g. 'I am starting the report now.' The past participle of a regular verb is formed by adding 'd' or 'ed' to the present tense of the verb, e.g.

rain   rained   It has rained hard today.
walk   walked   I have walked five miles across the fields.

Some irregular verbs form their past participle differently, e.g. 'given', 'written', 'spoken'.

(i) Verbal adjectives. Both the present and past participles can function as adjectives.

present participle   The secretary taking notes is very efficient.
('taking' is an adjective qualifying the noun 'secretary'; it is also a verb taking the object 'notes'.)
past participle   The notes taken by the secretary were used after the meeting.
('taken' functions as an adjective qualifying 'notes'.)

(ii) 'Misrelated' and 'unrelated' participles. Participles which are acting as adjectives *must* be attached to nouns, and to the right noun.

Having read the report, *he* was prepared to make the decision.
(He has read the report and he is prepared to make a decision.)

Thanking you for your letter, *we* are enclosing your order.
(We are enclosing your order and we are thanking you.)

One way of checking whether you have attached the participle to a noun is to turn the sentence round so that you start with the subject followed by the participle and ask yourself whether it still makes sense:

Walking into the room, the secretary gasped.
The secretary, walking into the room, gasped.
(The secretary is the same person who walked into the room and gasped.)

Misrelated participle: Careless writing often leads people into the trap of relating the participle to the wrong subject.

Self-check

Compare this sentence with the one above about the secretary.

Walking into the room, the secretary was already typing the memo.

If 'walking' relates to 'secretary', which it should according to the rules of sentence construction, then we are left with an absurd picture of the secretary typing while on the move! So, if it wasn't the secretary who was walking into the room, who was it? Someone else? The sentence must be expressed:

Walking into the room, *I* saw the secretary already typing the memo.

Now, in the above example because the possibility of secretaries typing while walking is rather remote, we can work out roughly what is meant, having recognized that something is wrong. However, sometimes the same error is committed but because it appears still to make sense, we misunderstand the sentence without realizing it. This is why it is so important to understand the rule and check your writing carefully. For example, let's go back to the gasping secretary:

Walking into the room, the secretary gasped.

Anyone who knows the rules about participles would be right in assuming that it was the secretary who walked into the room and then gasped. However, this is the kind of sentence that can easily and innocently be written by someone who does not know the rule and really meant: Someone else walked into the room which caused the secretary to gasp – which is quite another thing altogether.

Self-check

What about this one?

Unhappy about the decision, the meeting ended.

Who was unhappy about the decision?

We would be right in assuming from this statement that the meeting (i.e. all the members present) were unhappy about the decision. However, the truth of the matter is that it was the speaker who was the only one unhappy about the decision. To say what he really meant, he should have said:

> Unhappy about the decision, I realized that the meeting was ending.
> *Or:* Although I was unhappy about the decision, the meeting was ending.

Self-check

Now check numbers **11, 38, 44, 47, 49**.

They all contain participles: some used correctly and some used incorrectly. Can you work out which are wrong?

ANSWERS

11 Wrong. Who is doing the looking? Not 'the task' which is the subject of the sentence at the moment. The sentence must be recast if it is to be correct.

> *either*   Looking at it the next morning, we (or another pronoun) thought the task seemed easier
> *or*   When we looked at it the next morning, the task seemed easier.

38 Right. '*He* saw and *he* entered.'

44 Wrong. The bull wasn't cycling surely? A correct version would be:

> As I was cycling along the lane, the bull suddenly charged out in front of me.

47 The secretary could not be going into the office at the same time as she was typing. It must be someone else.

> 12 As I entered the office, the secretary could be seen . . .

49 Wrong. The manager is the subject of the sentence but he didn't steal the cash – 'I' did, so once again the sentence must be recast:

> Since I stole the cash, the manager had no option . . .

Unrelated participles

Another trap awaiting the careless writer is the unrelated participle. Instead of being related to the wrong noun or pronoun, which is bad enough, the participle is not related to anything at all.

> Having thanked the speaker for his contribution, there was nothing more to do.

Not only do we not know who thanked the speaker, but also we do not know who had 'nothing more to do'. The person who thanked the speaker? The speaker? The audience?

This error can also lead to absurd pictures:

> Putting the letter on the desk, there was an enormous crash and the ceiling fell down.

The unrelated participle is often related to errors of punctuation. For instance, a mistake commonly found at the beginning of letters leaves the sentence unfinished and the subject of the participle, at best, in the next sentence:

> Thanking you for your letter of 3 May, in which you ordered shelving. Unfortunately we are unable to complete your order at the moment.

The first 'sentence' is not a sentence because it has no subject and no verb. 'Thanking' is only a participle, i.e. a part of a verb, and not a main verb. The reader is left in mid-air. Eventually his curiosity about who or what might be doing the thanking is more or less satisfied in the second sentence when 'we' appears, but it is all very unsatisfactory and not guaranteed to create a very good impression of the writer or the writer's organization.

Self-check

How would you correct that example?

Either the two sentences must be joined together to make one:

> Thanking you for your letter of 3 May, in which you ordered shelving, we are unfortunately unable to complete your order at the moment.

Or, it would be even better expressed if two new sentences were produced:

> (We) Thank you for your order for shelving of 3 May. Unfortunately, we are unable to complete your order at the moment.

Similarly, the ends of letters often present the same problem if the hackneyed expression 'Thanking you in anticipation. Yours faithfully' is used. This is a legacy from the days when it was normal and correct to end a letter:

Thanking you in anticipation, we remain, dear sirs, your obedient and humble servants,

G. Pentwhistle & Sons.

Notice the punctuation. Though this expression is now outdated and should never be used, it is correctly expressed and punctuated as one whole sentence from 'Thanking' to 'Sons'.

Although most people would now drop 'we remain, dear sirs, your obedient and humble servants' some people still treat what is left as a sentence, putting a full-stop after 'anticipation' even though the clause no longer has a main verb, and leaving the reader in mid-air again. If in doubt therefore, it is probably better to avoid these expressions completely and use instead a straightforward sentence like:

We look forward to hearing from you.

Now let's turn to another problem. Beware! The present participle looks the same as a verbal noun (gerund) which serves a different function.

(iii) Verbal nouns (or gerunds). Verbal nouns, or gerunds as they are sometimes called, are verb forms which can function in a sentence, as their name suggests, as nouns. The words 'writing', 'dictating', 'selling', 'advertising' are examples of gerunds which can often occur in business messages!

Writing good reports requires skill.
He was congratulated for stepping in at short notice.

Self-check

Which of the following are present participles (or verbal adjectives) and which are gerunds (or verbal nouns)?

1 The man writing the letter is the managing director.
2 Writing the letter is the hardest job.
3 He does not like speaking in public.
4 Looking closely at the evidence, you will see that the conclusions are justified.

ANSWERS

1 'Writing' is a participle acting as a verbal adjective which

qualifies, or describes 'the man'.
2 In this sentence 'writing' is a gerund. It is acting as a noun and the subject of the sentence and as a verb taking the object 'the letter'.
3 Similarly in this sentence, 'speaking' is a gerund but this time it is acting as the object of the verb 'does not like'.
4 This one is more difficult. Don't be misled by finding 'looking' at the beginning of the sentence where the gerund often is if it is acting as the subject of the sentence. In this case, 'looking' is a participle acting as an adjective to qualify 'you'. The sentence could equally well read: 'You, looking closely at the evidence, will see that the conclusions are justified.'

Perhaps you didn't get them all right, but you should try to learn the difference because a common error arises from ignoring the difference.

Self-check

Is the following sentence correct?

He disliked me reading the memo.

Strictly speaking it is incorrect, because 'reading' functions as a noun and therefore, as with any other noun, the qualifying noun, or pronoun, in this case 'me', should be in the possessive form 'my'.

In other words, it wasn't that he disliked 'me' in the act of reading the memo; he disliked the act itself. The sentence should therefore read:

He disliked *my* reading the memo.

Similarly:

He regarded *my* leaving the company as a mistake.
The shop's opening was reported on the front page.

Of course, as with many other correct usages, too rigid adherence to the rule can lead to problems of style. In this case, the possessive form can lead to very awkward sounding sentences:

The manager complained about the treasurer's and the secretary's being so late for the meeting.

Owing to John's and David's falling ill, the completion of the project will be delayed.

Most educated people, despite knowing the rule, would probably omit the possessives in sentences like these, or better still, find another less cumbersome way to express them:

The manager complained that the treasurer and the secretary were both so late for the meeting.

Because John and David have fallen ill, the completion of the project will be delayed.

Self-check

Now check numbers **1**, **12**, **18** and **48**. Can you see what is wrong?

ANSWERS

1 Wrong. The 'sentence' is incomplete because there is no subject. A correct version would be: '(We) Thank you for your letter of 6 February in which you complained about the control mechanism.'

(Note: it is acceptable to leave out the pronoun 'we' or 'I' as it is understood.) Did you also notice that February needs an 'r' in the middle?

12 Wrong. We did not complain about 'them', but about the act of having taken the notice off the board. 'Having taken' is a gerund or verbal noun in this sentence so 'them' should be 'their'.

18 Wrong. The same mistake again. It should be: 'I do not remember *his* having told me about the meeting.'

48 Wrong. This is an example of an unrelated participle. 'Having opened' is not related or attached to anything in particular. Who opened the meeting? The same person or people that could not avoid the issue? A better version might be: 'Having opened the meeting, *I* had no way of avoiding the issue.'Or: 'The meeting having opened (or having been opened) there was . . .' which avoids the problem of stating who exactly was concerned, but does not leave a participle unattached.

(e) The subjunctive

> ### *Self-check*
>
> Is there anything wrong or strange about these two sentences:
>
> If I were in his place, I should resign.
> The committee recommended that the procedure be introduced.

The subjunctive mood of the verb used for hypotheses and commands has now almost disappeared from use but it is still retained to express a supposition, a wish or a doubt. In the two sentences above you may have thought that 'were' should have been 'was' and that 'be' sounded rather odd because we usually say 'I was' and 'the procedure is'. However, they are both perfectly correct uses of the subjunctive which have survived, and should be used if you wish to write correctly. The first is an example in common use of the subjunctive to express a hypothesis that is not a fact, and the second is an example of established idiomatic use of the subjunctive after any words of command or desire. The subjunctive is still therefore commonly used in the following examples.

(i) Wishing, hypothesis:

You are a very good speaker. I wish I were. (I *wish*, but I'm not.)

(ii) 'If . . . were' clauses. Note: where an ordinary condition is expressed, 'is' and 'was' can be used as usual but note the difference:

If the speaker *is* here, we can begin. (I don't know whether he is or not.)
If the speaker *were* here, we could begin. (But he is not here.)

(iii) Supposition:

Suppose he *were* to arrive late.

(iv) Command and desire. This use is particularly well established in modern business writing and formal English:

Public opinion demands that an inquiry *be* held.
I move that a chairman *be* appointed. (Always used in a formal motion at a meeting.)

It is suggested that traffic lights *be* installed to reduce the danger.
Hc has askcd that the ban *be* temporarily lifted.
He is anxious that the truth *be* known.

Note: in these examples an acceptable alternative is to use 'should be', but whichever form you choose, take care to be consistent, using instructions which are 'grammatically parallel', for example when listing recommendations.

Unfortunately, the following horrific example of inconsistency in recommendations, which appears all too frequently at the end of many reports, reveals not only the writer's unease with the use of the subjunctive, but also his inability to 'hear' the jarring effect of mixing structures:

It is recommended that:
1 A course be held to provide training for staff.
2 A training officer should be appointed.
3 Two staff will be seconded to organize the training course.

If you cannot grasp the rules about the subjunctive you will certainly be in good company, since many well-respected writers believe that rather than misuse it we should avoid it, and Somerset Maugham went even further when he said: 'The subjunctive is in its death throes, and the best thing to do is to put it out of its misery as soon as possible.'

However, even if you prefer to join the band of scholars devoted to the abolition of the subjunctive, you should never be guilty of saying: 'If I *was* you.' All sorts of people who are not at all familiar with the rules of grammar and have probably never heard of the subjunctive will frown on this error.

‖ *Self-check*
‖ Now check number **46**.

ANSWER

Yes; it should read: 'If I *were* you . . . (because I'm not you).'

(f) Tenses

The tense is that form of the verb or use of the verb which indicates the time of an action. The three main tenses are present, past and future: 'I walk' (present), 'I walked (past), 'I shall walk' (future).

Unfortunately the tense of the verb can cause difficulty but the whole subject of tenses is sufficiently complicated as to be worthy of a book of its own. However, the accurate timing of verbs is an important communication skill and it is worth becoming familiar with the different tenses and their uses so that you can write precisely what you mean. The verb must indicate the exact time of the action.

Self-check

Compare the different meanings indicated by:

They promised that they will pay.
They promised that they would pay.

In the first example, though they promised in the past they have not paid yet and are not expected to pay until some time in the future. In the second example, the act of paying was in the future at the time they promised, but may or may not have been done yet – a subtle difference which could have great significance!
Similarly:

I should like to have visited New York.
I should have liked to visit New York.

The first means that at the present moment, 'I wish I had visited New York', but the second means that at some time in the past I wanted to visit New York. Some people try to make it even more complicated (or simpler!) by writing instead of either sentence:

I should have liked to have visited New York.

Strictly speaking this has yet another meaning: 'At some time in the past I wished that I had visited New York at a time even further back in the past.' However, this meaning is usually not the one intended and is more likely to be the result of mere clumsy use of the past infinitive ('to have visited'), which should certainly not be used unless absolutely necessary to convey a very particular meaning.

Look back at number **12.** Many people might have written:

We complained about their taking the notice off the board.

But presumably the act of taking the notice off the board must have taken place further back in the past than the act of complaining, so it is more correct to say:

> We complained about their having taken the notice off the board.

Similarly in number **18**. If the act of remembering is taking place in the present, then the act of telling must have taken place in the past, so it is more correct to say:

> I do not remember his having told me about the meeting.

This brief selection of the complex range of meanings which can be conveyed by the use of different tenses should be enough to persuade you that, at the very least, considerable care needs to be given to the choice of tense, if you are to say what you really mean. However, if you are already completely bemused you might be happier referring to a basic explanation of English verbs. (See G. H. Vallins, *Good English* (1968), *Better English* (1953) and *Best English* (1963), Pan Books).

'Shall' and 'will'

A common error is to assume that 'shall' and 'will' are interchangeable without altering their meaning.

Future:

I shall	We shall
You will	You will
He	
She will	They will
It	

So, in a simple statement using the future tense:

> I shall be sitting the exams next month.
> He will be taking his exams later.

Determination:

However, if you wish to convey the meaning of determination in the future, 'shall' and 'will' are reversed:

> I will pass my exams. (I am determined to.)
> He shall go. (I shall see that he goes.)

Conditional:
'Should' and 'would' follow the same rules as 'shall' and 'will'.
They are used in conditional sentences referring to the present
time:

> I shall go if you will come with me.
> I should go if you would come with me. (There is doubt about going.)

However, all tenses take 'should' when it means 'ought to':

> He should go without me. (He ought to go without me.)

3 Problems with adjectives

Normally adjectives do not present too many problems but
frequent confusion arises over the difference between the comparative and superlative forms.

Comparative Used to compare *two* objects:
- normally formed by adding 'r' or 'er' to simple adjectives of
  one syllable and to a few of two syllables:

strong	stronger
wise	wiser
angry	angrier

- most adjectives of more than one syllable form the comparative by adding the word 'more' (or 'less') before the simple
  adjective:

careful	more careful
expensive	less expensive

> He is the stronger of the two boys.
> This car is more expensive than that one.

Superlative Used to compare *three or more* objects:
- normally formed by adding 'est' to adjectives of one syllable
  and to a few of two syllables:

fast	fastest
angry	angriest

- most adjectives of more than one syllable form the superlative
  by adding 'most' (or 'least') before the simple adjective:

| effective | most effective |
| variable | least variable |

This is the fastest car in the world.
That would be the least expensive method (of several methods).

> *Self-check*
>
> Choose the correct form of the adjective from those in brackets to complete these sentences:
>
> She was the .... of the two sisters. (more beautiful, most beautiful)
> This is the .... car in the range. (faster, fastest)
>
> Don't be misled by the presence of 'the' in the first sentence. Always concentrate on the number of objects being compared.

Other adjectives that deserve attention

(a) *'This', 'that', 'these', 'those'*: 'This' and 'that' are the only adjectives that have a plural form. 'These' and 'those' must be used with plural nouns:

wrong   *Those* kind . . .
right   *This/That* kind or *those* kinds . . .

'Them' is not an adjective and should never be used to qualify a noun:

very wrong   Can you pass me *them* books?

(b) *'Either', 'neither'*: 'Either' or 'neither' refers to one of two. 'Either' should be used with 'or', 'neither' with 'nor'.
(c) *'First', 'last'*: The words 'first' and 'last', when used with adjectives that express number, are placed before the adjectives:

The first three pages
The last ten issues

(d) *'Each other', 'one another'*: 'Each other' refers to two objects only; 'one another', to more than two:

The two women help each other.
The three women help one another.

(e) *'Above, below'*: 'Above' is normally an adverb or a preposition; but modern dictionaries are beginning to recognize its usage as an adjective. 'Below' is an adverb or a preposition; it is not recognized as an adjective and should not be used as one:

> *Below*, we could see the river in the valley. (adverb)
> The road ran *above*. (adverb)
> Put it *below* (*above*) the other. (preposition)
> The *above* comments must be checked. (adjective)
> *wrong* The *below* comments must be checked.

The word 'above' is sometimes used in combinations as in 'above-mentioned', 'above-listed'. Although correct they are usually avoided by careful writers as they create foggy English.

(f) *Numbers as adjectives*: see 'Using numbers', Appendix C.

(g) *Using the articles 'a', 'an', 'the*: 'A' and 'an' are indefinite articles used to describe a noun as anything in a particular class:

> *a* letter; *an* order

Note: use 'a' before nouns beginning with a consonant: 'a company'; 'a product'. Use 'an' before words beginning with a vowel sound: 'an employee', 'an angry man .

'The' is the definite article, so named because it selects a specific or definite individual or object from a particular class.

> The man who issues the order. (a specific man, a specific order)

Note: when two nouns in a sentence need different articles, e.g. 'a' and 'an', do not make one article do the duty of the other:

> Entries to the competition should be sent in an envelope or box (or *a* box).

When two separate things are intended, the article should be repeated:

> I was introduced to the chairman and the managing director (i.e. two people).
> I was introduced to the chairman and managing director (i.e. one person).

Be careful not to repeat the indefinite article unnecessarily:

> *wrong* They produced *a* further *a* hundred samples.
> *right* They produced a further hundred samples.

Self-check

Now check number **29** in the test. Did you spot it as an error the first time?

(h) *'Due'*: 'Due' is an adjective but despite the fact that it is often used as a prepositional phrase – 'due to' – this is regarded as an illiteracy and you should take care not to use it where 'owing to' or 'because of' is what you really mean.

> *right* Absenteeism due to illness is increasing.
> *wrong* Due to illness he missed the meeting.

In the first sentence 'due' is an adjective qualifying 'absenteeism' and the sentence could equally well read: 'Absenteeism, which is due to illness, is increasing.' However, in the second sentence 'due to' is being used as a prepositional phrase and should be replaced by 'owing to', 'because of', or 'as a result of'.

Self-check

Now check your answers to numbers **30, 32, 35, 42** and **43**.

ANSWERS

30 Right. 'Due' in this sentence is being correctly used as an adjective to describe 'he'.

32 Wrong. 'Due to' means 'because of' in this sentence so you must either say 'owing to the strike' or 'because of the strike'.

35 Wrong. There are only two brothers so the comparative should be used, not the superlative:

He is the taller of the two brothers.

42 Wrong. As we have already seen in this sentence there are all kinds of agreement problems but 'these' is an adjective which goes with a plural noun – 'these kinds' – or better still, 'this kind of problem'.

43 Wrong. Here again 'due to' should be 'owing to' or 'because of'.

(i) *'Less' and 'fewer'*: Frequently 'less' is confused with 'fewer'. 'Less' can only be used to describe a noun which is uncountable and is therefore used to describe the degree, the quantity or the extent of something; 'fewer', on the other hand, is used to describe the number:

less expenditure;   fewer expenses
less paper;   fewer papers
less money;   fewer pounds

Note: 'less' is always followed by a *singular* noun; 'fewer' is always followed by a plural noun.

Self-check

Now check your answers to numbers **23, 36, 45, 50**.

ANSWERS

23 Right. 'Paper' is singular, it cannot be counted and the sentence is concerned with the quantity or amount of paper, so 'less' is correct.

36 Wrong. In this case, we are concerned with the *number* of papers, so 'fewer' would be correct.

45 Wrong. Again we are concerned with a number of problems, so it should be 'fewer' problems.

50 Wrong. 'Fewer people' is correct but 'less questions' is wrong; it should be 'fewer questions'. Of course, as we have seen, this sentence is also wrong because the verb should be plural to agree with its subject 'people and questions'.

4 Problems with adverbs

(a) *'As . . . as', 'so . . . as'*: If equality is stated, use 'as . . . as'; if negative comparison is made, use 'so . . . as':

Profits are *as* good this year *as* they were last year.
Profits are not *so* good this year *as* they were last year.

(b) *'Farther', 'further'*: There is a great deal of controversy surrounding the correct use of these two words (which can both be used as adverb or adjective); 'farther' is usually preferred for reference to spatial distance, and 'further' for reference to time, quantity or degree:

He lives farther away than that man.
You will not succeed without further effort.

(c) *'Real'*, *'very'*: 'Real' is an adjective of quality. 'Very' is an adverb of degree. 'Real' must be used with a noun; 'very' to modify an adjective or an adverb:

As a singer, she has *real* talent.
This report is *very* (not *real*) good.
He spoke *very* (not *real*) slowly.

(d) *'Sometime'*, *'some time'*: 'Sometime' (one word) is an adverb meaning at one time or other not definitely known. 'Some time' (two words) is a phrase consisting of a noun 'time' qualified by the adjective 'some', indicating length of time:

They visited us sometime during last year.
They visited us for some time last year.

(e) *Placing adverbs*: Adverbs should be placed as close as possible to the words they modify. Frequently the wrong meaning is conveyed by careless positioning of the adverb. There is an important difference between:

He did not fly happily. (He did not like flying) *and*
Happily he did not fly. (. . . because the plane crashed.)

Self-check

How could you rearrange the words in order to avoid any doubt about the intended meaning?

'Happily, he did not fly' would remove any doubt.

Some adverbs ('merely', 'hardly', 'scarcely', 'too', 'also', 'almost', 'even' and, above all, 'only') need special care. 'I was only trying to help' is a common statement but what does it really mean? I was trying only to help or I was only trying, i.e. not helping but only trying. 'Only' can be placed in four different positions to give four different meanings to the following sentence.

Activity

Try it.

|| She has given £2000 to that charity.

Only she has given £2000 to that charity.
(She and nobody else has given that sum.)

She has *only* given £2000 to that charity.
(She has given money but not helped the charity in any other way.)

She has given *only* £2000 to that charity.
(She has given neither more nor less than the sum mentioned.)

She has given £2000 to that charity *only*.
Only to that charity has she given £2000.
(She has given money to no other charity.)

Self-check

Now check your answer to number **41**.

ANSWER

You might have been tempted to join 'some' and 'time' together, but in this sentence 'some' is an adjective describing 'time' and the two should therefore be written as two separate words.

Not only should single word adverbs be placed as closely as possible to the word they modify, but so also should groups of words acting as adverbs; these are called adverbial phrases or clauses.

Self-check

Look back at your answers to numbers **2, 21, 25**.

ANSWER

2 Wrong. This sentence is not so much wrong as ambiguous because we are left with the impression that the poor young lady is going to be married for only one year. This impression is caused by misplacing the adverbial phrase 'for one year'. In order to avoid any ambiguity it is necessary to move the phrase closer to the word it modifies – 'required':

Furnished accommodation is required for one year by young lady about to be married.

(Did you also notice that accommodation was spelled incorrectly in the original sentence?)

21 Wrong. Similarly in this sentence it sounds as if the pavement is getting longer because the adverbial clause 'which was getting longer' is too far away from 'a queue of people' which it really modifies. Note also the wrong spelling of 'queue' in the original sentence. ('Cue' is the spelling of the thing used to play billiards.) To avoid ambiguity the sentence must be reordered:

A queue of people, which was getting longer, stretched along the pavement.

25 Wrong. This is the same problem but rather more difficult to put right. At the moment we are not sure whether 'which he wrote last week' refers to the file or the letter. Slightly better might be:

This is the letter, which he wrote last week, from the file.

But this sounds rather awkward. In cases like this it is often better to start again and completely rewrite the sentence.

5 Problems with pronouns

Pronouns are useful since they act as substitutes for nouns and therefore reduce the need for repetition. However, their use is fraught with problems, if we are to ensure that we write correct English and above all English which is not ambiguous. We have already looked at some of the problems associated with pronouns while exploring the problems of other parts of speech, e.g. collective nouns, subject–verb agreement. Now let's look at others.

The main types of pronoun are:

personal   I, me, you, he, him, she, her, one, it, we, us, they, them
relative   who, whom, those, which, that
demonstrative   this, these, that, those, such, the other, the same
possessive   mine, yours, his, hers, its, ours, theirs, whose
interrogative   who? which? what? whom? whose?
reflexive and emphatic   myself, yourself, himself, herself, itself, oneself, ourselves, yourselves, themselves

Self-check

Now check number **19** in the test.

ANSWER

19 Wrong. 'Theirselves' does not exist as a pronoun, but is frequently invented as a pronoun to replace 'themselves'. This sentence also contains a spelling mistake. Did you spot it? 'Dissapointed' should be spelled 'disappointed'.

(a) Subject–object confusion

In English, unlike some other languages, most words do not change their form when they are being used as the object of a verb rather than the subject, e.g. 'The man hit the ball.' 'The car hit the man.'

In both these sentences 'the man' remains the same even though in the first sentence 'the man' is the subject of the verb and in the second sentence 'the man' is the object of the verb.

However, pronouns do change their form depending on their function in the sentence:

I walk. (*I* is the subject)
He walks towards me. (*me* is in the objective form because it follows a preposition *towards* and prepositions take the objective form)
Those books are mine. (*mine* is a pronoun in the possessive form)

Self-check

Which of the pronouns in the list on p. 401 can be used *only* in the objective form, i.e. as the object of the verb or preposition?

ANSWER

'Me', 'him', 'her', 'us', 'them', 'whom'.

One of the commonest errors is to use the subject instead of the object form, or vice versa:

Matthew and me went to the cinema.

If you take away 'Matthew and', it becomes obvious that you

would not say: 'me went to the cinema' so the sentence above should have read:

> Matthew and *I* went to the cinema.

Similarly:

> I booked seats at the theatre for my wife and I.

This sounds correct and in colloquial (i.e. everyday) English is frequently heard, but 'I' is governed by the preposition 'for' and you would never say 'for I', so the sentence, if written correctly, should read:

> I booked seats at the theatre for my wife and *me*.

A similar confusion seems to arise when comparing persons or things using 'than' or 'as'. The rule is that they can both be subject or object but they must both be in the same case:

> He is better than I at working alone. *right* (both subjective)
> He is better than me at working alone. *wrong* (*he* is subjective. *me* is objective)

One way to check is to insert the missing but understood 'am'. It then becomes obvious that you cannot say 'me am'

> ### Self-check
>
> Which of the following is correct?
>
> 1 It helped him more than I.
> 2 It helped him more than me.
> 3 He is as tall as I.
> 4 He is as tall as me.

Remember, each of the two things compared must be in the same case. The first sentence is therefore wrong because 'him' is an object so 'I' should be 'me'. Similarly the fourth sentence is wrong because 'he' and 'me' are not the same case. However, this last example demonstrates the 'I/me' controversy. Though it is incorrect, the last sentence sounds right and might be forgiven though noticed in spoken English. But although 'It is I' is correct because the verb 'to be' always takes the nominative case, you would probably be regarded as pedantic if you insisted on using it in spoken English. However, 'it is me', which is acceptable but incorrect in speech, would be regarded as improper in writing.

Self-check

Now check your answers to numbers **9**, **13** and **15**.

ANSWERS

9 Wrong. It should read: 'Please book the seats for my wife and *me*.'

13 Right. 'She cannot type as quickly as I (can).' In this sentence 'as quickly as' is an adverbial phrase describing *how* I type. 'Can' is understood, but if it had been written it would be clear that since we cannot say 'as quickly as me can' the pronoun in this sentence is correct.

15 Wrong. From the previous explanation it should be clear that the same rule applies in this sentence so it should read:

She does not remember the incident as well as I (do).

Although we may be forgiven for making these mistakes in everyday spoken communication, it is important to know the rules so that our more formal written English is correct.

(b) Who and whom

This subject–object confusion arises in the same way with 'who' and 'whom' which are relative pronouns.

'Who' is the subject and the equivalent of 'he' or 'they'.

'Whom' is the object and is the equivalent of 'him' or 'them'.

Apart from knowing the difference, the problem seems to be which one to use, because, as a relative pronoun, 'who/whom' refers back to its antecedent, or noun, but may function in its own clause in a different case from its noun:

She spoke to the man who/whom we hope will be the next chairman.

Although we would say 'She spoke to him' which seems to suggest 'whom' would be correct, or argued another way, in the subordinate clause 'we' might be thought to be the subject of the verb 'hope' making 'whom' the object; however, *the relative pronoun takes its case from its function in the part of the sentence to which it belongs*. Therefore to find out whether it must be 'who' or 'whom' we must isolate the clause in which the relative pronoun appears, make it a separate sentence and replace the relative pronoun with the right personal pronoun:

She spoke to the man. He (we hope) will be the next chairman.

In this way, it becomes clear that the equivalent relative pronoun must be 'who'.

|| *Self-check*

|| Now check your answers to numbers **10** and **16.**

ANSWERS

10 Wrong. As with the last example in the text, we must divide the sentence into two clauses:

He is the man. Him (we expect) to be the next chairman.
Or: He is the man. We expect him to be the next chairman.

Notice that this time the verb is the infinitive – to be – unlike the last example in the text. In that example the pronoun would have been 'he' but in the test sentence the pronoun must be 'him' so the equivalent relative pronoun must be 'whom'.

He is the man whom we expect to be the next chairman.

16 Wrong. 'Who' should be 'whom'. Again if we divide the sentence into two we get:

He is the only one. You could ask *him.*

So the sentence should read:

He is the only one whom you could ask.

(c) 'Its' and 'It's'

A very common error is to use 'it's' as a possessive pronoun – 'The cat was licking it's coat.' Personal pronouns in the possessive form do *not* require the apostrophe ('). The sentence should read: 'The cat was licking its coat.'
 'Its' is the correct possessive form of the personal pronoun 'it'.
 'It's' is the contraction for 'it is'.

(Note: the confusion probably arises because nouns *do* form their possessive with an apostrophe, e.g. 'the boy's book'; 'the boys' books'. Some people seem to be obsessed with using an apostrophe where it is incorrect and even use it when only a simple plural is required. The plural of 'company' is 'companies' *not* 'company's' which is the singular possessive form.

Self-check

Now check numbers **4, 14** and **33**.

ANSWERS

  4 Right. 'Its' without the apostrophe is correct in this sentence because 'its' is being used as the possessive form of 'it'.

14 Wrong. In this sentence 'its' means 'it is' and should therefore be 'it's'. (Note: it is normally better to avoid this contraction in formal writing anyway, so when checking through anything you have written something has gone wrong if you come across 'it's' at all.)

33 Wrong. 'Company's' should be 'companies' because it is a simple plural not a possessive.

(Did you also spot the spelling mistake in number **14**? 'Competitative' should be 'competitive'.)

Master the difference between 'its' and 'it's' (and the correct form of plural nouns and plural possessives) *now*! They are basic mistakes which will cause you embarrassment otherwise. If you are still confused turn to 'the apostrophe' in Appendix A.

(d) 'Their' and 'there' (and 'they're')

Another common but very basic mistake is to confuse 'their', 'there' and 'they're'.

'Their' is the possessive form of 'they', e.g. 'their coats', 'their ideas'.

'There' is an adverb of place, e.g. 'Here, there and everywhere.'

'They're' is a contraction of 'they are' (and should not, there-

fore, normally be used in written English).
NB '*They're* hot so they have put *their* coats in *there.*'

> *Self-check*
>
> Now check back to number **31** in the test. Did you spot the wrong 'their'?

(e) 'One'

The indefinite pronoun 'one' also tends to get people into a tangle. It is inadvisable to substitute 'you' for 'one' in formal writing. For instance, in a formal report the reader is made to feel under unjustified attack if he suddenly reads:

> It has to be said that you can never succeed completely

when all that is being referred to is people in general. However, it is possible to err the other way:

> One does not feel that one has the right to force one's opinion on others when one is not as directly involved as one would like to be.

Repetition of 'one' in this way sounds rather pompous and should be avoided by completely recasting the sentence in a different style.

However, in some cases 'one' is the right and proper pronoun to use, in which case care should be taken to maintain consistency in the pronouns used:

> *wrong* One is bound to agree that *you* can never completely eradicate the problem.
> *wrong* What could *one* do in the circumstances but consider *their* battle lost?

(f) Which pronoun refers to which?

A very common ambiguity is caused by careless use of pronouns, when the reader is left to guess which of several antecedents is referred to by the pronoun:

> She said her mother had moved when she got married.

Who got married? 'She' or 'her mother'?
As with other ambiguities the error can often cause amuse-

ment but in doing so it enables us to work out what was really meant:

> Please send me a form for cheap milk. I have a two month old baby and did not know about it until a neighbour told me

or, on a slightly more serious note:

> Mr Frank Dyer, prosecuting, told the court that he was one of a number of people involved in certain incidents which took place at the school that evening. He said he had gone with a friend to the Youth Club earlier that evening, but they had decided to go to a local pub on their motorcycles.

Presumably Mr Dyer, the prosecuting lawyer, was not the same person who was involved in certain incidents, nor the person who went to the youth club and then to the local pub on a motorcycle! The confusion arises because we are not sure to whom the pronoun 'he' refers.

All pronouns must clearly refer to the appropriate antecedents. In the passage above the antecedent of the first 'he' appears to be Mr Dyer, but obviously this cannot be the case. The correct antecedent should have been inserted to make it clear to whom the pronouns refer:

> Mr Frank Dyer, prosecuting, told the court that *Albert Dale* was one of a number of people involved in certain incidents which took place at the school that evening. He said *Dale* had gone with a friend to the Youth Club earlier that evening, but they had decided to go to a local pub on their motorcycles.

Exactly the same problem can arise with careless use of relative pronouns:

> This is the chapter from the book which he has just written.

Does '*which*' refer to 'chapter' or 'book'? Has he just written the chapter, or just written the book? In order to avoid this kind of ambiguity, it may be necessary to recast the sentence completely:

> This is the recently completed chapter from his book.

Moral: if you are to communicate exactly what you intend you must make sure that it is clear to which antecedents your pronouns refer.

(g) 'Which' and 'that'

The correct use of these two pronouns is difficult and complicated, but choosing the wrong one can completely change the intended meaning:

> *wrong* Sweets, which do not contain sugar should be given to diabetic patients.
> *right* Sweets that do not contain sugar should be given to diabetic patients.

In the first sentence the meaning seems to be that all sweets do not contain sugar, which is untrue. What is meant, and is better expressed by the alternative, is that only those sweets containing no sugar should be given to diabetics.

Sir Ernest Gowers in *The Complete Plain Words*, which explains the complexities of these two words in much greater detail, suggests a very useful general rule:

> On the whole it makes for smoothness of writing not to use the relative *which* where *that* would do as well, and not to use either if a sentence makes sense and runs pleasantly without.

Fortunately for us, he also says:

> The truth is that for nearly all writers, whatever their level of excellence, the ear is a reliable guide.

So take his advice when in doubt and try speaking the sentence aloud. More than likely you will be able to hear which one is correct, and whether it is possible to drop either without changing the sense.

For instance, in this sentence:

> He said that the report that he needed was that one

it would be possible to remove the first two 'thats' without altering the sense and it would sound a lot easier on the ear:

> He said the report he needed was that one.

Beware! Sometimes, particularly when writing in haste and using the words 'say' and 'think' which can generally do without 'that', it is easy to omit words which are essential to the sense of a particular sentence:

> The doctor said the patient was ill.

In order to make it absolutely clear that it is the patient who is ill and not the doctor, 'that' must be inserted into the sentence:

> The doctor said that the patient was ill.

Of course, if we really wanted to say that the doctor was ill, we would need to punctuate the sentence differently:

> 'The doctor,' said the patient, 'was ill.'

(h) Duplication of 'that'

It is also easy to insert 'that' more than once:

> He said that, in order to keep costs down, that it would be necessary to reduce the workforce.

The sentence needs one 'that' but not two.

Where it is necessary to repeat 'that' in a sentence, special care should be taken to remember which words introduced the first 'that':

> The general spoke to the troops in order to dispel the idea that they might be losing the battle, and that they should be attacking the enemy.

Put like this the general is likely to have had the opposite effect from the one intended. If we remove the first 'that' clause, we are left with:

> The general spoke to the troops to dispel the idea that . . . they should be attacking the enemy!

It is important always to check back to make sure that the constructions suit each part of the sentence, particularly with long complex sentences.

Self-check

Now check number **6**.

ANSWER

6 Wrong. At the moment it sounds as if all toys are dangerous. 'Toys *that* are dangerous should not be given to children' makes the meaning clearer.

6 Problems with prepositions and conjunctions

Prepositions and conjunctions are both 'connectives' and as their name suggests they are words used to connect ideas which are closely related.

In the following passage all the prepositions and conjunctions have been omitted.

> ### Self-check
>
> Insert the words which have been left out:
>
> They presented their recommendation (   ) us (   ) the first meeting of the committee, (   ) that was not, (   ) my opinion, the best moment (   ) its discussion.

In order, the words omitted are: 'to', 'at', 'but', 'in', 'for'.

> ### Self-check
>
> Which of these are prepositions and which are conjunctions?

(a) Functions of prepositions

A preposition is a word used to connect a following noun or pronoun to some other word or element in the sentence. In making the connection, the preposition always indicates the relationship:

> . . . *to* us *at* the first meeting *of* the committee.

The preposition is followed by its object, which is a noun, pronoun or the equivalent:

> . . . to *us* at the first *meeting* of the *committee*.

To identify the object of the preposition ask 'what?' or 'whom?' after the preposition:

To whom?	to us
At what?	at the meeting
Of whom?	of the committee

A preposition is always followed by an *object* so when the object is a pronoun it must be in the objective case:

> *right* So – to *me*
> *wrong* Not – to *I*

(i) Most commonly used prepositions:

aboard	along	behind	by	from	past	toward	with
about	amid	below	concerning in	round	under	within
above	among	beneath	down	into	through	underneath	without
across	around	beside	during	of	throughout until
after	at	between	except	on	till	up
against	before	beyond	for	over	to	upon

'But' when it means 'except' is also a preposition (see p. 414).
Some prepositions consist of two or more words:

instead of	contrary to
on account of	in reference to
in addition to	to the extent that
devoid of	from beyond

(ii) Prepositions and word order:
The old rule maintained that sentences should never end with a preposition. However, if this rule is applied too strenuously, it can lead to very awkward sounding sentences. Winston Churchill, in a successful effort to show how absurd the rule could be when taken too far, is renowned for having said: 'This is the sort of English up with which I will not put'.

Normally it is fairly easy to avoid putting the preposition at the end of the sentence. However it is more difficult to avoid when the verb in the sentence is a compound verb (i.e. made from a verb and two prepositions) where the last preposition is essential to the meaning of the verb, as in Sir Winston Churchill's example – 'to put up with'.

So let your ear be the best judge. If the preposition sounds best at the end of the sentence, leave it there.

However, ending a sentence with several prepositions can sound rather odd:

> 'What,' the small boy asked his mother, 'did you want to bring the book I didn't want to be read to out of up for?'

But it probably sounded perfectly understandable with the small boy's emphasis on the appropriate words.

Self-check

Which of these do you prefer?

Have you seen the house he lives in?
Have you seen the house in which he lives?
Have you seen the house he inhabits?

The first sounds perfectly acceptable, though perhaps the second would be better in written English, but the third just sounds pompous even though it is correct.

(iii) Prepositional idiom:
It is also important to use the right preposition, i.e. the preposition which is normally accepted as being the correct one:

He answered the teacher. (no preposition)
He had to answer *to* the committee *for* having failed to produce the report. (we answer *to* someone *for* doing something)
He substituted the tin trophy *for* the silver one.
The silver trophy was replaced *by* the tin one.
He replaced the silver trophy *with* the tin one.
He communicated his answer *to* the staff.
He communicated *with* his staff regularly.

(iv) Other prepositional idioms:

to be averse to	to be endowed with
to connive with	to gloat over
to culminate in	to be impervious to
to be deterred from	to be intent upon
to be devoid of	to be marred by
to dissent from	to be sensitive to

An even more common cause of uncertainty arises with verbs like 'compare' and 'to be different':

right Compared *with* her he is lazy.
wrong Compared *to* her he is lazy.
right This problem is different *from* that one.
wrong This problem is different *to* that one.
right He was indifferent *to* her plea.

(v) 'Among'/'amongst'/'between':
People often have difficulty determining which of these is correct. Most authorities on the subject seem to agree that 'amongst' is obsolete, and has now been replaced by 'among'. If

in doubt, therefore, use 'among'. However, don't confuse 'among' and 'between'. 'Among' is used where there are three or more items or people, whereas 'between' refers to two only.

(b) Functions of conjunctions

Conjunctions are words which are used to connect words, phrases and clauses:

> He will arrive at Heathrow *or* Gatwick. (connects words)
> He usually arrives in a long plastic mac *and* white tennis shorts. (connects phrases)
> His performance is improving, *but* his progress is slow. (connects clauses)

Note: in the example above 'but' is a conjunction. Compare its use in that sentence with its use in the following sentences.

> *But* for him, we would have lost the match.
> Everyone *but* the son was there.

In these last two sentences 'but' means 'except' and is therefore used as a preposition (see p. 412).

There are two sorts of conjunctions:

(i) *Coordinate conjunctions* which join elements of equal rank or grammatical relation:

> Men *and* women are treated equally here.
> She will take a long time, *but* she will complete the work.

The 'but' in the first example connects two nouns, and in the second connects two independent clauses. The principal coordinate conjunctions are these:

	and	likewise
	but	moreover
pure	for	neither–nor
conjunctions	neither	nevertheless
	nor	not only–but also
	or	notwithstanding
	accordingly	now
	as well as	so
	besides	so that
	both–and	still

consequently	then
either–or	therefore
furthermore	thus
hence	whether–or
however	yet

Note on punctuation: it is important to know which are the 'pure' conjunctions because you should use a comma to separate independent *clauses* which are in pairs or in series joined by a 'pure' conjunction:

> Men *and* women are treated equally here. ('and' is not joining clauses)
> First she planned the letter, *and* then she dictated it. (in this instance, 'and' is joining two independent clauses and so a comma is used)

Use a semi-colon, however, between independent clauses which are joined by a conjunction that indicates a greater change of thought than is indicated by a 'pure' conjunction. Typical of such conjunctions are:

> accordingly
> consequently
> hence
> however
> moreover
> nevertheless
> notwithstanding

> She did not work very hard; consequently she failed the exam.

Correlative conjunctions are coordinate conjunctions which are used in pairs:

> both–and
> either–or
> neither–nor
> not only–but also
> whether–or

Make sure that correlatives are placed *just before* the words or phrases connected:

> *right* Let me have either the report or the draft.
> *wrong* Let me either have the report or the draft.

Put another way, the words should always be balanced after each half of the correlative:

> *wrong* He will not only make a good secretary but also a good treasurer.
> *right* He will make not only a good secretary but also a good treasurer.
> *wrong* Either he will be promoted or sacked.
> *right* He will be either promoted or sacked.

The reason for this rule is that it helps to emphasize the two ideas clearly in the mind of the receiver. It is of course also an example of grammatical parallelism. (A good check is to see that the correlatives are followed by the same parts of speech: a pair of nouns, a pair of verbs, etc., e.g. 'a good secretary/a good treasurer'; 'promoted/sacked'; 'the report/the draft'.)

(ii) *Subordinate conjunctions* are used to join a subordinate or dependent clause to some word in the main clause:

> He was away from work *because* he was ill.
> He agreed to do it *on condition that* his family could accompany him.

The main subordinate conjunctions are:

after	so that
although	supposing (colloquial)
as	than
as soon as	that
because	though
before	till
if	unless
in the event that	until
in order that	when
inasmuch as	where
lest	whereas
on condition that	whether–or
provided	while
since	

Beware!

> No one doubted *that* (not *but that*) he was successful.
> He will try *to* (not *and*) come to the meeting.

'Like' and 'as':

'Like' is a preposition, but frequently it is used incorrectly as a conjunction instead of its corresponding conjunction 'as' which should be used to join clauses:

> *right* He looks like a kind man. (preposition)
> *wrong* It looks like they will come.
> *right* It looks as if they will come.
> *wrong* I wish I could write like he does.
> *right* I wish I could write as he does.

'Providing' and 'provided':
Strictly speaking 'providing' is a present participle and should not be used as a conjunction to replace 'provided'. However, dictionaries are beginning to reflect the more widespread use of 'providing' as a rough alternative to the more accurate 'provided':

> *less desirable* Providing he can chair the meeting I will present the report.
> *more desirable* Provided he can . . .

Self-check

Now check your answers to numbers **8, 15, 17, 22, 24, 26, 28**.

ANSWERS

8 Wrong. This is a very common mistake but will upset some people so it is important to use the right preposition:

He found the job very different *from* what he had expected.

Some people would even go further and write:

He found the job very different from that which he had expected

but this produces a rather pompous piece of English, even though it is correct.

15 Wrong. The sentence really means: 'She does not remember the incident as well as *I do*.' 'As' is therefore a conjunction not a preposition, so 'me' should be 'I'.

17 Right. If the sentence read 'Nothing succeeds like success does' we would have to replace 'like' with the conjunction 'as'.

22 Wrong. The two halves each side of the correlative conjunctions 'not only – but also' don't balance. To correct the sentence we must write:

Our trading had increased not only beyond our expectations but also beyond our hopes.
Or: Our trading had increased beyond not only our expectations but also our hopes. (This is correct but sounds rather more awkward than the first correct version.)

24 Wrong. As well as the mistake of not making the verb agree with its subject 'neither' which is singular, this sentence is also wrong because again 'like' is being used incorrectly as a conjunction and should be replaced by its corresponding conjunction 'as'.

26 Wrong. Again, 'like' is being used incorrectly as a conjunction and should be replaced by 'as if'.

28 Right. Here 'like' is being used correctly as a preposition introducing a phrase.

7 Problems with ellipsis

Ellipsis is the process whereby we leave out some words because they are 'understood' in a sentence. In this way we can avoid using the same word twice in a sentence and use one word to do the job of two, or sometimes more. So

The first examination was Economics, the second examination was Biology and the third examination was English

can be shortened by ellipsis to

The first examination was Economics, the second Biology and the third English.
Or: They had worked hard for and saved hard for their summer holiday

becomes

They had worked and saved hard for their summer holiday.

However, it is important that the words that are understood really are the same as the words in the sentence which are doing double duty. When this is not the case it is called faulty ellipsis, and without care this fault is easy to commit, as we have seen with the use of 'a' and 'an' (see p. 396).

Here are some examples of faulty ellipsis:

> *wrong* The police were preventing people coming and going from the scene of the accident.
>
> *right* The police were preventing people coming *from* and going *to* the scene of the accident. ('coming' and 'going' take different prepositions)

> *wrong* She swims as well, if not better than, her brother.
>
> *right* She swims as well *as*, if not better *than*, her brother. (the conjunction 'than' cannot take the place of 'as')

> *wrong* The pet shop owner said that he had black and white rabbits for sale.
>
> *right* The pet shop owner said that he had black rabbits and white rabbits for sale. (if this is what is meant, the omission of 'rabbits' after 'black' gives the impression that each of the rabbits was black and white)

> *wrong* His hair was dark but his eyes blue.
>
> *right* His hair *was* dark but his eyes *were* blue. (a singular verb cannot serve for an understood verb which is plural)

Self-check

Now check your answers to numbers **27** and **39** in the test.

ANSWERS

27 Wrong. The understood part of the verb must be the same as the part expressed in the sentence; so the sentence should read:

In my opinion he never has *been*, and never will *be*, a success.

39 Wrong. Similarly in this sentence, since 'as well' takes 'as' not 'than', the sentence should read: 'He writes reports as well *as*, if not better *than*, his boss.'

8 Problems with negatives

In English two negatives cancel one another out and produce a positive, just as in mathematics. In spoken English we often use double negatives: 'I shouldn't be surprised if he isn't coming' means 'I think he's coming'. Sometimes even in written English the use of two negatives creates an effect which would not be created by using the positive form:

> This is not to imply that the job is impossible

is not the same as

> This is to imply that the job is possible.

However, using negatives requires a great deal of care and skill or the communicator is liable to say the opposite of what he intended:

> There is no reason to doubt that what he says in his statement . . . is not true

when he meant to say: 'There is no reason to doubt that his statement *is* true.'

Even if you manage to work out the effect of multiple negatives and say what you mean, your receiver will be at best irritated at having to work out what you mean, and at worst completely and utterly confused.

(a) 'Hardly' and 'scarcely'

These words are virtually negative in meaning and therefore can cause the same problems as the more conventional negative forms if they are used with other negatives:

> *wrong* He hadn't scarcely the energy to go on.
> *right* He had scarcely the energy to go on.

Or with words that have a negative effect:

> *wrong*Without hardly another thought, he agreed to take on the responsibility.
> *right* With hardly another thought, he agreed to take on the responsibility.

Self-check

Now check your answers to numbers **37** and **40**.

ANSWERS

37 Wrong. It could be argued that this sentence is not so much wrong as ambiguous, but the word 'surprisingly' leads us to believe that he did something unusual. People usually deny that they are guilty so in this sentence we are surprised he *didn't* deny he was guilty. If the other negative – 'wasn't guilty' – is left in, we are left with a negative to spare, which means that he said he wasn't guilty which would not fit the tone of the sentence conveyed by 'surprisingly'. The sentence should surely then read: 'Surprisingly, he didn't deny that he was guilty (he admitted his guilt).' If you are completely confused, perhaps it proves the point about the confusion caused by multiple negatives – avoid them!

40 Wrong. Similarly 'without hardly' means 'with'. Are we to understand that he did have a thought? No; 'with hardly' is the right construction.

Revision

If you have worked carefully through all the sections in this chapter, now try the test again.

Come back to the test in a few weeks' time and see if you can improve your score.

Try to analyse where your particular weaknesses are. Verbs? Spelling? Agreement of verbs and subjects, or pronouns and their antecedents?

If you did well the first time, or feel that now you have been through the various problem areas, you are ready to move on to greater things, you might be interested in the following books which go into the subject of grammar and usage in much greater detail than is possible here:

Sir Ernest Gowers, *The Complete Plain Words,* Penguin Books, 1970
Eric Partridge, *Usage and Abusage*, Penguin Books, 1970
G. H. Vallins, *Good English*, Pan Books, 1968
—*Better English*, Pan Books, 1953
—*Best English*, Pan Books, 1963

Appendix A:
Punctuation made easy

Full stop

The strongest punctuation mark of all. Should be used:

1 At the end of a complete sentence (not a question or an exclamation).
2 At the end of an imperative sentence. ('Shut the door.')
3 After all initials and most abbreviations (N. R. Baines, etc., Feb., R.S.P.C.A.).
4 Between pounds and pence expressed in figures (£3.65).

Comma

The weakest pause mark, but the most important, since its omission can sometimes change the meaning of the sentence.

Don't pepper your sentences with commas – use the meaning of the sentence as a guide.

Never separate subject from verb by a comma.

Never separate verb from object or predicate by a comma.

Should be used:

1 To separate words or word groups in a series when there are at least three units: 'Sales are increasing, productivity is increasing, and profits are increasing.'
2 To separate a subordinate clause which precedes a main clause: 'Although we are not yet sure of the position, work will continue.'
3 To separate a relative clause whose removal would *not* change the basic sense of the sentence: 'This

product, which is one of our traditional lines, is not expensive.' Compare: 'The product that you have selected is not expensive.'

4 To separate a phrase or word of explanation from the rest of the sentence: 'London, the swinging city, stands beside the Thames.' Note: the rule here is the same as for relative clauses, so: 'He read the article "Management Training into the 1990s" before tackling the report.'

5 To separate coordinate *clauses* joined by one of the 'pure' conjunctions: 'and', 'but', 'or', neither', 'nor', 'for': 'He opened the safe, and took out the files.'

6 To separate an introductory phrase containing a verb from the main sentence: 'To complete the contract on time, we will need extra men.' Note: an introductory phrase without a verb has no comma following it, unless it is parenthetical: 'Following your request, here are the samples.'

7 To separate numbers (8,371,000).

8 Before a short quotation.

9 To mark a dependent word or word group that breaks the continuity of the sentence: 'The manager, his decision over-ruled, conceded defeat graciously.'

Semi-colon

 Marks a longer pause than a comma. A rather neglected punctuation mark, which is worth learning how to use. Should be used:

1 Between parts of a compound sentence when no conjunction is used: 'The comma is over-used in punctuation; the semi-colon is under-used.'

2 Between the clauses of a compound sentence before the so-called conjunctive adverbs: 'also', 'consequently', 'for', 'hence', 'nevertheless', 'on the other hand', 'otherwise', 'thus', 'however', 'therefore', etc., for these – unlike other conjunctions – do not join, but they do imply a close connection with the preceding clause: 'The matter had been discussed at length;

however, a decision had still not been made.'

3 Before the following expressions: 'as', 'namely', 'i.e.', 'e.g.', *viz*. when they introduce an illustration that is a complete clause or an enumeration that consists of several items: 'Business English should be concise; that is, as brief as is consistent with conveying a clear meaning.'

4 To separate the parts of a compound sentence when one or both parts already contain commas: 'The report will be finished today; the diagrams, tomorrow.' tomorrow.'

5 To separate serial phrases or clauses which have a common dependence on something that precedes or follows: 'They recommended that the department should be expanded; that a new manager should be appointed; and that work should start immediately.'

6 To emphasize parts of a series of clearly defined units: 'The true entrepreneur recognizes a great opportunity; moulds the resources necessary to take advantage of it; and creates a thriving business.'

Colon

 A stronger mark than the semi-colon, but used as an *introducer*. Should be used:

1 Between two independent groups not joined by a connecting word, when the first group points forward to the second: 'Success lies in two directions: better sales and higher productivity.'

2 To introduce a long quotation: 'In his inaugural address as President, John F. Kennedy said: "Ask not what your country can do for you; ask what you can do for your country." '

3 To introduce a list of items: 'He has good qualifications: a good business education, five years of work experience, and an excellent personal reputation.'

4 To separate independent clauses when there is sharp antithesis: 'Man proposes: God disposes.' But a semi-colon would be sufficient.

Question mark

It is equivalent to a full stop and should therefore be followed by a capital letter. Should be used:

1 After a direct question: 'Can you come to the meeting?' 'He asked, "Where is the letter?" '

  Should *not* be used after an indirect question; that is, one that does not require an answer: 'He asked where the letter was.'

  Need not be used after a courtesy question; that is, a sentence disguised as a question, but actually expressing a request or a command: 'Will you please let me know as soon as possible.'

2 After the individual parts of a speech, each of which might be expanded into a complete sentence: 'Have you finished the report? The illustrations? The binding?'

Exclamation mark

After a word, phrase or sentence to indicate strong emotion or to express sharp emphasis: 'No! That is not the point at all!'

Quotation marks

Are placed immediately before and after the actual words spoken or quoted. Should be used:

1 To enclose a direct quotation: 'He was reported as saying that "time is running out".'

2 To enclose both parts of an interrupted quotation: ' "Let us hope," he said, "that next year will be a better one for us all." '

3 To enclose the titles of subdivisions of published works (parts, chapters, sections, etc.) and the titles of magazine articles, reports, lectures and the like. Titles of books, newspapers, magazines, plays and other whole publications should be italicized. In typewriting, each word to be italicized is underlined: 'His

lecture "Communicate or Perish" was reproduced in *Management Today*.'

4 To enclose unusual or peculiar terms, words that are used in a particular sense, or words to which attention is directed to make the meaning clear: ' "Gobbledygook" is a term often used to describe foggy English in which a great deal of technical and business jargon is used.'

Note: when quotation marks are used with other punctuation marks, the rule is that punctuation marks go inside the quotation marks if they apply to the quotation or direct speech only, and outside when they apply to the whole sentence: 'He said, "Are you going?" 'Did he say, "I am going"? '

When both the whole sentence and the quoted words require a question mark, *one* question mark is made to serve both purposes, and is placed inside the quotation mark: 'Did he ask, "Are you going?" ' Note: where a quotation is included within a quotation, double quotation marks should be used for one quotation and single quotation marks for the other: 'The lecturer said, "The importance of good written English was summed up by Winston Churchill's words, 'Men will forgive anything except bad prose.' " '

Apostrophe

Beware of the apostrophe; it causes untold problems for people who do not seem to know the correct use of 'it's' and 'its'. 'It's' stands for 'it is'. 'Its' stands for 'belonging to it'.

Should be used:

1 To indicate possession (by a noun):
(a) 'man' – '*man's* hat': singular noun not ending in 's' adds ''s' to show possession.
(b) 'Charles' – '*Charles's* hat': singular noun ending in 's' adds ''s' to show possession. (Some people do not like the effect of double 's' and therefore add only an '. But this can cause other mistakes, so it is safer to

add ''s' to all singular nouns, whether they end in 's'
or not.)

(c) 'men' – *'men's'*: plural noun not ending with 's'
adds ''s' to show possession.

(d) 'boys' coats' – plural noun ending with 's' merely
adds ' to show possession.

Note: 'Fortnum and Mason's store' (joint possession),
'Matthew's and Abigail's premium bonds' (individual
possession), 'my brother-in-law's house' (one
brother-in-law), 'my brothers-in-laws' houses' is correct but better would be 'the houses of my brothers-
in-law'.

2 To indicate missing letters: 'haven't', 'can't', 'isn't'.

3 To indicate contracted dates: 'the swinging '60s'.

4 To indicate the plural of letters and numbers: 'Your
handwriting is not very clear: your u's are difficult to
distinguish from your n's.' 'How many 9's in 36?'

   But omit the apostrophe in punctuated abbreviations and in 'collective' dates: 'M.P.s', '1960s'.

Dash

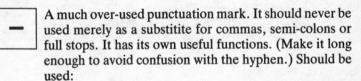

A much over-used punctuation mark. It should never be
used merely as a substitite for commas, semi-colons or
full stops. It has its own useful functions. (Make it long
enough to avoid confusion with the hyphen.) Should be
used:

1 As a separator, to indicate that a sentence has been
broken off, or to indicate a new direction of thought:
'We used a similar campaign for the Marsh account –
but of course you'll be familiar with it, won't you?'
'The Prime Minister admitted the desperate need for
housing, hospitals, schools – thereby, you may think,
invalidating her policy of public spending cuts.'

2 To mark a parenthesis or apposition: 'One director
attended the party – Mr Gideon.' 'He asked for only
one document – the Walker contract.'

3 To give strong emphasis: 'Those who voted against
him – and there were many – still spoke warmly of his
courage.'

4 To mark off a contrasting or summarizing statement: 'Accuracy, brevity and clarity – such are the qualities of good business writing.'

Parentheses (round brackets)

 Distinguish between round and square brackets. Round brackets should be used:

1 To mark off explanatory or supplementary material: 'Commas are the weakest marks for this purpose; dashes are stronger; round brackets (parentheses) are the strongest.' 'In future advertisements (watch out for them in the press) we will give dates and times of free trial sessions.' 'The trend this year is encouraging (see figure 3a).'

2 To enclose numbers or letters in enumerations in the text: 'The report is written in three parts: (1) the introduction, (2) the body, and (3) the conclusion or terminal section.'

3 To express an amount in numbers previously expressed in words: 'The annual salary will be five thousand pounds (£5000).'

Brackets (square)

 Square brackets should be used to enclose explanation, comment, or criticism inserted by someone other than the person quoted: 'The economy [of Britain] has never looked worse.'

Omission marks (or ellipses)

 Signify the omission or deletion of letters or words in quoted material. Three marks (. . .) signify an omission that does not end in a full stop; four marks (. . . .) signify an omission that does end in a full stop: 'Man . . . is a being born to believe.' – Disraeli.

Hyphen

1 To indicate the division of a word at the end of a line (see Appendix D).

2 To join parts of certain compound words. There appear to be no definite rules; however, the following guides represent current practice:

(a) With prefixes 'ex', 'self' and 'vice': 'ex-managing director', 'self-centred'.

(b) To join a prefix to a proper noun: 'pro-British'. Note: it is not used with short prefixes like 'co', 'de', 'pre', 'pro' or 're' except to prevent misinterpretation or mispronunciation: 'co-op' for 'co-operative', 'recover' – to regain, but 're-cover' – to cover again.

(c) Between two or more words serving as a single adjective before a noun: 'first-class mail'; 'forty-hour week'; 'up-and-coming company'. Note: when an adverb ending in 'ly' is used with an adjective or a participle, the compound is usually not hyphenated: 'highly regarded employee', 'universally held view'.

(d) To join numbers, quantities and fractions: 'a one-third share' but 'one third of the total sum', 'a ninety-nine-year lease'.

(e) To express a series of hyphenated compounds dependent on a common element which is omitted in all but the last compound: 'short- and long-term objectives'.

(f) To join a single letter to another word: 'X-rays'; 'H-bomb'; 'Z-cars'.

(g) To separate repetitions of certain letters: 'semi-invalid'; 'taxi-ing'.

(h) To avoid ambiguity: 'the sweet-shop girl'; 'the black-bearded politician'.

When in doubt – consult a dictionary.

The 'rules' of punctuation given above are frequently a subject of debate, and like much of English language usage constantly undergoing a process of change. For a more comprehensive examination of the irregularities and exceptions, try *Mind The Stop* by G. V. Carey (Pelican edn, Penguin Books, 1971).

Appendix B:
Using capitals

Try to use capitals as little as possible. However, use capital letters:

1 For proper names – a proper name is the name of an *individual* person, place, company, ship, product, etc.: 'Maximilian Forsythe-Rhodes'; 'the British'; 'Concorde'; 'the Houses of Parliament'.
2 To start a sentence or quotation.
3 For names of days of the week and months of the year but *not* for seasons: 'Wednesday'; 'March'; 'spring'; 'autumn'.
4 For the titles of books, magazines, films and so on: *The Dogs of War*; the *Daily Mirror* (but note: *The Times*); *Management Today*.
5 For the particular and not the general: 'the Chairman, Managing Director and senior directors'; 'Avon County Council' – but when you refer to them a second time – 'the council deferred the decision'.
6 For points of the compass which name a particular geographical area; but *not* when they express direction: 'You travel north-east to get to the North-East'; 'the Far East'; 'far eastern crafts'; 'southern Britain'; 'North America'.
7 For divisions of knowledge when you use them as titles of specific courses; but *not* when they are used to refer to studies in general or common divisions of knowledge: 'I am taking Principles of Marketing and Personnel Management as well as some economics and politics.'

Appendix C:
Using numbers

General rule Write numbers from one to nine as words; from 10 upwards write them as figures.

Exceptions
1 *Beginning a sentence* Numbers are *always* spelled out when they begin a sentence. Try not to start sentences with complicated numbers; e.g. 'Fifty-three million nine hundred and eighty-five thousand three hundred and sixty cars were produced last year.'(!)
2 *Round numbers* These should be spelled in full, except when they are used in the same sentence with other numbers that cannot be expressed in words conveniently:
'We cancelled the meeting ten days ago.'
'The report contained more than fifty pages.'
'These machines range in price from £50 to £13,500.'
3 *Adjoining numbers* When one number immediately follows another, it is best to spell out the smaller number, or the first number: 'ten 40-seater coaches'; 'four 25p notebooks'; 'twelve 2p pieces'.
4 *Numbers in parallel constructions* Write all the numbers in figures, unless all are small or are round numbers that can be written easily in words. If the first word is a number, it may be written out, even though the rest of the numbers are written in figures; but it may be possible to recast the sentence so that the first word is not a number:
'She ordered 65 diaries, 43 ring binders, and 125 felt-tip pens.'
'One hundred and sixty-two men, 75 women and 53 children were in the plane when it was hijacked.'

'When the plane was hijacked there were 162 men, 75 women and 53 children on board '

5 *Sums of money* Write sums of money in figures except in legal documents: £53; £5.36; 36p.

6 *Ordinal numbers* Ordinal numbers in lists are in figures – 1st, 2nd, 3rd; the date is in figures – 4th February 1982; but elsewhere in words – first, second, third.

7 *Quantities and measurements* Quantities and measurements are usually written in figures.

Appendix D:
Line-end division
of words

General rule Try to divide according to the sense of the words, if possible keeping enough of the whole word on the first line to imply the meaning.

Never divide:

- a proper noun
- one or two letters at the beginning or end of a word
- short words of two syllables
- at the end of three consecutive lines
- in legal documents
- words of one syllable and their plurals
- on the last line of a paragraph or page
- in the middle of figures
- between initials of names

Use the following suggestions as a guide:

1 In words ending in '-ing', divide before the '-ing'.
2 When the final consonant is doubled before '-ing', divide between the consonants.
3 Divide before '-sion', '-tion', '-cian'.
4 Divide before '-tial', '-cial'.
5 Divide before a suffix of *more* than two letters: 'disab-ility'; 'depart-ment'; 'separ-ate'.
6 Divide after a prefix of *more* than two letters: 'mis-under-stand'; 'com-mittee'.
7 Where there are two consonants between two vowels, divide after the first consonant: 'main-tenance'; 'obser-vation'.
8 Where there are three consonants between two vowels, divide after the first consonant: 'frus-trated'.

9 Divide between two vowel sounds (unless a diphthong) or after the first vowel when followed by a diphthong: 'strenu-ous'; 'circu-itous'.

10 Where the suggestions above do not apply, divide according to syllables: 'atti-tude'; 'complem-entary'.

Note: these suggestions will often make it possible to divide a word in different ways.

Appendix E: Commonly misused and confused words

accept: to receive, to give an affirmative answer
except: to exclude, to omit, to leave out

advice: counsel, recommendation (noun)
advise: to suggest to, to recommend (verb)

affect: to influence, to alter (verb)
effect: to bring about (verb)
effect: result or consequence (noun)

all ready: prepared
already: previously

all right: completely right
alright: OK (coll.) – considered by some as incorrect usage of 'all right'

altogether: completely or thoroughly
all together: in unison, in a group

among: refers to three or more
between: refers to two only

amount: quantity (of uncountable material)
number: a total of countable units

anyone: any person in general
any one: a specific person or item (e.g. any one suggestion)

complement: that which completes or supplements
compliment: flattery or praise, expression of regard

confidant: person in whom one confides (noun)
confident: positive or sure (adjective)

continual: taking place in close succession, frequently repeated
continuous: without stopping, without a break

council: an assembly of people (noun) – similarly, councillor
counsel: to advise (verb), advice (noun), legal adviser – similarly, counsellor

credible: believable or acceptable
creditable: praiseworthy
credulous: gullible

currant: fruit
current: belonging to present time, motion of air or water

dependent: depending, relying (adjective)
dependant: one who depends on another for support (noun)

discreet: prudent, circumspect
discrete: separate entity, individual

disinterested: neutral, not biased
uninterested: not concerned with, lacking interest

disorganized: disordered
unorganized: not organized or planned

eminent: outstanding, prominent
imminent: very near, impending, threatening

farther: refers to geographical or linear distance
further: more, in addition to

formally: according to convention
formerly: previously

imply: to hint at, or to allude to in speaking or writing
infer: to draw a conclusion from what has been said or written

its: a possessive singular pronoun
it's: a contraction for 'it is'

less: smaller quantity of uncountable material
fewer: a smaller total of countable units

licence: permission, authorization (noun)
license: to permit, to authorize (verb)

maybe: perhaps (adverb)
may be: indicates possibility (verb)

moral: a principle, maxim, or lesson (noun); ethical (adjective)
morale: a state of mind or psychological outlook (noun)

oral: by word of mouth
verbal: in words whether oral or written

personal: private, not public or general
personnel: the staff of an organization

practical: not theoretical, useful, pragmatic
practicable: can be put into practice (should not be used to refer to people)

practice: action, performance, habitual action (noun)
practise: to put into practice, to perform (verb)

proceed: to begin, to move, to advance
precede: to go before

principal: of primary importance (adjective), head of a college, original sum, chief
principle: a fundamental truth

stationery: writing paper or writing materials
stationary: not moving, fixed

their: belonging to them (possessive of 'they')
there: in that place (adverb)
they're: a contraction of the two words 'they are'

weather: climate or atmosphere
whether: introduces the first of two alternatives
wether: a castrated ram

who's: a contraction of 'who is'
whose: possessive of 'who'

your: a pronoun (possessive)
you're: a contraction of 'you are'

Appendix F
Ten (simple?) rules
of spelling

1 *i* before *e* except after *c*, when the sound is *ee*:

achieve, receive, piece, perceive

Except:

seize, weird, weir, sheik

Note: the words 'neighbour', 'height', 'weight', 'heir', 'their', are not exceptions, since the sound is not *ee*.

2 Words ending in a silent *e* drop the *e* before a vowel when forming compound words but not before a consonant:

love – lovable – loving; move – moving
but: like – likely; safe – safely

Except: the *e* is retained
    (a) after *c* and *g* to soften the sound:

noticeable, knowledgeable, manageable

    (b) for reasons of distinction:

singing, singeing
dying, dyeing

Note. the *e* is dropped before consonants in words of one syllable:

due – duly; true – truly

ana judgement and judgement
    acknowledgment and acknowledgement } *both acceptable*

3 Words ending in *l* take *ll* when *ly* is added:

hopeful – hopefully
faithful – faithfully

4 Words ending in a single vowel and a single consonant double the final consonant before adding *-eo, -ing, -er*:

win – winning   commit – committed
run – running   refer – referring

but: feel – feeling

as long as the stress is on the final or only syllable.
  If the accent is not on the last syllable, the consonant is not doubled:

differ – differing
alter – altering

Except:

worship – worshipping
travel – traveller

5 When the word begins with *s* the *s* is retained after *mis-* and *dis-*:

misspelling, dissolve, dissatisfy, dissuade

but: mislead, disappoint, disappear

6 When *all, full, till* and *well* are used to form compound words they usually drop one *l*:

full – fulfil   careful
skill – skilful   until
well – welfare

Except:

farewell, well-being

7 Words ending in *-ceed, -cede, -sede*

pro
  ex } ceed   super – sede
suc

All others take *cede*:

concede, intercede, precede

Note:
proceed but procedure
proceedings

8 Words ending in *-our* usually drop *u* before *-ation*, *-ate* and -*ous*:

humour – humorous
vigour – vigorous – invigorate

Note: 'humor', 'color' are American spellings.

9 Words ending in *y* preceded by a consonant change *y* to *i* when a syllable is added:

merry – merrily
lady - ladies
rely – relied
likely – likelihood

10 *c* changes to *s* when the noun is used as a verb:

practice (I am going to do some practice)
practise (I am going to practise)

licence (I have a driving licence)
license (I am licensed to drive)

advice (Can I give you some advice?)
advise (Can I advise you?)

Appendix G: Commonly misspelled words

absence
accessible
accommodate
achieve
acquainted
advertisement
agreeable
all right
among
appearance
arrangement

beautiful
beginning
believed
benefited
business

certain
choice
colleagues
coming
committee
commitment
comparative
competent
competitive
conscientious
conscious
correspondence
criticism

decision
definite
disappointed
disappear

eighth
embarrassed
environment
especially
essential
excellent
exercise
expenses
extremely

faithfully
familiar
February
forty

gauge
government
guard
guarantee

height

immediately
independent
instalment

knowledge

library
losing
lying

maintenance
management
miniature
minutes

necessary
noticeable

occasionally
occurrence
omitted
opinion

parallel
parliament
personal
personnel
planning
possesses
preceding
privilege
procedure
proceed
professional
pronunciation
psychological

quantitative
quiet
quite

really
received
recommend
receipt
relieved
responsibility
restaurant

scarcely
secretary
separately
similar
sincerely
successfully
supersede
surprising

tendency
transferred
twelfth

unconscious
undoubtedly
unnecessary
until
usually

valuable
view

Wednesday

A final word

Throughout this book and its companion volume *What Do You Mean, 'Communication'?* we have concentrated on the basic principles that lie behind effective communication in business, but you will have discovered that there is no magic lamp that you or I can rub to make you an effective communicator. It is a question of being aware of the nature of communication and the principles which govern the process, and then being prepared to make the effort to put those principles into practice.

If you are willing to think sensitively when you communicate and always keep the other person – the receiver – constantly in mind both before you communicate and while you are communicating, you will automatically discover the answers to those familiar questions. What shall I say? How shall I say it? What does he mean?

In other words, communication is a selfless process in which, to stand any chance of success, we have to fight constantly our natural instinct to be self-centred. We have to guard against the very natural inclination to concentrate on ourselves, on what *we* want to say, and try instead to consider the other person and focus on what we *need* to say and do, both to help him understand what *we* mean and to help him tell us what *he* means.

Real communication, then, is a two-way process. We must be prepared to listen as much as speak and we must listen effectively to what is really being said – and to what is not being said. We must be conscious of what may be communicated between the lines when we listen and read, and when we speak and write – in other words we must be aware of the total message. Above all, we need to be constantly aware of the potential difficulties that

beset communication, and alert to the ways in which we can
strive to overcome them, or at least reduce their effect.

We will not always succeed. Communication is by nature a
human and therefore an imperfect process, but our efforts to
improve will be rewarded in countless ways. In any case, just
trying to understand how communication works and how we can
try to perfect our ability to communicate effectively can in itself
be a rewarding task.

Index

THE PROBLEM BUSTER'S GUIDE

THE PROBLEM BUSTER'S GUIDE

Mike Allison

Gower

First published 1993 by
EstoQual Enterprises
This edition published by
Gower Publishing Limited
Gower House
Croft Road
Aldershot
Hampshire GU11 3HR
England

Mike Allison has asserted his right under the Copyright, Designs and Patents Act 1988 to be identified as the author of this work.

British Library Cataloguing in Publication Data

Allison, Mike
    The problem buster's guide
    1. Problem solving   2. Management science
    I. Title
    658.4'03

    ISBN 0 566 07761 2

Typeset in 11pt Times by Raven Typesetters, Chester and printed in Great Britain at the University Press, Cambridge

CONTENTS

LIST OF FIGURES

LIST OF TABLES

PREFACE

The purpose of this book is to provide a comprehensive kit of methods to convert problems into improvements. We shouldn't be afraid of problems. Without them, there would be little or no incentive to make improvements.

The current interest in problem solving stems largely from attempts by industry at improving productivity, to meet foreign competition. The popular problem-solving material has evolved mainly from methods used in quality management. These tend to be logical and analytical in nature. These methods are not ideally suited to creativity, but they are important, because much of what we do *is* logical and analytical. By combining creative methods with analytical approaches, we get the best of both worlds – new ideas and practical ways of implementing them.

There is a huge demand for new ideas and the demand will continue to increase. People in industry particularly, and in other activities as well, will have more problems to solve in future. Being equipped with techniques for problem solving will make for better results in all spheres of human activity. There is enormous satisfaction in solving problems and helping others. Armed with problem-solving techniques, everyone can make a difference to the world and thus improve the quality of life.

The approach of this book is, not only to show ways to solve problems which have been proven effective, but also to encourage the reader to develop her or his own approach. Rigid 'one true way' approaches to problem solving are not encouraged, although they may be useful at a very elementary level. The scope of this book is sufficient for most managers in industry, designers, facilitators, improvement team members and people with a sense of curiosity. No special preparation is necessary to understand these methods.

One of the emerging themes for coping with life is 'holism', meaning proper balance between the many things we have to do and making sure we lead a worthwhile life. This balance is a theme applied in this book to the problem-solving approach.

I am grateful to the following people for their assistance in developing this book:

My colleagues, Tony Pilli and John York, for incisive observations about the initial drafts.

My wife, Jan, for patience and a fresh approach to understanding.

Mike Allison

INTRODUCTION

Turning our problems into opportunities

Opportunities present themselves to us every day. Whether you are walking down the street, working in an office or enjoying a well-earned holiday, opportunities are all around us. Why is it then, that so many opportunities are missed – not taken advantage of? The answer is that we often turn an opportunity into a problem. Because we don't know how to take this opportunity, we create barriers and turn a positive situation into a negative one. It's time to alter this way of thinking. Through this book, we will show you how to take advantage of an opportunity, rather than waste it.

Issues that will be confronted in this book

There's no shortage of problems to be solved – high levels of pollution, pressure of population growth, diminishing resources and so on. What we must realize is that these problems *can be solved*. Imagine the improvements we could make to our society if everyone was confident and capable of solving problems. It does take hard work, but work which is extremely rewarding. There is immense satisfaction in turning a problem into an opportunity.

Most of the information on problem solving published so far has been for industry. Not surprisingly, that information has concentrated on methods and techniques which involve logic and analytical approaches. Now we must go beyond these approaches and apply more creative methods towards problem solving. Some work has already been done on creativity, but very little has been used for industry and quality management, where most of the activity is based.

There's a growing awareness that most people in industry tend to be 'logic dominant', meaning those people tend to use the skills which are usually associated with parts of the brain which use logic and analysis. What could be achieved if these people allowed other parts of their brains to make a bigger contribution to problem solving – the parts usually associated with emotion and creativity? We'll be looking at ways to do this, as well as how to improve our logical brain talents. These two approaches will enable us to expand dramatically our problem-solving skills. The techniques are not difficult to learn, but there are no 'easy steps'. You can't solve a problem without working hard at it.

How to use this book

We all approach our work differently. That's why the material in this book has been organized so that there are several ways for the reader to study it.

We suggest that you read the whole of Part I, which explains each method and gives examples of how to use it. This Part also shows the various stages in problem solving and how they are linked together, and discusses some of the traps and pitfalls you may encounter.

The sequence indicated in the book should not be regarded as a rigid formula. Some problems need to be tackled differently and the text includes many examples of special situations.

Part II is designed as a restatement – in abbreviated and standardized form – of the techniques described in Part I. It includes a summary of the problem-solving steps and a checklist of questions to help you take a fresh look at intervals during the problem-solving process. In addition there are two matrices showing the roles of the different problem-solving methods and the way they relate to one another.

You may wish to read more about problem solving. The reference section contains details of books on particular aspects.

Finally, the index covers the complete text. When selecting a method for a specific application, it's helpful to consult both parts of the book.

PART I

THE ART OF
PROBLEM BUSTING

Chapter 1

RECOGNIZING PROBLEMS

Key concepts and methods:

- Problem visibility
- Problems and symptoms
- The Five Whys
- Not all problems have to be solved

'An Organisation will meet its death when all its problems are gone'

Toshio Doko
Former Chairman of the Federation of Economic Organisations of Japan

How visible is the problem?

One of the most fascinating things about humans is the way we perceive things. We have a strange duality of behaviour – needing variety for stimulation, but resisting change. About 100 years ago, Russia changed to the Gregorian calendar, which is in use throughout most of the world today. The peasants thought they were being robbed of several days of life, because of the adjustments to the date. Hundreds were killed in the riots. The change was too much to handle.

Biologists have shown that animals adapt to *gradually changing* conditions so well that threats to their existence may be ignored. We often behave like this. In industry, it's common for serious problems to be ignored while relatively trivial matters get urgent attention. We do much the same with social matters. Why is this? We get used to the serious problems because they have been with us for so long, we have adapted to them. On the other hand, if some change comes along to alter the status quo, we sit up and take notice. It's the old adage of the squeaky wheel getting the most attention.

There's another reason why we don't notice problems when we should. We are so busy doing our 'regular jobs' (production) that we don't notice or don't have time for other things, like problem recognition. Incidentally, another reason we notice changes from the status quo is that we are adapted to this. Our eyes make rapid, tiny movements, scanning for changes in our surroundings – is that a wild beast about to leap on us? The effects of millions of years of evolution are strong and very much a part of our nature that we need to understand.

Does this attitude to problems happen in areas of human endeavour other than industry? You bet it does. The world was considered to be flat for hundreds of years. The evidence that it was round existed, but it was difficult for people to break out of the established ways of thinking. The view of the flat earth was reinforced by folklore. Even the maps showed warning signs that ships would fall off the edge! This was despite the fact that nobody had actually observed an edge.

Problems and symptoms

One of the most common mistakes in problem solving is to try and solve a symptom. You can't do that. Here is a simple example. You are making toast for breakfast. The toast gets burnt. Here is a problem – the toast doesn't taste nice if it's burnt. So the problem is fixed by scraping the burnt layer off the toast. Wrong! All that happened is that the symptom was removed. The burnt layer was a symptom of a toasting system that isn't working. To fix the problem, you need to remove the *cause* of the burning. Then the symptom doesn't keep coming back.

Many situations exist where the observer attacks the symptom rather than the problem in a similar manner to the example. It's a sure bet the symptom will keep coming back. In industry, it's often found that operators are 'warned to take more care'. The same thing happens over and over again. The symptom is that something went wrong. The knee-jerk reaction is to blame the operator. But no attempt is made to find the *cause* of the problem, which is not often the operator. In society, we have considerable resources devoted to reducing drink driving and its effects. We should ask ourselves whether drink driving is a cause or a symptom. By enquiry like this, we soon find that observed conditions or behaviours may be both symptoms and causes. See the Relations Diagram for further details.

How can we be sure we are working on a problem and not a symptom? There's a marvellously simple method which can be used to test for a problem or a symptom. The bonus is that this method often finds the cause as well. If the solution is sufficiently clear (and it often is), the problem can quickly be solved.

The Five Whys

Figure 1.1   *The Five Whys*

The method is the five whys. Simply keep asking **Why?** until the cause is exposed. For example, for the burnt toast, the dialogue goes something like this:

Why was the toast burnt?
Because the toast was in too long.

Why was the toast in too long?
Because the setting was wrong.

or:

Why was the toast burnt?
Because the toast was in too long.
Why was the toast in too long?
Because the bread stuck.
Why did the bread stick?
Because it was cut too thickly.

We got to the bottom of the problem for the first set in just two questions. This is an example of a flexible rule. Five Whys is just a guideline. Obviously it makes no sense to keep asking why if the answer has been found. But on the other hand, if the answer hasn't been found after five whys, keep on asking. If you haven't uncovered something which can be dealt with to make the problem go away permanently, you may be trying to fix the symptom. Ask whether the problem could come back after you have eliminated the visible evidence of it. The second set of questions and answers could lead on to trying machine-sliced bread. Note that the Five Whys could take different paths, depending on the viewpoint of the person answering the questions.

A word of warning about the Five Whys. It works well for simple problems where there is a single cause of the problem. It also works well when used with other methods such as the *cause and effect diagram* and the *relations diagram*. But beware of thinking that the problem is fixed when the Five Whys has found a cause. Many problems in life usually have multiple causes, particularly the major ones. It's the major problems which have the greatest pay-off. As we shall see, Five Whys can be used together with several other methods.

Not all problems have to be solved

This statement might seem strange at first, but some problems are of a transitory nature. When we were living in caves and hadn't discovered fire, nightfall was a problem. We couldn't see and would bump into things. The problem was too difficult to solve with the available technology, so the solution was simply to lie down and wait until it went away – which it did. The sun rose quite reliably the next day and we could see again. A variant of this occurs when some condition is perceived as a problem, but the 'problem' would go away if we simply changed the perception of the people who see the situation as a problem.

Sometimes we are tempted to work on 'problems' which, if solved, might make matters worse. For example, all humans die. Some people have accepted this as a problem and are working on ways to solve it. In the United States, many dead people have been deep frozen, in the hope that a way will be found to bring them back to life in the future. If you saw the film *Ice Man*, where a 40 000 year old frozen man was brought back to life, you would have some idea of how we would cope with a future world. Except today's 'Ice Man' would only have to wait about 200 years to be faced with an utterly alien world – such is the rate of change.

Chapter 2

DEFINING
PROBLEMS

Key concepts and methods:

- Working on the right problem
- Problem formulation
- Broadening definition
- Creativity

Which is the problem and which the symptom, the breakdown of the family or the decline of religious standards? Perhaps the question is wrong.

Working on the right problems

Once we are satisfied that solving a problem is in our best interests, we need to get down to the serious business of defining the problem. There are two main reasons for doing this:

- to be sure we are working on the real problem
- to open up opportunities for breakthrough solutions.

We need to be sure we are working on the right problem, because the *symptom* may deceive us into thinking we know the *problem* when we really don't. Doctors are always faced with this difficulty. The complexity of the human body is such that a symptom may be the same for a variety of different complaints. Until the job of diagnosis has identified the *real problem*, the doctor doesn't know which remedy to use. So we should take care to ask some questions which will lead us through a diagnosis of what the real problem may be which is manifesting itself with the symptoms we see.

Suppose a fuse keeps blowing on an electrical appliance. It's tempting to conclude that the fuse is too low a value for the job. That would be dangerous, because the designers are likely to have thought about what is the correct value. Quite likely there is something wrong with the appliance which causes excessive power consumption. Our questioning might go something like this:

- Do other, similar, appliances keep blowing fuses?
- Can we show a connection between the fuse blowing and some other condition in the appliance?
- Does the way we have described the problem correctly identify it?

At the same time, we want to make sure we have explored the best possible solution – not just a solution which gets rid of the irritation caused by the problem. This is where we have the opportunity to break through to a new level of thinking. Breakthrough thinking is closely related to lateral thinking, made famous by Dr Edward de Bono. This sort of thinking is useful right from the start of a problem-solving process and at all subsequent stages.

Problem formulation

We can get our breakthrough thinking by carefully formulating the problem. Here's an example of how it works. Years ago, an American industrial engineer was asked to make improvements to a warehouse where sacks were being filled with pig feed. It was a typical operation of weighing feed from a hopper into sacks, stitching up the sacks, moving them to pallets, then into storage

Figure 2.1   *Problem formulation*

and eventually on to a truck for transportation to the customers.

The engineer could have easily earned his fee by making a few re-arrangements of the warehouse. Likely improvements would be to measure the frequency of operations and make sure the most frequent operations were the shortest paths. However, the engineer decided to think about the problem carefully. He used Problem Formulation to progressively redefine the problem in broader and broader terms. This is the essence of getting breakthrough thinking. Never accept a problem at face value! The engineer redefined the problem like this:

Start	**End**
Feed in the mixing bin	Bags of feed in the warehouse
Feed in the mixing bin	Bags of feed loaded on delivery truck
Feed in the mixing bin	Feed in customer's storage bins
Feed ingredients in field	Feed in customer's storage bins
Feed ingredients in field	Feed in pigs' stomachs

Notice how each redefinition or formulation of the problem moved away from the narrow confines of the original problem to a broader formulation which opened up more ideas. The last formulation could be satisfied by letting the pigs loose in the field! Now that may not be feasible – the feed might be grown a long way from where the pigs are. But the third formulation led to a breakthrough in how stock feed was handled. There was no need to fill the sacks at all! A much more efficient way was simply to fill a bulk transporter with the feed and off-load it at the customers' premises.

Today, we wouldn't think of doing it any other way. But the idea of bulk feed transport only came about because of the approach the engineer took. Try this on your next problem at work or at home. It opens up so many opportunities. The essence of the method is to show 'Start' as an early stage in the process – a condition you are trying to move from – and 'End' as the final stage of the process – a condition you want to arrive at.

Dr de Bono's lateral thinking is similar. He deliberately introduces a disturbance into the thinking process to force a more radical approach. One way he does this is to turn the problem upside-down. For example, if designers of the Concorde supersonic airliner had tried 'landing the aircraft upside-down' as a disturbance, they might have been inclined to try putting the cockpit underneath the body of the aircraft so it didn't need a hinged nose to allow the pilot to see the runway when the aircraft lands at its steep angle. Of course, there might need to be a way of keeping the crew safe if the landing gear failed. An aircraft was built during World War II which had cockpits both under and above the body.

Here are some more examples of formulating problems in broader ways:

broader start	start	end	broader end
	waste material	dumped waste	useful materials
	hungry people	people fed	hunger removed
passengers at home	passengers at airport	passengers in plane	passengers at destination
voters at home	voters in polling booth	ballot papers completed	votes cast

Notice how the broadening process opens up opportunities for radical new solutions, such as voting by computer. The counting could be done in a few minutes!

The importance of making opportunities for breakthrough thinking is greater than all the other methods in this book. It is here that the flashes of inspiration lead to huge improvements in our lives. But it needs work. Unless we make a conscious effort to do it, the pressure of everyday work will win and the opportunity will be lost.

It's worth looking at another aspect of creativity. Dr de Bono and other writers[1,2] have suggested that humour is an important part of creativity. When we find something funny, it's often because of its bizarre or unexpected relationship to something else. The essence of a good joke is that we leap in thought from one subject to another. The leap seems to be the thing that brings on laughter. That's very much like what we try to do in creativity. We deliberately force a shift in thought patterns by introducing an artificial distraction. Problem formulation and lateral thinking are two methods of distraction. Making a joke out of the problem might be another way. Try getting a good joke teller on your team. She or he might just bring about a new way of looking at the problem, leading to a breakthrough. Who says problem solving can't be fun?

Chapter 3

MAPPING THE PROBLEM

Key concepts and methods:

- Matrix data analysis
- Matrix diagram
- L-shaped matrix
- Guide to problem-solving approach

'.... I can only feel that I had been so taken by the magic of statistical methods that I had forgotten to pursue the nature of quality control itself.'
Shigeo Shingo

Another job for us in problem solving is to make sure we have a clear picture of what we are dealing with. Here's an example of where rules are not a good idea. I've put this job after problem formulation, but it could just as well go before it. Often the two go hand-in-hand. Instead of relying on rules, it's best to keep looking at the problem afresh and ask 'what's the best approach at my present level of understanding of the problem?' After all, the level of understanding is continuously changing as we learn more about it. An approach suitable when we know little may not be useful when we have a better understanding.

Matrix data analysis

Figure 3.1   *Matrix data analysis*

To help understanding, we have to make the best use of available information. There may not be much information at the start. One useful method to improve understanding is a 2 by 2 matrix diagram. This simple graphical method lets us show the relationships between two variables that we are dealing with. It covers a lot of our needs, but not all. The 2 by 2 matrix is also useful just to show how we see a problem – even if we don't have any measurements.

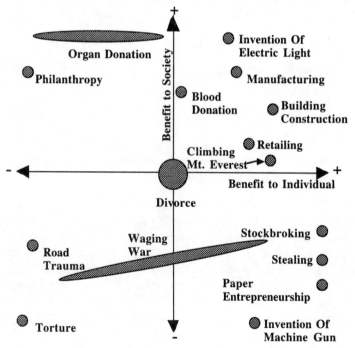

Figure 3.2   *2 × 2 matrix diagram – social and individual benefits*

This may be sacrilege to those who insist on measurements for everything, but some things don't have measurements. For simple problems, the 2 by 2 matrix diagram may not be necessary.

Figure 3.2 shows an example of a 2 by 2 matrix used to show an individual's perception of a situation. The purpose of the example matrix is to show which human activities are beneficial to society and which are harmful. This may help in a project to show how we reward, encourage or discourage different activities.

Teams can cluster around a whiteboard to develop this. The electronic whiteboard has to be one of a team's best gadgets. You can alter it as much as you like, then get a copy of the end result. Incidentally, if you have an ordinary whiteboard, there are now special devices to take a picture of the whiteboard and produce a copy. These devices are about the size of a 35mm slide projector, so they are portable.

How the Matrix is constructed:

● Choose two variables which describe the issues of interest – in this case the individual benefits of an action and the corresponding social benefits.
● Show one on the horizontal line and one on the vertical line. Give a plus sign for a positive benefit and a minus sign for a negative effect.
● For each idea which comes to mind, show a point or an area which best describes it.

The example matrix isn't intended to be factually correct – only to show how the individual or team who prepared it sees the situation. A map like this might be helpful to governments in deciding the best course of action in any complicated situation. Notice how some of the areas are stretched out, because there are uncertainties and wide differences, depending on circumstances. For this matrix, the general interpretation would be to encourage activities in the top half, particularly the top right hand quarter, because these benefit both individuals and society. Activities in the lower half would be discouraged, particularly those in the lower left, where both society and individuals suffer disadvantage.

Now the problem is seen in this mapped-out form, it may take on a different appearance in the minds of the people involved in problem solving. The very definition of the problem may change.

Perhaps the 2 by 2 matrix will show something that was not obvious at first. These constant changes in view during the problem solving process are good. It means progress is being made. It's important to keep reviewing in the light of each new development.

The matrix diagram

Another method for mapping out the problem is the matrix diagram (Figure 3.3). There are several types of matrix diagram, but by far the most commonly used version is the 'L-shaped' matrix – so called because one leg of the L contains one set of attributes and the other leg of the L contains another set. This method shows the relationship between two or more sets of attributes. For example, we might want to know which parts of the organization have something to do with a type of problem. The matrix diagram lets us show this by placing the types of problem in one leg and the departments in the other. Where the rows and columns of the matrix intersect, we show the nature of the relationship. It might be no relationship, or a weak or strong relationship.

Figure 3.3   *The matrix diagram*

Figure 3.4 shows a matrix diagram used to show the relationship between patient admission/discharge problems in a hospital and the departments of the hospital. This approach gives a clear picture of where to concentrate the efforts in further investigation. In the example, there are more primary responsibility symbols under Nursing Administration than any other function. Hence, concentrating efforts in this area is likely to pay dividends sooner than efforts in Customer Contact, where there are only communications/reports.

The size and scope of the problem may be taking on new dimensions at this stage. Often, when people are asked to start

Department/Individual/Function \\ Problem	Customer Contact	Ward Nursing Staff	Porters	Admissions Officer	Medical Staff	Nursing Administration	Relatives	Ancillary Services
Bed Moves	△		○	△		◎		
Lack Of Policy Understanding		○			◎	◎	△	
Not Enough Beds Available	△	○		○		◎		
Patients Discharged Wrong Time	△	○		○	◎		△	
No Staff To Make Up Beds		△	◎	○		○		
No Linen		△				◎		
Pending Admissions Not Known	△					△	○	
Comms - Admission Officer/Nursing Staff		○		◎		◎		
Delay-notify Admis. Officer-imp. Discharge	△	◎		△		△		
No Delivery - Pharmacy Supplies						○		◎

◎ Primary Responsibility   △ Communications/Receive Reports

○ Secondary Responsibility

Figure 3.4 *L-shaped matrix for admission/discharge problems*

projects to solve problems, they are asked to prepare a chart showing the time schedule. This is one of the really laughable aspects of Western management. How can we know the length of time it will take before we begin? If the problem was really simple, we might know, but then the chart would be a waste of time. Think of the problem of developing fusion power. This enormously complex problem has been under investigation for many years – the timing chart must have been redrawn many times. It's good to have a plan for review after there's been time to gather information and make a first assessment, but rarely can the solution be predicted.

With changing scope, the problem should be re-examined. Perhaps the process needs to go back to an earlier step to see if it could be handled better now.

The work so far should now give a picture of roughly how big the problem is and what sort of skills are needed to solve it. Some problems are best dealt with by individuals, some need teams. Knowing when to use which approach is the job of the person in charge of the project. If there are many jobs to be done, a team approach divides the work into manageable chunks. There may need to be a main project team and several teams to work on components of the problem.

Recently, I saw an example of the wrong approach to problem solving. The company involved decided teamwork was important and used an 'N Easy Steps' approach. This was assumed to be the *one true way* to solve problems. The team involved gave a very impressive presentation of how they tackled the problem. Each member gave a well rehearsed talk on her or his part in the work. The job proceeded in the specified step by step approach. The trouble was the team took six weeks to solve a problem which any self-respecting tradesperson could have solved on the spot.

Had a person with the right technical skills been assigned to the problem, he or she would have recognized a likely cause from the appearance of the problem symptoms. Then the tradesperson would have proceeded directly to a new line of investigation which would have uncovered the basic cause very quickly. This was a problem suited to a technically qualified person. Others are better solved by teams which bring a wide variety of skills to the process. Someone has to make the decision which is the better way to approach the problems and the decision cannot be made without some idea of what the problem is about and what the relative benefits are from each approach. Table 3.1 is a guide to help make the decision.

Remember to remain flexible in approaching a problem. If there is some special knowledge that the problem solver possesses, then this should be used to choose the best approach.

If there are many components to a problem, each needing a team to tackle them, then there is a need for co-ordination. The difficulty with these complex problems is that teams are needed to work on the components of the problem, but the overall project leader mustn't lose sight of the total picture. There is an ever present danger of the teams solving the components but the components not working to solve the total problem.

Table 3.1   *Guide To Choosing An Approach To Suit The Problem*

Problem Type	Recommended Approach	Example
One place, consistent symptoms	Technical specialist to make initial assessment and report back – often solves problem on the spot	Photocopier suddenly producing different results
One place, inconsistent symptoms	Team of technical specialist initial assessment and person working on the proess to make initial assessment and report back	Photocopier sometimes produces defective copies
Any place, familiar symptoms	Team of local people and facilitator to take fresh approach (previous approaches have tried to fix the symptom)	Arguments about which TV programme to watch
Several places, consistent symptoms	Team of technical specialist, representatives from several areas to make initial assessment	Particular make of washing machine develops faults
Several places, inconsistent symptoms	Team of technical specialist, management representative to gather more information and report back	Same make of washing machine lasts well in some places, fails early in others
Broad problems, affect many areas	Draw team from variety of areas, gather information without fear of criticism or punishment	Poor morale

In this type of situation, the overall project leader needs to keep bringing the team leaders together and taking a fresh look at the total problem. The focused approach of the individual teams helps concentrate the effort on identified components, but the project team consisting of team leaders has the job of looking at the big picture. Both the main project team and the component teams need to constantly look for a 'better view of the situation', as new knowledge develops.

Another factor which emerges from handling bigger problems is that solutions to component problems may have to be traded off with other solutions. What is best for a component may not be best for the overall problem. For example, a company has a problem with not making enough profit from its production. It is known that the cost of spares for maintaining machines has gone up sharply and machines are out of action too often. The manager decides to tackle the problem on two fronts. Two teams are formed. One team has to find a way to reduce the cost of purchased spare parts. Another has to find a way to reduce the time that machines are out of action while being maintained. Both components of the overall problem are important, but they are classic cases of one destroying another. The team looking for cheaper parts will likely find a source of cheap but unreliable parts. The team looking to reduce machine downtime will want to buy parts which have a long life – these may be expensive. To produce the best result, the teams need to pool their information and work out which mixture gives the lowest total cost. The overall project leader should know about concepts such as life cycle costs.[3]

Chapter 4

BREAKING DOWN THE PROBLEM

Key concepts and methods:

- Affinity diagram
- Team participation
- Task groupings

How do you build a Cathedral? – One brick at a time

In Chapter 3, the 2 by 2 matrix helped map out our ideas and went some way to showing what are the component parts of a problem. As the problem-solving process progresses, the elements are better defined. The bigger the problem, the more elements it is likely to have. A problem may be big, not just because of its complexity, but because of strong emotional feelings which make it difficult to deal with. Both these barriers to problem solving can be dealt with using a remarkable method developed by the Japanese Union of Scientists and Engineers (JUSE). The method is called the Affinity Diagram.

I've found this method to be useful in manufacturing, health, service, interpersonal relations and the home. It's easy to learn and when people see it for the first time, they are usually amazed at its effectiveness. Another advantage is that it equalizes the inputs of team members when there are dominant or shy people in the group. We'll see how in a moment.

Teams often find that, as well as the complex or emotional difficulties involved with a project, it is hard to get started. An example project might be 'How to move our factory to another suburb'. The project is complex, large and riddled with emotional difficulties. Time for the *affinity diagram*.

The affinity diagram

The affinity diagram is unlike almost every other popular method for problem solving. This is because it favours the right side of the brain. Most of the others make use of the left side of the brain. Most people tend to use one side of their brains in thinking. The left side involves logical thinking, analysis and language. The right side is used for emotions, behaviour and overall comprehension.

Figure 4.1   *The affinity diagram*

To use the affinity diagram, we first have to state carefully the central subject. It's very important that the subject is expressed as a generality. For example, let's take the move to another suburb.

Suppose we said 'How can we move our factory to another suburb, by next month?' From the way we have stated this subject, it focuses on a one month time-frame. This might have been suggested by a senior manager, without the benefit of analysing the problem. Instead, try 'What are the issues surrounding the movement of our factory to another suburb?' You could even leave out the time-frame at this stage. It will emerge quite naturally from the process of using the affinity diagram.

The broad statement allows free development of ideas. Let's assume a team has been formed, consisting of representatives from all the main departments of the company. A good way to structure the team for this type of problem (and most others where both management and operators are affected) is to have management and operators involved. Without such a mixture, the team will produce a one-sided and unrealistic output. It may also be an unworkable output, which is of no use to anybody. Now get the team to write out ideas with the issues statement in mind. Have the team write the ideas in large letters, on sticky notes. The ideas should have about six words, for clarity. When each team member has about five ideas, you're ready to start the fascinating process of the affinity diagram. For the first time a team uses the affinity diagram, a facilitator should be on hand to assist and explain the method.

The team places all the sticky notes with ideas on a whiteboard. If you don't have a whiteboard, the wall will do, but sticky notes don't stick very well to wallpaper or cloth. Here's an important rule: the process is best done in silence. This has the effect of eliminating emotional bias. It also disarms any dominating member and makes it easier for quiet members to contribute.

Each member in turn moves the sticky notes into groupings. Not logical categories, but groupings where the sticky notes just seem to belong. We are using feelings here, so it's important for the team members not to spend too much time thinking about where they're putting the sticky notes. Each member can make as many moves as he or she thinks fit, before handing over to the next member. After a very few turns, the team will find there's little or no desire to change the position of the sticky notes. There might be one or two sticky notes which haven't been placed in groupings. These are called 'lone wolves'. Consensus has been reached and nobody feels upset. It's easy to underestimate the power of this method. It has been used to resolve quite bitter disputes, with great success.

Once the process of arranging the sticky notes is done, the team can talk again. Now we need a title to summarize each category. One of the sticky notes might be suitable, or a title can be made up. For example, there may be several sticky notes saying things like:

- How will we avoid a lengthy shutdown?
- Need to replace resigned staff
- Setting up machines.

The team might decide to give this grouping a title like 'Continuity of Production'. There could be groupings within groupings. Continuity of production might have sub-groupings for transport coordination, staff recruitment, training, installation, etc.

Figures 4.2, 4.3 and 4.4 show the steps for the affinity diagram.

The affinity diagram gives us order out of chaos. Now we can examine how to use the ideas in the groupings to do detailed problem solving. If we were really working on the factory move problem, we would probably form teams to tackle each grouping from the affinity diagram.

Using multiple teams to attack the problem-solving job is one way to give the speed of completion which is so important in today's fast moving world. The first enterprise to solve a problem is usually the one which wins the lion's share of the market.

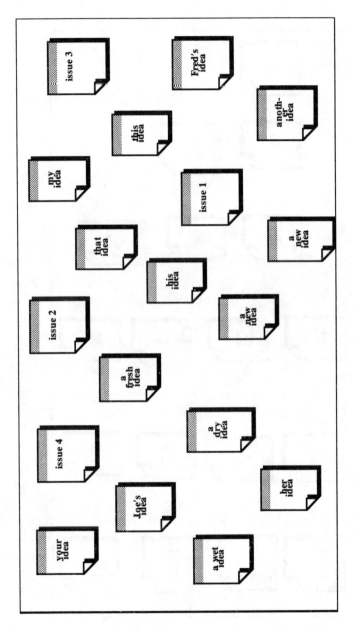

Figure 4.2 *Affinity diagram Step 1 – collect issues*

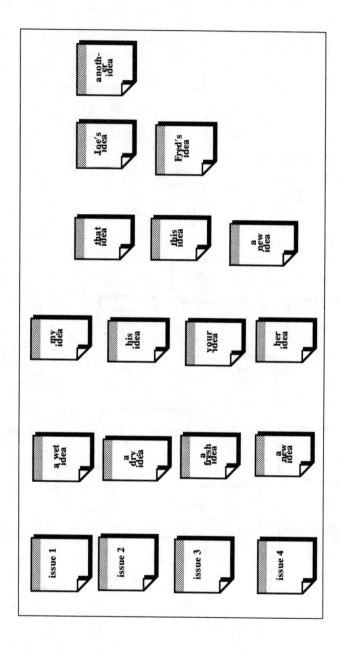

Figure 4.3 *Affinity diagram Step 2 – arrange in groupings*

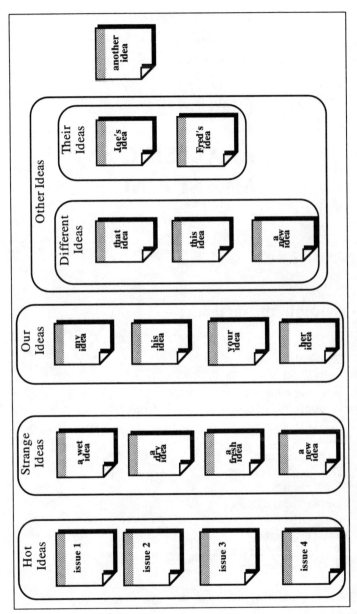

Figure 4.4 *Affinity diagram Step 3 – name groupings*

Chapter 5

ANALYSING AND MEASURING

Key concepts and methods:

- Data collection
- Tally chart
- Ranking data
- Histogram
- Sturgess' Rule
- Run chart
- Scatter diagram
- Design of experiments
- Flow chart
- Deployment chart
- Check-list
- Measles chart
- Cause and effect diagram
- Relations diagram

Unless we measure, how can we know what we are dealing with?
Unless we analyse, why bother to measure?

Collecting data

Up to now, we've concentrated on being sure we are working on the right problem, maximizing our potential for breakthrough solutions and breaking the task into manageable pieces. Once we are down to the level of individual elements of the problem, and often before we can be sure what the nature of the problem is, we need facts to help guide our thinking and let us measure how much improvement we have made.

There are three kinds of data we may wish to collect. The first kind is essentially a count of how many times we see events. We call this *attributes data*. Examples are how often a customer has to wait for service, how many things were made incorrectly or what type of property a problem has.

The second kind is measurement on a comparative scale, called *ranking*. This kind of measurement is used when there is no way to express the measurement in units. For example, it may be possible to say only that customers prefer flavours in a certain order, or that one patient is more aggressive than another. We can't run a tape measure over the thing we are measuring.

The third kind of measurement is on a continuous scale. This is sometimes referred to as *variables data*. Examples are the temperature of an oven, the length of a bar or the mass of an object. These measurements can be restricted by the accuracy of our measuring equipment and we may not be able to show enough difference to be sure of what we are dealing with.

How should we collect these measurements?

The counted measurements are easily dealt with by means of a *tally chart*, which typically looks like Figure 5.1. The comparative data are simply shown as a *ranking*, as in Figure 5.2.

Type Of Word	How Many Times In Error
Technical Words	√√√√√ √√√
Personal Names	√√√√√ √√√√√ √√√√√ √√√√
Adjectives	√√√√√ √√√√√ √√
Place Names	√√√√√ √

Figure 5.1   *Tally chart for spelling errors*

Colour	Rank
Red	1
Green	2
Blue	3
Orange	4
Grey	5
Black	6
Purple	7

Figure 5.2   *Ranked data*

Measurements on a continuous scale can simply be made for each item and recorded. For clear presentation, the measurements should be arranged to show how many in a range. When measurements are arranged like this, the resulting picture is called a histogram.

The histogram

Figure 5.3   *Histogram*

To construct a histogram, measurements need to be grouped in ranges. For example, there might be ranges of 1 to 5, 6 to 10, 11 to 15 and so on. The number of measurements falling in each range is called the frequency. Then the ranges are shown along the horizontal axis and the frequencies on the vertical axis. This gives the typically pyramid shape of the histogram. To know how many ranges there should be, Sturgess' Rule can be used. This gives the number of cells or ranges as:

No. of cells = $1 + 3.3 \log_{10}(N)$
where N = number of measurements

Here are some measurements which have been made. Table 5.1 shows them as raw measurements.

Table 5.1 *Measurements*

3	6	1	8	4	3	6	3	4	2
4	5	3	3	7	6	3	5	3	4
6	3	7	3	3	4	1	3	5	3

Figure 5.4 shows them in a tally chart. Sturgess' Rule is applied to work out how many ranges there should be:

No. of cells = $1 + 3.3 \log_{10}(30) = 5.87$ say 6

The highest measurement is 8 and the lowest is 1. With six cells to hold this range of measurements, a suitable set of ranges would be as shown below. Note each cell is about 1.3 units wide, which is the range (8) divided by the number of cells (6):

0.1 – 1.3	1.4 – 2.6	2.7 – 3.9
4.0 – 5.2	5.3 – 6.5	6.6 – 8.0

Cell Limits	How Many Measurements
0.1 – 1.3	√√
1.4 – 2.6	√
2.7 – 3.9	√√√√√ √√√√√ √√
4.0 – 5.2	√√√√√ √√√
5.3 – 6.5	√√√
6.6 – 8.0	√√√

Figure 5.4 *Tally chart*

It's a good idea to make the number of decimal places in the cells one more than the number of decimal places in the measurements. This makes sure there are no uncertainties about which cell to put a measurement in.

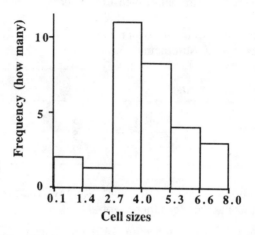

Figure 5.5 *Histogram of measurements*

Figure 5.5 is a histogram of the measurements grouped together. The histogram shows the way in which the measurements cluster around the middle and how much they spread out from the middle. There is more information in measurements on a continuous scale than there is with counted or comparative data.

The run chart

Another aspect of measuring is to know how much the measurement varies with time. A simple way to do this without the need for mathematics is to use the *run chart*. The run chart simply shows how the measurement moves up and down on the measurement scale with time. A clear indication of what's going on can often be gained from drawing a run chart. As the problem-solving team becomes more skilled, methods like the control chart can be used. The *control chart* is like a run chart, but with the addition of scientifically calculated limits to show when the measurements are outside the expected variation.

Suppose we had been measuring the daily count of dropped

Figure 5.6   *The run chart*

and damaged parts in a factory operation. The operator suggests placing a soft mat under his feet, because the part is difficult to handle and is often dropped. By putting a line on the chart where the change was made, we can evaluate the effectiveness of the change. Figure 5.7 shows an example of a run chart for the situation described. So a run chart can also double as a method for evaluating the effectiveness of a problem solution (see also chapter 9).

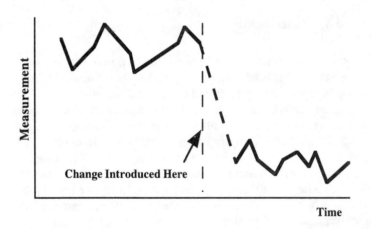

Figure 5.7   *Run chart – reduction in measurement following a change to the process*

Scatter diagrams

Sometimes we can have measurements of inputs to a process and outputs from the process at the same time. This is really helpful, because it gives us understanding of how inputs affect outputs.

Usually, just knowing how the output varies doesn't lead us to a
solution. When we plot the relationship between two measurements like this, it is called a *scatter diagram*, because it shows
how much or how little scatter there is between the two measurements. Figure 5.8 shows a scatter diagram.

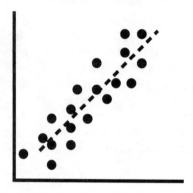

Figure 5.8   *Scatter diagram*

The shape of the relationship between the two variables helps us
to understand what is happening. Figure 5.9 shows some different
relationships which may be found in scatter diagrams.

In Figure 5.9(A), the dots are all over the place. It doesn't seem
to matter what strength of solution is used, the effectiveness is not
predictable from the strength. We say there is no relationship.

Figure 5.9(B) shows that as the strength of solution is
increased, the effectiveness also increases. There is a positive
relationship here and it is pretty well a straight line or linear relationship. Of course, there is still some variation, but we can
clearly make a useful prediction.

Figure 5.9(C), on the other hand, reveals the effectiveness
decreasing as the solution strength increases. Some things in
nature do behave this way, although we might be surprised at such
a result with cleaning solutions. It pays to ask questions when
something doesn't behave as expected.

Figure 5.9(D) is similar to 5.9(C), but the relationship is not linear. Sometimes complicated processes are going on in the things
we measure and a non-linear relationship is the result.

Figure 5.9(E) shows the relationship changing from negative to

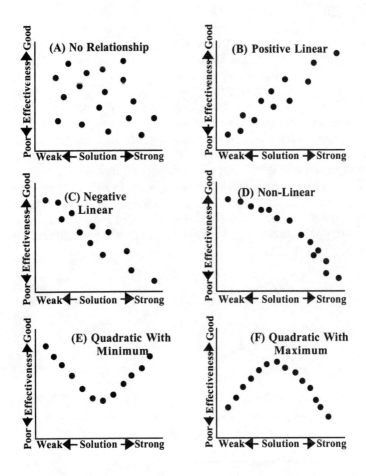

Figure 5.9 *Scatter diagrams – different cleaning solutions*

positive, with a minimum effectiveness point. Often processes and materials behave this way, perhaps for complicated reasons. It is important to know where the minimum point is. It could mean danger.

Figure 5.9(F) is the opposite. Here, it might be important to get the best out of the cleaning solution by carefully specifying what strength to use.

Design of experiments

Scatter diagrams demonstrate a simple relationship between two variables. When there are more than two variables involved, there is a special way to find out how changes in input affect output. For example, if temperature, time and pressure could all influence output, how would we know how much influence each has? Sometimes, changing more than one input at a time has an effect greater than the effect of changes in each, independently. This is called an interaction effect. The study of how changes in multiple inputs affect outputs is called *Design of experiments* (DOE). There are many books dealing with DOE[4]. The subject is a little more complex than other methods for improvement, but very powerful. The use of DOE is symbolized in this book by the drawing in Figure 5.10, which shows the graphs for different settings of inputs.

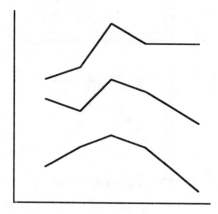

Figure 5.10　*Design of experiments*

Suppose we wanted to get the most out of a baking process where the temperature, time and mixture could all be varied. We could just change one of these at a time and measure the effect. We might find an improvement from doing this measurement.

　　Perhaps we would find that if the mixture and temperature were both varied, we got even better results. How would we know when the best combination of temperature, time and mixture was being used? Only by a designed experiment could we be sure. We would also need a designed experiment to avoid an enormous amount of testing.

It's enough for most people to remember that DOE can give a big improvement in a process. It's best to talk to a statistician or somebody else trained in DOE before starting on a project. By working with people who have these skills, the best approach can be worked out.

Narrowing down to where it is

An important part of problem solving is to find out:

- where things are going wrong
- when things are going wrong
- whether particular people are involved
- what systems are involved.

Unless we do this, the problem will remain a collection of vague generalities. Of course, we must be careful not to be seen as being on a witch-hunt. We should know which people are involved, so that we can have them on the team and also in case they need training. When people need training, it is not their fault – it is management's fault that the training wasn't given in the first place. Problem solvers have to work hard at getting that message across.

The flowchart

One of the best methods for doing all of these things is the process *flow chart*. In Part II, it is clear this method plays more roles than any other, so it is very powerful, yet simple to use. Figure 5.11 shows a simple example of a flowchart.

Figure 5.11 *Flowchart*

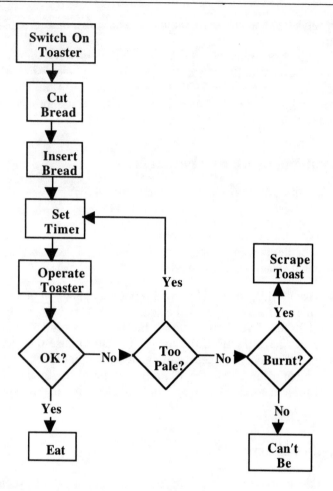

Figure 5.12   *Flowchart – making toast*

The flowchart can be modified to show us who is involved. By putting the symbols in columns to represent people in the process doing the steps in the flow, we create a *deployment chart*. This helps to see if a particular person is associated with the problem. For example, if a person who is colour-blind is asked to put red caps on one type of container and brown caps on another, it wouldn't be surprising if they made a mistake. Many colour-blind people don't know they have this condition. It's up to managers to make sure this is tested for when the job demands it. Figure 5.13 shows a deployment chart.

The deployment chart pictures the way in which the work is divided up. If we mark the boxes to show where problems happen, we may be able to narrow the problem down to a particular operation or a particular person. The chart also gives a picture of the workload and the order of events. There's a lot of information in the chart to help problem solving.

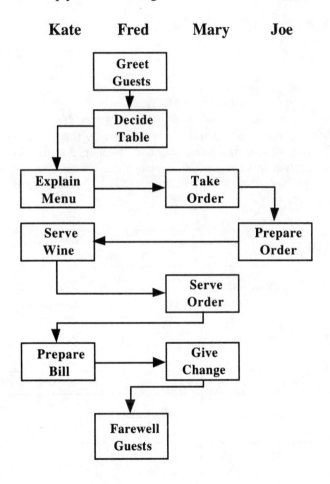

Figure 5.13   *Deployment chart – restaurant service*

When using a flowchart or deployment chart and check marks, it's just as important to think about the boxes which don't have marks as it is to think about those with marks. Perhaps the reason why the marks don't appear in certain places is that the conditions there prevent it.

φρεδ	卅 III
θοε	I
Μαρψ	IIII
Ωενδψ	II
θιμ	卅 I

Figure 5.14 *Checklist*

We also need to know about the *times* at which problems occur. Some problems are definitely influenced by time. For example, it's well known that more accidents happen due to slipping in winter than in summer. Other associations with time are not so obvious and we need measurements to help us understand what's going on.

Time	Problem Type				
	Missing	Broken	Blunt	Cracked	Undersized
	Worksheet	Tools	Tools	Castings	Parts
Morning	√	√√		√√√	√
Lunch-time		√	√		
Afternoon	√	√			√√
Evening	√	√		√	
Conference	√√√√√	√√√	√√√√	√√	√√√
Night Shift	√	√		√	√

Figure 5.15 *Checklist of problem types and times*

Checklist

The checklist or checksheet is very effective for recording times when things go wrong. It can also be used to record what kinds of events happen. Figure 5.15 shows a checklist of problem types and times.

Simply keeping records like the checklist lets us see a lot of information. The beauty of the checklist is that it does some analysis for us as we record it. We can see at a glance that a lot of problems of all types occur during the conference between shifts. Perhaps machines are left unattended. We might need to go a layer deeper to find this out, but we have improved our knowledge of the situation greatly from just knowing there are 'problems'.

The measles chart

A special kind of checklist is one where we match up the counted happenings with a location. To use the measles chart, all we require is a picture of the subject of interest. It might be a casting (as in Figure 5.16), a rubber glove or a patient in a hospital. We need to know where the problem is happening, so we use the picture of the subject as a map. Each time the problem occurs, we mark where it happens on the picture. If there are different kinds of problems, we can use different symbols for each kind. Very quickly, we build up a picture of where the problem happens most often. This may let us see the solution straightaway. For example, a casting might have a lot of cracks near a sharp corner. There shouldn't be sharp corners on castings. The solution would be to remove it in the pattern.

Figure 5.16   *Measles chart*

Figure 5.17 shows a measles chart used in a shirt factory. The crosses were marked on a replica of a shirt whenever stitching faults were discovered. Very quickly, operators could see where faults were happening and could turn their attention to finding out the causes.

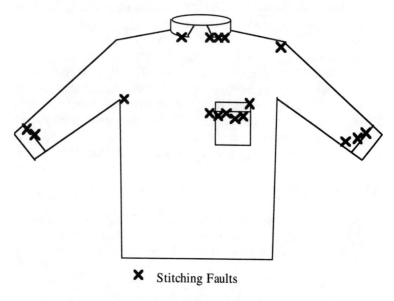

✖   Stitching Faults

Figure 5.17   *Measles chart for shirt manufacture*

Now we have some information about the problem, it's time to work on causes of the problem. Unless our early work on problem formulation led us to a different path, finding the causes of problems is the main effort in most problem-solving situations. We must often dig deep to arrive at causes. We have already seen one technique – the Five Whys. This simple technique should never be overlooked. For example, we could start by looking at our flowchart and asking 'Why does [the problem] happen more often at work station X?' This may lead us directly to the cause.

Cause and effect diagram

Another method for finding causes is the cause and effect diagram. Developed by Dr Kaoru Ishikawa, this diagram can be applied to a wide range of problems. It is sometimes called the 'fishbone diagram', because it looks a bit like the skeleton of a fish.

Figure 5.18   *Cause and effect diagram*

What the cause and effect diagram does for us is to get our ideas down on paper (or a whiteboard, or butchers' paper), so we can put those thoughts in order. In Figure 5.19, the effect or problem is the subject matter. From this 'head of the fish' we draw a 'spine'. From the 'spine' we draw main 'bones' with the headings 'cause 1', 'Cause 2', and so on. In the early days of using cause and effect diagrams, these headings used to be 'Men', 'Machines', 'Materials', 'Methods'. You can see the purpose, but it was too restrictive for applications other than manufacturing. In the health industry, for example, users might want to have headings such as 'Staff', 'Procedures', 'Ward Conditions', 'Equipment'. The differences are not great, but it always helps to speak in the language of the user.

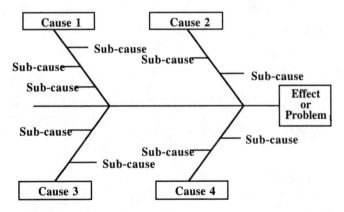

Figure 5.19   *Cause and effect diagram also known as fishbone diagram (developed by Dr Kaoru Ishikawa)*

To use the cause and effect diagram, assemble a team of people who are familiar with the problem and the process in which it is detected. We could just brainstorm ideas, or write down on sticky notes what we think the likely causes might be. The sticky notes can be placed on the fishbone on a whiteboard. As the first ones are placed, a name needs to be put in place of 'Cause 1', and so on. For example, it might be 'Information' or 'Equipment'. Placing the ideas on the fishbone may trigger further ideas. For each bone coming off the main bones, the question should be asked 'Why?'. This may take the process to another level. When the team has run out of ideas, it is likely there will be several appearances of some ideas under different headings. This just shows the cause affects several areas. The team could vote on which are the most promising causes to work on or, better yet, use some measures which we'll be looking at soon.

Figure 5.20 shows how a fishbone diagram might look in a study of ways in which household electricity bills might be reduced.

Note that in most uses of the fishbone, we are finding likely causes, not *the* cause. If there is a single cause, it is likely that simple Five Whys questioning will arrive at the solution – if we know it. Generally, we are really only saying what our *opinion* is

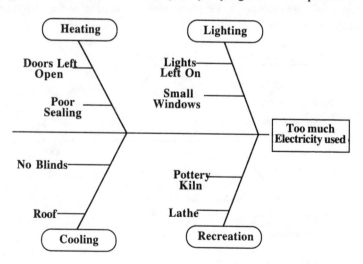

Figure 5.20   *Fishbone diagram – electricity use*

as to the actual cause. When there are multiple likely causes, fixing them will *improve* the process, but will not necessarily cause the problem to vanish. Rarely can we locate *all* the causes. It is wishful thinking to imagine that we can. The problem of developing fusion power is an example. Some problems are so big, it will take decades to get them under control.

Another technique for digging out the root causes of problems is the *relations diagram*. One of the JUSE 'seven management tools', the relations diagram is a method which is easy to learn and can be used individually or in groups. It's best to work in groups, with people from all the areas affected by the problem.

Relations diagram

Figure 5.21 *Relations diagram*

With the relations diagram, we need to start with a clear statement of the problem. Unlike the affinity diagram, the relations diagram is logical. A statement like 'Why holiday pay is late' makes sense. We are trying to find out what the causes are, not just the issues surrounding late holiday pay. The issues would be OK for the affinity diagram.

We write this in the centre of the whiteboard. Butchers' paper is not very good for the relations diagram, because we're going to draw a lot of lines and change them around. An electronic whiteboard is useful, or any handy surface if you have an infra-red camera to produce a copy of the finished work.

Ideas could come from an affinity diagram exercise or from brainstorming. The ideas should be written on sticky notes. As with the cause and effect diagram, new ideas may come from putting them on the relations diagram. Look at the sticky notes. Ask what leads to the central problem. Take those ideas which seem to lead directly to the problem and place them around the central problem. Draw arrows connecting the causes to the central problem. Then ask what leads to the causes surrounding the central problem, and repeat the arrows.

The team may need to have several attempts at reaching agreement on what causes what. That's why the whiteboard is important. There's a lot of rubbing out and repositioning of the sticky notes. The important thing here is to build up a chain of cause and effect. Working outwards from the central problem, we find the central problem is the result of the causes around it. These causes are the results of other causes further out, and so on. When we can't find any more connections, the outermost causes are root causes.

Instead of voting for the most likely cause, we look for the root causes with the most arrows coming out of them. Some causes lead to *several* other causes, which eventually lead to the central problem statement. These root causes with multiple arrows are the

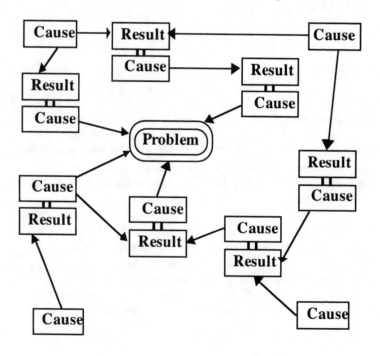

Figure 5.22   *Relations diagram – result/cause*

key causes for the team to concentrate on. Of course, we shouldn't ignore a cause with fewer arrows, if our knowledge and judgement tell us it's important.

Figure 5.22 shows how first-level causes are the result of second-level causes, and so on. Figure 5.23 shows a simple relations diagram with an identified root cause which leads to several other causes. Again, beware of assuming all the causes have been eliminated. When we test the effectiveness of any changes, we will have a better idea of whether the problem is really fixed. So long as there is improvement, the work is worthwhile.

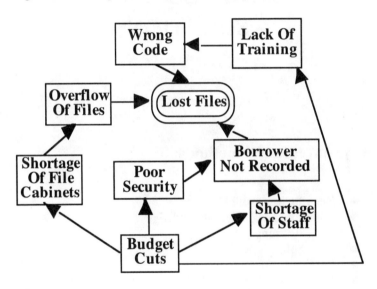

Figure 5.23   *Relations diagram – causes of lost files*

Chapter 6

DEVELOPING SOLUTIONS

Key concepts and methods:

- Keeping it sensible
- Traps and pitfalls with knowledge
- Brainstorming
- Morphology chart
- Reclassification chart
- Mandalas
- 'Other hand' writing
- Lateral thinking
- Pareto diagram
- Prioritization matrices
- Decision tree

'It won't work' – a million doubters

Keeping it sensible

As we develop information about problems, we must keep our

wits about us to avoid thinking the process is all over. At each stage of our work, we need to do a short review of where we stand. Here is a short checklist of questions to keep the problem solving project on track:

- Is the problem still real?
- Would the problem still be there if we changed the environment?
- Is the cause we think we have found always true?
- Are there other causes?
- Is there any other way to deal with the problem?
- Has anyone else solved this or a similar problem?
- What might a similar problem look like?
- Is this an area which needs special expertise?
- Are we trying to solve the user's problem, or somebody else's?

If we keep asking these questions, we won't find ourselves trying to solve an impossible problem or being led astray by forgetting to keep our eyes on the basic purpose of the project.

To know or not to know

Another trap in problem solving is to be careless about the application of knowledge to a problem.

Knowledge is a two-edged sword. In the right place and at the right time, it may give the best way to solve the problem. At other times, it can be a handicap. The reason knowledge can hold us back is that it tends to prevent open thinking. It's remarkable how we develop a mindset that things *have to be a certain way*. We want problem solvers to keep trying radical new ideas for the best chance of a real breakthrough.

Following is an interesting list of quotations from the past which show how difficult it was for 'knowledgeable' people of the day to accept change. Today's knowledge may be tomorrow's ignorance.

New ideas – the difficulty of acceptance

'Drill for oil? You mean drill into the ground to try and find oil? You're crazy.' *Drillers whom Edwin L. Drake tried to enlist to his project to drill for oil in 1859*

'This "telephone" has too many shortcomings to be seriously considered as a means of communication. The device is inherently of no value to us.' *Western Union internal memo, 1876*

'Heavier-than-air flying machines are impossible.' *Lord Kelvin, president, Royal Society, 1895*

'The horse is here to stay, but the automobile is only a novelty – a fad.' *Bank president advising Horace Rackham (Henry Ford's lawyer) not to invest in Ford Motor Company, 1903*

'Professor Goddard does not know the relation between action and reaction and the need to have something better than a vacuum against which to react. He seems to lack the basic knowledge ladled out daily in high schools.' *1921 New York Times editorial about Robert Goddard's revolutionary rocket work*

'The wireless music box has no imaginable commercial value. Who would pay for a message sent to nobody in particular?' *David Sarnoff's associates in response to his urgings for investment in the radio in the 1920s*

'Who the hell wants to hear actors talk?' *H. M. Warner, Warner Brothers, 1927*

'We don't like their sound, and guitar music is on the way out.' *Decca Recording Co., rejecting the Beatles, 1962*

'So we went to Atari and said... "What do you think about funding us? Or we'll give it to you. We just want to do it. Pay our salary, we'll come work for you." And they said "No." So then we went to Hewlett-Packard, and they said "...we don't need you. You haven't got through college yet."' *Apple Computer Inc. founder, Steve Jobs, on attempts to get Atari and H-P interested in his and Steve Wozniak's personal computer*

A further example of the difficulty in predicting the future of an idea is IBM's early attempts to predict the market for mainframe computers. At one stage, it was confidently stated that the world-wide market for mainframe computers was just six!

On the other side of the coin, knowledge can open up solutions and ideas which are very unlikely to occur to someone who lacks that knowledge. For example, if the problem involves physical principles which are unknown to the group, it is unlikely that an appropriate solution will be developed. Here's an example of a problem which needs knowledge to solve it. When a satellite is launched from a space vehicle, how can we make sure it ends up pointing in the right direction? Sophisticated rocket and control systems could be used, but these are expensive and clumsy. Knowledge of gravitation tells us that the force of gravity varies according to the square of the distance between the earth's centre and the satellite. After extending a boom from the satellite, gravity will cause the boom to point to the earth's centre. It works rather like a pendulum. A few other tricks are needed to make it work, but in essence it's quite a simple solution.

When knowledge is used to increase ideas, the thinker must be open-minded, not closed like those who said the car would never replace the horse. Remember, most of the people who rejected progress in the list above were prominent in their field. An example of a knowledgeable thinker with an open mind was Nikola Tesla who was an exceptionally gifted scientist and engineer, able to visualize ideas in action, using his knowledge to open up new opportunities. He patented many devices and tested his ideas in his mind before building prototypes. Such people are very rare.

We can be trapped into taking the wrong approach to a problem if we don't have the right knowledge. Here is an example of a rather little known science. Ergonomics is the study of the relationship between people and their environment. It is used in industry to make sure people can do their work comfortably and with minimum error. Part of ergonomics is an interesting field called 'looking without seeing'. It is possible for people to overlook important information because they cannot see it, despite the fact they are looking for it. Sounds strange? It's a very common problem. People are still blamed for not seeing things they are supposed to, because many managers are unaware of the ergonomics of seeing. For a bit of fun, have a look at Figure 6.1. What do you see? Most people see a bunch of strange looking shapes. After a while, you will suddenly see a word.

Figure 6.1   *Looking without seeing*

This is an example of looking without seeing. Sight is an enormously complex function and we make far too many assumptions about what people can see and what they can't see. There is some research being done into this phenomenon, but it is in its infancy.[5]

So it seems the ideal problem solver would have broad knowledge and needs to be flexible in thought and open minded.

Brainstorming

Figure 6.2   *Brainstorming*

For most problem solving teams, the first method to use in getting ideas is brainstorming. This technique has been around for a long time, but still works well.

To run a brainstorming session, gather together people who are knowledgeable about the process under study. Relax the group by doing something quite different from everyday work. Doing puzzles of a light nature helps. The leader of the session writes out the subject for brainstorming, which might be 'How can we reduce errors in completing leave forms?'. The group is asked to call out ideas and these are recorded on a whiteboard or flip chart. The key principle is that we are looking for quantity not quality of ideas. The best ideas can be selected and the poor ideas rejected after the quantity has been offered. When the group has run out of ideas, it's time to decide on the best ideas. A method might be for allocation of five points for the best, four for the next, and so on. Alternatively, simply, take a count of votes for the best ideas. These rules help to ensure a successful brainstorming session:

- Suspend judgement
- No misfits
- Freewheel.

Suspend judgement simply means do not pass comment on anything that is suggested. Such interruptions prevent a free flow of ideas and may inhibit people from freely offering suggestions. The judgement is made after the list is complete.

It is important not to have people in the group who may be disruptive or inhibit others, perhaps because of personality clash or disposition towards harsh criticism. An atmosphere of 'no blame' is important.

Freewheeling refers to maintaining a free flow of ideas, without grabbing on to the previous idea. It is permissible to trigger new ideas from previous ones, but the leader should discourage excessive concentration on a particular direction of idea formation. Tricks such as shouting out 'carrots' or some equally neutral word can often trigger a new wave of ideas.

A variation of the brainstorming technique is used where people are uncomfortable with the idea of offering their ideas in public. In this technique, each member of the team works in silence, individually brainstorming ideas and writing them down. Each member is then asked to contribute one idea, working in round-robin fashion, until all the ideas have been recorded on a flip chart. Of course, the ideas can also be submitted anonymously. This method helps to overcome the natural reticence of some people.

Expanding creativity

To get the best out of our problem-solving projects, we need to be able to expand our ability to suggest new ways of doing things. There are several methods available to us to do this. One simple and interesting way is to use a *morphology chart*. It sounds like something out of a medical journal, but is quite easy to use. If you've seen one of those tables that lets you match any word in one column with any word in the next, you'll have no trouble using a morphology chart.

Morphology chart

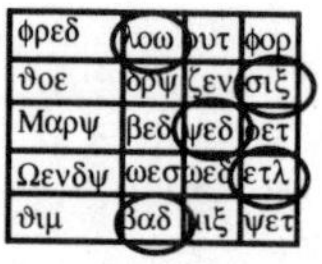

Figure 6.3 *Morphology chart*

For any process, we can break the process down into the elements or attributes of which it is made up. For example, suppose we needed a better way to toast bread. The attributes might be:

- power (which might be electricity, gas, or solar)
- capacity (which might be one slice, two slices, a whole loaf)
- speed (which might be leisurely, instant, fast)
- method (which might be direct, reflected, convection).

If we take any one of each attribute and combine it with any of another and so on, we get 81 ideas from this little table. Some may be nonsense, but one might be a breakthrough. Figure 6.4 shows the resulting morphology chart.

We could try a gas powered, whole loaf capacity toaster which works at a fast speed and uses direct heat. Not sure how the details would work, but the concept could be useful for catering, where large quantities of toast are needed at once. No good trying to work with hundreds of pop-up toasters!

ATTRIBUTE	FORM		
Power	electricity	gas	solar
Capacity	one slice	two slices	whole loaf
Speed	leisurely	instant	fast
Method	direct	reflected	convection

Figure 6.4 *Morphology chart – making toast*

I've used this method in designing components for cars and it's amazing how many ideas it generates. Without the method, it's very hard to force our minds to come up with new ways to do things.

Reclassification chart

Figure 6.5 *Reclassification chart*

Another method to help creativity is the reclassification chart. What this does is to list the classification of certain parts of a design, product or idea and use this to create new classes of parts. The method can be used with groups or by individuals. Here's how it works. Identify the basic elements of the subject. Classify each of these in terms of what it does. Then reclassify these elements and think of new components to do their functions.

Figure 6.6 shows reclassification of the parts of a cut-throat razor. The new whole is a safety razor. The reclassification process starts by identifying the components of a cut-throat razor. These are a blade, handle and strop. The classification of the blade is cutting. This is reclassified as two functions – cutting edge and edge stiffness (you need to think about what the classified function really does). New parts to provide these functions are a flexible blade with a clamp to provide the stiffness. A similar approach is used for the handle and the strop. The result is potentially a new invention.

Existing Whole	Existing Part	Existing Classification	New Classification	New Part	New Whole
	Blade	Cutting	Cutting Edge	Flexible Blade	
			Edge Stiffness	Blade Clamp	
Cut-Throat Razor	Handle	Control	Angle Control	Clamp Edges	Safety Razor
			Stroke Control	Handle	
	Strop	Sharpening	Maintenance Of Edge	New Blade	

Figure 6.6   *Reclassification chart – cut-throat razor*

Remember, the reclassification chart won't invent new things. Only humans can do this. The chart is just an aid to invention. But it can be very effective in opening up avenues of thought.

Computers can help creativity by storing, sorting and displaying information. Computers have a large capacity for information and don't get bored sorting through huge lists of possible ways to do things. If there is a concordance generator program in the computer, this allows ideas (perhaps generated in a brainstorming session) to be shown in combinations. What it does is to arrange the ideas as a list with alphabetical and phrase orders. Sometimes this can trigger new ideas.

The most powerful way to generate new ideas is to bring the creative part of our brains into play. Most of us use the logical part of our brains in everyday work. This is because our society is dominated by logical behaviour (contrary to what might appear to be the case!). Think about the way we test people. Logic and number skills are highly prized, and work with computers is as logical as anything can get. Are the tests fair in evaluating people who have intuitive or artistic skills? They have a role to play and often see through problems in a way that logical people are unable to.

Most of us are right-handed. The brain is divided into two hemispheres, with the opposite side of the body being controlled by each hemisphere. So a right-handed person writes under the direction of the left side of the brain. This side of the brain also happens to be the side which deals with logic, numbers and reason in most of us. The right side of the brain deals with emotion and the 'whole picture' for the majority of us. In our everyday work, the left side is involved in most of the activity. If we could bring the right side of our brains to the fore, we could look at problems in a very different light. We would be more creative. There are a couple of remarkably simple methods to help us do this. Why these have not been more widely used is difficult to understand, because the knowledge of how to do it is not new.

Mandalas

The first method is used to simply quieten the logical part of the brain and allow the intuitive part to come to the fore. The method is called a *mandala*. A mandala is simply a pattern which contains little or no information to feed the logical part of the brain.[6] When we look at the middle of a mandala, the absence of logical information and the overall appearance of the pattern make our

Figure 6.7   *Mandala*

intuitive brains active in order to try and understand the shape. Figure 6.7 shows a mandala. To use it, just move it in front of your vision until it fills your whole field of view. Stare at the dot in the centre for a few minutes. Avoid trying to analyse the shapes as geometric. Your intuitive or right brain is now active!

Looking at mandalas is good relaxation, even if you don't want to work on new ideas.

When people are asked for ideas with the intuitive brain active, they offer different ideas from those when the logical part of the brain is more active. This increases our range of ideas. It also makes sure we provide feelings, which is important when dealing with emotional or difficult issues. We are unlikely to do this when the logical part of the brain is dominating our thoughts and behaviour.

'Other hand' writing

Here is another method which is so powerful you will think another person provided the ideas. In a typical problem-solving activity, you have written down ideas about the problem while the logical brain was dominant. Take about eight minutes using a mandala to bring the intuitive brain to the fore. Now write down some more ideas about the same subject, but using your 'other hand', that is the hand you do not normally write with. If it is too difficult to write with your 'other hand', try using Scrabble letters to make the words. This isn't quite so good, because it isn't as spontaneous as writing. Your 'other hand' writing may be hard to read, but the ideas are quite different from those you wrote out with your usual hand. This experience is quite startling for most people. You may also find that your ideas suggest you are unsure of yourself and have self-doubts. This is the emotional part of the brain coming to the fore (at least for 95 per cent of the population).

Figure 6.8   *'Other hand' writing*

Lateral thinking

Dr de Bono made lateral thinking famous. In this book, I've called it lateral/breakthrough thinking. That's because breakthroughs to new ways of doing things can happen when we think laterally. It's hard to over-estimate the value of this approach in problem solving. Some of Dr de Bono's illustrations of lateral/breakthrough thinking make people wonder why they hadn't thought of the idea. We looked at the importance of breakthrough thinking earlier, because often the best time for breakthrough thinking is when the problem is being defined.

Figure 6.9   *Lateral/breakthrough thinking*

Lateral thinking involves forcing a movement away from the current mindset to other possible ways of doing things. For example, a team has to solve a problem with defence. The problem involves having sufficient weaponry to deter a potential aggressor. There is not enough money in the budget. The discussion moves to 'smart' weapons which are more destructive for less money. The mindset is on destroying the enemy. Lateral thinking breaks this mindset and moves to another level. Coming back to the link between humour and creativity, somebody might joke in frustration: 'Perhaps we should fire cans of beer at them, so they will be too drunk to fight'. This triggers a new line of (lateral) thinking: what if we look at making the enemy ineffective, rather than killing the enemy? There might be a range of ways to do this which are cheaper, more effective and humane.

So lateral thinking can lead to solutions which are not just an improvement, but a huge jump to a completely new approach which wins hands down on many counts. Here are some big improvements which are so great we would never consider going back to the old way:

Old Way	New Way
Solid tyres	Pneumatic tyres
Hand crank	Self-starter
Typewriter	Word processor
Pony express	Mobile phone
Coal	Natural gas
Scythe	Combine harvester

It's interesting to think about the extent to which these improvements came about through evolution and through breakthrough or lateral thinking.

As an aside, it's easy for us to forget the significance of inventions in the advance of humanity. Jacob Bronowski, in his TV series 'The Ascent of Man', raised a startling point when he said that the inventions of the brass bedstead and cotton underwear were two of the most significant inventions in history. He went on to explain to his audience that each of these inventions greatly reduced the level of disease, which had decimated populations before. People used to sleep on piles of rags on the floor – a haven for vermin. The brass bedstead stopped this. Before cotton, people used to wear woollen underwear which was filthy and harboured more vermin. Cotton underwear was easy to wash and less hospitable to vermin. Makes sense when it's explained, but it's not obvious.

We can use the flowchart to help us find creative solutions, too. The chart is used to show how we do it now. Then we think about what the chart would look like if the process worked the way we would like it to. This triggers thinking about ways to improve the process. By the same token, we can think about better ways to do the job and use the flowchart to show what improvement we have made.

Think about the process we go through in getting off an aircraft and finding our way to the hotel. Figure 6.10 shows how it happens at present. It's a pretty tiresome process that's left many a traveller with ragged nerves. If you have a high-pressure assignment to complete, the last thing you need is hassle getting to your accommodation.

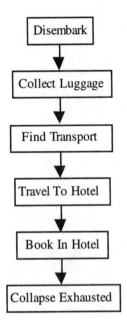

Figure 6.10 *Getting from airport to hotel – old way*

What Figure 6.10 shows us is that the process takes place one step at a time. You can't find transport until you've collected your luggage. You can't book into the hotel until you've arrived there. If we look at the flowchart, we can ask why we can't do some or all of the steps at the same time. For example, somebody could be collecting our luggage while we rested or made telephone calls to our family or business contacts. Figure 6.11 shows an improved way to process arrivals from an airport to a hotel.

Figure 6.11 looks different from Figure 6.10, because we have several activities happening at the same time. This saves time and makes for better travel. In industry, there are many opportunities like this. When separate jobs are done at the same time, we call it 'parallel processing', because the boxes in the flow chart are in parallel. The old way was 'serial processing', because the jobs took place one after the other. One large utility saved hundreds of thousands of dollars by doing its accounting work in parallel instead of serially. An interesting idea in Figure 6.11 is that booking into the hotel is done at the same time as travelling to the hotel. How can this be done? Well, what about having hotel staff on the bus, booking people in as they travel? Lateral thinking could help to develop ideas like that. A good memory can help, too. I'll let you into a secret. I saw the idea in a video on involving employees in managing business. It seemed like a good idea, so it stuck in my mind. Now you know it too.

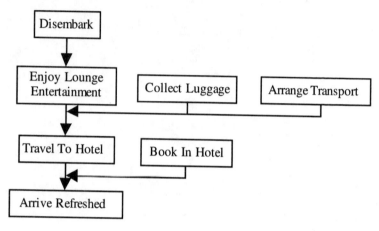

Figure 6.11   *Getting from airport to hotel – new way*

Now a story which shows how lateral thinking can make a big difference to the effectiveness of an idea. In 1901, an American inventor demonstrated a 'wonder machine' for removing dust from carpets. The machine blew air on to the carpet, forcing the dust out. At that time, people used to remove dust from carpets by hanging the carpet on a clothes line and beating it with a wide stick. The machine was an extension of that idea. The result was choking clouds of dust.

The demonstration was watched by a man called Hubert Cecil Booth, who later was credited with inventing the vacuum cleaner. Booth suggested to the inventor of the blowing machine that it would be better to suck the dust out of the carpet, but the inventor said it was impossible to do so. Booth tried the principle by placing his lips on the back of an armchair and sucking. The resultant mouthful of dust nearly choked him.

If the inventor of the blowing machine had 'turned the problem upside-down', in the way Dr de Bono suggests, he would have invented the vacuum cleaner.[7]

Choosing the best solution

With a properly defined problem, carefully analysed and a range of solutions offered, we are faced with deciding the best solution. Typically, we have to balance the following factors:

● cost to implement
● time to implement
● difficulty of implementation (resistance, technical complexity)
● benefits.

The Pareto diagram or 80:20 rule

If the factors are not too complicated (use your judgement, there is no easy rule to apply here), the Pareto diagram is a simple but powerful way to decide which way to go. The Pareto diagram is based on the work of the Italian economist Vilfredo Pareto and popularized in quality control work by Dr J.M. Juran.[8] The Pareto diagram shows a clear division between the 'vital few' items which account for 80 per cent of the cost, problem, and so on, and the 'useful many' which account for the remaining 20 per cent. Sometimes the principle is called the '80:20 rule'.

If a Pareto diagram were made showing the likelihood of a solution working or the estimated effectiveness, the diagram might look like Figure 6.12.

In the diagram, items A and B dominate the scene. They are bigger than all the rest put together. This is fairly typical of lots of things in nature and in human affairs. It's well known that a small part of the population have most of the wealth of nations. That was the original use for Pareto's study – to show the distribution of wealth. The same is true of the popularity of solutions, the effectiveness of methods, the cost of alternatives. So the Pareto diagram can help to clarify these things.

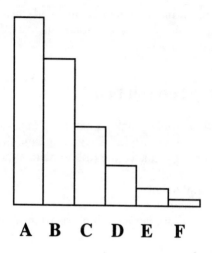

A   B   C   D   E   F

Figure 6.12   *Pareto diagram*

The way in which information is put into the Pareto diagram is important. Suppose the team was trying to decide initially on which problem to tackle. One way is to list all the things gone wrong and start with the one which happens most. This will make quite a dent in the count of problems. But what about the cost impact of problems? If there are a thousand ten cent problems and a single one-hundred-thousand dollar problem, it would be madness to put resources into anything other than the expensive problem. There needs to be care in choosing the units for a Pareto diagram.

The Pareto diagram can also be used as a method for the analysis stage of problem solving. If the first line causes of a problem are shown on the Pareto diagram, the Five Whys can be used to cascade each cause down to further causes. The trick is to concentrate on the top one or two causes for the most effective use of resources. Figure 6.13 shows how this works for falls of hospital patients.

The biggest source (or cause) of falls is from bed. In turn, falls from bed are cascaded down to another Pareto diagram which shows getting out of bed is the biggest cause of falls from bed. This can be cascaded down further, if necessary, i.e. what are the

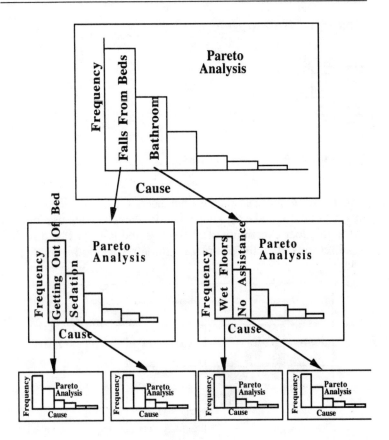

Figure 6.13   *Repeated Pareto analysis*

causes of patients getting out of bed? Similarly, the second biggest source (or cause) of falls was in the bathroom. The Pareto of causes for falls in the bathroom shows wet floors as the biggest cause. We could then ask 'Why are the floors wet?' and make a Pareto of the causes.

When the choice between solutions is complicated, involving many factors such as time, money, resources, effectiveness, it's better to be more objective. This is even more important if the project is large. Here is a tool which allows us to do this.

Prioritization matrices

Figure 6.14   *Prioritization matrices*

Prioritization matrices enable a balanced, objective decision to be made, but it does take a good deal of time and effort to use them. If there are clear overriding priorities e.g. the job must be done for legal reasons, then the prioritization matrix method is not appropriate.

	Criterion 1	Criterion 2	Criterion 3	Criterion 4	Criterion 5	Total across rows (% of grand total)
Criterion 1		5	1/10	1/10	1/5	5.4 (0.08)
Criterion 2	1/5		1/5	1/10	1/5	0.7 (0.01)
Criterion 3	10	5		1/10	1/5	15.3 (0.21)
Criterion 4	10	10	10		1/5	30.2 (0.42)
Criterion 5	5	5	5	5		20 (0.28)
Column total	25.2	25	15.3	5.3	0.8	Total across columns 71.6 grand total

1 Equally important
5 Significantly more important
10 Exceedingly more important

1/5 Significantly less important
1/10 Exceedingly less important

Figure 6.15   *1 – Criteria ranking matrix*

Assuming the work has been done to determine the tasks, there are three basic steps in this process. First, the criteria for decisions are decided. These should be clear judgements. For example, 'Easy to learn'. The first step is to find the relative importance of each criterion compared to the others.

The criteria are placed in an L-shaped matrix, as shown in Figure 6.15. The relative importance is read across the rows. In the example, Criterion 1 is significantly more important than Criterion 2.

In the example, there are only a few criteria. Some do not have much perceived importance compared to others. It might be appropriate to discard these criteria, particularly if there are many criteria to deal with.

The next step is to compare the options under consideration (the ideas it is desired to implement) against the weighted criteria. This has to be done for each criterion. Hence the value in discarding criteria which have little weight.

	Option A	Option B	Option C	Option D	Option E	Total across rows (% of grand total)
Option A		1/5	1/10	1/5	1/5	0.7 (0.01)
Option B	5		1/5	1/10	1/5	5.5 (0.09)
Option C	10	5		1/5	1/5	15.4 (0.25)
Option D	5	10	5		1/5	20.2 (0.33)
Option E	5	5	5	5		20 (0.32)
Column total	25	20.2	10.3	5.5	0.8	Total across columns 61.8 grand total

1 Equal by Criterion
5 Significantly better   1/5 Significantly worse
10 Exceedingly better   1/10 Exceedingly worse

Figure 6.16   *2 – Rank options by each criterion*

Figure 6.16 shows the process for one criterion only. This leads to weights for each of the options.

The output from the previous two matrices then goes into the final matrix, which compares all options against all criteria. In Figure 6.17, all the options and all the criteria are brought together.

Criteria / Options	Criterion 1	Criterion 2	Criterion 3	Criterion 4	Criterion 5	Total across rows (% of grand total)
Option A	.01x.08 =.0008	.07x.01 =.0007	.13x.21 =.0273	.12x.42 =.0504	.02x.28 =.0056	.0848 (.09)
Option B	.09x.08 =.0072	.02x.01 =.0002	.4x.21 =.084	.03x.42 =.0126	.09x.28 =.0252	.1292(.14)
Option C	.25x.08 =.0200	.3x.01 =.0003	.08x.21 =.0168	.13x.42 =.0546	.21x.28 =.0588	.1505(.17)
Option D	.33x.08 =.0264	.25x.01 =.0025	.25x.21 =.0525	.3x.42 =.1260	.09x.28 =.0252	.2326(.26)
Option E	.32x.08 =.0256	.36x.01 =.0036	.14x.21 =.0294	.36x.42 =.1512	.36x.28 =.1008	.3106(.34)
Column total	.0800	.0073	.2100	.3948	.2156	Grand Total 0.9077

Figure 6.17   *3 – Rank options by all criteria*

The method obviously lends itself to a spreadsheet approach on a personal computer.

Another type of decision which often has to be taken with projects is assessment of risk. In fact, this might need to be done before looking at a prioritization matrix. It depends on the circumstances of the project. Often, when a decision to market some new idea or product is taken, it's best to assess the risks.

The decision tree

Figure 6.18   *Decision tree*

The *decision tree* is useful for dealing with problems where the implementation depends on what happens at various stages. It helps to make the decisions about which way to go. For marketing, it can help with the transition from a pilot market to a larger market and all the cost implications that go with such projects.

Where decisions are involved in marketing or implementation, there are two fundamental types of decision:

● those where the choice is made by the decision-maker
● those where the choice is a matter of chance and not under the control of the decision-maker.

For example, suppose a company had developed a new way to record sound, using a biological memory. It works well, but they are not yet sure whether the public will be keen to buy a product which is so radically different. If a decision were taken to market the product in a particular area, that decision would be under the company's control. The decision whether to actually buy would be under the control of the potential customers (to the extent that advertising does not influence them).

In a decision tree, decisions under the control of the decision-maker are shown as squares and decisions under outside control ('chance') are shown as circles. Figure 6.19 shows the decision tree for our imaginary product launch.

Suppose the company initially chooses from abandoning the project, launching in a limited area or a full market campaign with a pilot launch. Each is a decision for the company to make. Abandoning the project generates no income and is labelled as such. Launching in the limited market may succeed or fail and the probability of each is assigned to the legs of the tree. Each out-

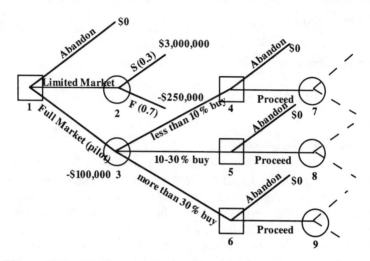

Figure 6.19   *Decision tree for a product launch*

come has a resultant income, which can be negative. It's important for managers to know the effect of different outcomes. Of course, nobody really knows what the probabilities are – it's up to experienced people to use judgement. This means the decision tree is a mixture of subjective and objective methods. Not a bad compromise for the real world, in which there is much uncertainty. If the pilot market is tried, there can be three outcomes of interest to the company.

The tree is built up in this way until all the outcomes of interest are charted. The diagram shows dotted lines out of the last three nodes, to show the chart is not finished. The chart enables users to see which approaches involve the greatest financial risk, when critical decisions need to be made and – if charts are made with different risk assessments – how sensitive the project is to the accuracy of risk assessment. This last point may be crucial in deciding how to assess the risk. For example, a special study might be needed to assist the process of estimation.

Voting

A final method for deciding which solutions to adopt is by voting. In fact, this is the most common method used in practice. Voting is based on opinions. It is a poor substitute for facts. It's acceptable to use voting if the facts are not available, but the superiority of facts should be kept in mind.

Chapter 7

PLANNING AND MANAGING THE IMPLEMENTATION

Key concepts and methods:

- Process decision program chart
- Mistake-proofing
- Tree diagram
- Arrow diagram
- Quality function deployment
- Managing change
- Force field analysis

'The operation was successful, but the patient died' – Anon.

Some of the best ideas have never been implemented because of failure to look at three key points about putting ideas into use:

- making sure they will work in practice
- having a plan for implementation
- managing change.

With the speed that ideas, services and products come to market, it is more important than ever to make sure there are no 'bugs' in the products about to be unleashed on the public. The same applies to ideas. Luckily, there are a couple of methods which help us to do this.

Process decision programme chart

To help find ways that our solutions may go wrong, we can use a method which glories in the name of the process *decision programme chart* or, mercifully, PDPC. The PDPC looks at the potential ways that a concept may fail in application and places countermeasures to overcome these possible pitfalls. Figure 7.1 shows a PDPC for a health industry application.

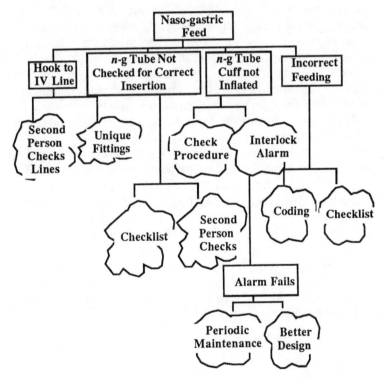

Figure 7.1 *Process decision programme chart (PDPC): possible ways in which a naso-gastric feed can be incorrectly given*

The way to set up the PDPC is to ask 'How could this go wrong?' and then 'What could be put in place to stop that?'. The process is repeated until there is a general consensus that the likelihood of further failure is minute. How do we know when we have reached this point? Usually it's a matter of judgement, but it is possible to apply reason, even when we are dealing with human safety. For example, if a process could cause death to an operator if it malfunctions, what should be the level of risk for a malfunction?

A digression here points out a common failing with figures. If we look at statistics for accidents, we are often given the wrong impression, because the figures seem to suggest certain types of activity are more dangerous than they seem to be. For example, more people are killed in road accidents within a short distance of their homes than they are on long journeys. Why is this? Simply, because they are exposed to the hazard more often in the *many* short journeys from home. There is a way to express risks which is objective. Any form of accident statistics can be made meaningful if we express them in the risk *per person-hour* of exposure. Then the high absolute rate of accidents in the home starts to look more sensible. The risk per person-hour of exposure is very low, but we are there so much more than anywhere else that the actual number of accidents is large.

So, now this is known, we can look at the risks per person-hour of exposure of the process. Most people would agree that if the risk is brought down to no higher than the risk per person-hour of exposure to living at home, we have done all that is reasonable.

It's also important that we make our solutions proof against the 'Murphy's Law' events which always seem to frustrate our best efforts. In manufacturing, clerical processing, health and service industries alike, things go wrong even after we are sure we got the method right. Out of manufacturing comes a superb idea which dramatically reduces the error rate in both factory and administrative processes.

Mistake-proofing

Figure 7.2   *Poka-Yoke*

I'll describe how mistake-proofing works in manufacturing, then look at how the principles can be applied to other industries. Mistake-proofing has been used for decades, but only in the last ten years or so has it become known outside the field of industrial engineering. The technique is known in Japan as Poka-Yoke (pronounced 'poker-yolk-eh'). It grew out of earlier work known as Baka-Yoke or 'fool-proofing'. The name change arose when it became clear that people working in a process are not fools, but human error is commonplace.

The technique was refined by Shigeo Shingo.[9] The genius of Shingo was to make the distinction between an error and a resulting defect. Making a mistake does not have to translate into a physically wrong act. The trick is to have some intervention which catches the error before it can translate into a defect.

In manufacturing, Shingo used gadgets to stop machines from working if something had been missed out by the operator. The same philosophy can be used with white collar work, the health industry, tourism, law, government. It just needs mapping on to the new environment. Figure 7.3 shows one of Shingo's early devices to help prevent an operator forgetting parts to be placed in switches. Just by placing the parts in a dish acted like a physical checklist.

Similar reasoning to the manufacturing environment can be employed with a set of medical devices to be used, a number of clerical tasks to be completed or a set of operations to be carried out in servicing a hotel room. As each is done, it can be transferred to the 'output' dish, which may be a physical dish for medical devices, a checklist ticked for clerical operations or a prepackaged, ordered set of materials for servicing the hotel room. In each case, the process is set up so that the order is built into the process, not something which people have to remember. We all have to cope with many more interruptions today and interruptions are sure to make people forget where they were.

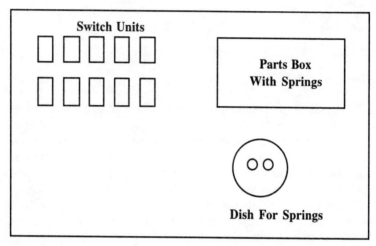

Figure 7.3   *Early Poka-Yoke device. The dish serves as a 'checklist', providing feedback if the operator has forgotten to fit a spring to one of the switch units in a pair.*

Organizing and planning for implementation

We've got our ideas organized, we've mistake-proofed the process and feel sure this solution to the problem is going to be a winner. How is it going to happen?

Without a plan, we're planning to fail. There is another method in the Seven Management Tools from Japan, which is useful for both planning and problem solving. We'll look at it now.

The tree diagram

Figure 7.4 *Tree diagram*

The tree diagram allows us to show in detail what things are related to the problem or the desired end goal. Here's how it works.

We write our desired goal on the left-hand side of a whiteboard. Another way would be to write the problem instead of the goal. Then we look at the related facts. For example, we might be interested in cutting down on how much sugar we eat. On the left side of the board, we put 'reduce sugar intake' in a box. We decide that two things relate to reducing sugar intake:

● Eat less.
● Select foods with less sugar.

We write these down in boxes to the right of the first goal. We could use sticky notes instead of writing on the board. Each of these in turn will have things related to them. We might decide that 'Selecting foods with less sugar' is supported by:

● Have list of low sugar foods.
● Buy from health food shops.

Now, these new boxes may have supporting actions. We keep on writing things in the boxes until the tree shows the level of detail we think is enough. Figure 7.5 shows an example of a tree diagram.

We might want to collect some more data to confirm that our thoughts about the problem specification are on the right track. For example, if we thought that poor data collection by agents was leading to errors in insurance policies, we might set up a sampling of policies to confirm this.

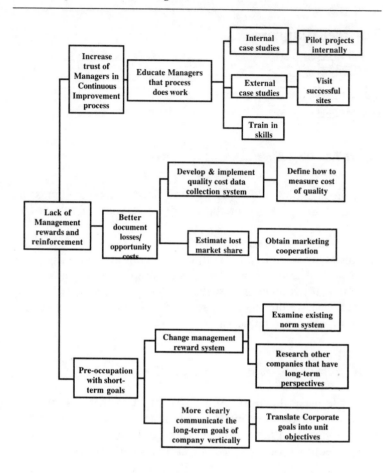

Figure 7.5   *Tree diagram: ways to deal with the lack of management
rewards and reinforcement for continuous improvement*

The tree diagram shows the sequence of events to make things
happen, so it's a planning method. The sequence property is very
important, because this is often poorly planned for. It also shows
the cause relationship between actions or events, so it's a problem-solving method as well.

The arrow diagram

Figure 7.6   *The arrow diagram*

For problems which need considerable planning, the arrow diagram is useful. Although this is one of the Seven Management Tools, it is directly taken from critical path method. Only large projects will need an arrow diagram, for which a detailed description will be found in specialist books. The basic principle is that all tasks are related in a diagram which shows which jobs must be done before others can start. For example, in building a house, the roof work cannot commence until the frame is up.

The arrow diagram is usually maintained using a computer program which calculates the minimum and maximum times for each job and shows which ones are 'critical': that is, if those jobs are delayed, the whole project will be delayed.

When we are dealing with problem solving at the marketing level, there is a special method to help manage the job.

Quality function deployment (QFD)

We'll only look at an overview of QFD, because it's quite specialized and there are plenty of books about this method.[10,11]

QFD takes the requirements of the customer and carries them step-by-step through the various development stages or functions of an organization, without losing sight of what the customer wants. The tool used to do this is the House of Quality. A condensed form of the House of Quality is shown in Figure 7.7. The name is derived from the appearance of the diagram. The House of Quality overcomes the difficulties in the traditional approach to product development of the marketing department saying what is to be designed, the design department telling manufacturing what is to be made and manufacturing handing to sales what it has produced. The House of Quality can also be used for more general work than product development. Any requirements, be they product features or planning elements, can be dealt with using the House of Quality.

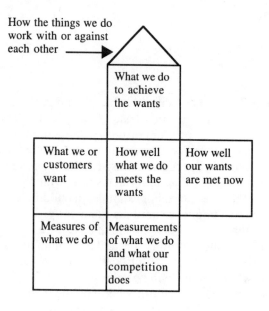

Figure 7.7 *The House of Quality*

A brief example of use for the House of Quality is shown in Figure 7.8. A team has decided to review how well their methods satisfy their needs in teamwork. First, the wants are placed in the left-hand rows. The team is the customer in this case. Then, the tops of the columns are filled in with the tools used to achieve the wants. The next step is to look at how well each of the tools satisfies the wants. The central matrix shows this. Symbols are placed at the intersections of the tools with the wants. A double circle might signify a strong relationship between the want and the tool. A single circle might signify a moderate relationship and a cross might signify that a negative relationship exists.

The box for how well our wants are met might be filled in using the simple scoring system shown. The 'roof' of the house shows how the various tools work with or against each other and the measurements at the bottom of the house show a similar scoring of the tools against the agreed measures. The House of Quality is an excellent means of forcing teamwork and can be used whenever a fairly large project involves trade-offs between benefits and costs.

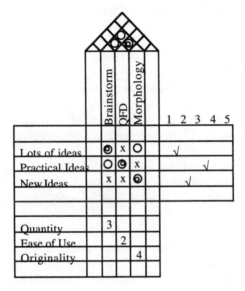

Figure 7.8   *The House of Quality: teamwork*

Managing change

Managing for change is a hot topic for the 1990s. We are not good at this in the West. We need to be more aware of how difficult change is and how to help people cope with it. Here are some topics managers and facilitators of change need to be aware of:

- the difficulties people have in coping with change
- the importance of managing for change
- how the effects of these difficulties cause poor performance
- how change can be made to happen more easily.

It's only recently – a few years ago – that we realized managing for change was a subject of its own. We've been busy doing *technical* things to get quality moving, but the human side has been largely forgotten.

How difficult is change for individuals? Much more than most people realize. Try a simple test. Clasp your hands together. Make a note of which thumb is on top. Now, unclasp your hands and clasp them together again, but with the other thumb on top. It isn't easy, is it? Now, if it's so hard to make a little change like that, we shouldn't be surprised if major changes in our work cause much bigger problems.

What's required to make change happen? For change to happen, as well as taking care to inform people, we have to overcome the financial and emotional cost to people of making that change. There are three conditions we must have to overcome these costs:

- There must be dissatisfaction with the current situation.
- There must be a vision of the desired future state.
- There must be a plan of how to get to the desired future state.

If any of these are missing, or aren't strong enough to overcome the financial and emotional cost of change, then we'll have trouble making change happen. All people affected by change should be involved in decisions about change. This makes it harder to resist change, because they're a part of it. We could look at change management as planning the movement between three stages of the process. The first stage is to unfreeze people's thinking. We do this by making people aware of new ideas and arousing their interest. We need to be aware of and overcome the forces which make people resist change. For example, distrust, conflict between individual and organizational goals, lack of resources. The next stage is for people to try out the new ideas. This helps them move through the 'grieving' process. The third stage is to re-freeze, where the new ideas are adopted.

So, what must we do to manage change? It's best explained by an example. Let's look at a typical situation in industry. The plant isn't big enough for today's work. Executive management wants to move to a new plant, 50 kilometres from the present site. All the usual notices are put up. Middle management is asked to prepare a plan for the move. What gets moved first? How will we minimize disruption to production? Who will move and who will quit? How will we train new people? It's a big job. But there's no mention of managing for change.

After a few weeks, nothing's happened. The managers seem to be frozen in their tracks. Why has nothing happened? Quite likely, the managers are in the denial stage of the grieving process. Nothing will happen until something causes the managers to move forward from where they are. This is where change management comes in.

The *change agent* – that is, the person who manages change – must intervene. The change agent could be an expert from outside the company. In the future, we'll need lots of change agents *within* the company. So, managers could be trained to be change agents.

The first job for the change agent is to unfreeze the managers from their present state. The managers probably don't want to talk about the change, but we'll look at a way to overcome this problem. The change agent helps the managers to see what the issues and concerns are. There'll be some things about the change which the managers like and some things they don't like. The trick is to bring these out in the open, so they can be dealt with separately.

The affinity diagram could be used to draw the issues out in the open. The theme could be: 'What are the issues surrounding the move to the new site?'

When the issues have been placed on the whiteboard, the groupings provide a basis for discussion of subjects which may not have been discussed openly because of fear of a superior or worry about other managers' opinions.

Force field analysis

Figure 7.9 *Force field analysis*

Now we're ready to see what the Change Agent does to deal with the issues. Force field analysis is a technique which makes use of the fact that there are always two sides to a problem. Otherwise we wouldn't have a problem. Our minds are confused by two kinds of influences:

- Driving forces
- Restraining forces.

Figure 7.10 shows how the force field analysis method works. Driving Forces support the change. Most managers would see the extra space at the new plant as being a Driving Force. It makes life better. Restraining Forces oppose the change. Some of the managers may have a longer journey to get to the new plant.

The level of the problem is too high   The level of the problem is too low

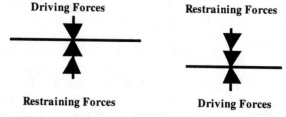

Driving Forces   **Restraining Forces**

Restraining Forces   **Driving Forces**

(upward Restraining Forces stronger   (downward Restraining Forces stronger
than downward Driving Forces)   than upward Driving Forces)

Figure 7.10   *Force field analysis*

The issues from the sticky note work need to be separated into Driving Forces and Restraining Forces. It's quite likely that the groupings already gave some clues to this. Some likely Driving Forces:

- an opportunity to improve plant layout
- better access to the site
- better materials handling.

Some Restraining Forces which the managers might identify:

- difficulty in recruitment of labour
- greater distance for transportation to the main market
- feelings of helplessness.

To help move towards achieving the change, we require a strategy of minimizing the Restraining Forces and maximizing the Driving Forces. We need to involve the managers in this. The change agent can work with the managers to get ideas on how the Restraining Forces can be minimized and how the Driving Forces can be maximized.

One way to do this is to look at the issues and see what are the causes of the issues. Each issue is placed in the centre of the whiteboard and dealt with one at a time. The group is then asked 'What causes the issue?'. For example, if a feeling of helplessness was the issue, the managers might suggest 'lack of information' or 'not enough control over timing'. When several of these causes have been placed around the issue and joined to the issue with arrows, the change agent asks another question: 'What are the causes of each of the causes you've just written down?' These causes are put outside the first causes and arrows drawn to show the relationships.

This process is repeated until the group can't think of any more causes. The causes with the most arrows are likely to be underlying causes of the issues.

By doing this work for both the Driving and Restraining Forces, we produce a list of things to do to enhance the Driving Forces and reduce the Restraining Forces. The ideas need to be evaluated to see which will work best. Then an action plan can be made to carry out the ideas.

In our example, we might get these ideas to reduce resistance to change:

- Get government assistance for hiring people.
- Look at ways to transport faster or shorten response time.
- Give managers more authority to use new methods.

In a similar way, we might find these ideas on how to enhance the forces driving change:

- Involve the workforce in plant layout, so the information will be better and the workforce will be involved.
- Use the improved access to bargain with transport companies.
- Use the latest technology to get extra benefits from materials handling.

Because the managers are involved in arriving at these actions, change is easier on two counts. The managers have brought their fears out in the open so they can be dealt with. The managers are involved in the processes to reduce resistance and enhance the Driving Forces. It's hard for people to resist their own ideas!

The managers should now consider what they think the Driving and Restraining Forces would be if the actions were taken. The new forces should show a big move to supporting the change. If not, the strategy isn't right. It might be necessary to work out the plan again. Better to discover the mistake during planning, than during implementation.

What we've done is to re-freeze the manager's new thoughts about the change. These new thoughts are positive. They're action oriented and make the managers more comfortable with the change.

When the actions have been taken, the change agent should help the managers to review the situation to see how effective the actions have been. If they've not been as effective as expected, it's time to find out what the Driving and Restraining Forces are now. It can happen that opinions alter as actions are taken.

Chapter 8

DOING IT MY WAY
OR TEAMWORK?

Key concepts and methods:

- Individual work
- Teamwork
- Storyboarding
- Complexity in work
- Team member roles

'None of us is as good as all of us'
Ray Kroc of McDonald's

In the last few years, many texts and speakers have extolled the virtues of teamwork. There's no doubt that teamwork has been badly neglected in the West. Good teamwork can produce better results than individuals working alone. Teamwork is definitely the way to go if individuals are all pulling in different directions.

But it's not always best to work in teams.

Let me explain this heresy. Many problems are quite simple to solve. The teamwork approach for these problems is simply a waste of resources. What's worse, the team will take longer to solve the problem than the right individual. Examples are:

- An appliance is not working – it is not plugged in.
- A user is having trouble with a software package – a work-mate knows the package well.
- The car is making an unusual noise – a friend is a car enthu-siast.
- The washing machine is leaking – the mechanic said on his last visit that the seal may need replacing, but you couldn't afford it at the time.

In all these examples, personal resources or networking with friends and other contacts provides *single individuals* who can solve the problem. These individuals are usually some sort of technical specialist.

For problems where the solution is simple – like the appliance not being plugged in – it's silly to form a team. A little more thought may be needed for other problems, but a good question to ask is, 'Who do I know who is good at working with....?' If the solution is clear to the technical specialist, then using that special-ist is the fastest way to solve the problem. If it isn't clear, then it may be time to take a look at forming a team.

As a general rule of thumb, if teamwork is being used exclu-sively, then it's worth leaning in the direction of using individuals, to counter the current mindset.

Another matter which should occupy our minds in problem solving is the question of whether there is a single cause of the problem we are experiencing. Usually, single causes are associ-ated with simple problems. Complex problems often have multi-ple causes, which may need the efforts of both teams and technical specialists to unlock the secrets to the solution. We have this insa-tiable desire for simple solutions and single cause solutions. In the 1980s, the swing to simple solutions to complex problems left us with a legacy of even more complex problems to solve. Figure 8.1 shows our difficulty with this.

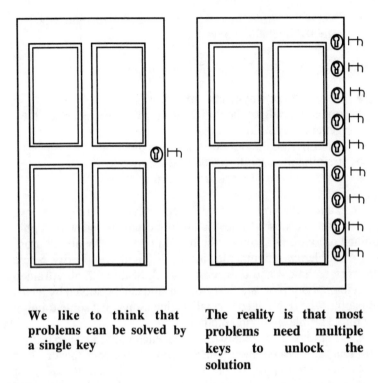

We like to think that problems can be solved by a single key	The reality is that most problems need multiple keys to unlock the solution

Figure 8.1 *The reality of problem solving*

Teamwork

The rest of this chapter deals with a subject which to most enterprises is almost as new as change management. We are not used to working in teams. In the West, we have emphasized the individual as all-important. Only now is literature emerging to point out the dangers of such a narrow view.

When is teamwork better than an individual working on the problem?

- When the issues are complex and affect several people or areas.
- When individual technical specialists are not sure of the answer or have run out of steam.

- When the problem is known to several people who are affected by the outcome.

Some of the conditions for good teamwork are:

- awareness of why teamwork is important
- understanding of the difficulties teams experience and the general psychology of teams
- making sure the right people are in the team
- training in the skills needed for teamwork
- providing the support structures for teams.

If we exanine the problems which need solving in companies, we see several reasons why teams are important – and why highly trained individuals shouldn't be relied upon to solve all the problems. Problems in companies are of different complexity. Some are very technical and do need the work of a few highly trained individuals. But most are fairly simple and can be solved by teams of people who don't need specialist education – just some training in simple problem-solving methods.

Another reason for Teamwork is that each individual can bring a different slant to a problem. This can provide the edge that cracks a problem one individual can't solve. To quote the late Ray Kroc of McDonald's: 'None of us is as good as all of us.' It's especially important to make sure the right mix of people is in a team. All too often, teams are made up of management or supervisors and people working in the process are excluded. A team of managers and supervisors simply won't see the problem the way it really is. The solution may not be acceptable to the workforce, either.

Most Western nations don't work well in teams because of their culture. But there are deeper reasons why all people have difficulty working in teams. These have to do with the make-up of humans. David Suzuki has described us as 'stone age people, trying to cope with modern technology'.[12] Because we've had more past experience with clubs than pens, we all have some trouble adapting to team conditions. We react to situations which are new in a 'fight or flight' mode, with the adrenalin pumping and hostility rising. Not a good basis for teamwork.

When a team forms, there are four stages of development which the team may go through. These are often called:

- forming
- storming
- norming
- performing.

During the forming stage, there's some nervousness among the members. They may be a bit excited about doing something new and proud at having been chosen for the team, but there'll be fear and anxiety about the job they are about to start. Possibly team members have been chosen who don't like each other. There might be some rivalry between departments.

During this stage, the team may waste time on matters which aren't relevant to the task. They're distracted easily by side issues. The group doesn't deal with feelings, because the group isn't ready to handle these issues. There's not much care about other members of the group. This obviously isn't a very effective team.

In the next stage, storming, we see the differences in members' temperaments coming to the surface. Members' confidence will rise and fall as the various members speak, and perhaps make others feel positive or negative about the team process. The members begin to take risks and experiment with new ideas. There may be conflict over who has authority, because individuals are competing for power over the group. But people are starting to listen to each other. Different people will have different styles and approaches. The team has to learn to cope with these differences.

In the third stage, norming, the team is settling down. The team members may see the interests of the team as more important than getting the job done. Minority viewpoints are discouraged. Both these behaviours can work against progress, unless properly managed. The team is now able to resolve conflict between members and is confident enough to set its own ground rules about team behaviour. These ground rules are quite important for smooth functioning of the team. Ground rules might cover how to give each member a fair hearing, types of behaviour and language allowable and simple administration rules.

In the fourth stage – performing – the members of the team now understand each other. The team can work through group problems. Loyalty to the team has developed. This loyalty can be a barrier to good results, as the loyalty might interfere with decisions.

For example, a decision might involve a choice between an outsider and one of the team members to do an important job. The team's loyalty to its member could cause the team to choose the team member, when the outsider was a better choice.

The team can deal with complex tasks effectively and is creative about dealing with disagreements. There's openness, honesty and trust. The team is flexible and can change procedures to meet different needs. In this stage, the team is able to function efficiently.

Most teams *never progress* beyond the forming stage. So what can be done to get teams to the performing stage? The difficulties teams have are perfectly normal, so we shouldn't criticize them, but should plan to have a facilitator present who understands what's happening.[13] Following are a few things the facilitator can do to help the teams progress:

- Make sure all members attend meetings regularly.
- Coach members to do pre-meeting preparation.
- Help the team to plan meetings which are long enough to do the work.
- Redesign tasks to allow goals to be met.
- Give members responsibility for specific parts of the project.
- Bring others into the team when different skills are needed.

An excellent way to communicate the project's progress is the use of a *storyboard*. A storyboard is simply a step-by-step record, using pictures, of what the team has done. The storyboard uses the diagrams of problem solving to make the record. It might start by showing the problem definition, with perhaps a picture of a problem-solving method for summarizing information. As the team progresses, the storyboard might show a cause and effect diagram to say they've worked on causes of the problem.

So the storyboard shows progress, as well as a record of what was done. This means it's another way to communicate with management. The storyboard shouldn't become a tedious chore. It isn't important to have precise diagrams. It's better to use them as icons, showing in principle what's been done. Figure 8.2 shows an example storyboard.

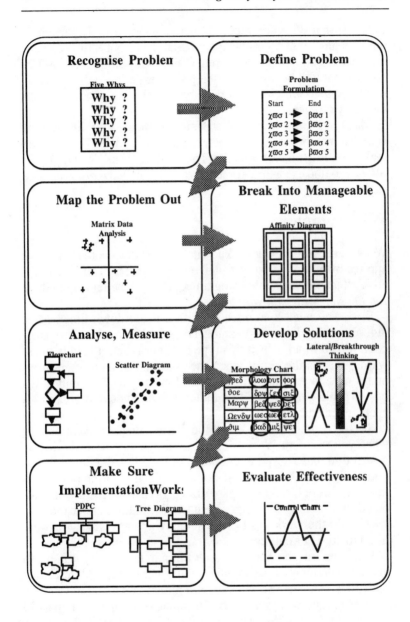

Figure 8.2 *Storyboard – quality improvement project*

Interpersonal skills are important in teamwork. Simply participating in teams with a competent facilitator present will give team members good skills in communicating with others. It won't be quick but it will be lasting. When people experience the improvement in results which comes from better handling of other people, they don't forget.

Managing time is one of the most difficult jobs for a team. Usually, members still have their regular work to do. This can be a real stumbling block for teams. There's a very simple and powerful way to find extra time for teamwork. It's called *work sampling*.

Work sampling

Work sampling has been known for decades, but used to be applied by putting the stop-watch on other people. This had a negative effect on the people being timed. Here's a better way to do it. *Put the stop-watch on yourself.*

First, you need a stop-watch with a count-down timer. Most digital watches have this feature. Try to pick one with a repeating count-down timer. When this type of timer is set, it counts backwards, sounds the alarm when the count ends, then resets itself and counts down again. Set the countdown to, say, 37 minutes. It's best to avoid multiples of 15 minutes, because you may lock into a cycle of tea and meal breaks.

Set the counter going. When the alarm sounds, make a note of what you're doing. Very soon, a pattern will start to build up. You'll find that a surprising amount of time is spent doing things you really shouldn't be doing. For example, if your job is a draftsman, you were hired to prepare drawings. If you're drawing, calculating, checking a design reference or thinking about the best way to do the work – all of those activities are what you were hired to do. Let's call this *real work*.

But suppose you had to phone the purchasing department to chase the drawing office supplies which were promised for Friday but still haven't arrived. You weren't hired to do that. Let's call an activity of that type *complexity*. The amazing thing is that up to 90 per cent of the working day for white collar workers is chewed up by complexity.

When your measurements show what kind of complexity your

time is being spent on, you can attack complexity and remove it. Think of the potential savings. Here's an example of complexity which can be removed. Your measurements show a lot of time is spent moving between floors to use the photocopier. This may be the justification you need to get a photocopier on your floor. Then the wasted time is saved. Figure 8.3 shows a typical result of work sampling and the complexity identified.

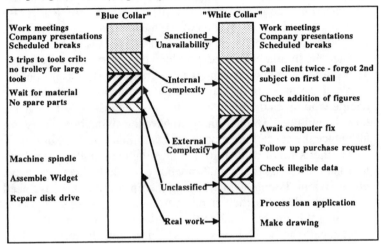

Figure 8.3 *Complexity in work*

I've found that team members who are genuinely interested in participating jump at the chance to use work sampling to find out how to get more productive time. Others invent excuses not to do the measurements. They usually don't want to do the team job.

Another important skill for teamwork is knowing how to run meetings. The main skills needed are:

- stating the aim of the meeting
- setting agendas
- establishing the roles
- controlling the meetings.

It's surprising how many meetings start without an aim or agenda. Yet both are basic to running a meeting. Without an aim or agenda, we have to ask 'Why are we here?' If people don't know in advance of the meeting what they are going to discuss, they can hardly be blamed for not bringing information on the topics.

Roles should be established, so people know what they're expected to do and to make sure all the work gets done. There has to be a *team leader*. (More about the leader shortly.) Somebody has to take the minutes. Another needs to *monitor* the meeting to make sure it's keeping to time. And of course there should be a *chairperson*. The chairperson doesn't have to be the leader. By enabling everybody to do something, the team spirit is reinforced. It is too much to expect one person to do all of these jobs.

The jobs should be rotated, provided that everybody is comfortable doing each task. By the way, a great way to ensure people arrive at the meeting on time, and avoid drawing short straws to decide who takes the minutes, is to have the last person to arrive take the minutes. Another hint is to have the switchboard operator announce the start of the meeting a few minutes beforehand.

Another kind of control for the meeting is to make sure behaviour isn't affecting the team. Somebody should be keeping an eye on behaviour. People who are being disruptive or aggressive need to be reminded that their behaviour should change. The person watching this might be called the *gatekeeper*. Another job for the gatekeeper is to watch for people who dominate the meeting. This may be quite unintentional, but it doesn't allow full exchange of ideas.

The chairperson should make sure there's consensus on issues and that proper evaluation of ideas is made. And, of course, the meeting should do some work on the agenda for next time.

The *facilitator* has the important job of giving guidance and training to the team. This means coaching the members in what they'll experience as a team, showing the team how to run meetings and giving training in use of problem-solving methods. The facilitator is sometimes called the *quality adviser*. Whatever the name, the facilitator is an outsider to the team and can remain neutral on issues which cause friction.

A good level of skill is needed to be an effective facilitator. As well as being good at dealing with people, the facilitator has to have presentation skills to train the team and needs a clear understanding of the technical information which is part of quality management. The facilitator may also give training in the use of problem-solving methods.

The facilitator guides the team so that it concentrates on the process underlying the problem. Without this guidance, the team may try to fix the symptoms or won't get beneath the surface of the problem.

The *leader* (who is not necessarily the chairperson) is responsible for making sure there are written records of what the team has done. As well as this, the leader provides contact with the rest of the organization. The leader may have to assist members to find time, by talking to the members' supervisors about the importance of the project and arranging for their release for teamwork.

A difficulty for the team leader is to avoid being seen as the boss. This is much harder for the leader who is normally the supervisor of the team. If the leader comes from outside, he or she is better able to do this. In either case, the leader has to make a big effort to avoid dominating the meetings of the team.

Another job for the team leader is to make sure the team reviews the meetings to see how they can be improved. It only takes a few minutes at the end of the meeting to check on this and receive suggestions as to how the meetings could be made better.

When the time comes to implement ideas, the team leader can make use of normal authority to help implement the project.

Team members should make sure they contribute to all the meetings. They should also put in time between meetings, to gather data or try out ideas. Many teams fail because they only work on the project at meetings. The real work of projects is usually at the workplace.

At the end of the project, the team members should make a presentation of their findings to management and perhaps to other teams. These presentations are important for two main reasons. They build confidence and skill in communicating. They give team members a chance to give information to management – something which doesn't often happen in most Western companies.

To ensure productive meetings, team members need to develop discussion skills. These are some of the things to be learned:

- Making sure each member understands what is being talked about.
- Controlling people who tend to dominate the meeting.
- Listening positively.

- Sticking to the point.
- Managing time.
- Knowing when to close discussion.
- Reaching consensus.
- Improving the meeting.

There are many new approaches to teamwork which involve openness, trust and other factors which are difficult for many managers to accept. Modern texts on this subject should be studied by managers who want to have effective teams.[14,15]

Humility

A widespread problem with teamwork is lack of humility. It could also be called a lack of honesty, when we think about what it means. Most people are slow to admit they don't understand what's being said. For open and honest exchange of ideas, we can't have this. So, each member needs to ask whenever something is not clear. This also helps the other members, as they probably don't always understand either.

People who dominate meetings must be managed. It's hard for people who are quiet or shy to speak up when somebody else seems to always have all the right words. All members should play a part in seeing that each team member gets a fair hearing.

When we hear another point of view, we usually try to discredit it or defend our own point of view. In a team meeting, it's important for all members to listen carefully to others' points of view. Instead of attacking the other member's views, it's better to state what's good about those views. This is a great way to start off a team meeting. When people force themselves to listen positively to others, the process of discovering facts is helped enormously. Team members feel better about saying what they really think when the right atmosphere has been set.

It's hard not to wander off the point at some time. By having somebody responsible for looking out for this, a team can control a meeting. If the job of controlling the meeting is shared like this, all members have a job to do and the chairperson can concentrate on getting input from members.

Chapter 9

EVALUATING EFFECTIVENESS

Key concepts and methods:

- Customer satisfaction
- Control chart
- Graphical presentation and analysis

Is the customer satisfied?

A problem-solving project is not complete until the implemented solution is demonstrated to work effectively. How can we be sure the solution is effective? Some things take years to show up as a problem. As with the job of debugging solutions, we have to satisfy the mythical 'reasonable person'.

We took measures early in the problem-solving cycle to be sure of what we were talking about. These same measures should be taken after the solution is in place and bedded down. In fact it may be useful to take measurements, several times, to see if it is bedding down.

The control chart

Figure 9.1 *The control chart*

A useful method for measuring the effectiveness of solutions, at least for repetitive processes, is the *control chart*. Developed in the 1920s and 1930s, this method has had a resurgence of popularity in recent years. It needs a little more calculation than most methods and is like a sophisticated run chart.

Rather than duplicate what appears in many publications, I'll point you to books on how to prepare control charts and just discuss where the charts fit in with testing the effectiveness of solutions.

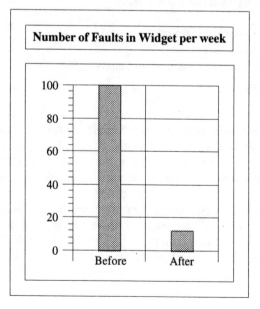

Figure 9.2 *Control chart showing improvement – 1*

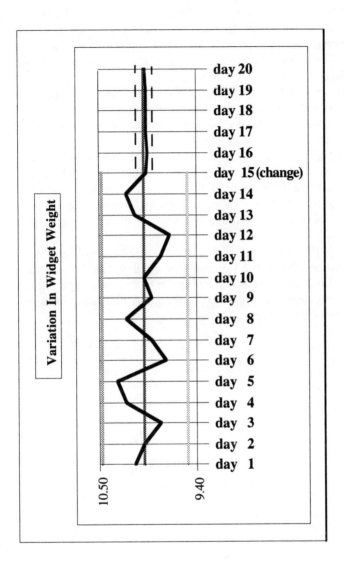

Figure 9.3   *Control chart showing improvement – 2*

An easy-to-follow source of information on control charting is *Quality Control by Statistical Methods*.[16] This book contains some techniques which few, if any, other introductory books have tackled. For those who want to go further, there are many books on advanced control chart techniques.[17,18] For situations where measurements cannot be made on a continuous scale, especially in the service industries, there are special techniques available.[19] If at all possible – and it usually is – graphical methods are the best way to show what's going on.[20]

We're usually interested in showing that there's been a real improvement in some measure of the problem. It might be a simple reduction in the number of occurrences, a smaller variation or an increase in customer rating against the competition. Typical examples of reporting on these measures are shown in Figures 9.2, 9.3 and 9.4.

What if the evaluation shows that the solution isn't effective? The team will have to go through the cycle again, but this time armed with more knowledge. Using the techniques shown in this book, particularly the mistake-proofing and PDPC methods, it's very likely the solution will be effective.

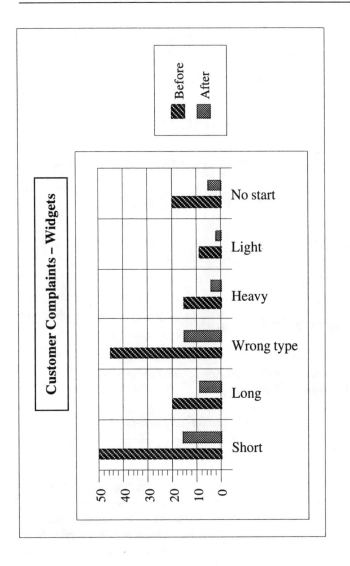

Figure 9.4 *Control chart showing improvement – 3*

Chapter 10

PROBLEM BUSTING IN PRACTICE

Key concepts and methods:

- Main steps
- Mindsets, myths and manna from heaven
- Traps and pitfalls

  'From CVS to BVS' – Dr Michael Hewitt-Gleeson
  (from Current View of the Situation to Better View of the Situation)

The steps shown in previous chapters are summarized here. These are guidelines only. There is no easy step model for every case. The key to success with problem solving is to stay flexible and learn as many techniques as possible. The more techniques you know, the more situations you can handle and the greater your flexibility. There's an old saying that if the only tool people are taught how to use is a hammer, every problem looks like a nail.

Here's a summary of the main steps:

- Recognizing problems
- Defining problems

- Mapping the problem out
- Breaking the problem down into manageable elements
- Analysing, measure
- Developing solutions
- Planning and managing the implementation
- Evaluating effectiveness.

For continuous improvement, a solution should never be seen as the end of the problem. However, the reality of limited resources and oceans of problems means that most problems will be dealt with until they have been reduced to a tolerable level, then a different problem will be tackled. Eventually, the general level of problems should be reduced to the point where further improvements can take place.

There are several books which can further expand your problem-solving ability[21,22,23,24,25].

Mindsets, myths and manna from heaven

In problem solving, it's difficult to over-emphasize the importance of an open mind. Most of us, if challenged, would say we have open minds. Think about how male attitudes to women have changed in the last five years. Gay men are now regarded quite differently, by most people, than was the case a few years ago.

For centuries, the world was considered to be flat and to challenge that view was to invite fearful retribution. We can discuss more subjects today, but there are still many areas of human activity where virtually no thought has been given to why we behave as we do.

As problem solvers, we need to be aware of how powerful mindsets can be. We should think about myths which get in the way of problem solving and we have to accept the fact that problem solving is hard work. To many, this is seen as unpleasant, but hard work is satisfying if it produces a result which moves us forward. The more problem solving we do, the better we become at it, just like any skill.

Let's consider a couple of examples of how mindsets, myths and 'manna from heaven' have held us back.

Mindsets are established ways of thinking. Usually these exist because of the way we were brought up. If we look hard enough, we can all find examples of our own mindsets. Most of us would have been brought up to believe that it's bad manners to interrupt when somebody else is speaking. But it's *not always* bad manners to do so. Unless the building is on fire or there is some other compelling reason *which takes the responsibility for the decision away from us*, most of us don't feel comfortable about interrupting people when they are speaking. This means an important point may be forgotten, if we are supposed to provide comments.

It's the mechanism by which we interrupt which is intrusive. What if there was a way to interrupt somebody which was not intrusive? Modern telephones have a facility called 'knocking' which, by means of a tone, lets the user know somebody else wishes to talk. If we could introduce a form of 'knocking' which could be recorded and the idea in the would-be interrupter's mind could also be recorded, wouldn't that make it easier to exchange ideas and information? We could take it further and think of a system which had varying degrees of interruption, depending on the urgency. When we think about it, the 'rule' about not interrupting isn't very sound, but we stick with it and a person who does interrupt isn't well regarded. In team situations, a simple signalling system could overcome the taboo against interrupting. For example:

- One raised finger means 'I want to make a point which will help this process'. (Speaker can finish the line of reasoning.)
- Two raised fingers (don't laugh) means 'I want to make a point which is critical to getting this process right'. (Speaker should stop at end of sentence.)
- Three raised fingers means 'There is an emergency. You must stop talking immediately'. (Speaker to stop instantly.)

This isn't the best system, just a suggestion. Each group should work out its own system.

Myths are beliefs we hold for which nobody can remember the reason. For example, I was brought up in a country where a little over 300 years ago certain people were burnt to death because of their appearance, dress or the colour of their pets. Seriously! I'm talking about burning witches at the stake. This happened in England, where some women were classified as witches for the flimsiest of reasons, such as possessing a black cat. Why should anyone be classified as a witch? Presumably there was a reason, but is anyone alive who can remember? I doubt it. Historians will be able to provide some reasons, but how can we be sure the accounts weren't biased by the people who produced the reasons in the first place? Earlier, whole towns were put to the sword in the name of religion. We must be able to distinguish myths from facts when working on problem solving.

'Manna from heaven' is a particular problem in the West. We have been brought up from an early age to assume that we have 'rights'. What is a right? According to my dictionary, a right is that which is due to anybody by just claim. We speak of 'human rights', but this is meaningless in a country where people are starving. What law of nature confers 'rights' upon us? Do we have a 'right' to a pension, a job or a home? It's becoming increasingly obvious that we don't and we'll have to find a new set of values to replace these.

It's a good exercise to think about how governments go about the process of problem solving. Would it be an improvement to use methods such as shown in this book? The answer, and what you may be prepared to do about it, has a strong bearing on the quality of life for us all in our complicated society and turbulent future.

Some traps and pitfalls

Whenever we think, we have to recognize the mindsets, myths and manna from heaven, to give ourselves the best chance of coming up with new ideas. Some more observations about barriers to thinking:

- When we take sides, we drive out objectivity.
- When we say 'it won't work', we close our minds.
- When we say 'There are no problems', we are killing progress.
- When we say 'It's not my fault', we hide from self-examination.
- When we say 'Heads will roll for this', we inhibit people from working on the problem – the job is to avoid punishment.

- When we say 'They don't know' (referring to workers, customers, etc.), we are throwing away important sources of ideas.
- When we see too many problems, we become numb and unable to act.
- When we look to others to solve the problem, we demean our own abilities.

There are other traps and pitfalls which prevent us from getting the most out of ideas. Sometimes, a good idea will not be followed through because the proposed solution doesn't seem workable. *Instead of looking for another way to implement the idea, we throw out the idea with the implementation.*

Perhaps the most common error in problem solving is to assume there is *only one cause* of the problem. Few problems have only one cause. Attacking only one of many causes may make an improvement, but it falls far short of the potential benefits.

An interesting human failing is the way we go along with proposals we don't really agree with. It's the business of not offending which we looked at before. This phenomenon has been named 'The Abilene Paradox'. A family was asked if they would like to drive to Abilene on a hot day. Abilene is a small and not very exciting town in the US, which is rather like a dust bowl in summer. To avoid giving offence, all agreed, despite the fact that everybody thought it was a bad idea. We may do the same in problem-solving situations.

Another source of errors in problem solving is assuming that things are being done the right way at present. A problem may arise simply because the job is not being done the way it is supposed to be done. The effect is regarded as a problem which must be solved. If the way of doing the job were checked out, chances are, doing it the right way would eliminate the problem. Instead, the problem-solving team goes through a lengthy process of solving the problem. Of course, the team might come up with a better way of doing the job. But with resources scarce, the energy of the team could probably be put to better use elsewhere.

Overlooking the obvious is another common way of failing to arrive at a proper solution to a problem. Recently, I heard people complaining that a particular software package wouldn't work properly. It wasn't possible to print from the new software. After some energy and time had been spent talking about the ways in which the software could be causing the problem, somebody thought to check the connection of the printer to the port on the back of the computer. Sure enough, the plug was hanging on by one corner only. As soon as the printer was plugged in properly, the problem vanished.

How many service calls have been made to fix TV sets which were not plugged into the mains? How much waste is caused in industry through overlooking the obvious?

PART II

USING THE
TECHNIQUES

Summary of main steps

Summary of the main steps (remember, it's not *always* the best sequence):

- Recognizing problems
- Defining problems
- Mapping the problem
- Breaking down the problem
- Analysing and measuring
- Developing solutions
- Planning and managing the implementation
- Evaluating effectiveness

Checklist of questions

Checklist of questions to ask regularly during the problem solving process:

- Is the problem still real?
- Would the problem still be there if we changed the environment?
- Is the cause we think we have found always true?
- Are there other causes?
- Is there any other way to deal with the problem?
- Has anyone else solved this or a similar problem?
- What might a similar problem look like?
- Is this an area which needs special expertise?
- Are we trying to solve the user's problem, or somebody else's?

Method selection matrix

Key:
●   Strong relationship
○   Moderate relationship
(Blank) Little relationship

Problem or need

Problem or need	Affinity diagram	Arrow diagram	Brainstorming	Cause and effect diagram	Checklist	Control charts	de Bono's 'Po'	de Bono's Six Thinking Hats	Deployment chart
Allow for different personalities	○							●	
Allow for human factors			○	○	○				
Compare methods, defects					○	○			
Deal with opposing influences									
Decide priorities									
Defect prevention			○	○					○
Discover characteristics									
Discover causal linkage	●			●	○	○	○		○
Encourage lateral thinking							●		
Generate many ideas			○					○	
Handle chaos	●								
Handle unmeasurable information									
How is time spent?		●	○	○	○				○
Invent new ways to do things			○				○		
Involve passive people								○	
Prediction		○				○	○		
Prevent intermittent errors			○	○					○
Quantify causal linkage					○	●			
Ranking features					○				
Relate discrete factors	○			○					○
Satisfy customer needs					○				
Workplace layout			○	○					○

Design of experiments	Ergonomics	Five Whys	Flow diagram	Force field analysis	Histogram	Matrix data analysis	Matrix diagram	Measles chart	Morphology chart	Pareto diagram	PDPC	Poka-Yoke	Prioritization matrices	Quality function deployment	Reclassification chart	Relations diagram	Run chart	Scatter diagram	Tree diagram	Work sampling
○	●		○					○	○		○	○	●		○		○		○	○
●			○	○	○	○		○		○								○		
				●			○						○							
										●		●								
		○	○					○			●	●			○				○	
●				○	○			○												
○	○	●	○				○		○		○			○					○	○
									○						○					
									●						○					
		○	○										○							
				○		○	○	●												
			○		○					○			○			○		○		●
									●						●					
○						○			○		○						○	○		
	●	○					○			○	●				○					
●						○		○						○				○		
						○				○				○	○					
○	○	○		○				○						○		○			○	
						○								●						
	○		○																	

A typology of problem-solving methods

	Descriptive	Analytical	Organizing/planning	Mistake proofing/preventive	Creative/expansive
Affinity diagram	X		X		
Arrow diagram			X		
Brainstorming		X			X
Cause and effect diagram		X			
Checklist	X	X			
Control chart		X			
Decision tree			X		
DOE		X			
Flowchart	X	X	X		
Force field analysis		X	X		
Histogram	X				
Lateral/breakthrough thinking			X		X
Mandalas					X
Matrix data analysis		X			
Matrix diagram	X				
Measles chart	X	X			
Morphology chart		X	X		X
'Other hand' writing					X
Pareto diagram		X	X		
PDPC		X		X	X
Poka-Yoke		X		X	X
Prioritization matrices		X	X		
Problem formulation		X	X		X
QFD		X	X		X
Reclassification chart		X			X
Relations diagram		X			
Run chart	X				
Scatter diagram		X			
The Five Whys		X			
Tree diagram		X	X		

The Five Whys

Why ?
Why ?
Why ?
Why ?
Why ?

Figure A.1 *The Five Whys*

Applications

- Gets to the root cause of problems.
- Encourages an explorative culture.
- Team with many diagrams to enhance problem-solving process.
- Avoids 'blaming' atmosphere.

Advantages

- Extremely simple to apply.
- Very wide applicability.
- Can be used by individuals and groups.
- Suitable for all industries (manufacturing, service).
- Requires no charts.

Disadvantages

- May be seen as intrusive if not used with discretion.
- May lead to premature solution of problems if used without other means of discovery.

Special Requirements

- Tact in use.

How to use

- When a problem presents itself, think about what the problem is and phrase the problem to yourself. For example, the toast is burnt.
- Ask 'Why is the toast burnt?' (You can ask this of yourself or another participant.)
- Listen for the answer, e.g. 'Because the bread stuck'.
- Ask why the answer is so, e.g. 'Why did the bread stick?'
- Repeat the questioning until the underlying cause is found. This may take more than Five Whys, but not often.

Problem formulation

Figure A.2 *Problem formulation*

Applications

- Ensures problems rather than symptoms are solved.
- Develops innovative approaches.

Advantages

- Forces a thorough analysis of the situation.
- Develops a habit of challenging the status quo.

Disadvantages

- Can be irritating for minor problems.
- Requires a good deal of personal discipline.

Special requirements

- Conditions for reflection.

How to Use

- Gather a group of people with knowledge of the subject.
- Think about the real nature of the problem.
- Write down progressively broader statements of the subject by considering 'start state' and 'end state'.
- Use the statements to trigger ideas on better ways to provide the product or service.

Matrix data analysis

Figure A.3   *Matrix data analysis*

Applications

● Shows two-dimensional relationships.
● Finds clustered data.
● Obtains consensus as to qualitative relationships.

Advantages

● Easy to learn.
● '2 × 2' concept familiar to many people.
● High visibility.
● Suitable for all industries (manufacturing, service).
● Wide application.

Disadvantages

● Usually only a step on the way to a solution.
● Usually qualitative rather than quantitative.
● Requires a fairly high degree of control by facilitator with inexperienced groups.

Special requirements

- Requires whiteboard or computer graphics package.

How to use

- Gather a group of people with knowledge of the problem.
- Consider the characteristics to be analysed. For example, the group might wish to study the relationship between the importance of speed of service and cost, for various customers. One axis of the diagram is marked from high to low on speed of service, the other is marked from high to low on cost.
- Get the group to write in examples of pairs of information, preferably from measurements, but from experience if this is all that is available.
- Look for trends or clustering of pairs, especially if the customers can be identified by age or some other social classification.
- The analysis should enable a product or service design or marketing strategy to be adopted which makes use of the information shown.

The matrix diagram

Figure A.4 *Matrix diagram*

Applications

- Shows relationships between departments/functions and problems.
- Maps out where things are happening.
- Shows strength of relationships.
- Shows multiple relationships.

Advantages

- Easy to learn.
- High visibility.
- Suitable for all industries (manufacturing, service).

Disadvantages

- More complicated matrices difficult to understand.

Special Requirements

- Spreadsheet pro-formas may be needed.

How to use

- Gather a group of people with knowledge of the problem.
- Think about what needs to be shown in the matrix diagram. For example, if the relationship between types of faults and work groups is to be shown, the types of fault can be listed in the rows. The work groups are listed in the columns.
- The group should think about how the various work groups influence or are involved in the types of faults. For example, the purchasing work group would have a strong influence on the quality of items purchased from suppliers. Prepare codes for the influences or involvements.
- At the intersection between each type of fault and each work group, the group inserts a suitable code. Some intersections may not have a code at all (no influence or involvement).

The affinity diagram (sometimes called a KJ)

Figure A.5 *Affinity diagram*

Applications

- Maps out the elements of a large problem or task.
- Allows all people to participate on an equal footing.
- Brings the creative part of the brain into play.
- Identifies elements of a problem which may be missed in other methods.

Advantages

- Easy to learn.
- Disarms dominant people.
- High visibility.
- Suitable for all industries (manufacturing, service).
- Involves the whole team.
- Allows non-measured data to be handled.

Disadvantages

- Takes some time to prepare.
- Visibility could cause discomfort to some participants.
- Only the first step – doesn't actually *solve* problems.
- Restricted as to size of team for optimum results.

Special requirements

- Requires a facilitator for early sessions.
- Requires a largish free space for sticky notes.

How to use

- Gather participants who have knowledge in the field to be studied.
- Write the central issue on a whiteboard in the format 'What are the issues surrounding (the subject)?'
- Participants write ideas (5 or 6 words) on sticky notes.
- Place sticky notes on whiteboard or other working space
- *Without talking*, arrange sticky notes in groupings 'where they seem to belong'.
- Provide titles for the natural groupings.
- Use the completed affinity diagram to gather more ideas.

The histogram

Figure A.6   *Histogram*

Applications

- Studies distribution of measurements.
- Finds possible mixed populations.
- Shows middle of distribution.

Advantages

- Easy to create.
- Simple to read.
- High visibility.
- Gives first level of statistical analysiss

Disadvantages

- Some calculations required.
- Will not reveal effect of time on measurements (see run chart).
- May be misleading if cell sizes are unsuitable.

Special requirements

- Important to choose cell sizes carefully (refer Sturgess' Rule).

How to use

- Decide on measurements for the subject being studied, e.g. heights of customers. Take the measurements.
- Decide on the number of cells and the cell limits for the measurements. This can be done with Sturgess' Rule.
- Count the number of observations in each cell, by noting whether each measurement falls in a cell interval. Note that several computer packages, including spreadsheets, will do this automatically and with less likelihood of error than when done by people.
- Draw the histogram and use to show how the information is distributed.

The run chart

Figure A.7 *Run chart*

Applications

- Studies effect of time on processes.
- Finds opportunities to eliminate special causes of variation.
- Shows if there are obvious cyclic variations.

Advantages

- Easy to use.
- Helps prepare for control charting.
- High visibility.
- Suitable for all industries (manufacturing, service).
- Requires virtually no statistical training.

Disadvantages

- Less sensitive than a control chart.
- May result in false conclusions (through over-enthusiasm in interpretation of the process measurements).

Special requirements

● Requires some care in choosing the method of measurement.

How to use

● Choose a measurement unit for the subject being studied (e.g. time, weight, number of errors). This is used on the vertical axis.
● Choose a unit for the horizontal axis (e.g. time in days, weeks or sequence number).
● Take measurements at each agreed time interval and record any events which may be important, such as temperature changes, cold winds, shift changes.
● Plot the measurements so that each measurement is shown on the vertical axis, with its corresponding time on the horizontal axis.
● Study the plot as it grows and look for sudden shifts. Can these be related to something which happened at that time (e.g. there may be peaks at 11 am every day)?

Scatter diagram

Figure A.8 *Scatter diagram*

Applications

- Studies relationships of variables.
- Finds unsuspected behaviours of processes.
- Shows variability.

Advantages

- Easy to construct.
- High visibility.
- Minimum use of computations.

Disadvantages

- Strength of relationships not quantified.
- May lead to false conclusion if variables plotted are not physically related.

Special requirements

- Important to involve process experts, process operators and statistical experts at set-up.

How to use

- Decide on the relationship to be studied. For example, you might want to know how the temperature of a process is related to the output.
- Decide on the measures, e.g. temperature in degrees Celsius and output in kilograms.
- Over a period of time, take measures of each at the same time, e.g. when the temperature is 250° C, the output might be 400 kg and when the temperature is 300° C, the output might be 450 kg. Repeat this for a range of temperatures.
- Plot the pairs of observations on the scatter diagram.
- Study the scatter and decide whether there is a relationship and if so, what kind of relationship. The assistance of a statistician may be needed in some cases.

Design of experiment

Figure A.9 *Design of experiment*

Applications

- Minimizes costs in processes with multiple inputs.
- Determines relationships between inputs and outputs.
- Makes processes robust against variation in inputs.

Advantages

- Extremely powerful techniques.
- Applicable to a wide range of problems.
- Potential for large improvements and/or savings.

Disadvantages

- Highly mathematical.
- Difficult to learn.
- Needs both process expert and statistician for best results.

Special requirements

- Expert assistance.

How to use

- Unless trained in the techniques, obtain the services of a statistician or other person who knows how to apply the method. In summary:
- Develop a concept of what factors affect the process.
- Conduct a screening experiment to find out the strongest (main) influences.
- Develop a model for the process, including interactions between factors.
- Verify the effect of changes in variables (factors) on the process output.
- Decide where to place the effort for control of the influencing factors.

The flowchart

Figure A.10 *Flowchart*

Applications

- Study of sequence in processes.
- Finds opportunities for parallel steps in place of serial.
- Records group's perceptions of processes.
- Used with check marks to record where problems are located.
- Used with time measurements to analyse process cycle time.
- Shows where feedbacks and critical steps are located.
- Arranges in columns showing operators/functions to create a deployment flowchart.

Advantages

- Easy to learn.
- Simple to follow.
- High visibility.
- Suitable for all industries (manufacturing, service).
- Multiple uses.

Disadvantages

- May take a long time to prepare.
- May restrict innovation (through association of symbol with step in process).

Special requirements

- During construction, it is important to involve people working in the process.

How to use

- Gather together people who have knowledge of the process or problem.
- Choose a quiet, comfortable room with recording facilities (whiteboard or butchers' paper).
- Optional – if the group is stressed, warm up with a few puzzles.
- Ask the team how the process starts.
- Draw in symbols on the chart as the steps are stated. Make sure all agree before moving on to the next step.
- When the flowchart is complete, ask the team to check that nothing has been missed.
- Post the flowchart on a wall for additions and alterations to be made.

The checklist

φρεδ	卌 III
ϑοε	I
Μαρψ	IIII
Ωενδψ	II
ϑιμ	卌 I

Figure A.11 *Checklist*

Applications

- Studies causes of problems.
- Measures frequency of occurrence.
- Shows analysis immediately.
- Collects data on demand for goods and services.

Advantages

- Easy to learn.
- Simple to complete.
- High visibility.
- Suitable for all industries (manufacturing, service).

Disadvantages

- Limited to count data (attributes).
- Could be seen as a criticism of operator.

Special requirements

- Needs care to make sure measures do not appear to assign blame.

How to use

- Decide what needs to be studied. For example, you might want to know how often customers ask for each of five different products at a sales counter.
- Prepare a table like Figure A.11, with the names of the products in the left hand column.
- Each time a customer asks for one of the products, make a check mark against the appropriate name. Use 'five-bar gates', crossing through four check marks each time the fifth count arrives.
- When enough information is gathered, count the check marks and use the information to decide which product is most in demand.

Measles chart (defect concentration diagram)

Figure A.12 *Measles chart*

Applications

- Studies location of problems.
- Used with flowchart to record where problems are located.

Advantages

- Easy to learn.
- High visibility.
- Suitable for most industries (manufacturing, service).

Disadvantages

- May be seen as assigning blame.
- Can take some time to accumulate data.

Special requirements

- Important to avoid creating atmosphere of blame.

How to use

- Draw a picture (a rough sketch will do) of the subject being studied, e.g. if a shirt, show the sleeves, collar, cuffs, etc.
- Decide on the types of defect being looked for and assign a symbol to each, e.g. a cross for a mark, a dot for a loose thread and a star for defective sewing.
- Each time a defect is observed, mark the chart with the appropriate symbol, in the area where it was seen.
- When enough information is gathered, use the chart to show where defects are happening most and which types occur where.

The cause and effect diagram (fishbone diagram)

Figure A.13 *Cause and effect diagram*

Applications

- Studies causes of problems.
- Shows how causes are related.
- Records group's perceptions of problems.
- Used with Pareto diagrams to probe deeper into main causes.

Advantages

- Easy to learn.
- Simple to read.
- High visibility.
- Suitable for all industries (manufacturing, service).

Disadvantages

- May take a long time to prepare.
- May restrict ideas on relationships, due to structure.

Special requirements

- Important to involve people working in the process in using the method.
- Main cause categories need choosing carefully.
- Facilitator needed to guide team.

How to use

- Gather together a group of people who know about the process. Make sure there are operators as well as technical experts and managers.
- A facilitator is usually needed for this method, to guide the group in placing ideas on the diagram.
- State the problem or desired result e.g. 'error-free forms'.
- Place the statement in the 'head' of the cause and effect (fishbone) diagram.
- Place main categories on four to six main bones, such as 'training', 'environment', 'design', 'information'. The categories will vary from task to task. If they are not right first time, the process will soon sort them out.
- Ideas may be taken from a previous brainstorming session and the group can place them on the chart, or the ideas can be generated and placed directly on the chart. It's useful to take the latter way and concentrate on what leads to each of the main causes.
- When all ideas are on the chart, it can be left on display for a couple of days for people to add new ideas, or proceed directly to next step.
- The group decides which causes are the most important, so work can be done on these.

The relations diagram (interrelational digraph)

Figure A.14 *Relations diagram*

Applications

- Studies relationships of causes.
- Identifies principal causes.
- Discovers root causes.

Advantages

- Fairly easy to learn.
- Forces questioning of relationships.
- High visibility.
- Suitable for all industries (manufacturing, service).
- Involves the whole team.

Disadvantages

- Takes some time to prepare.
- Restricted as to size of team for optimum results.

Special requirements

- Need whiteboard to allow for iterations.

How to use

- Gather a group of people with knowledge of the problem.
- State the central problem by writing it in the middle of a whiteboard in the form e.g.' late pay', 'customers have to wait', or 'out of stock'.
- Get the group to write causes of the central problem in positions around the central problem. Make sure they ask 'Why is pay late?', etc.
- Prepare a second 'layer' of causes by asking why each of the causes happens.
- Repeat the process for each 'layer' of causes, until ideas run out.
- Draw arrows to show which causes lead into results, which in turn cause other results.
- Look for the causes with the most arrows coming out of them. These are the most powerful contributors for immediate attention.

Brainstorming

Figure A.15 *Brainstorming*

Applications

- Generates large quantity of ideas.
- Involves the team in finding solutions.
- Records group's perceptions of processes.

Advantages

- Easy to learn.
- Group involvement.
- High visibility.
- Suitable for all industries (manufacturing, service).

Disadvantages

- Quiet people may be inhibited.
- May restrict ideas (if inappropriate people are involved).

Special requirements

- Important to involve people working in the process in brainstorming.

● Requires a recorder, preferably a facilitator, and quiet accommodation.

How to use

● Gather together people with knowledge of the subject matter. Make sure to include operators as well as managers and technical experts.
● Use a comfortable, quiet room, free from distractions. Do not allow interruptions. Make sure there is somebody who can write fast to record ideas. Check that nobody in the group is likely to cause friction or inhibit others from participating. If the group is stressed, do some 'warm-up' puzzles.
● Write the problem on the whiteboard in the style 'How to get good widgets'.
● Ask the group to call out ideas. Record these *without making any comment* (even those which have been called out before).
● If the group starts to run out of steam, encourage more input by asking 'What's related to the last idea?'
● After the ideas have all been submitted, the group can assess the merits, weed out the duplicates and decide which are the best.

Morphology chart

Figure A.16 *Morphology chart*

Applications

● Generates new ways to do things.

Advantages

● Generates many ideas.
● Applicable to design of products and services.

Disadvantages

● Many ideas generated may be meaningless.
● Requires technical knowledge of process or design elements.

Special requirements

● Concordance generator.

How to use

- Gather a group of people with knowledge of the subject, or work as an individual.
- List the elements or attributes of the subject, for example toasting bread involves power, capacity, speed, method.
- Make a table showing the various forms the attributes of elements might take.
- Generate many ideas by combining any form of each attribute with forms for other attributes.
- Examine the list to see if there are any 'smart' ideas which are also practical.

Reclassification chart

Figure A.17 *Reclassification chart*

Applications

● Generates new ways to do things.

Advantages

● Builds on existing techniques.
● Applicable to design of products and services.

Disadvantages

● May miss opportunity for breakthrough.
● Requires technical knowledge of process or design elements.

Special requirements

● Whiteboard.

How to use

- Gather a group of people with knowledge of the subject.
- Make a table which shows how the existing 'whole' subject is broken down into parts and their corresponding classifications e.g. the blade of a cut-throat razor is classified as 'cutting'.
- Extend the table to show a new classification e.g. the blade may be reclassified into separate elements of 'cutting edge' and 'edge stiffness'.
- Further extend the table to show the new parts which provide the new classifications.
- These activities lead to a new whole, such as a safety razor.

Mandala

Figure A.18   *Mandala*

Applications

● Quietens the analytical side of the brain, ready for creative work.

Advantages

● Shifts away from most common mode of working.
● Effective fairly quickly.

Disadvantages

● Requires uninterrupted quiet.
● Not suitable for people with psychological problems.

Special requirements

● Quiet room.
● Prepared patterns.

How to use

- Find a quiet place.
- Select a mandala and move it in front of your vision until it fills your whole field of view.
- Stare at the centre of the mandala for a few minutes.
- Avoid trying to analyse the shape.
- Try different problem solving methods while in this 'right brain' state.

'Other hand' writing

Figure A.19   *'Other hand' writing*

Applications

- Generates ideas which do not normally occur in analytical mode.
- Ensure creative side of the brain is used.

Advantages

- Generates new ideas.
- Dramatic expansion of output.

Disadvantages

- Unsuitable for people with psychological problems.
- Requires a high degree of acceptance by peers.

Special requirements

- Quiet room.
- Screening of participants to avoid disturbance.

How to use

- Make sure you are relaxed and not under stress for this. One way is to use the mandala.
- In a brainstorming or general ideas session, use the hand you do not normally write with to list your ideas. If this is too difficult, Scrabble letters can be used with the 'other hand', but some of the spontaneity is lost.
- Use the ideas to see another (often more emotional) viewpoint of the problem or subject.

Lateral/breakthrough thinking

Figure A.20 *Lateral/ breakthrough thinking*

Applications

- Escapes from conventional thinking.
- Generates radical approaches.

Advantages

- Allows new directions of thought.
- Easy techniques to apply.

Disadvantages

- Requires acceptance of principle by users.
- Requires management willingness to try new ways.

Special requirements

- Quiet room.
- Facilitator to trigger new thoughts.

How to use

- Gather a group of people with flexible minds – not necessarily experts.
- Phrase the problem in a broad way, so as not to be specific about how it works, e.g. when thinking about how to prevent something happening, try rephrasing the problem in terms of 'eliminating the ill effects' of the event.
- Use humour to assist the group in jumping to new styles of thinking.

The Pareto diagram (80:20 rule)

Figure A.21   *Pareto diagram*

Applications

- Shows priority of causes, problems.
- Organizes effort for further work.
- Shows baseline and improvement results.
- Selects projects for attention.

Advantages

- Extremely simple concept.
- Useful at all levels of an organization.
- High visibility.
- Suitable for all industries (manufacturing, service).
- No statistical analysis.

Disadvantages

- May give misleading signals (e.g. if count is shown and some problems are much more expensive than others).

Special requirements

- Need to verify that visibility will not cause a perception of blame.

How to use

- Decide on a unit of measure for the subject, e.g. count, dollars, mass.
- Arrange the measures in descending order, e.g. if cost of various errors were being studied, it might be:
    error B – $21 000
    error D – $18 000
    error E – $ 9 000
    error A – $ 8 000
    error C – $ 4 000
- Use the chart to show which are the 'vital few' for attention.

Prioritization matrices

Figure A.22   *Prioritization matrices*

Applications

- Determines the best choice among projects.
- Makes highly objective decisions in complex situations.

Advantages

- Obtains team consensus.
- Applicable to a wide range of problems.

Disadvantages

- Very time-consuming.
- Difficult to learn.

Special requirements

- Electronic spreadsheet.

How to use

- Gather a group of people with knowledge of the problem.
- Decide on the criteria to be used in selecting candidate proposals, projects, etc. , which are called 'options'. The criteria might be 'ease of implementation', 'low cost', 'short time', etc.
- Make a matrix of all the criteria in both rows and columns.
- The group decides the relative importance of each criterion against the others. The decisions should be consistent and the matrix allows this test to be done.
- Sum the relative importance across the rows to see the ranking of the criteria.
- If there are only a few criteria, some of the unimportant ones may be dropped, to simplify the process.
- For each criterion, compare the options to show which is better, worse or equal. Calculate the relative score for each option.
- Finally, make a matrix showing each option against each criterion, calculating the combined score. Sum the rows to show the overall ranking and select the highest ranking options.

Decision tree

Figure A.23 *Decision tree*

Applications

● Determines course of action in complex project with risks and variable outcomes.
● Obtains consensus decisions in complex situations.
● Decides a marketing strategy 'in the laboratory'.

Advantages

● Very objective.
● Involves whole team.

Disadvantages

● Very time-consuming.
● Somewhat difficult to learn.

Special requirements

● Expert knowledge and/or senior people to authorize risk assessments.

How to use

- Gather a group of people with knowledge of the project.
- Decide what the options are, under the control of the project team, for the project to take different paths, such as limited trial, full production, abandon.
- Decide the outcomes which are controlled by outside influences, such as the market. Assign probabilities to these various outcomes.
- Draw a tree showing the decisions under control of the team and by outside influences. Calculate the cost of different paths, where possible.
- Test the sensitivity of the model by altering some of the more difficult decisions to decide probabilities and see what happens to the outcomes.
- Use the tree to study the various possible outcomes and to plan for alternative actions.

Process decision programme chart (PDPC)

Figure A.24 *PDPC*

Applications

- Debugs processes at the design stage.
- Analyses how a process or design may fail and produces countermeasures.

Advantages

- Provides high confidence in a design or process.
- Allows all team members to contribute.

Disadvantages

- Somewhat time-consuming.
- Requires a high level of technical skill in the technology under study.

Special requirements

- Whiteboard or other recording means.

How to use

- Gather a group of people with knowledge of the problem.
- Draw a tree structure, starting with the condition under study at the top. For example, the group might be interested in knowing what errors could cause a parking meter to malfunction.
- The various potential faults are listed as boxes under the top box, for example 'full of coins', 'wrong type of coin'.
- For each box, the group thinks of ways to overcome the problem, for example 'larger coin box' or 'more frequent emptying'. These are called *countermeasures*.
- Where possible, treat the countermeasure as a subject for similar analysis – how could it go wrong and what countermeasures could be put in place to prevent this?
- When all the countermeasures have been examined, use the list to decide improvements to the process or design.

Mistake-proofing (Poka-Yoke)

Figure A.25 *Mistake-proofing (Poka-Yoke)*

Applications

- Designs processes to prevent mistakes happening.
- Makes zero defects possible.
- Takes quality beyond the capabilities of statistics.

Advantages

- Eliminates opportunities for errors.
- Usually inexpensive to apply.
- Allows operators to contribute.

Disadvantages

- Usually requires some technical expertise.
- May distract the team from other opportunities.

Special requirements

- Electro-mechanical equipment fairly often required.

How to use

- Gather a group of people with knowledge of the problem, including technical experts in mistake-proofing.
- Think about the reasons why things go wrong e.g. a data entry clerk gives the computer a date for return of a hire car which is before the day of pick-up.
- Develop mistake-proofing which prevents the cause of the error from taking effect e.g. program the computer to test for errors such as the previous example and prompt the operator for correction.

The tree diagram

Figure A.26 *Tree diagram*

Applications

- Shows the sequence of implementation activities.
- Discovers the activities to cause a step in the process to be effective.

Advantages

- Fairly easy to learn.
- Very focused – forces questioning about effectiveness of actions.
- High visibility.
- Suitable for all industries (manufacturing, service).
- Involves whole team.

Disadvantages

- Fairly time-consuming.
- Assumes team's inputs represent the best way.
- Some people find difficulty with the directional nature of the method.

Special requirements

- Requires a whiteboard for best application.

How to use

- Gather a group of people with knowledge of the problem.
- State the key objective at the left-hand side of a whiteboard as a desired end state, such as 'quick service to customers'.
- Get the group to show on the right-hand side of the key objective what has to be done to make the key objective happen. Make sure they ask 'If we do this, will we achieve the key objective?'
- For each of the actions identified in the previous step, repeat the process for each of the actions.
- Continue this process until no further actions can be identified.
- The completed tree diagram is an action list in the order needed to get to the key objective, working from the right-hand side.

The arrow diagram

Figure A.27 *Arrow diagram*

Applications

● Controls the execution of a project.
● Plans for resource allocation.

Advantages

● Highly structured approach to projects.
● High level of detail.

Disadvantages

● Very time-consuming to set up.
● Requires maintenance.

Special requirements

● Software.

How to use

- Make a list of all the jobs which need to be done to complete a project.
- Decide which tasks must be done before others can start. For example, in building a house, the roof cannot be done until the walls are up.
- Estimate how long each task takes.
- A diagram can be drawn and calculations of when tasks start and end, but it's much easier to use a computer program to work these out.
- The completed and calculated arrow diagram shows which jobs are 'critical' i.e. any delay in these will delay the whole project, which jobs are dependent on others being done and which jobs can be allowed to 'float' in the schedule.

Quality function deployment (QFD)

Figure A.28   *QFD*

Applications

- Ensures the 'voice of the customer' is heard in the design process.
- Speeds up the design/implementation process.
- Reduces iterations in design.
- Studies the effectiveness of means to achieve goals.

Advantages

- Involves all departments.
- Ensures the customer requirements are paramount.
- 'Forces' teamwork.

Disadvantages

- Very time-consuming.
- Somewhat difficult to learn.
- Requires a major 'selling' job in most Western organizations.

Special requirements

- Proformas

How to use

- Collect information on what the customer really wants, using the language of the customer.
- Break these wants down into basic functions of the product or service.
- Determine what product or service design elements will be used to meet the customer needs.
- Use the 'House of Quality' to show how each customer need is satisfied by the design elements.
- Benchmark the company's performance on customer needs against competitors.
- Show in the 'roof' of the House of Quality how the design elements interact.
- Select target performance measures based on the strengths and weaknesses of the competition, degree of importance to the customer and the technical difficulty/cost of providing the features.

Force field analysis

Figure A.29 *Force field analysis*

Applications

- Maximizing or minimizing effects.
- Managing change.

Advantages

- Easy to learn.
- Involves whole team.
- Effective for manufacturing and service industries.

Disadvantages

- Requires preparatory work to identify forces.
- Requires consensus on direction of forces (different people may perceive forces as being in opposite directions).

Special requirements

- Quiet room.

How to use

- Gather a group of people with knowledge of the subject.
- State the issue to be analysed, e.g. moving to a new location.
- Get the group to write lists of the forces opposing the issue and those supporting it.
- Draw a force field analysis diagram showing the forces in each direction.
- Study the lists to see how the opposing forces might be minimized and the supporting forces maximized.

The control chart

Figure A.30 *Control chart*

Applications

- Studies variability of processes.
- Finds opportunities for elimination of special causes.
- Indicates trends, cyclic behaviour.
- Verifies improvements.

Advantages

- Statistically sound.
- Powerful signalling device.
- High visibility.
- Versions available for attributes and variables.

Disadvantages

- Requires computations.
- May be misleading if applied to the wrong population (e.g. variables to non-normal).
- Not sensitive to small but sustained shifts (refer Cusum chart).

Special requirements

- requires proforma.
- statistical support desirable.

How to use

- Decide on the measurement for the subject, e.g. size in mm of a part being made on a machine.
- Select the appropriate type of chart for the measurement and the method of sampling[†].
- Take measurements over a period of time with conditions known to be typical of operations. Record any significant events, such as change in temperature or personnel[†].
- When enough information is gathered, calculate the control limits and plot the readings[†].
- Study the chart to see if the process is stable and if special causes can be related to some corresponding event[†].

† Refer to statistical texts for details of the selection of charts and the way to calculate chart limits.

REFERENCES

1. Adams, James L., *Conceptual Blockbusting*, 3rd Edn, Penguin, 1987.
2. Koestler, Arthur, *The Act of Creation*, Danube Edition, Hutchinson, 1976.
3. Juran, Dr J.M., *Juran on Planning for Quality*, The Free Press, 1988.
4. Barker, Thomas B., *Quality by Experimental Design*, Marcel Dekker, Inc., 1985.
5. Triesman, Anne, 'Features and Objects in Visual Processing', *Scientific American*, November 1986, pages 106–115
6. Zdenek, Marilee, The *Right-Brain Experience*, Corgi, 1985.
7. Pile, Stephen, *The Book of Heroic Failures*, Futura Publications, 1982, page 36.
8. Juran, Dr J.M., *Juran's Quality Control Handbook*, 4th Edn, McGraw-Hill, 1988.
9. Shingo, Shigeo, *Zero Quality Control: Source Inspection and the Poka-Yoke System*, Productivity Press, 1986.
10. Day, Ronald G., *Quality Function Deployment: Linking a Company with its Customers*, ASQC Quality Press, 1993.

11.   King, Bob and Akao, Yoji, *Better Designs in Half the Time*, GOAL/QPC, Methuen, 1988.
12.   Suzuki, David, *Inventing the Future*, Allen & Unwin, 1990.
13.   Scholtes, Peter R., *The Team Handbook*, Joiner Associates, Inc., 1988.
14.   Mink, Oscar, Mink, Barbara and Owen, Keith, *Groups at Work*, Educational Technology Publications, 1987.
15.   Mink, Dr Oscar G., Shultz, Dr James M. and Mink, Dr Barbara P., *Developing and Managing OPEN ORGANIZATIONS*, Organization and Human Resource Development Associates, Inc., 1986.
16.   Knowler, Lloyd A. *et al.*, *Quality Control by Statistical Methods*, McGraw-Hill, 1969.
17.   Duncan, Acheson J., *Quality Control and Industrial Statistics*, 4th Edn, Irwin, 1974.
18.   Grant, Eugene L. and Leavenworth, Richard S., *Statistical Quality Control*, 4th Edn, McGraw-Hill, 1972.
19.   Siegel, Sidney, *Nonparametric Statistics for the Behavioural Sciences*, McGraw-Hill, 1956.
20.   Tufte, Edward R., *The Visual Display of Quantitative Information*, Graphics Press, 1987.
21.   Adams, James L., *The Care and Feeding of Ideas*, Addison-Wesley, 1986.
22.   Adams, James L., *Conceptual Blockbusting*, 3rd Edn, Penguin, 1987.
23.   de Bono, Edward, *Six Thinking Hats*, Penguin, 1986.
24.   Argyris, Chris, *Reasoning, Learning and Action – Individual and Organizational*, Jossey-Bass, 1982.
25.   Burns, Marilyn, *The Book of Think*, Little, Brown and Company, 1976.

INDEX

The David Solution

How to Reclaim Power and Liberate Your Organization Through Empowerment

Valerie Stewart

As Jean Jacques Rousseau neglected to say: 'Organizations were created free, but everywhere they are in chains.' Whether you work in the private or public sector, in service, retailing, manufacturing or utilities, Valerie Stewart's book will help you to demolish the blockages that prevent people in your organization from consistently delivering peak performance.

Written in a direct and entertaining style and enlivened with anecdotes, parables and case studies, it will show you: how to bust the bureaucracy; how to avoid paralysis by analysis; how to break down the barriers of organizational empire; how to empower junior managers; how to put customers first (yes, truly); and how to create an enabling culture.

| 1993 | 176 pages | 0 566 07420 6 |

A Gower Paperback

A Systematic Approach to
Getting Results

Surya Lovejoy

Every manager has to produce results. But almost nobody is trained in the business of doing so. This book is a practical handbook for making things happen. And whether the thing in question is a conference, an office relocation or a sales target, the principles are the same: you need a systematic approach for working out

- **exactly what has to happen**
- **when everything has to happen**
- **how you will ensure that it happens**
- **what could go wrong**
- **what will happen when something does go wrong**
- **how you will remain sane during the process.**

This book won't turn you into an expert on critical path analysis or prepare you for the job of running the World Bank. What it will do is to give you the tools you need to produce results smoothly, effectively, reliably and without losing your mind on the way.

1994   192 pages   0 566 07541 5

A Gower Paperback

The Goal

Beating the Competition

2nd Edition

Eliyahu M Goldratt and Jeff Cox

Written in a fast-paced thriller style, *The Goal* is the gripping novel which is transforming management thinking throughout the Western world.

Alex Rogo is a harried plant manager working ever more desperately to try to improve performance. His factory is rapidly heading for disaster. So is his marriage. He has ninety days to save his plant - or it will be closed by corporate HQ, with hundreds of job losses. It takes a chance meeting with a colleague from student days - Jonah - to help him break out of conventional ways of thinking to see what needs to be done.

The story of Alex's fight to save his plant is more than compulsive reading. It contains a serious message for all managers in industry and explains the ideas which underlie the Theory of Constraints (TOC) developed by Eli Goldratt - the author described by Fortune as 'a guru to industry' and by Businessweek as 'a genius'.

As a result of the phenomenal and continuing success of *The Goal* there has been growing demand for a follow-up. Eliyahu Goldratt has now written ten further chapters which continue the story of Alex Rogo as he makes the transition from Plant Manager to Divisional Manager. Having achieved the turnround of his plant, Alex now attempts to apply all that Jonah has taught him, not to crisis management, but to ongoing improvement.

These new chapters reinforce the thinking process utilised in the first edition of *The Goal* and apply them to a wider management context with the aim of stimulating readers into using the technique in their own environment.

| 1993 | 352 pages | 0 566 07418 4 |

A Gower Paperback

Gower Handbook of Management Skills

2nd Edition

Edited by Dorothy M Stewart

The second edition of this bestselling handbook brings together the expertise of thirty three specialists. Between them they cover the whole range of personal skills needed by today's managers. The original text has been radically revised and updated, and a complete section has been added on how to run the main specialist functions.

Part I deals with personal skills and includes chapters on self-development and career planning. Part II covers 'people skills', including leadership, teambuilding and communication. Part III - new for this edition - looks at the particular problems of managing departments such as production, personnel, marketing and finance. Part IV addresses the skills required for running a successful business.

Each chapter contains an introduction and detailed guidelines and ends with a checklist of key points and suggestions for further reading. For the practising manager - or the would-be manager - *Gower Handbook of Management Skills* represents a one-book library which, widely used, cannot fail to improve effectiveness.

1994 576 pages 0 566 07614 4

A Gower Paperback

Problem Solving in Groups
2nd Edition
Mike Robson

Modern scientific research has demonstrated that groups are likely
to solve problems more effectively than individuals. As most of us
knew already, two heads (or more) are better than one. In
organizations it makes sense to harness the power of the group both
to deal with problems already identified and to generate ideas for
enhancing effectiveness by reducing costs, increasing productivity
and the like.

In this revised and updated edition of his successful book, Mike
Robson first introduces the concepts and methods involved. Then,
after setting out the advantages of the group approach, he
examines in detail each of the eight key problem solving
techniques. The final part of the book explains how to present
proposed solutions, how to evaluate results and how to ensure that
the group process runs smoothly. With its practical tone, its
down-to-earth style and lively visuals, this is a book that will appeal
strongly to managers and trainers looking for ways of improving
their organization's and their department's performance.

1993   176 pages   0 566 07415 X

A Gower Paperback

Right Every Time

Using the Deming Approach

Frank Price

Over the five years since the publication of Frank Price's book
Right First Time the business landscape of the Western World has
undergone an upheaval - a Quality Revolution. This explosion of
interest in the management of quality has not just affected the
manufacturing sector but has influenced all areas of industry; and
with diverse effects. In *Right Every Time* the author not only
examines the content of quality thinking, the statistical tools and
their application to business processes; he also explores the context,
the cultural climate, in which these tools are put to work, the
environment in which they either succeed or fail. The core of the
book consists of a critique of Deming's points - which the author
refers to as the new religion of quality - and an examination of the
pitfalls which act as constraints on quality achievement.

This is more than a 'how to do' book, it is as much concerned with
'how to understand what you are doing', and the book's message is
applicable to anybody engaged in providing goods or services into
markets where 'quality' is vital to business success. There can be
no doubts concerning the benefits of quality control, and in this
important and highly readable text Frank Price reveals how such
visions of excellence may be transformed into manufacturing
realities.

1993   192 pages   0 566 07419 2

A Gower Paperback